WHERE'S *the*

BIRTH

CERTIFICATE?

WHERE'S *the*

BIRTH

CERTIFICATE?

THE CASE THAT BARACK OBAMA IS NOT ELIGIBLE TO BE PRESIDENT

JEROME *R.*
CORSI *Ph.D.*

 WND Books

WHERE'S THE BIRTH CERTIFICATE?
The Case That Barack Obama Is Not Eligible to Be President
by Jerome R. Corsi, Ph.D.

Published by WND Books
Washington, D.C.

Copyright © 2011
Jerome R. Corsi, Ph.D.

Book designed by Mark Karis

WND Books are distributed to the trade by:
Midpoint Trade Books
27 West 20th Street, Suite 1102
New York, NY 10011

WND Books are available at special discounts for bulk purchases. WND Books, Inc. also publishes books in electronic formats. For more information call (541) 474-1776 or visit www.wndbooks.com.

ISBN 13 Digit: 978-1-936488-29-2

Library of Congress information available

Printed in the United States of America

TO THE MEMORY OF

JUDGE JOHN JOSEPH SIRICA

AND

THE MILLIONS OF AMERICANS
*who continue to believe the
Constitution trumps a cover-up*

CONTENTS

PART 3 — THE CONSTITUTIONAL GAMBIT

FOREWORD

By the standards of most of America's media establishment, the subject matter of this book is the stuff of wild conspiracy theories, irresponsible conjecture, and worse. But then, that's the same media establishment that wildly and irresponsibly advocated for the election of Barack Obama as president.

The issue at hand centers around one simple and profound question: Has Barack Obama proven he is constitutionally eligible to serve as president of the United States?

This book by my good friend and WND senior staff reporter, Jerome Corsi, provides the unequivocal and definitive answer—no.

As the publisher of this book as well as the chief executive officer of WND, the news organization that has investigated this subject more exhaustively than all other media outlets combined, I can assure the reader that the question of constitutional eligibility has never been about a documentable *foreign* birth by Obama. Instead, it is about the conspicuous lack of documentation of a *domestic* birth.

It seems preposterous on its face that a politician could win the presidency of the United States without clearly establishing his bona fides as a "natural born citizen." But that is, in fact, exactly what Obama did. This book proves it.

Common sense suggests that since Obama *still* hasn't provided any of the documentation necessary to proving his eligibility – and has spent millions in legal fees avoiding doing so – that he probably doesn't meet the simple requirements. Why else would he go to such lengths and be so combative about it, if he could quell the controversy by simply producing a long-form birth certificate as Americans are routinely required to do?

And make no mistake about it, in spite of the media establishment's lockstep denials, the controversy is raging.

A CNN poll in 2010 showed 58 percent of Americans to be doubtful about Obama's "official" nativity story.

Here are some simple facts to keep in mind as you plow into this thorough investigation of what we know and what we don't know about Obama's origins and eligibility to serve in the highest office in the most powerful country in the world:

• No federal or state government agency or institution vetted Obama's requirements for office before he became a candidate for the presidency, during his campaign or subsequently.

• The United States Senate did take up the question of eligibility for his opponent, John McCain, and concluded unanimously, with an affirmative vote by Obama himself, that he was qualified to hold the office because *both* his parents were U.S. citizens. Obama could not meet the same test, if indeed his parents were, as he contends, Barack Hussein Obama, Sr. of Kenya and Stanley Ann Dunham.

• To this day, no hospital in the United States claims to be the birthplace of America's first black president. One hospital that did make the claim for the purposes of fundraising, quickly backtracked on the assertion when confronted by questions from WND.

• Hawaii public officials have offered contradictory claims about their knowledge of Obama's birth – all the while maintaining a veil of secrecy around the one document that would provide the basis for answering the question of eligibility.

So, why all the mystery?
Why all the secrecy?
Why all the intrigue?

Where's the birth certificate?

It's this simple, unanswered question that has dogged Obama throughout his term of office.

It has become the source of innumerable jokes on late-night television. And it may well cost him any chance for re-election in 2012.

For the first time, someone has put all the pieces of this fantastic story together in one place.

Who better than Jerome Corsi, the two-time No. 1 *New York Times* bestselling author, political scientist, Harvard Ph.D. and investigative journalist – the man who went to Kenya in search of the truth and got detained by military authorities there for his trouble? He has also visited Hawaii where he has hired private detectives to help him in his quest for the elusive birth certificate. He has traveled to Chicago to meet with those who knew Obama during his community organizing years and as a budding politician. All told, *Where's the Birth Certificate?* is the result of more than three years of research – much of it very unpleasant for the author.

Now Corsi goes beyond asking questions.

Where's the Birth Certificate? ups the ante for those Americans tired of the stonewalling by Obama and his administration.

This book makes a compelling case that Obama is, indeed, constitutionally ineligible for the office of the presidency.

That's not a minor technicality.

That's a finding that has real-world implications and ramifications for every American.

Already, distinguished military servicemen and officers have refused deployments because of their serious concerns about whether or not the commander-in-chief is legitimate and is issuing lawful orders. Some have faced courts-martial and prison sentences.

This is not a fringe issue – unless you consider 58 percent of Americans to be on the fringe.

It's about constitutional propriety. It's about the minimal established standards for holding the most powerful office in the world. It's about national security. It's about the rule of law. And it's about the integrity of future presidential elections.

— *Joseph Farah, CEO & Editor-in-Chief of WND*

INELIGIBLE FOR COMMAND

Is the 44th president of the United States of America, Barack Hussein Obama, illegally occupying the Oval Office?

The question is jarring, almost surreal, and of course intensely controversial. Yet with repeated national polls revealing that more than half of all Americans suspect the answer is "yes," it's a question that demands a serious and informed response.

This book will demonstrate conclusively that no legal authority has ever verified Barack Obama's legal eligibility to be president, that glaring inconsistencies and blackouts in his life narrative have caused widespread doubts among the American populace, and that, in fact, a compelling body of evidence exists that Obama is not a natural-born citizen as is required of all presidents by Article 2, Section 1, of the Constitution.

This book further establishes the case that Barack Obama, aided by his media collaborators, has conducted one of the most audacious cover-ups ever perpetrated at the highest level of American politics.

By the time you finish reading, you will understand the need to block Obama's bid for re-election in 2012 unless he releases all documents relevant to his birth, his educational past, his employment history, and his political career.

Until now, Obama and his supporters have done everything possible to suppress and ridicule any serious attempt to investigate his constitutional qualifications to hold the nation's highest elective office.

Whereas *Washington Post* reporters Bob Woodward and Carl Bernstein were heralded by the cultural establishment in the 1970s, largely because they probed lies and cover-ups on the part of Republican President Richard Nixon, investigative reporters today are excoriated if they dare press Obama for the public release of dozens of documents kept under seal relating to his identity and life history.

Why are his medical records being kept hidden? Why are his educational records, including his student loan applications, so protected by privacy restrictions that it is a crime to possess them unless they are obtained under the tight restrictions of authorized access imposed by the Department of Education?

What about his travel records? His law school writings? His parents' marriage records?

The list goes on.

All too often, documents relating to Obama's past turn out to be conveniently lost or reported destroyed when they are not sealed away and officially protected from public view. The list of suppressed, lost, or otherwise unavailable documents is so long that I have devoted an appendix to cataloguing them and examining why they are most likely being purposely withheld (see Appendix A, page 316).

While refusing to release even the most basic documents regarding his past, including the original long-form birth certificate, which would identify the attending physician and the hospital where he was born, Obama has confidently relied upon a compliant and biased media to protect him from scrutiny.

The longer the cover-up continues, the greater the erosion in the public's trust that President Obama has told the truth about his past.

More than two years into the Obama presidency, public opinion polls continue to demonstrate that the majority of Americans have questions about the place of Obama's birth. His refusal to come clean with requested documents has moved concerns about his presidential eligibility from the fringe of American politics increasingly to center stage.

There are other compelling issues. Aside from Obama's total evasion of the birth certificate question, for example, what about the fact of his father having Kenyan citizenship at the time Obama was born? As we will document here, a State Department Web site concedes Barack Obama was a dual citizen of the Commonwealth of Great Britain at birth, because his father was then a Kenyan citizen. Does this fact alone compromise Obama's presidential eligibility as a "natural-born citizen" of the United States? A significant body of legal precedent says it does.

The lesson of Watergate is that presidents who engage in cover-ups are walking down a very risky path. Once the American public wakes up to the reality that the White House is intentionally withholding important truths, a president may risk impeachment and removal from office unless the truth is finally told. Nixon protested famously that he was "not a crook," almost as determinedly as Obama and his supporters have insisted that the short-form Certification of Live Birth posted on the Internet is the "best evidence" he was born in Hawaii. In the end, Nixon was forced to resign from office, while Obama's future in the White House, of course, has yet to unfold.

On August 4, 2010, President Obama's 49th birthday, a CNN poll showed the majority of Americans expressing doubts about the president's eligibility, with an astonishing 6 out of 10 people uncertain that he was born in the United States.[1] Only 42 percent of those questioned said they had absolutely no doubts that the president was born in the United States. "It's surely not what the leader of the free world wants for his birthday," CNN reported. "But, for a stubborn group of Americans, conspiracy theories about President Obama's birthplace are the gifts that keep on giving."

CNN neglected to mention that the same news agencies, watchdog groups, and pundits that ridiculed those questioning Obama's eligibility had stridently demanded answers to the same questions about John McCain during the 2008 presidential campaign.

The fact is, the American public knows less about President Obama's admittedly complicated life history than it has known about any other president in modern history. Bill Clinton may have been reluctant to have his passport records examined too carefully, especially for the years when he was dodging the draft during the Vietnam War, but there is no question he was born at Julia Chester Hospital in Hope, Arkansas, on August 19, 1946.

During a televised interview on August 29, 2010, NBC Nightly News anchor Brian Williams asked Obama why more than one-fifth of Americans responding to recent polls believe he is a Muslim.

Oddly, Obama answered the question about his faith with a reference to his birth certificate: "Well, look, Brian, I—I would say that I can't spend all my time with my birth certificate plastered on my forehead. (LAUGHS) It—it is what—the facts are the facts. And so, it's not something that I can, I think, spend all my time worrying about."[2]

Since Obama was not even asked about his birth certificate, his answer, viewed psychologically, could suggest he is self-conscious about his truthfulness regarding facts surrounding his birth.

In any event, the argument of this book is clear: Viewed objectively against the Constitution's "natural-born citizen" requirement, a wealth of evidence suggests Barack Obama is ineligible for command.

At a minimum, by 2012, formal governmental procedures and mechanisms likely will be put in place demanding that Obama and all future presidential candidates present their birth documentation openly so their eligibility as natural-born citizens can be determined beyond doubt. Only then should their names be placed on the presidential ballot.

I began working on this book in June 2008, when the DailyKos.com first posted online a short-form Certification of Live Birth, arguing it was Obama's authentic birth certificate issued by the Hawaii Department of Health.

I have continued researching the Obama birth controversy since that day, traveling both to Kenya and Hawaii in search of Obama records.

I have spent thousands of hours researching the birth controversy and publishing many of my key findings on WND, the news agency for which I work full-time as a senior staff writer, as the work progressed.

I have searched the Library of Congress in Washington, D.C., both for newspaper accounts in Hawaii concerning the time Barack Obama, Sr. spent attending the University of Hawaii and examining the Jackie Robinson papers to expose fabrications in the story of how Barack Obama, Sr. came to Hawaii. I have worked with the archives and records sections of the University of Washington in Seattle to pin down the details of the time Ann Dunham, Barack Obama's mother, spent there. I have filed Freedom of Information Act requests and worked with others to file their FOIA requests, seeking the public release of archived documents on Obama.

Yet, a shocking number of relevant documents in government archives concerning Obama and those close to him have either been destroyed by the government or remain under seal, unavailable for public inspection.

I have interviewed many people close to Obama in childhood, though a great many more decline to talk.

Given the documentary evidence that continues to be uncovered, it should be clear by the conclusion of this book that much of President Obama's official nativity story is a fabrication.

I write in the conviction that Obama has usurped the office of the presidency by waging a skillful public relations campaign to suppress the facts about his actual birth circumstances.

If he is not eligible to be president, he is also ineligible to command the armed forces defending this nation—a challenge several brave members of the military have dared to make, putting themselves at risk, and in at least one case actually losing his own liberty—in court-martial proceedings brought against them for refusal to obey orders.

Those of us who believe the Constitution of the United States is worth preserving, protecting, and defending intend to continue pressing the Obama eligibility argument until Barack Obama is either removed from office or forced to reveal the truth.

THE UNDOCUMENTED WORKER
IN THE OVAL OFFICE

Who is Barack Obama, and why is the American public forbidden from examining key documentation from his past?

The U.S. Constitution demands that every president of the United States must be a "natural-born citizen." Shouldn't Americans therefore be allowed to see and inspect all documents that pertain to Barack Obama's—or any presidential candidate's—eligibility, including his hospital-generated birth certificate listing the doctor attending his birth and the name of the hospital where he was born? At its most fundamental level, any attempt to conceal such vital personal documents that bear directly on a candidate's legal qualifications for the presidency is an assault on the Constitution itself.

Moreover, the fact is, politicians conceal documentary evidence only when the contents are so toxic that their revelation might threaten the viability of their careers. Barack Obama is no exception. Will the current charade continue, with an endlessly stonewalling Obama being given a pass to run for re-election without establishing his legal eligibility, simply because he got away with it the first time around?

Following are three vignettes that demonstrate the extent of the ongoing cover-up Obama has perpetrated to conceal his true identity, not just regarding his birth records, but regarding a wide range of records, including passport records, his student loan files, with unanswered questions remaining even over the Social Security number Barack Obama is currently using.

As you read these vignettes, ask yourself: Should American citizens have to risk losing their jobs or being prosecuted just because they want to see for themselves the president's passport records or his student loan file to ensure he is legitimately holding office? Why would the White House stonewall answering questions concerning the president's most basic identity documents, such as why his Social Security number was issued in a state where the president never resided?

American presidents and presidential candidates routinely divulge documents regarding their past. It's expected, and for obvious reasons: If they desire to be elevated to the most powerful elected position in the world, the public has a right to know all about them, to assure they are making a wise selection as leader. Why then should Obama, who campaigned on a standard of openness and transparency, be allowed by a compliant, politically motivated press to withhold biographically relevant documents when others aspiring to the presidency have asked for and received no similar privilege? American voters have the right under the Constitution to ask why they cannot examine key documents from Obama's past, especially with regard to the threshold question of his legal eligibility to be president.

Intrigue on the Potomac:
The State Department Breach of Obama's Passport Records

In March 2008, during the presidential campaign, two unnamed contract employees for the State Department were fired and a third was disciplined for breaching the passport file of Democratic presidential candidate and then-Senator Barack Obama.

In breaking the story, the *Washington Times* noted that all three had used their authorized computer network access to look up and read Obama's records within the State Department's consular affairs section that "possesses and stores passport information."[3]

The *New York Times* reported two days later that the security breach had involved unauthorized searches of the passport records not just of Senator Obama, but also of then-presidential contenders Senators John

McCain and Hillary Clinton. The report attributed the breaches to "garden-variety snooping by idle employees" that was "not politically motivated."[4] But according to the paper, Obama was concerned.

"One of the things that the American people count on in their interactions with any level of government is that if they have to disclose personal information, that is going to stay personal and stay private," Obama told reporters. "And when you have not just one, but a series of attempts to tap into people's personal records, that's a problem, not just for me, but for how our government is functioning."

The report noted that the files examined were likely to contain sensitive personal information, including Social Security numbers and addresses, as well as passport applications and other biographical information that would pertain to U.S. citizenship. Only at the end of the article did we find out that State Department spokesman Sean McCormick had emphasized that the most egregious violation appeared to have been made against Obama.

Obama was the only one of the three candidates whose passport file had been breached on *three* separate occasions—January 9, February 21, and March 14, 2008. Moreover, all three offending employees had obtained Obama's files, while the passport files of McCain and Clinton had been accessed only once each.

The *New York Times* noted the two offending State Department contract employees who were fired had worked for Stanley, Inc., a company based in Arlington, Virginia, while the reprimanded worker continued to be employed by the Analysis Corporation of McLean, Virginia. The newspaper gave no background on either corporation, other than to note that Stanley, Inc. did "computer work for the government." Stanley Inc. turned out to be a 3,500-person technology firm that had just won a $570 million contract to provide computer-related passport services to the State Department. It also turned out that John O. Brennan, a former CIA agent who was then serving as an advisor on intelligence and foreign policy to Senator Obama's presidential campaign, headed the Analysis Corporation.

By Saturday, March 22, 2008, the *Washington Times* reported that the State Department investigation had focused on the contract worker for the Analysis Corporation because he was the only one of the three involved in breaching the passport records of both Senators Obama and McCain, the two presidential candidates whose eligibility as "natural-born" citizens under Article 2, Section 1, of the Constitution, were in question.[5]

In keeping with the official story that the motive for the passport breach was simply mischief, the three State Department contract employees received relatively light penalties: Two were fired and one was reprimanded.

Although the State Department promised a full-scale investigation, the public was kept in the dark. The department's Office of Inspector General issued a 104–page investigative report on the incidents in July 2008, stamped "Sensitive But Unclassified," that was so heavily redacted as to be near worthless to the public.[6] Scores of lengthy passages were blacked out entirely.

One investigative reporter, Kenneth Timmerman, said a well-placed but unnamed source told him the real point of the passport incidents was to cauterize the Obama file, removing from it any information that could prove damaging to his eligibility to be president. According to this theory, the breaches of the McCain and Clinton files were done for misdirection purposes, to create confusion and to suggest the motives of the perpetrators were attributable entirely to idle curiosity.[7]

Within a few days, a new case surfaced unexpectedly, providing evidence that breaching passport files was an offense being perpetrated by State Department personnel on an ongoing and regular basis. The case involved Leiutenant Quarles Harris, Jr., age twenty-four. (Harris spelled his first name "Leiutenant," distinct from "lieutenant," the military or police rank. Harris, a petty drug dealer and identity-theft criminal, never held rank in any military, police, or fire organization.)

On March 25, 2008, at approximately 9:30 p.m., Officer William A. Smith, Jr. of the D.C. Metropolitan Police Department's Narcotics Special Investigation Division stopped an oncoming vehicle that had tinted windows he believed were in violation of D.C. law. Smith found the driver, Harris, as well as his female passenger, had been smoking marijuana and that Harris had stuffed in his jacket pocket a large Ziploc bag containing thirteen smaller bags filled with marijuana. A search of the vehicle turned up nineteen different credit cards with names not belonging to Harris or his female passenger, as well as eight U.S. Department of State passport application computer printouts, also in names different from Harris and his female passenger.[8] The officers further discovered four of the names on the passport applications matched the names on the credit cards. A check with American Express while Harris was still on the scene of the traffic stop indicated that some of the American Express cards in Harris's possession, but not in his name, had recently been used and that American Express had placed a "Fraud Alert" on the cards.

Officer Smith brought Harris to the D.C. Metropolitan Police Sixth District, where agents of the Secret Service, State Department, and Postal Service questioned him. Harris' involvement in passport application theft clearly made him no ordinary petty criminal. His statements revealed that breaching passport records at the State Department had developed into major criminal activity conducted on an ongoing basis by employees with access to the State Department's Passport Information Electronic Records System, or PIERS. Harris also had information relating to the employees who had accessed Obama's passport records, and was cooperating with government officials.

Despite the prosecutors' objections, the judge released Harris the next day on personal recognizance, ordering him to return to court for a hearing in June.

Unfortunately, Harris did not live to attend the court hearing.

On Thursday, April 17, 2008, Harris was found murdered in Washington, D.C., killed by a single bullet to the head in what appeared to be a drive-by shooting.

The *Washington Times* reported that a "key witness in a federal probe into passport information stolen from the State Department was fatally shot in front of a District church" at close range, around 11 p.m.[9]

Harris was found slumped dead at the steering wheel of his car, in front of the Judah House Praise Baptist Church in the northeast section of the District of Columbia, according to Commander Michael Anzallo, the head of the Metropolitan Police Department's Criminal Investigations Division.

A police officer patrolling the neighborhood at the time of Harris's death heard gunshots and ran to the scene, only to find Harris dead inside his car. The Metropolitan Police admitted a "shot spotter" device had been used to locate Harris in the shooting, although police officials declined to say whether his death was a direct result of his cooperation with federal investigators.

No available evidence links Harris's crimes or his murder with the breach of Obama's passport records by State Department contract employees. Properly viewed, Harris can be dismissed as a foot-soldier selling marijuana and peddling/using credit cards fraudulently obtained via passport-related identity theft. Yet, there is more to the story than petty criminal activity. Obviously, Harris got himself way over his head when he decided to work with the State Department officials accessing PIERS to obtain passport records without authorization. Equally obvious was that by being willing to cooperate with police, Harris risked becoming a threat to his accomplices and co-conspirators within the State Department.

But by withholding his passport records from the public, Obama has created not only a political but also an economic motive for State Department contract employees to access them. Unpublished Obama passport records would be a valuable commodity to political operatives conducting opposition research and willing to break the law to obtain information, as well as to foreign intelligence operatives wanting to obtain the information as a lever to influence U.S. foreign policy. To the extent Obama's passport files might contain information that would compromise his eligibility to be president, the black-market value of his records escalates.

The ABC affiliate WJLA-TV in D.C. reported that Cleopatria Harris, mother of Leiutenant Quarles Harris, believed her son was murdered to silence him from cooperating with the federal investigation.

As this book goes to print, the D.C. Metropolitan Police have no suspects in the murder of Leiutenant Quarles Harris, Jr. At the same time, the State Department has never revealed publicly what was discovered in the breach of Obama's passport records, and the three individuals who illegally accessed presidential candidate passport records have never come forward to divulge what they found.

The story did not end there.

Two weeks after the news broke that Obama's passport records had been accessed, candidate Obama made the surprise disclosure at a private fundraiser on April 7, 2008, that he had traveled to Pakistan during his college years.[10]

Jake Tapper, ABC News senior White House correspondent, commented that Obama's Pakistan disclosure was "news to most of us." "It was odd we hadn't heard about it before," Tapper added, "given all the talk of Pakistan during this campaign."[11] According to the Obama campaign, reported Tapper, Obama had visited Pakistan in 1981, the year he transferred from Occidental College to Columbia, and had visited his mother and sister, Maya, in Indonesia on the same trip.

Why was Obama coming forward now, for the first time, with news that he had traveled to Pakistan?

Did he use an Indonesian passport to travel to Indonesia and Pakistan in 1981, as many researchers have speculated, and was he concerned the public disclosure of his passport records might end up revealing such information?

"I traveled to Pakistan when I was in college," Obama is heard saying on the poor-quality audiotape of the San Francisco fundraiser. "I knew what Sunni and Shia was [sic] before I joined the Senate Foreign Relations Committee."

At any rate, John Brennan was certainly not punished for the incident, even though his contract employee was identified as the central focus of the investigation—the only one of the three initial suspects who had accessed the passport records of both candidates with eligibility questions in their backgrounds—namely, Obama and McCain.

After the inauguration of President Barack Obama, John Brennan joined the White House as Assistant to the President and Deputy National Security Advisor for Homeland Security and Counterterrorism.

The fact is, had Obama made a full and complete disclosure of his State Department passport file to the American public, no one seeking to obtain his passport or travel records would ever have had a motive for committing the crime of searching State Department records without authorization.

The key question remains unanswered: What information is in the passport file that Barack Obama will not allow the American public to see?

The Davenport Nine: The Department of Education Breach of Obama's Student Loan Records

Not only is it dangerous to look up President Obama's passport records without authorization, the examination of his student loan records has resulted in federal criminal prosecution of nine defendants in Davenport, Iowa.

A defense attorney representing one of the nine characterized the Department of Justice's actions as political prosecution. "The only reason my client was prosecuted by the federal government was that he happened to look up the student loan records of Barack Obama," says attorney David R. Treimer of Davenport, Iowa.

Treimer represented John Phommivong, the twenty-nine-year-old son of parents who fled Southeast Asia during the Vietnam War. He was charged in the U.S. District Court in the Southern District of Iowa with a criminal misdemeanor under 26 U.S.C. Section 1030, a broadly worded section of the federal code devoted to computer fraud that carries a maximum penalty of one year in prison and a $100,000 fine. Phommivong also looked up student loan records for Angelina Jolie, Brad Pitt, and John Wayne, according to his attorney.

"Nobody seemed to care if they were looking up the student loans of well known celebrities in 2007, including Obama," attorney David Treimer explained. "But the moment they looked up Obama's records after he was president, the FBI descended upon them."

All nine of the defendants, including Phommivong, were employees of Arlington, Virginia-based Vangent Inc., a private contractor that assists the Department of Education in researching student loan cases.

Treimer said he had no idea if the Obama student loan records included any irregularities or any information that would indicate Obama had applied for loans as a foreign student.

Ultimately, all the defendants pleaded guilty, except two. For the two who went to trial, the juries found them guilty. All were given light sentences of modest fines, probation, and community service, and none has ever disclosed publicly what was found in Obama's student loan files.

Despite repeated requests to allow public access to his college records, Obama has consistently refused to release any, including from Occidental College, Columbia University, and Harvard Law School. Remarkably, Americans have never seen a single application Barack Obama submitted to a college, university, or graduate school, no course schedule or grade transcript, and no information about any student loans he might have applied for or received.

At issue regarding Obama's student loan records is whether he ever used the time he spent in Indonesia with his mother and Indonesian stepfather,

Lolo Soetoro—from around six years old until he was approximately ten—as grounds to apply for loan assistance as a foreign student. Particularly in question is Obama's application to Occidental, where he roomed with Pakistani foreign students. Had Obama applied for admission as a foreign student? Had Obama applied for student loans as a foreign student? If Obama had a foreign student status at Occidental, Columbia University, or Harvard Law School, that fact might compromise his "natural-born citizen" status and thus negate his eligibility to be president. The dearth of documents evidencing Obama's college education gave rise to a popular e-mail hoax declaring Obama's Occidental records had been found and claiming he had received financial aid for foreign-born students.

Still, the key question from the Davenport case remains unanswered: What is in Barack Obama's student files that he is so determined to keep hidden from the American public?

Obama Uses Social Security Number Issued in Connecticut—Whose Social Security Number Is Barack Obama Using?

Two private investigators working independently have been asking why President Obama is using a Social Security number set aside for applicants in Connecticut while there is no record he ever had a mailing address in that state. In addition, the records indicate the number was issued between 1977 and 1979, yet Obama's earliest employment reportedly was in 1975 at a Baskin-Robbins ice cream shop in Oahu, Hawaii.

WND has copies of affidavits filed separately in a presidential eligibility lawsuit in the U.S. District Court of the District of Columbia by Ohio licensed private investigator Susan Daniels and Colorado private investigator John N. Sampson. The investigators believe Obama needs to explain why he is using a Social Security number reserved for Connecticut applicants that was issued at a date later than he is known to have held employment.

The Social Security Web site confirms the first three numbers in the Social Security ID currently being used by Obama, 042, fall within the sequence of the first three numbers that the Social Security administration reserves for the state of Connecticut, 040–049. "Since 1973, Social Security numbers have been issued by our central office," the Social Security Web site explains.[12] "The first three (3) digits of a person's social security number are determined by the ZIP code of the mailing address shown on the application for a social security number."

"I doubt this is President Obama's originally-issued Social Security number," Daniels told WND. "Obama has a work history in Hawaii before he left the islands to attend college at Occidental College in California, so he must have originally been issued a Social Security number in Hawaii."

Robert Siciliano, president and CEO of IDTheftSecurity.com and a recognized expert on identity theft, agrees the Social Security number should be questioned. "I know Social Security numbers have been issued to people in states where they don't live, but there's usually a good reason the person applied for a Social Security number in a different state," Siciliano told WND.

WND asked Siciliano whether he thought the question was one the White House should answer. "Yes," he replied. "In the case of President Obama, I really don't know what the good reason would be that he has a Social Security number issued in Connecticut when we know he was a resident of Hawaii." Siciliano is a frequent expert guest on identity theft on cable television networks, including CNN, CNBC, and the Fox News Channel.

WND has further confirmed that the Social Security number in question links to Obama in the online records maintained by the Selective Service system. Inserting the Social Security number, his birth date and his last name produced a valid Selective Service number identified with Obama. Interestingly, as soon as WND published this information, the Selective Service Web site was changed so that attempts to identify Obama's Selective Service number from his Social Security number were blocked.

Take a look at Exhibit 1, seen on page 142, which shows a screen of the Selective Service cross-verification of the Social Security number that President Obama is currently using.

To verify that the Social Security Administration issued Social Security number in question for applicants in Connecticut, Daniels used a Social Security number verification database. She found that the two Social

Security numbers immediately before and immediately after the Social Security number Barack Obama is currently using were issued in Connecticut between the years 1977 and 1979.

"There is obviously a case of fraud going on here," Daniels maintained. "In fifteen years of having a private investigator's license in Ohio, I've never seen the Social Security Administration make a mistake of issuing a Connecticut Social Security number to a person who lived in Hawaii. There is no family connection that would appear to explain the anomaly."

Does the Social Security Administration ever re-issue Social Security numbers?

"Never," Daniels said. "It's against the law for a person to have a re-issued or second Social Security number issued."

Daniels said she is "staking my reputation on a conclusion that Obama's use of this Social Security number is fraudulent."

There is no indication in the limited background documentation released by the Obama 2008 presidential campaign or by the White House to establish that Obama ever lived in Connecticut. Nor is there any suggestion in Obama's autobiography, *Dreams from My Father*, that he ever had a Connecticut address. Also, nothing can be found in the public record that indicates Obama visited Connecticut during his high-school years. Barack Obama, Sr. had completed his education at Harvard and returned to Kenya in 1965, more than a decade before the Social Security number was issued. There is nothing on the public record that would indicate Barack Obama, Sr. ever had a Connecticut address.

Sampson's affidavit specifies that as a result of his formal training as an immigration officer and his twenty-seven-year career in professional law enforcement, "It is my knowledge and belief that Social Security numbers can only be applied for in the state in which the applicant habitually resides and has their official residence."

Daniels told WND she believes Obama had a different Social Security number when he worked as a teenager in Hawaii prior to 1977. "I doubt this is President Obama's originally-issued Social Security number," Daniels told WND. "Obama has a work history in Hawaii before he left the islands to attend college at Occidental College in California, so he must have originally been issued a Social Security number in Hawaii."

The published record available about Obama indicates his first job as a teenager in Hawaii was at a Baskin-Robbins in the Makiki neighborhood on Oahu. Politifact.com, a Web site typically supportive of President Obama, claims Obama worked at the Baskin-Robbins ice cream store in 1975 or 1976, prior to the issuance of the Connecticut Social Security number Obama is currently using.[13]

"It is a crime to use more than one Social Security number, and Barack Obama should have had a Social Security number to have worked at Baskin-Robbins," Daniels insisted. "Under current law, a person is not permitted to use more than one Social Security number in a lifetime."

Another anomaly in the law enforcement databases searched by Daniels and Sampson is that the date 1890 shows up in the field indicating the birth of the number holder, along with Obama's birth date of 08/04/1961. A third date listed is 04/08/1961, which appears to be a transposition of Obama's birth date in an international format, with the day listed before the month.

Daniels said it appears the number Obama is using was previously issued by the Social Security Administration.

After an extensive check of the proprietary databases she uses as a licensed private investigator, Daniels determined that the first occurrence of Obama's association with the number was in 1980. Daniels assumes, but cannot prove, that Obama took on a previously issued Social Security number that had gone dormant due to the death of the original holder.

"The number President Obama is using today, was evidently issued previously by the Social Security Administration," Daniels said. "A person born in 1890 would have been eighty-seven- to eighty-nine years old when they got the Social Security number issued in 1977–1979 in Connecticut. If the person originally issued the Social Security number died and no one claimed Social Security death benefits, there may be no traceable record in the Social Security database to determine the identity of the person born in 1890 who was originally issued the card."

Daniels pointed out that Social Security numbers that go dormant and are not traceable to the original holder are ideal targets for identity thieves.

Why would someone eighty-seven- or eighty-nine years old want a Social Security number for the first time?

"One reason might have been for medical care," Daniels explained. "Getting government-paid medical care typically requires having a Social

Security number. There is no other reason for somebody to get a Social Security number at that age. In the 1970s, many women who had been housewives raising families applied for the first time to get a Social Security number because they needed to get medical benefits under programs such as Medicare."

Daniels has been a licensed private investigator in Ohio since 1995.

Sampson formed his private investigations firm, CSI Consulting and Investigations, in 2008. He previously worked as a deportations law enforcement officer with the U.S. Department of Homeland Security.

Since WND first published this investigation on May 11, 2010, the Obama White House has refused to answer any questions regarding President Obama's Social Security number.[14]

To date, Barack Obama's application for a Social Security number must be included among the scores of documents concerning his background and identity that he has refused to release to the American public.

PART ONE

THE OBAMA BIRTH CONTROVERSY

THE "FIRST BIRTHERS" ATTACK MCCAIN

Republican Candidate's Eligibility Assailed by Democrats and Obama Supporters

Long before all the mockery and ridicule started to be heaped on those raising questions about Barack Obama's constitutional eligibility to be president, Democratic Party operatives and dedicated Obama supporters were the first "birthers," insisting that John McCain was not eligible to be president as a "natural-born citizen."

The "birther" attack against John McCain was actually carried out first and loudest by Obama-supporting "mainstream media" sources, including ABC, CBS, NBC, the *New York Times*, the *Washington Post*, and FactCheck.org. In stark contrast to today, the eligibility issue was quite popular when Obama's opponent in the 2008 presidential campaign was the focus of attention.

When historians look back on this period, the hypocrisy of Democratic Party operatives, Obama supporters, and their accomplices in the establishment press will be inescapable. The eligibility issue was not toxic at all when John McCain was the target of attack, but only became so when the focus shifted to the Democratic hopeful. Then, in true Saul Alinsky-fashion, Obama's sympathizers on the left began deriding those who dared ask the same questions about Obama's eligibility that Obama's supporters had first raised about McCain.

This is a story President Obama and his team do not want told. They would prefer that American voters forget about the attack they launched against McCain, raising many of the very issues that would end up doing more damage to Obama. Fortunately, anticipating all of this, WND made dozens of screen captures of media stories attacking McCain on eligibility issues before they could be removed from the Internet.

Believe it or not, John McCain requested that a resolution be passed by the House and Senate affirming that he was eligible to run for president under Article 2, Section 1, of the Constitution.

Senator Barack Obama refused to do the same.

Meet Law Professor Jonathan Turley, "Father of the Birthers"

Almost a full six months before questions about Obama's eligibility started to appear, Jonathan Turley—a law professor at the George Washington University Law School in Washington, D.C.—began a full-scale assault on McCain's eligibility. On his personal blog, Turley describes himself as "a nationally recognized legal scholar who has written extensively in areas ranging from constitutional law to legal theory to tort theory." Noting that he has written more than three dozen academic articles appearing in leading law journals, he adds that he's the "second most cited law professor in the country," having published more than 750 articles in such newspapers as the *New York Times, Washington Post, U.S.A. Today, Los Angeles Times,* and *Wall Street Journal.*[15]

On February 28, 2008, Turley published an article titled "Does John McCain Have an Alexander Hamilton Problem? A Constitutional Challenge May Loom Over McCain's Eligibility for President."[16] The reference to Hamilton was to remind readers that Hamilton was born on the British West Indian island of Nevis, which has never been part of the United States, meaning Hamilton was not a natural-born citizen. In fact, one theory behind the inclusion of the "natural-born citizen" clause was that it was intended to prevent Hamilton from becoming president. Hamilton, however, would have been grandfathered in to eligibility by the language in Article 2, Section 1, specifying that citizens at the time the Constitution was adopted were eligible to be president.

John McCain was born in 1936 in the Panama Canal Zone, where his father was stationed as an officer in the U.S. Navy. Turley wrote that "absent a constitutional amendment, the question remains whether McCain can claim natural-born status." Turley suggested that the Constitutional Convention inserted the natural-born citizen requirement into Article 2, Section 1, "in part to block Hamilton by his detractors—although this may be apocryphal." More likely, Turley argued, was that "people like [John] Jay were concerned with a preference among some to have a King, including some foreign princes who might rule the nation."

Since there was no doubt that both of McCain's parents were U.S. citizens at the time of his birth, Turley focused on the location, claiming the candidate needed to be born on U.S. soil. In a nearly identical article published the next day—titled "McCain's Constitutional Dilemma: Native Son But Not Natural-born?"—Turley suggested McCain was "a foreign born citizen given his birth in the Canal Zone."[17] Writing that there "has never been a president sworn into office who was not born in one of the fifty states," Turley argued that McCain's case "would be a very close question." His conclusion was that, "A strong argument can be made that the Framers considered natural-born to refer to birth on U.S. soil." Turley was charging that McCain likely was ineligible to be president under Article 2, Section 1, the very argument that prompted Obama partisans to coin the pejorative term "birthers" to describe those who dare ask similar questions of their champion.

Turley's bias is obvious when we examine his comments concerning Arnold Schwarzenegger. Clearly favoring the prospect that Schwarzenegger might run for president, Turley published an article on August 20, 2007, just six months before his attack on McCain, arguing that Article 2, Section 1 reflected the insecurity of a young United States "surrounded by foreign conspiracies—real and imagined." When it came to a candidate Turley found politically acceptable, he argued that Article 2, Section 1, "was written for a different people and a different time." The eligibility provision, he charged, "now strikes a decidedly xenophobic note in an otherwise inclusive document." Even more sharply, he suggested, "the exclusion is an insult to the immigrants who built this nation—20 million since 1907."[18]

Pointing out that Article 2, Section 1, would prohibit from being president more than 700 immigrants who received the Medal of Honor, as well as former secretaries of state Christian Herter born in France, Henry Kissinger born in Germany, and Madeleine Albright born in the Czech Republic, Turley argued the natural-born citizen requirement should be eliminated.

"The provision reads like a constitutional version of an American Kennel Club certification for the purebred president," he wrote. "The fact is that we are a nation of mutts with the blood of countless ethnic groups coursing through our veins." He ended with the taunt: "If you want a pure breed, buy a dog."

Yet, when it came to opposing McCain's presidential candidacy, Turley did not hesitate to argue that the Republican likely was disqualified under Article 2, Section 1, because he had been born in the Canal Zone.

Those who think Turley's challenge to McCain's candidacy was not serious should consult an August 2008 article by University of Arizona law professor Gabriel J. Chin, titled, "Why Senator John McCain Cannot Be President."[19] In 1937, Chin noted that Congress passed a statute granting citizenship to any person born in the Canal Zone on or after February 26, 1904, who had at least one U.S. citizen parent. "This Act made Senator McCain a United States citizen before his first birthday," Chin wrote. "But again, to be a natural-born citizen, one must be a citizen at birth. Since Senator McCain became a citizen in his eleventh month of life, he does not satisfy this criterion, is not a natural-born citizen, and thus is not 'eligible to the Office of President.'"

Professor Chin was unwilling to compromise on the issue. On one hand, he wrote that as a matter of public policy, McCain should be allowed to be president because presidential candidates "who obtained their citizenship after birth are no more likely to be disloyal than those born citizens." Still he was opposed to McCain's eligibility. Why? Because, he insisted, "The Constitution forbids it."

"The rule of law would be mortally wounded if courts, Congress, or the executive could legitimately ignore provisions of law they deemed obsolete under the circumstances," Chin wrote. "It would be a grim moment in history if the very oath to 'preserve, protect, and defend the Constitution' that made a person President was also a falsehood that defied the document."

For Turley, these arguments were irrefutable. "Panama was never U.S. soil," he wrote in an article published March 6, 2008. "It is different in that sense from embassies or even territories. If such military installations are U.S. soil, it raises a host of even more difficult questions. For example, when illegal immigrants have a child in the United States, the child is a U.S. citizen. Does that mean that foreign citizens who give birth at United States military hospitals or installations are entitled to U.S. citizenship for the child? How about U.S. ships or aircraft?"[20]

It is important to note that the law professors arguing McCain was not eligible to be president were not scorned by the political establishment as "wing-nut" crazies, nor were they ridiculed as "birthers." Instead, their arguments were taken so seriously that Harvard law professor Laurence Tribe and former solicitor general Ted Olsen co-signed a letter refuting the legal scholars challenging McCain's eligibility. The two had argued the Florida recount case in the 2000 presidential election before the Supreme Court, with Tribe representing Al Gore and Olsen representing George W. Bush.[21]

Tribe and Olsen advanced the argument that the Panama Canal Zone was sovereign U.S. territory at the time of McCain's birth. "Historical practice confirms that birth on soil that is under the sovereignty of the United States, but not within a State, satisfies the Natural-born Citizen Clause," Tribe and Olsen wrote. Noting that Barack Obama was born in Hawaii on August 4, 1961, two years after Hawaii became a state on August 21, 1959, they argued, "We find it inconceivable that Senator Obama would have been ineligible for the Presidency had he been born two years earlier."

The letter noted that Senator Barry Goldwater, Republican Party presidential nominee in 1964, had been born in Arizona before its statehood and that Charles Curtis, vice president under President Herbert Hoover, was born in the Territory of Kansas on January 25, 1860, one year before Kansas became a state.

Still, the fact that Tribe and Olsen felt compelled to cross partisan lines to co-author the letter reflects the gravity of the eligibility challenges McCain's legally trained critics were raising in the early months of 2008.

February 28, 2008: Start of a Coordinated Attack on McCain

In an article published February 25, 2008, months before the Republican Party nominated McCain for president, FactCheck.org raised questions about McCain's eligibility without raising similar questions about Obama. The piece (see Exhibit 2, page 142) led off with the question, "How can Panamanian-born McCain be elected president?" FactCheck argued that although McCain met the natural-born citizen requirements, were he to win the presidency, the issue "could be challenged in the courts."[22]

A flurry of mainstream media news pieces popped up three days later, in what appeared to be a coordinated effort to raise questions about McCain's eligibility.[23]

On February 28, Carl Hulse wrote an article (see Exhibit 3, page 143) in the *New York Times* titled, "McCain's Canal Zone Birth Prompts Queries About Whether That Rules Him Out."[24]

Noting that neither Congress nor the Supreme Court has ever resolved definitively the issue of what constitutes "natural-born," Hulse turned McCain's eligibility into a question of whether he was born on American soil. "Almost since those words [natural-born citizen] were written in 1787 with scant explanation," he wrote, "their precise meaning has been the stuff of confusion, law school review articles, whisper campaigns, and civics class debates over whether only those delivered on American soil can be truly natural-born."

Hulse concluded by observing, "To date, no American to take the presidential oath has had an official birthplace outside the 50 states."

Picking up on the *New York Times* piece, NBC News ran a feature (see Exhibit 4, page 144) on the same day, posing the question, "Born in the U.S.A.?"[25]

Linking to Hulse's article in the *Times*, NBC pointed out that McCain was born on a military installation in the Canal Zone.

The same day, the *Wall Street Journal* published a Law Blog column (see Exhibit 5, page 145) authored by Dan Slater asking, "Does John McCain Have a Birthplace Problem?"

"In 1936, McCain was born at the Coco Solo Air Base, in the then-American controlled Panama Canal Zone, to Jack McCain, a Navy officer, and Roberta McCain," Slater wrote. "If McCain wins the 2008 election, he'd be the first American to take the presidential oath who has an official birthplace outside the 50 states."

Not to be outdone, CBS News speculated the same day (see Exhibit 6, page 146) that McCain's eligibility question "could conceivably end up before the Supreme Court," adding, "And you thought counting chads was a circus."[26]

The next day, February 29, 2008, the *Sunday Times* in London published (see Exhibit 7, page 146) a similar piece titled "McCain's Panama Birth Prompts Eligibility Probe by His Campaign."[27]

"Many experts argue that the nation's founders could never have intended to exclude the children of those serving in the military," reporter Hannah Strange wrote, "but as all presidents to date have been born within the 50 states there is no legal precedent."

Continuing the theme, on February 29, NBC correspondent Pete Williams published (see Exhibit 8, page 147) on the MSNBC Web site "McCain's Citizenship Called into Question."[28]

"Sen. John McCain, R-AZ, and his advisers are doing their best to brush aside questions—raised in the liberal blogosphere—about whether he is qualified under the Constitution to be president," Williams wrote. "But many legal scholars and government lawyers say it's a serious question with no clear answer."

Williams pointed out that "many legal scholars say the Canal Zone never was sovereign U.S. territory." He cited a February 1978 speech to the nation on the Panama Canal Treaty in which President Jimmy Carter claimed, "We have never had sovereignty over it. We have only had the right to use it. The U.S. Supreme Court and previous American presidents have repeatedly acknowledged the sovereignty of Panama over the Canal Zone."

Responding to Media Attacks, Senate Affirms McCain Is Eligible

On April 10, 2008, ABC's Jake Tapper published a piece on the network's Web site (see Exhibit 9, page 148) noting that the Constitution "does not define 'natural-born Citizen,'" and adding, "McCain was born in the Panama Canal Zone to parents who were U.S. citizens, but some scholars have questioned that it suffices."[29]

In the process of raising questions about McCain's eligibility, Tapper was still among the first to report that Senate Democrats were preparing to introduce a non-binding resolution expressing the sense of the Senate that McCain qualified under Article 2, Section 1, to run for president.

The next day, April 11, the *Wall Street Journal's* Law Blog published a piece confirming that Senators Patrick Leahy, D-VT, and Claire McCaskill, D-MO, had introduced just such a non-binding resolution.[30] Senators Hillary Clinton and Barack Obama, both at that time contenders for the Democratic Party presidential nomination, co-sponsored the bill.

The central argument of the resolution was "that there is no evidence of the intention of the Framers or any Congress to limit the constitutional rights of children born to American citizens serving in the military or to prevent those children from serving as their country's president." The resolution, introduced to the Senate as Senate Resolution 511, passed unanimously on April 30, 2008.

Despite Resolution, Demands Continue for McCain's Birth Certificate

But this was not enough to stop liberal activists and the establishment press from continuing to question McCain's eligibility.

In an article published in the *Washington Post* on May 2, 2008, reporter Michael Dobbs questioned (see Exhibit 10, page 149) whether Senate Resolution 511 was sufficient to prove that McCain was a natural-born citizen.[31]

The Senate resolution, Dobbs wrote, "is simply an opinion that has little bearing on an arcane constitutional debate that has preoccupied legal scholars for many weeks."

Dobbs noted that at the time the article was published, "three pending cases are challenging McCain's right to be president" because of his birth outside the United States.

While acknowledging that a senior McCain campaign official had shown reporters a copy of the candidate's original birth certificate, issued by the Canal Zone hospital, something the Obama presidential campaign and White House have persistently refused to do, he nevertheless questioned why McCain did not release the document to the press generally.

Shifting ground to attack not simply the fact of McCain's birth in the Canal Zone, the *Washington Post* moved to challenge his birth records. "Curiously enough, there is no record of McCain's birth in the Panama Canal Zone Health Department's bound birth registers, which are publicly available at the National Archives in College Park," Dobbs noted. "A search of the 'Child Born Abroad' records of the U.S. consular service for August 1936 included many U.S. citizens born in the Canal Zone but did not turn up any mention of John McCain."

Moreover, asserted Dobbs, according to a State Department manual, U.S. military installations abroad cannot be considered "part of the United States," and, "A child born on the premises of such a facility is not subject to the jurisdiction of the United States and does not acquire U.S. citizenship by birth." He further observed that there are few precedents for someone born outside the fifty states running for president, noting that the best example the McCain camp "has been able to come up with" is Vice President Charles Curtis, born in the Territory of Kansas in 1860, before Kansas became a state.

On May 12, 2008, PolitiFact.com published an article (see Exhibit 11, page 150) authored by Robert Farley called, "Was McCain born in the U.S.A.?"[32] Again, the argument was shifting to demand an examination of McCain's long-form birth certificate identifying the hospital where he was born and the doctor who attended the birth.

"Some Internet bloggers have speculated that McCain wasn't actually born in the Coco Solo military hospital in the Panama Canal Zone," Farley wrote, "but rather a nearby off-base hospital, in Panama."

The suggestion was that the off-base hospital might not qualify as U.S territory, hence invalidating a key premise that supported McCain's eligibility. PolitiFact also groused that McCain had not released his long-form birth certificate publicly, although it has steadfastly neglected to mention that the Obama campaign has refused all inquiries for Barack Obama's hospital-generated long-form birth certificate.

Noting that the question of McCain's eligibility is "rooted in legal opinions," not in facts, PolitiFact begged off giving McCain's eligibility question a truth rating, claiming, "PolitFact's customary True-False ratings don't quite fit here."

The influential Web site also dismissed congressional resolutions affirming McCain's eligibility, quoting Atlanta attorney Jill Pryor, "who twenty years ago wrote a nineteen-page paper" in the *Yale Law Journal* in which she argued that Congress' interpretation of the natural-born citizen clause is not binding on the courts.

Then, on June 12, the leftist DailyKos.com posted a piece (see Exhibit 12, page 151) by blogger "andyfoland" called "The Bombshell on McCain's Birth Certificate," claiming McCain had "no interest in releasing his birth certificate" because he "actually wasn't born in the United States." Moreover, "andyfoland" argued, "McCain has done a good job keeping the public at large from catching on that he was born in Panama."[33]

The *New York Times* rekindled the controversy (see Exhibit 13, page 151) in a July 11, 2008, article by law reporter Adam Liptak, with contributions from Carl Hulse, titled, "A Hint of New Life to a McCain Birth Issue."[34] The story brought to public attention the law journal article of Arizona law professor Gabriel J. Chin discussed above. As noted earlier, Chin had asserted that a 1937 law conferred citizenship on children of American parents born in the Canal Zone after that date, but that McCain didn't become a U.S. citizen until just before his first birthday.

"In his paper and in an interview, Professor Chin, a registered Democrat, said he had no political motive in raising the question," the *Times* wrote, although Newsbusters.org characterized it as "a meaningless, but prominently placed, 900-word story to further chip away at John McCain's stature." Newsbusters noted the *Times* had yet to print an article addressing growing questions about the validity of Obama's birth certificate.[35]

Keeping the bandwagon moving, UPI published a July 11 story (see Exhibit 14, page 152) headlined "McCain Not Natural-born Citizen, Prof Says," mirroring the *Times* story about Gabriel Chin's legal analysis.[36]

"A lawsuit challenging McCain's qualifications is pending in a federal court in Concord, N.H.," the UPI report stated. Evidently, lawsuits challenging McCain's eligibility were highly newsworthy—a sharp contrast, as we shall soon see, to the disdain the mainstream media displayed for any lawsuit that would question Obama's eligibility.

In July 2008, Snopes.com, yet another supposedly independent fact-checking Web site, classified as "undetermined" (see Exhibit 15, page 153) the claim that McCain isn't qualified to be president as a natural-born citizen because he was born in Panama.[37]

"As much as we'd like to dismiss this one as just another frivolous election season rumor, it's impossible to make any definitive statement about Senator McCain's presidential eligibility because the issue is a matter of law rather than a matter of fact, and the law is ambiguous," Snopes wrote.

Yet only a month before, in June 2008, Snopes had confidently disqualified as "false" the assertion that Obama wasn't eligible to be president, declaring instead that Obama was unquestionably a natural-born citizen within the meaning of Article 2, Section 1.[38]

On September 18, 2008, after McCain had won the Republican Party presidential nomination, Law.com reported that a San Francisco federal judge had ruled that McCain's assertion of U.S. citizenship was "highly probable," though carefully qualifying how the judicial ruling was characterized, thus keeping the issue alive.[39]

Obama Supporters Question McCain Birth Certificate and Birth Hospital

Nearly a year after the 2008 presidential campaign had ended, the Internet continued to buzz with stories generated by the political left questioning whether McCain was born in the Panama Canal Zone, without reporting that similar issues were being raised about whether Obama was born in Hawaii.[40]

In stark contrast to Obama, McCain's campaign staff released both a long form and a short form of his birth certificate. Immediately, bloggers opposed to McCain's presidential aspirations jumped on the documents to search out evidence of forgery or other information that might disqualify him. For example, a question had been raised as to how McCain could have been born in the Coco Solo Naval Hospital in 1936 when the hospital was not built until after 1941. Executive Order 8981, signed by FDR on December 17, 1941, laid out the boundaries of the land on the military base that would eventually be the hospital building site.[41] The nearest hospital to the base was in Colon, in the Republic of Panama, not on the U.S. military base and therefore not a part of the U.S.-administered Canal Zone.

Copies of McCain's long-form (see Exhibit 16, page 154) and short-form (see Exhibit 17, page 155) birth certificates surfaced publicly in *Hollander v. McCain*, a lawsuit filed in the U.S. District Court to challenge whether McCain was a natural-born citizen.

As recently as April 2010, a blogger posting as "Dr. Conspiracy" published on the pro-Obama Web site ObamaConspiracyTheories.com a two-article analysis arguing that both the long- and short-form McCain birth certificates were forgeries. His argument rested largely on an examination of discrepancies in the typeface of data entered on the documents, an effort reminiscent of the document analysis that destroyed the career of CBS News anchor Dan Rather, whose famously botched investigation had focused on the record of George W. Bush's participation in the Texas Air National Guard during the Vietnam War.[42] Moreover, objections were raised that the long-form birth certificate showed McCain born in the Colon Hospital, in the Panama Canal Zone, not on the Navy base hospital.

The mystery was solved when a review of the archival record showed there was a small hospital at the Coco Solo submarine base in 1936, and also revealed the name of the U.S. Navy physician who signed McCain's birth certificate.

Reporter Michael Dobbs, who earlier questioned McCain's birth qualifications, explained in the *Washington Post* that a senior McCain campaign official showed him a copy of the candidate's birth certificate issued by the "family hospital" in the Coco Solo submarine base.[43] McCain's grandfather, Dobbs pointed out, commanded the Coco Solo Naval Air Station in 1936, and his father was the executive officer of a submarine based there. Captain W.L. Irvine signed the birth certificate. "I have now checked that name against the Naval Register for 1936," Dobbs wrote, "and I find that William Lorne Irvine was director of the medical facility at the submarine base in Coco Solo, Panama Canal Zone, during that time." Linking to the relevant entry (see Exhibit 18, page 155), Dobbs concluded, "I think this effectively disposes of any remaining doubts that McCain was born inside the Canal Zone."

The issue of McCain's eligibility to be president became moot on November 4, 2008, the day he lost his presidential bid. In sharp contrast, the issue of Obama's presidential eligibility was not settled in his favor simply by winning the election. Rather, by dodging the issue during the campaign, Obama allowed eligibility questions to grow, remaining unanswered despite two more years of intensified examination. Should Obama run for re-election in 2012, the fact that he was president for one term does not prove he was ever eligible for that office. Indeed, he will have a difficult time being re-elected, particularly if millions of voters conclude he withheld inconvenient documents intentionally, fabricated materially important parts of his official birth narrative, and advanced specious legal arguments as a strategy to confuse an honest eligibility debate.

In the final analysis, those questioning McCain's eligibility had a weak argument. There has never been any doubt that McCain was born as the child of two U.S. citizens. Two nationally prominent constitutional lawyers—Tribe, a staunch supporter of Democratic Party politicians, and Olsen, an equally stalwart advocate for Republicans—agreed that the Canal Zone was under U.S. sovereignty when McCain was born there. The Senate concluded the Founders never meant to exclude from the presidency the child of two U.S. citizens born outside the United States because the family was involved in military service to the nation. What more remains to be examined? Navy records support that McCain was born at the family hospital on the military base in the Canal Zone. McCain is a natural-born citizen within the meaning of Article 2, Section 1, of the Constitution.

In sharp contrast, Barack Obama has never come forward to allow his birth history to be subject to equal scrutiny.

Consider:

• While then-Senator Obama co-sponsored the Senate resolution on McCain's eligibility, he and his supporters failed to pursue a Senate resolution on his own eligibility.

• Obama has refused to release his own long-form birth certificate, insisting instead that the short-form online Certification of Live Birth posted by partisan Web sites like FactCheck.org is his "birth certificate," the document he relies upon to prove he was born in Hawaii.

• To dodge the implications of Obama's dual citizenship at birth, Obama supporters have advanced specious arguments, contending that somehow he was a natural-born citizen by virtue of the 14th Amendment, even though that amendment had never been purported to redefine Article 2, Section 1's "natural-born citizen" requirement to be president.

• While McCain made public his long- and short-form birth certificates, Obama has hidden behind a complicated, contradictory and largely undocumented birth story while passport records, adoption papers, student loan applications, and other key documents remained sealed.

Nevertheless, the attack on McCain's eligibility has served a useful purpose in exposing the hypocrisy of the liberal-left political establishment.

Law Professor Jonathan Turley, justly termed the "Father of the Birthers" because of his leading role in claiming McCain was not a natural-born citizen, is never ridiculed as a "birther" for raising questions about where McCain was born.

Instead of confronting Obama eligibility arguments head-on and producing the documentary evidence needed to allow an honest evaluation, many of the same news agencies and self-proclaimed watchdog groups that pressed McCain's eligibility issue point fingers and laugh derisively at defenders of the Constitution who continue to pursue the inquiry.

Turley's hypocrisy is obvious in light of his open support of a possible presidential run by Arnold Schwarzenegger. The good professor saw no contradiction when he attacked the natural-born citizen requirement in the governor's case as xenophobic, championing the left's globalist perspective that as a nation of immigrants, America has grown beyond the national security and loyalty concerns that drove the Founders to insert the eligibility requirement into the Constitution.

The mainstream media went along for the ride, doing their best to publicize and amplify leftist attacks on McCain's eligibility while scorning as "birthers" and "crazies" anyone seeking to raise the exact same sorts of eligibility challenges regarding Obama.

· 2 ·

ABERCROMBIE & GLITCH

While the mainstream media showed little or no interest in Barack Obama's eligibility, citizens clearly had concerns, as demonstrated by an astonishing memo issued just months after Obama's inauguration by the Congressional Research Service, a public policy arm of Congress.

Prompted by a barrage of e-mails, letters, and phone calls from constituents to senators and Congress members, the April 3, 2009, document sought to provide a ready response for Capitol Hill staffers.

Remarkably, the memo stated that no one in the federal government, including Congress, had asked to see Obama's long-form, hospital-generated birth certificate during the 2008 campaign. The CRS explained there were no federal or state laws requiring officials to demand that the document be submitted.

Authored by Jack Maskell, the legislative attorney in the CRS's American Law Division,[44] the memo noted that many citizens had asked their representatives why Obama "has not had to produce an original, so-called 'long' version of a 'birth certificate' from the State of Hawaii" and wanted to know "how federal candidates are 'vetted' for qualifications generally."

The CRS explained that "there is no federal law, regulation, rule, guideline, or requirement that a candidate for federal office produce his or her original birth certificate, or a certified copy of the record of live birth, to any official of the United States Government; nor is there a requirement for federal candidates to publicly release such personal record or documentation."

Furthermore, the memo said, "There is no specific federal agency or office that 'vets' candidates for federal office as to qualifications or eligibility prior to election."

Nearly halfway through Obama's term—with some polls showing more than half of all Americans doubting Obama's claim that he was born in the Aloha State—the questions still had not gone away, and the big media remained uninterested.

That was when a self-proclaimed friend of Barack Obama's parents declared that, as Hawaii's new governor, he would use the authority of his office to put to rest a growing controversy he believed threatened the president's chances for re-election in 2012.

Countering the "Dark Side"

Neil Abercrombie, a former nineteen-year congressman, vowed shortly after his December 6 gubernatorial inauguration that he would try to release additional records on Obama from his state's Department of Health vault to prove the president was born in Hawaii and qualifies for the presidency as a natural-born citizen.

Abercrombie's announcement led to a spate of interviews in which he condemned "birthers" who question Obama's constitutional eligibility.

In an interview with Hawaii News Now,[45] the news department shared by three Honolulu television stations, Abercrombie blamed the "dark side" for the controversy and expressed optimism he would be able to answer at least some of the questions surrounding Obama's birthplace.

He told the *New York Times*[46] he had initiated conversations with Hawaii's attorney general and the chief of the state's Health Department about how he could release more explicit documentation of Obama's birth.

Abercrombie maintained he was acting on his own initiative, without consulting the White House, which declined to comment to the *Times*.

In an interview with CNN,[47] Abercrombie insisted he would push the matter forward whether or not the White House was privately worried that his quest would serve only to bring more attention to the issue.

"We haven't had any of those discussions," Abercrombie said of the White House. "It's a matter of principle with me. I knew his mom and dad. I was here when he was born. Anybody who wants to ask a question honestly could have had their answer already."

A native of Buffalo, N.Y., the seventy-two-year-old Abercrombie arrived in 1959 to study sociology at the University of Hawaii. As a teaching assistant, he met Obama's father, a native of Kenya, whom he described as a good friend.

A reporter asked Abercrombie if one option was to ask Obama to waive his privacy rights so that a copy of his birth certificate could be released publicly.

The governor cut off the question.

"No, no, no—it's not up to the president," he said. "It has nothing to do with the president. It has to do with the people of Hawaii who love him, people who love his mom and dad. It has to do with respect the office of the president is entitled to. And it has to do with respect that every single person's mother and father are entitled to."

Pressed on whether he might unilaterally release a copy of Obama's original birth certificate, Abercrombie made clear that he was waiting for his cabinet officials to report back to him on what he could legally do before proceeding, CNN reported.

"Obviously, I'm going to do what is legally possible," he said.

He told the *Los Angeles Times*,[48] he was bothered "that some people who should know better are trying to use this for political reasons."

"Maybe I'm the only one in the country that could look you right in the eye right now and tell you, 'I was here when that baby was born,'" he said.

Playing Hardball

Abercrombie's investigation caught the attention of Obama supporter and self-proclaimed "enemy" of "birthers" Chris Matthews, anchor of the nightly MSNBC "Hardball" program. Matthews devoted a segment to the controversy December 27, noting a *New York Times*/CBS News poll that said only 58 percent of Americans were willing to say Obama was born in Hawaii as the president claims.[49]

Matthews displayed a copy of a Hawaii long-form birth certificate from 1961 and compared it with a copy of the Certification of Live Birth that Obama supporters posted on the Internet during the 2008 presidential campaign, when the issue first was raised.

"Why has the president himself not demanded that they put out the initial documents?" Matthews asked his guests, *Chicago Tribune* columnist Clarence Page and David Corn of *Mother Jones* magazine.

"What do you do about those other 43 percent" who either don't believe Obama was born in Hawaii or don't know? the host asked. "Why isn't Abercrombie on the right trail here, to at least go to the [23 percent who aren't sure]? Obviously the nut cases on the far right who hate this guy aren't going to ever admit that you're right. But why not get to the people who are confused?"

What was new, said Matthews, was "the mere fact that a newly elected governor of Hawaii, [Obama's] home state—and it is his home state, I completely agree with you—has begun this effort."

"Now everybody on the right knows he's begun the effort. Every newspaper person knows it. You guys know it. I know it," Matthews continued. "So we're going to be peering out of the corner of our eye in the next couple of weeks, 'How's Abercrombie doing on his expedition to find the original document, with signatures all over it, like all our birth certificates, like this one here that somebody who was born one day before—has all kinds of signatures on it, it's an actual Photostat?"

Matthews was referring to the hospital-generated birth certificates of twin daughters born to Eleanor Nordyke at Kapi'olani Hospital on August 5, 1961, one day after the purported day of Obama's birth at the same hospital. The Nordyke birth certificates were featured in a July 2009 WND report.[50]

The Nordykes's certificates include information missing from the short-form document for Obama published online, including the name of the hospital, the name of the attending physician, the name and address of the parents, the race of the parents and the race of the baby, the exact time of birth and the weight of the baby at birth.

"Don't we want to know if he can find it?" Matthews continued in his December 27 segment. "I don't understand why the governor just doesn't say, 'Snap it off, whoever's over there in the department of records, send me a copy right now.' And why doesn't the president just say, 'Send me a copy right now'? Why doesn't (press secretary Robert) Gibbs and (senior adviser David) Axelrod say, 'Let's just get this crappy story dead'?"

Matthews' guests insisted the president doesn't care.

But an incredulous Matthews responded: "The president doesn't care that 43 percent of the country doesn't think he's an American?"

So Where Is the Birth Certificate?

A few weeks later, the *Honolulu Star-Advertiser* published[51] an interview with Abercrombie in which it asked for an update on the governor's quest to resolve the "birther" issue.

Abercrombie said in the January 18 interview that at that moment his investigation was showing a recording of the birth "actually exists in the archives, written down." But he apparently had not found the long-form birth certificate he was seeking.

> **Star-Advertiser:** You stirred up quite a controversy with your comments regarding birthers and your plans to release more information regarding President Barack Obama's birth certificate. How is that coming?
>
> **Abercrombie:** I got a letter from someone the other day who was genuinely concerned about it; it is not all just political agenda. They were talking on Olelo last night about this; it has a political implication for 2012 that we simply cannot have.
>
> (Abercrombie said there is a recording of the birth in the State Archives and he wants to use that.)
>
> It was actually written I am told, this is what our investigation is showing, it actually exists in the archives, written down ...
>
> ... What I can do, and all I have ever said, is that I am going to see to it as governor that I can verify to anyone who is honest about it that this is the case.
>
> If there is a political agenda then there is nothing I can do about that, nor can the president.

Essentially, Abercrombie was reporting what everyone with half an interest in the issue already had heard: There is something "written down" in

Hawaii's records about Obama's birth. But what, exactly, Abercrombie still was unable to say. His answer—a tacit admission that he couldn't produce documented proof of eligibility—caught the attention of a sleeping media.

A WND story on the interview[52] was linked by the *Drudge Report* and followed by coverage by ABC News,[53] United Press International,[54] and the *Daily Mail* of London,[55] among others. Just two days later, talk radio icon Rush Limbaugh opened his top-rated program noting WND's story and asking why Abercrombie appeared to have no support from the White House in his publicized quest to resolve the issue.[56]

"Where's Obama? Where's the White House? Is this guy flying alone? Neil Abercrombie on his own on this? So much of this is difficult to fathom, to believe," the king of talk radio said.

Puzzling over Abercrombie's investigation, Limbaugh pointed out the governor's knowledge of the "ins and outs of electoral politics" as a veteran of two decades in the House of Representatives.

But Abercrombie made a mistake, Limbaugh said, in announcing his investigation in December before he was sure he could produce the proof.

Nobody had "come forward to definitively prove it."

"In fact, most government officials have apparently done their best to seal it all off," he said. "Whatever there is, they've sealed it all off, and they've tried to pooh-pooh any interest in it. And they have attempted to impugn those who have interest in it."

For liberals, Limbaugh said, the issue of whether Obama is a natural-born citizen is no big deal, "It's merely a presidential, constitutional requirement."

After all, as far as liberals are concerned, he said, the Constitution is an "impediment to them."

James Taranto, editor of the *Wall Street Journal*'s influential "Best of the Web" blog, who had urged conservatives to steer away from the "birther" issue because it could tar the movement and jeopardize Republican electoral success, caught the significance of Matthews' stance and Abercrombie's "investigation."

"So we now have three or four liberal Democrats—the 'Hardball' trio and possibly the Aloha governor—taking what had been a birtherian position in favor of releasing the archival certificate," wrote Taranto.[57]

Taranto added that his "view has long been that the birthers are playing a sucker's game—that they are aiding Obama by making it easier for his supporters to depict his critics as wackos and divert attention from real questions about his political character. This change in liberal attitudes may be a sign that the game is no longer working to Obama's advantage. It could be that his baneful policies have led more Americans to harbor doubts about his very legitimacy."

Meanwhile, even the legacy media were beginning to take notice. An ABC News report stated, "Despite his assurance to end the controversy, the governor has yet to present the document."

ABC led its story with, "Officials in Hawaii say they have located President Obama's birth certificate indicating that he was born in the state, but have yet to produce the document at the heart of a long-simmering conspiracy theory."[58]

Back in Abercrombie's Hawaii, a columnist writing in an award-winning, independent online news and opinion journal founded by veteran Hawaii reporters asserted the governor "has utterly failed to prove Obama was born in Hawaii."

Robert Paul Reyes, in the *Hawaii Reporter*,[59] said state officials "need to track down only one document: The original Obama birth certificate with the name of the hospital and the doctor, his or her signature."

"How difficult can it be for the governor of Hawaii to track down one document? He can dispatch hundreds of state employees to search for Obama's birth certificate," the columnist said.

Reyes argued that "to state that 'officials have tracked down papers indicating that President Obama was indeed born in Hawaii' falls woefully short of proving that Obama is a citizen of the United States."

He concluded: "Show us the money! Show us the birth certificate!"

Radio Daze

The story of Abercrombie's apparent inability to find the birth certificate took on new life when celebrity journalist Mike Evans, a friend of the governor's for decades, declared in radio interviews January 20 that Abercrombie had personally admitted to him that his quest had failed.

Evans said Abercrombie had told him that after mobilizing gubernatorial staff and wielding the power of his office, including the use of a search warrant, the governor concluded there is no birth certificate in Hawaii for Barack Obama.

A recording of Evans' interview with the *Morning Show* on KQRS radio in Minneapolis documented Evans claiming he had been "talking to Neil's office" the day before.[60]

"Neil promised me that when he became governor, he was going to cut through all the red tape," Evans noted. "He was going to get Obama's birth certificate once and for all and end this stupid controversy that he was not born in the United States."

But now, after conducting his search "to get rid of that question" of whether or not Obama was born in Hawaii, Evans told the radio show, Abercrombie "has some egg on his face; I mean, now he admits publicly there is no birth certificate."

Evans declared: "Yesterday, talking to Neil's office, Neil says that he's searched everywhere using his powers as governor at the Kapi'olani Women's and Children's Hospital and Queens Hospital, the only places where kids were born in Hawaii back when Barack was born, and there is no Barack Obama birth certificate in Hawaii—absolutely no proof at all that he was born in Hawaii."

But not long after the interview was reported by WND, Evans backtracked.

In an interview with Fox News January 26, he insisted he "misspoke,"[61] explaining that he had not talked to Abercrombie since he became governor.

"I was on 34 radio stations that morning. [KQRS] was the only station where I said, instead of saying, 'The hospital said there's no birth certificate.' I misspoke and said, 'Neil said that.'"

But recordings of other interviews Evans made that day revealed otherwise.

In an interview with 590 KLBJ in Austin, Evans was even more explicit than in his Minneapolis interview, stating not that he had talked to "Neil's office," but to Abercrombie himself. And he even quoted the governor.[62]

"Yesterday I talked to Neil. Said that he searched everywhere using all of his power as governor. Looking at Kapi'olani Women's and Children's

Hospital and Queen's Medical Center where children were born back in that day. And he said, 'Mike, there is no Barack Obama birth certificate,'" Evans said.

A KLBJ host then asked: "I thought the holder of the certificate said it was locked up, that she had seen it."

"Well," replied Evans, "the governor demanded to see it, went to the hospitals, sent all of his people, a search warrant, and he could not get it."

Evans also told the audience of KOOL FM in Phoenix, "Yesterday I talked to Neil ... said he has searched everywhere using his power as governor ... there is no Barack Obama birth certificate."

WND columnist Jack Cashill, author of the 2011 exposé *Deconstructing Obama*,[63] said that after listening to numerous clips of interviews Evans conducted that day, he concluded Evans appeared to be reading from a script and ad-libbing.[64]

"I suspect that he repeated the Abercrombie claim on all thirty-four stations," Cashill said, concluding that it was possible not only that Evans' backtrack was a lie, but that someone "had gotten to him," warning him to retreat.

The Minneapolis interview clearly showed, at the least, that either Evans or Abercrombie has an abysmal memory.

Evans said Abercrombie told him his first recollection of Obama was when Obama was playing in a T-ball league, at the age of about five or six.

"I go, 'What about before that?'" Evans recalled. "And he goes, 'Well, I really don't remember him much before that,' which I thought was very odd."

Abercrombie, on the other hand, had told the *Los Angeles Times* in December, "Maybe I'm the only one in the country that could look you right in the eye right now and tell you, 'I was here when that baby was born.'"[65]

A few days later, Abercrombie's clarification to the Associated Press only further called into question his account of Obama's childhood.

Abercrombie explained that he didn't exactly see Obama's parents with their newborn son at the hospital, but that he "remembers seeing Obama as a child with his parents at social events."[66]

The problem with that statement is that school records show Ann Dunham took the infant Obama with her to Seattle just weeks after his birth to enroll at the University of Washington.

The next year, 1962, Barack Obama, Sr. left Hawaii for good to study at Harvard in Massachusetts, before his son was a year old. Ann Dunham did not return to Hawaii until after Barack Obama, Sr. left to go to Cambridge, Massachusetts.

Head Fake?

In the monologue that opened his January 21 show, Limbaugh wondered aloud whether, despite Abercrombie's claims to the contrary, the White House was behind the governor's investigation.

"I would think that if Abercrombie is gonna do this, he's not the Lone Ranger. He's gotta be calling the White House, 'Okay, look, we have a potential problem here. I want to find this thing and I want to make it public.'"

If that happened, Limbaugh continued, "somebody at the regime did not say, 'No, don't do it,' because Abercrombie is still alive. If they had said, 'No, don't do it,' and Abercrombie is still doing it, I don't even want to think of the consequences of that."

Could Obama be "toying" with birthers, seeking to expose them, Limbaugh wondered, as "a bunch of Looney Tune kook right-wingers"?

Limbaugh said he wouldn't put it past the White House to concoct a scheme to lure in birthers, build up anticipation, then suddenly have the birth certificate show up somewhere.

What worries him, he said, is that Hawaii's previous director of health, Dr. Chiyome Fukino, issued an official statement June 27, 2009, stating that she had "seen the original vital records maintained on file by the Hawai'i State Department of Health verifying Barack Hussein Obama was born in Hawai'i and is a natural-born American citizen."

"So the director of health for Hawaii says [she] personally saw it. Now, out of the blue here comes the new governor, Abercrombie, saying he can't find it. Now (sigh), folks, I'm just warning you: Be very, very careful on this. Something here is just not right."

The next day, the Associated Press reported[67] that Abercrombie's spokeswoman announced the governor had given up his pursuit.

Was it because there there was no birth certificate to be found? Did the White House shut down the sorry saga? According to the spokeswoman, Abercrombie stopped because the state attorney general told him privacy laws bar him from disclosing an individual's birth documentation without the person's consent.

But if that explanation is to be believed, then apparently Abercrombie had not been listening to Hawaii officials who had been saying the exact same thing constantly for two years.

"There is nothing more that Gov. Abercrombie can do within the law to produce a document," said spokeswoman Donalyn Dela Cruz. "Unfortunately, there are conspirators who will continue to question the citizenship of our president."

Health Department spokeswoman Janice Okubo confirmed, according to the Associated Press, that Obama's name is found in its alphabetical list of names of people born in Hawaii, maintained in bound copies available for public view.

That information, called index data, shows a listing for "Obama II, Barack Hussein, Male," according to the department's Web site.

"The index is just to say who has their records within the department. That's an indication," Okubo said. "I can't talk about anyone's records."

"There's No Birth Certificate."

Meanwhile, just two days later, WND published a story featuring a notarized affidavit by a former senior elections clerk for Honolulu in 2008, Tim Adams, swearing that there is no long-form, hospital-generated birth certificate on file with the Hawaii Department of Health and that neither of Honolulu's hospitals has any record that Obama was born in their facility.[68]

Adams was employed at the City and County of Honolulu Elections Division from May 2008 through September 2008.

His position was senior elections clerk, overseeing a group of fifty to sixty employees responsible for verifying the identity of voters at the Absentee Ballot Office. It was in this capacity that Adams became aware of the search for Obama's birth records.

"During the course of my employment," Adams swears in the affidavit, "I became aware that many requests were being made to the City and County of Honolulu Elections Division, the Hawaii Office of Elections, and the Hawaii Department of Health from around the country to obtain a copy of then-Senator Barack Obama's long-form, hospital-generated birth certificate."

As he inquired about the birth certificate, he says, his supervisors told him the records were not on file at the Hawaii Department of Health.

"Senior officers in the City and County of Honolulu Elections Division told me on multiple occasions that no Hawaii long-form, hospital-generated birth certificate existed for Senator Obama in the Hawaii Department of Health," Adams' affidavit reads, "and there was no record that any such document had ever been on file in the Hawaii Department of Health or any other branch or department of the Hawaii government."

In a telephone interview, Adams told WND it was common knowledge among election officials where he worked that no original, long-form birth certificate could be found at the Hawaii Department of Health.

"My supervisor came and told me, 'Of course, there's no birth certificate. What? You stupid,'" Adams said. "She usually spoke well, but in saying this she reverted to a Hawaiian dialect. I really didn't know how to respond to that. She said it and just walked off. She was quite a powerful lady."

Moreover, Adams was told that neither Queen's Medical Center nor Kapi'olani Women's and Children's Hospital had any records of Obama's birth at their medical facilities.

"Senior officers in the City and County of Honolulu Elections Division further told me on multiple occasions," stated Adams, "that Hawaii State government officials had made inquires about Sen. Obama's birth records to officials at Queen's Medical Center and Kapi'olani Medical Center in Honolulu and that neither hospital had any record of Senator Obama having been born there, even though Governor Abercrombie is now asserting and various Hawaii government officials continue to assert Barack Obama Jr. was born at Kapi'olani Medical Center on August 4, 1961.

"We called the two hospitals in Honolulu: Queens and Kapi'olani," Adams said. "Neither of them have any records that Barack Obama was born there."

Who's My Father?

In his autobiography, *Dreams from My Father*, Obama mentions he had his birth certificate among other items "folded away" but indicated there may have been a problem with the document.

When his father died in 1982, lawyers contacted anyone who might have claim to the estate.

According to *Dreams*, Obama, Sr. had children with at least four different women, including two Americans. Ruth Nidesand—an American whom Obama, Sr. married after he separated from Barack Obama, Jr.'s mother—had two children, including a son named Mark.

Amid questions about the paternity of many of the children, Obama, Jr. told his half-sister Auma in *Dreams*, "Unlike my mum, Ruth has all the documents needed to prove who Mark's father was."[69]

Did Ann Dunham have no proof that Barack Obama, Sr. was the father of her son?

Is that the real reason why, three decades later, an attempt by Hawaii's highest authority to settle once and for all the facts surrounding the birth of the president of the United States turned out looking like he was on a fool's errand?

· 3 ·

A DUAL CITIZEN AT BIRTH

**Why Barack Obama Is Not a Natural-Born Citizen Under
Article 2, Section 1 of the Constitution**

The Constitution specifies in Article 2, Section 1, that: "No Person except a natural-born Citizen, or a Citizen of the United States, at the time of the Adoption of this Constitution, shall be eligible to the Office of President."

The Constitution does not define the term "natural-born Citizen," nor does it constitute or appoint a governmental entity to assure this requirement is met for each presidential candidate. Put simply, the Constitution did not designate a mechanism for verifying the birth credentials of presidential candidates.

By specifying natural-born citizen, the Constitution establishes a higher eligibility threshold for president than mere U.S. citizenship. One can be a citizen of the United States and yet not be a natural-born citizen under Article 2, Section 1. A good example is Arnold Schwarzenegger. Born in Austria, the former California governor is a naturalized American citizen, but not a natural-born citizen, and therefore would not be eligible to run for the presidency. A naturalized American citizen is, by definition, not natural-born.

The purpose of this chapter is to define natural-born citizen as the Founders understood it and intended it, and to show that there are legitimate questions about Barack Obama's eligibility for the presidency simply because his father, as a citizen of Kenya, was a British citizen at the time Obama was born. Through his father's citizenship, Obama was a "dual citizen" of Britain and the United States of America at birth, a situation America's Founding Fathers considered highly problematic to natural-born citizenship under the meaning of Article 2, Section 1.

Previous Constitutional Challenges to Presidential Eligibility

Before we examine the Founders' conception of natural-born citizenship, understand that Barack Obama is by no means the first presidential candidate in U.S. history to have his eligibility challenged on these grounds.

Perhaps the most notable previous case was Chester Alan Arthur, a Republican elected vice president under James Garfield who ascended to the presidency after Garfield was assassinated by Charles J. Guiteau on July 2, 1881. A close examination of concerns over his presidential eligibility reveals that problems with Arthur's family history bear a striking resemblance to questions about Obama's.

Some historians say Arthur lied about his father's citizenship in order to claim he was eligible under Article 2, Section 1, to run for vice president, with the ever-present possibility of suddenly being elevated to the presidency. William Arthur, the future president's father, was born in Ireland in 1796 and emigrated to Canada in 1818 or 1819. In recent years, microfiche records have surfaced proving William Arthur was naturalized in New York and became a U.S. citizen in August 1843, when his son, Chester Arthur, the future president, was either thirteen or fourteen.

So, Chester Arthur was a British citizen at birth by virtue of his father's citizenship (Ireland had joined with Great Britain in 1801) and a dual citizen of the United States, by virtue of the citizenship of his mother, Regina Melvina, who was born in Vermont. William and Regina eloped in Canada and married in 1821. Chester, their fifth child, was born October 5, 1829, in Burlington, Vermont, though there was a question for some time as to where he was born.

Prior to the 1880 election, the Democratic Party, desiring to investigate Arthur's eligibility, hired lawyer A. P. Hinman, who in 1884 published a book titled *How a British Subject Became President of the United States.* Hinman argued that Arthur was not a natural-born U.S. citizen because he was a British subject at birth, a result of his father's citizenship in the United Kingdom. Hinman also argued, incorrectly, that Chester Arthur had been born in Canada, or possibly in Ireland, but not in Vermont. Had Arthur been born outside the United States, he undoubtedly would have been doubly disqualified from being president—both because his father was a British citizen when Chester was born, and because he was born on foreign soil.

Throughout his life, Chester Arthur did what he could to obscure his personal history, reportedly burning all his papers before his death. No birth certificate for Chester Arthur exists, because at the time of his birth it was not common practice to issue them. The question of Arthur's birthplace was not settled until 1975, when U.S. historian Thomas Reeves' definitive history of Arthur, titled *Gentleman Boss,*[70] validated Hinman's conclusion that Arthur's father was born in Ireland. He corrected Hinman, however, by using family history notations in the family Bible to establish that Chester had been born in Vermont.

The salient question is this: Was the fact that Chester Arthur's mother was a U.S. citizen when he was born and that he was born in Vermont sufficient to make him a natural-born citizen under the meaning and original intent of Article 2, Section 1?

Had the naturalization papers for Chester Arthur's father surfaced in the run-up to the 1880 presidential election, would Chester Arthur have been nominated for vice president?

As was the case with Chester Arthur, Barack Obama's father was a citizen of the British Empire when Obama was born. Thus, both presidents were dual citizens at birth.

Moreover, questions continue to be raised over whether Barack Obama was born in Hawaii, much as rumors circulated that Chester Arthur was born in Canada, or possibly in Ireland.

Arthur intentionally obscured his birth circumstances to bury questions about his eligibility to be president, much as Obama continues to withhold from the American public key documents regarding his birth, including his original hospital birth certificate.

Arthur's candidacy for president is not the only one prior to Obama's in which Article 2, Section 1, of the Constitution was an issue.

• Senator Charles Curtis, Republican Party vice presidential candidate for Herbert Hoover in the 1928 presidential election, served as the nation's 31st vice president from March 4, 1929, to March 4, 1933. Curtis was born in Topeka, Kansas Territory, on January 25, 1860, a year before Kansas became a state on January 29, 1861.

• Senator Barry Goldwater, 1964 Republican Party presidential nominee, was defeated by President Lyndon B. Johnson. Goldwater was born in Phoenix, Arizona Territory, on January 2, 1909, three years before Arizona became the 48th state, on February 14, 1912.

• Michigan Governor George Romney, unsuccessful aspirant for the Republican Party 1968 presidential nomination, was born in Mormon colonies in Mexico on July 8, 1907.

• Senator Lowell Palmer Weicker, Jr., unsuccessful candidate for the 1980 Republican Party presidential nomination, was born in Paris on May 16, 1931.

The status of all four as natural-born citizens under the meaning of Article 2, Section 1, was questioned because they were either born outside the United States, or in a U.S. territory before the territory was a U.S. state.

One difference between these four cases and that of Chester Arthur was that with Curtis, Goldwater, Romney, and Weicker, there was no doubt that both parents were U.S. citizens when their future-candidate children were born. Even though none of the candidates was born in a U.S. state, all were born subject to the jurisdiction of the United States, because their parents were citizens.

The Founders, Natural Law, and the Meaning of "Natural-Born Citizen"

America's Founding Fathers, assembled in 1787 at the Constitutional Convention in Philadelphia, were fearful that foreign influences could destroy the republic they were seeking to establish. As historian Forest

McDonald has pointed out, Elbridge Gerry of Massachusetts wanted to prevent foreigners from becoming citizens, "taking the position that naturalized citizens would always have divided loyalties."[71] The Founders believed it critical that the nation's chief executive and commander in chief possess undivided loyalty to the United States. They wanted this loyalty to be established at birth, such that no circumstance regarding that birth could indicate loyalty to a foreign country.

John Jay, president of the Continental Congress from 1778 to 1789 and the first Supreme Court chief justice, wrote the following in a July 25, 1787, letter to George Washington, presiding officer of the Constitutional Convention: "Permit me to hint, whether it would be wise and seasonable to provide a strong check to the admission of Foreigners into the administration of our national Government; and to declare expressly that the Command in Chief of the American army shall not be given to nor devolve on, any but a natural-born Citizen."

Jay is thought to have written this in response to speculation that the Constitutional Convention was attempting to erect a monarchy that ultimately could be headed by a foreign ruler. At any rate, shortly after Jay wrote the letter, the "natural-born Citizen" language was introduced into the draft of the Constitution by the Committee of Eleven and was adopted with no debate.[72]

In the 18th century, the term natural-born citizen derived from an understanding of natural law—the universal, self-evident law America's Founding Fathers presumed came from God. Natural law was seen as God's law that ruled human affairs, distinct from positive law, which specified statutes written by human beings to govern human behavior. The Founders would have understood that positive law, to the extent it was correct and bore authority, had to derive from and be consistent with natural law. Writers in the natural law tradition, including Swiss philosopher and diplomat Emerich de Vattel, profoundly influenced the thinking of the Founding Fathers.

The term natural-born citizen appears first in a treatise Vattel wrote in 1758 titled *Law of Nations: or, Principles of the Natural Law Applicable to the Conduct and Affairs of Nations and Sovereigns*. In Chapter 19, Section 212, Vattel specified:

> The citizens are the members of the civil society, bound to this society by certain duties, and subject to its authority; they equally participate in its advantages. The natives or natural-born citizens are those born in the country of parents who are citizens.

He continued:

> As the society cannot exist and perpetuate itself otherwise than by the children of the citizens, those children naturally follow the condition of their fathers, and succeed to all their rights. The society is supposed to desire this in consequence of what it owes to its own preservation, and it is presumed as matter of course that each citizen, on entering into society, reserves to his children the right of becoming members of it.

Vattel again emphasizes the concept that natural-born citizens are those born in the nation to parents who are citizens of the nation:

> The country of the fathers is therefore that of the children, and these become true citizens merely by their tacit consent. We shall soon see whether, on their coming to the years of discretion, they may renounce their right, and what they owe to the society in which they were born.

Vattel concluded:

> I say that, in order to be of the country, it is necessary that a person be born of a father who is a citizen; for, if he is born there of a foreigner, it will only be the place of his birth, and not his country.

Thus, the point of requiring that presidents be natural-born citizens was to prevent foreigners, or those whose allegiance could be attributed to the jurisdiction of foreign sovereigns, from ever being chief executive with the awesome powers of commander in chief.

Using Vattel's definition, natural-born citizen is not a vague concept. Rather, applied to the U.S. Constitution, a natural-born citizen is someone born in the United States to parents who are United States citizens. Given this definition, a person born in the United States to one U.S. citizen parent and a second who is a citizen of another country would not qualify. Obama's situation is precisely this: He says he was born in Hawaii to a

Kenyan father and a U.S. citizen mother.

The assertion that a presidential candidate should be disqualified for being born on foreign soil was arguably weaker if both parents were U.S. citizens when the child was born. Under Vattel's definition, if the child's birth location were under U.S. jurisdiction at the time and both parents were U.S. citizens, the child was arguably a natural-born citizen. So, according to Vattel, Charles Curtis and Barry Goldwater would be considered natural-born citizens, provided we consider the territories of Kansas and Arizona to have been part of the United States before they were granted statehood.

Had George Romney or Lowell Weicker advanced as presidential candidates, their birthplaces would have become an issue under Article 2, Section 1.

With regard to John McCain, whose Democratic critics in 2008 investigated whether he was born at a civilian hospital in the Canal Zone or in a U.S. Navy hospital, some believed birth outside the Navy base would have disqualified him from running for president.

There can be no doubt the Founding Fathers were familiar with Vattel's *Law of Nations*. On December 9, 1775, Benjamin Franklin wrote to Vattel's editor, C.G.F. Dumas, in France: "I am much obliged by the kind present you have made us of your edition of Vattel. It came to us in good season, when circumstances of a rising state make it necessary frequently to consult the law of nations. [I]t has been continually in the hands of the members of our Congress, now sitting, who are much pleased with your notes and preface, and have entertained a high and just esteem for their author."[73]

The First Congress in 1790—whose members included twenty delegates to the Constitutional Convention, eight of them members of the Committee of Eleven that drafted the natural-born citizen clause—passed the Naturalization Act of 1790 (1 Stat. 103, 104), which provided: "And the children of citizens of the United States that may be born beyond the sea, or out of the limits of the United States, shall be considered as natural-born citizens."[74] If we incorporate this into the meaning of Article 2, Section 1, it becomes less important for natural-born citizenship that the person is born in the United States, as long as his parents are both U.S. citizens. This interpretation might have allowed Romney and Weicker to be eligible for president despite being born on foreign soil. Still, it is questionable whether being born in Vermont would make Chester Arthur qualified or whether being born in Hawaii would qualify Barack Obama, because of the foreign nationality and presumed allegiance of their fathers.

Critics who object to interpreting the meaning of natural-born citizen in Article 2, Section 1, as a term of natural law have argued that there is "no source to which an appeal can be made to determine what natural law is."[75] This argument, however, would not make sense to the Founding Fathers, who were familiar with philosophers such as Thomas Hobbes, John Locke, and David Hume, all of whom wrote extensively of natural law as derived from classical Greek and Roman philosophy. While Hobbes, Locke, and Hume all differed in their exact definitions and applications of natural law, the concept that natural law derived from God and was imbued in human nature was held in common. Moreover, Vattel is careful not to leave the term natural-born citizen vague, but to define it carefully as applying to those born in the nation to parents who are citizens of the nation.

Critics also object that it "makes no sense for a nation of immigrants to consider 'natural allegiance' to be determined by where their fathers came from." Yet, consider that in Article 2, Section 1, the Founders stipulated as eligible for the presidency not only "natural-born Citizens," but also "Citizens of the United States, at the time of the Adoption of this Constitution." Foreigners, including persons born to one or more foreign parents who were not citizens at the time the Constitution was adopted, were not eligible to be president. This was the entire point. The Founding Fathers wanted to exclude foreigners from the presidency because they were distrustful of elevating to chief executive of the nation or commander in chief anyone who by birth might bear allegiance to a foreign nation. That someone was born to a foreign parent reflects no fault of their own, of course, but the Founding Fathers were distrustful that a dual citizen at birth would owe his undivided loyalty to the United States of America.

One final point is grammatical in nature. In writing the natural-born citizen clause of Article 2, Section 1, observe that the Founding Fathers capitalized "Citizen," such that the phrase read "natural-born Citizen." In 18th-century English grammatical tradition, the principle was that the noun "Citizen" was being modified by the phrase "natural-born," which served to further qualify the understanding of "Citizen." That is, to be eligible for president, it was not sufficient that a person be a citizen; he also had to be natural-born. The point is that not all citizens are natural-born, but only natural-born citizens are eligible to be president. The phrase "natural-born Citizen" was intended to specify that "natural-born" constituted a sub-class within the larger class of "Citizens."

To modern thinkers, the idea of restricting the presidency to natural-born citizens can seem archaic or xenophobic, especially when the United States is itself a nation of immigrants. Still, the clause remains in Article 2, Section 1, and has never been modified or removed by constitutional amendment, even if some today think it would be wise to do so. As long as the natural-born citizen eligibility requirement remains in the Constitution, Americans have an obligation to take the entire phrase seriously and to apply its standard rigorously, without exception.

Barack Obama—a Dual Citizen at Birth

During the 2008 campaign, supporters of Barack Obama fought hard to prove he was not then a citizen of Kenya. But they could not deny that his father was a citizen of Kenya at the time the son was born. And because Kenya in 1961 was part of the British Empire, making Barack Obama, Sr. a British citizen, that in turn made Barack Obama, Jr. an Imperial subject at the time of his birth, and a citizen of Kenya and of the British Commonwealth from 1963 on, when Kenya gained independence from Great Britain.

Even FactCheck.org, which consistently championed Obama's 2008 presidential candidacy, was forced to make these admissions. On August 29, 2008, FactCheck asked: "Does Barack Obama have Kenyan citizenship?"[76] The question was asked rhetorically, as a leaping-off point for refuting a *Rocky Mountain News* article that had claimed Obama was still a Kenyan citizen in 2008, when he was running for president.[77]

FactCheck began by admitting Obama was indeed a citizen of the Commonwealth of Great Britain by virtue of his father's citizenship:

"When Barack Obama, Jr. was born on August 4, 1961, in Honolulu, Kenya was a British colony, still part of the United Kingdom's dwindling empire. As a Kenyan native, Barack Obama, Sr. was a British subject whose citizenship was governed by the British Nationality Act of 1948, which also governed the status of Obama, Sr.'s children:

> **British Nationality Act of 1948 (Part II, Section 5):** Subject to the provisions of this section, a person born after the commencement of this Act shall be a citizen of the United Kingdom and Colonies by descent if his father is a citizen of the United Kingdom and Colonies at the time of the birth.

In other words, at the time of his birth, Barack Obama, Jr. was both a U.S. citizen (assuming he was born in Hawaii) *and* a citizen of the United Kingdom and Colonies, or the UKC, by virtue of being born to a father who was a citizen of the UKC.

FactCheck went on to argue, "Obama's British citizenship was short-lived." Since Kenya gained independence from the United Kingdom on December 12, 1963, the Web site noted, Chapter VI, Section 87, of the Kenyan Constitution conveyed Kenyan citizenship upon Barack Obama, Jr. again through his father's Kenyan citizenship:

> As a citizen of the UKC who was born in Kenya, Obama's father automatically received Kenyan citizenship via subsection (1) [of the Kenyan Constitution Chapter VI, Section 87]. So given that Obama qualified for citizen of the UKC status at birth and given that Obama's father became a Kenyan citizen via subsection (1), it follows that Obama did in fact have Kenyan citizenship after 1963. So The Rocky Mountain News was at least partially correct.

FactCheck determined that the *Rocky Mountain News* was only partially correct because the Kenyan Constitution in effect at independence prohibited dual citizenship for adults. That is, Kenyan citizens possessing citizenship in more than one country automatically lose their Kenyan citizenship when they turn twenty-one, unless they formally renounce any non-Kenyan citizenship and swear an allegiance to Kenya. The Kenyan Constitution required Obama to choose whether to keep his U.S. or his Kenyan citizenship within a two-year window of achieving his twenty-first birthday, by no later than August 4, 1984.

Following this legal logic, FactCheck concluded:

Since Sen. Obama has neither renounced his U.S. citizenship nor sworn an oath of allegiance to Kenya, his Kenyan citizenship automatically expired on August 4, 1984.

Nevertheless, FactCheck, a consistent supporter of Barack Obama's presidential campaign, was admitting that Obama was a dual citizen at birth.

Even Obama's own 2008 campaign Web site, FightTheSmears.com, reprinted (see Exhibit 19, page 156) FactCheck's assertion that Obama was a dual citizen at birth by virtue of his father's British citizenship.[78]

And yet, the whole point of drafting the natural-born citizen requirement was to prevent those born with foreign citizenship from ever becoming president. Thus, even if Obama were born in Hawaii as he claims, it's possible he would not be eligible for president because of his dual citizenship status at birth.

State Department Admits Obama was a Dual Citizen at Birth

Through August 2010, the State Department maintained a "counter-misinformation" page on an America.gov blog that attempted to "debunk a conspiracy theory" that Obama was not born in the United States, likening the topic to believing space aliens visit earth in flying saucers.[79]

Ironically, in its attempt to debunk the Obama birth certificate controversy, the State Department author actually confirmed that Obama was a dual citizen of the U.K. and the United States from 1961–1963, and a dual citizen of Kenya and the United States from 1963–1982, making Obama a dual citizen until he was twenty-one years old. The implication is that Obama's dual citizenship ended in 1982, the year of his twenty-first birthday, seeing as he did not renounce U.S. citizenship and swear allegiance to Kenya, as required by the Kenyan Constitution to retain that nation's citizenship.

"Interestingly," said the State Department Web site, "FactCheck.org determined that Obama was originally both a U.S. citizen and a citizen of the United Kingdom and Colonies from 1961 to 1963 (because his father was from Kenya, which gained its independence from the British Empire in 1963), then both a U.S. Citizen and a Kenyan citizen from 1963–1982."

Evidently, the State Department was unaware that Obama's dual citizenship status might compromise his "natural-born" status, even if documentary evidence of his birth were made public.

After WND reported on this development,[80] the State Department removed the page discussing Obama's birth certificate from the Internet, without explanation.

Anticipating this development, WND captured a screen shot (see Exhibit 20, page 157) of the page before it was taken down.

Reminiscent of George Orwell's *1984*, this State Department "counter-misinformation" office (see Exhibit 21, page 158) appears intent on propagating the accepted U.S. government-approved view on a wide range of controversies branded dismissively as "conspiracy theories," including questions about President Obama's presidential eligibility.

Its modus operandi? Dismiss and discourage serious discussion of Obama's birth certificate by lumping the issue in with conspiracy theories holding that the moon landing was a hoax, that flying saucers and alien life regularly visit earth, that there were multiple shooters in the JFK assassination, and that the anti-Semitic "Protocols of the Elders of Zion" was a legitimate document.

The entry on Obama's birth controversy was written by Todd Leventhal, identified as the chief of the counter-misinformation team for the U.S. Department of State. The office appears to have been established originally "to provide information about false and misleading stories in the Middle East," as described in an online biography of Leventhal.

"Todd Leventhal is the Department's expert on conspiracy theories and information—stories that are untrue, but widely believed," the State Department explains on America.gov. "He enjoys reading obituaries, which tell the personal stories of people who have shaped the fabric of American life." According to America.gov, Leventhal's qualifications for the job at America.gov include that he "worked for Voice of America for seven years and bikes to work year-round."

Remarkably, the government's article cites FactCheck.org, indicating that the State Department felt comfortable relying on the left-leaning Web site as an authority on the Obama birth controversy. Leventhal's entry was also very similar to the comparable entry at the Obama 2008 presidential campaign Web site, FightTheSmears.com.

Apparently, the State Department merely parroted what the Obama campaign said, rather than conducting an even-handed and original inquiry.

Still, the Department of State is the U.S. government agency responsible for issuing passports and, as such, should be the final administrative arbiter of all questions pertaining to citizenship. That the department admitted Obama was a dual citizen at birth should be interpreted as an authoritative conclusion of the U.S. government.

It is noteworthy that the State Department did not ridicule the issue when Democratic Party operatives and other Obama supporters were questioning McCain's eligibility to be president during the 2008 campaign, not even when McCain's critics got down to questioning whether McCain was born in a hospital on the Navy base or in a hospital off the Navy base in Colon in the Republic of Panama.

The purpose of the American Revolutionary War was to win political independence from Great Britain. How ironic would it be for the Founding Fathers who crafted Article 2, Section 1, to realize that two centuries after independence the American republic would end up being ruled by Barack Obama, a British citizen at birth through the Kenyan nationality and citizenship of his father? Even more pointedly, is it unfair to ask whether Barack Obama has indeed demonstrated a disturbing level of loyalty and allegiance toward his "other" country at birth, Kenya?

Obama's Ties to Kenya Remain Strong

Obama remains enormously popular in Africa and has been described as "one of its illustrious sons." On January 21, 2009, the *Sunday Times* in London reported that at the time of Obama's inauguration as U.S. president one man was quoted as saying, "This man is Jesus. When will he come to Kenya to save us?"[81]

Obama has also maintained a strong personal commitment to Africa, often identifying himself with the continent as his father's homeland. "I have the blood of Africa within me, and my family's own story encompasses both the tragedies and triumphs of the larger African story," Obama said when visiting Ghana in July 2009, according to a report by ABC's Jake Tapper.[82]

The *New York Times* reported that in Ghana an announcer called out, "The first black president of the United States. Africa meets one of its illustrious sons, Barack Obama."[83] The newspaper noted that Ghana's president introduced Obama to the parliament as "a long-lost relative," declaring, "You've come home."

On August 3, 2010, in a town-hall meeting at the White House with 120 young leaders from nearly fifty countries in sub-Saharan Africa, President Obama said, "I don't see Africa as a world apart; I see Africa as a fundamental part of our interconnected world."[84]

Obama Eligible to Run for President, in Kenya!

Looking to the future, Kenya's new constitution, passed by a 67 percent "Yes" vote on August 4, 2010, President Obama's birthday, was written so as to make Obama not only eligible to recover his Kenyan citizenship, but also so that he would be eligible to run for president—in Kenya! This point is relevant in a discussion of whether Obama is a natural-born citizen under the U.S. Constitution, because a key reason the Founding Fathers included the eligibility clause involved their determination to avoid having a chief executive of the United States who had divided loyalties to another nation by virtue of their birth.

In the newly ratified Kenyan constitution,[85] Chapter 3, Section 14(1), entitled "Citizenship by birth," reads: "A person is a citizen by birth if on the day of the person's birth, whether or not the person is born in Kenya, either the mother or father of the person is a Kenyan citizen." Obama qualifies. As we have pointed out, on the day Barack Obama was born, August 4, 1961, his father, Barack Obama, Sr. was a Kenyan citizen, thereby conferring on his son Kenyan citizenship.

Next, Chapter 3, Section 16, of the Kenyan Constitution specifies, "A citizen by birth does not lose citizenship by acquiring the citizenship of another country." This language makes clear that U.S. citizenship is not an impediment for Barack Obama also being a Kenyan citizen; the new Kenyan constitution allows for dual citizenship.

Finally, Chapter 14, Section 14(5) reads, "A person who is a Kenyan citizen by birth and who, on the effective date, has ceased to be a Kenyan citizen because the person acquired citizenship of another country, is entitled on application to regain Kenyan citizenship."

So, all Barack Obama would need to do to make his Kenyan citizenship effective once again is to apply for his citizenship to be reinstated. But is he qualified to run for president of Kenya under the new Kenyan constitution?

Interestingly, the Kenyan constitution does not demand that a candidate for president be "a natural-born citizen," as does Article 2, Section 1, of the U.S. constitution. Consider the following sections of the new Kenyan Constitution ratified in 2010:

- All that is required in Chapter 9, Part 2, Section 137(1)(a) to qualify to run for the presidency of Kenya is that a person be a citizen by birth, a qualification Obama meets because his father was a Kenyan citizen when Obama was born.

- Chapter 9, Part 2, Section 137(1)(b) also requires that a presidential candidate be qualified to stand for election as a member of parliament.

- Chapter 8, Part 2, Section 99(2)(c) requires that to qualify as a candidate for parliament, a person must only have been a citizen for the ten years immediately preceding the date of the election.

Since Obama is a Kenyan citizen by birth under terms of the new Kenyan constitution, he qualifies to be a member of the Kenyan parliament now, a condition that equally qualifies Obama to run for president of Kenya.

Even under the most stringent requirement, all Obama would need to do is to reapply to Kenya to make sure his Kenyan citizenship is current; in the process, Obama would not need to renounce his U.S. citizenship, since the new Kenyan constitution allows Kenyan citizens to be dual citizens of foreign countries.

Obama Spent Millions to Get Kenya's New Constitution Ratified

Speeches about an "interconnected" Africa are not just presidential happy-talk. An investigation by three Republican congressmen, Representatives Chris Smith of New Jersey, Ileana Ros-Lehtinen of Florida, and Darrell Issa of California, has revealed the Obama administration secretly spent $23 million of U.S. taxpayer dollars in Kenya to fund a "Yes" vote on a referendum on a comprehensive new constitution that would increase access to abortions in Kenya and establish legal status for Shariah, or Islamic law, tribunals. The U.S. Agency for International Development admitted to the expenditures in July 2010.

Meanwhile, the White House used Vice President Joe Biden's June 2010 Kenya trip and the office of U.S. Ambassador to Kenya Michael E. Ranneberger to spread the message that a "Yes" vote would allow the White House to open the floodgates and allow millions of dollars of additional U.S. government aid and private investment capital to flow into Kenya.

According to Representative Smith's office, the inspector general of the U.S. Agency for International Development had identified ten USAID-funded programs with direct ties to supporting the "Yes" vote the Obama administration had funded in Kenya, including:

- $91,106.66 to the Central Organization of Trade Unions to "marshal a coalition of pro-Constitution individuals, institutions, and organizations to drum up political support for the Proposed Constitution by organizing a public rally at the historic Kamukunji Grounds, Nairobi."

- $94,193.33 to the Provincial Peace Forum in the Rift Valley Province to "build on previous activities in the North Rift as an entry point for a YES campaign on the constitution. Specifically, this activity will serve to gain buy-in for the new proposed constitution by getting the professional elites' commitment."

"Despite denials, the Obama administration's funding to support passage of the controversial Kenyan proposed constitution is clear," Jeff Sagnip, spokesman for Representative Smith, told WND prior to its passage.

"It constitutes U.S. monetary interference in a sovereign nation's voting process. If passed the constitution would dramatically alter existing pro-life laws."

Sagnip pointed out that the new constitution would water down the existing constitution that prohibits abortion except to save life, and instead would permit abortion when "in the opinion of a trained health professional, there is need for emergency treatment or the life or health of the mother is in danger, of if permitted by any other written law." Sagnip characterized the language as "obviously vague" and riddled with "blatant loopholes."

The new constitution also gave legal status to what are known as "Kadhi Courts," constituting an Islamic judicial structure within the overall structure of the Kenyan legal system, to resolve disputes between Muslims under Islamic law.

During the 2007 campaign for president of Kenya, Raila Odinga, the presidential candidate of the Orange Democratic Party, and like Obama's father a Luo tribesman, had signed an initially undisclosed memorandum of understanding with radical Muslims in Kenya to expand Islamic law within Kenya in exchange for Muslim support of his presidential candidacy.

· 4 ·

CITIZEN OBAMA?

Is Obama a Natural-Born Citizen Under the 14th Amendment?

The controversy over Barack Obama's eligibility to be president will almost certainly continue until he authorizes the release of his original birth certificate, solidly documenting when and where he was born and who his parents truly were.

Yet, even if this document's eventual release provides authoritative evidence he was born in Honolulu as he claims, the constitutional eligibility question might not be settled on all counts.

The current controversy raging over "birthright tourism" and "anchor babies"—referring to children whose foreign mothers come to America, legally or illegally, for the express purpose of having their child here because of the many benefits that follow—dramatizes a key question regarding Obama's presidential eligibility: Does simply being born on American soil, to parents loyal to another nation or even here illegally, automatically make one a "natural-born citizen"?

A "native-born citizen," yes. But not necessarily "natural-born." Both the "birthright citizenship" and "Obama eligibility" issues bring us directly to the 14th Amendment.

The Obama camp has gone to considerable lengths to convince the public there is no difference between being a citizen and a natural-born citizen, or that one's place of birth, in and of itself, somehow automatically confers natural-born citizenship status via the 14th Amendment. The goal of this tactic is to deflect public focus from consideration of the foreign citizenship of Obama's father.

Indeed, Obama supporters have made exhaustive attempts to blur the lines between "native-born citizens" and "natural-born citizens," to advance their position that Obama is natural-born simply because he was born in Hawaii.

The real question with respect to the 14th Amendment is not whether Obama is a natural-born citizen, but whether he is a citizen at all. If it turns out he was not born in Hawaii as he claims, he might not have been a U.S. citizen at birth, let alone a natural-born citizen.

As we will see shortly, the 14th Amendment's requirements for being considered a citizen of the United States are particularly difficult to meet when the individual has only one parent who is a U.S. citizen.

That Barack Obama and his supporters have attempted to obscure the all-important distinction between being a citizen and a natural-born citizen is obvious from the campaign's 2008 presidential Web site. Examine the screen capture (see Exhibit 22, page 159) from FightTheSmears.com from August 2009.

Under the headline "The Truth about Barack's Birth Certificate," we read: "Senator Obama was born in Hawaii in 1961, after it became a state on August 21st 1959. Obama became a citizen at birth under the first section of the 14th Amendment." It then quotes the relevant language of the 14th Amendment: "All persons born or naturalized in the United States, and subject to the jurisdiction thereof, are citizens of the United States and of the State wherein they reside."

As noted in the treatise "Obama Presidential Eligibility—An Introductory Primer" by Stephen Tonchen, some Obama supporters apparently believe there are only two kinds of American citizens: naturalized and natural-born. A naturalized citizen is not a U.S. citizen at birth, but becomes one after successfully completing a naturalization process. A natural-born citizen, according to this view, is anyone who is a U.S. citizen at birth. Tonchen summarizes the argument of Obama supporters as follows: "Since President Obama was born in the United States and was therefore a U.S. citizen at the time of the birth, he is a natural-born citizen, regardless of his parents' citizenship."[86]

In other words, Obama sympathizers want to equate "native-born" with "natural-born." Thus they blur important distinctions to suit their agenda, characterizing a short-form Certification of Live Birth as a "birth certificate" and concluding that since it states Obama was born in Hawaii, he is a native-born citizen of the United States. The slide into the final conclusion is equally easy: Because Obama is a native-born citizen, he is a natural-born citizen, qualified by the 14th Amendment to be eligible for the presidency under Article 2, Section 1, of the Constitution, or so Obama supporters would like us to believe.

This is a skillful attempt to redirect the argument. Obama and his defenders want to transform the eligibility question into a matter of whether Obama is a citizen under the 14th Amendment. If that succeeds, then the eligibility impediments arising from the foreign citizenship of Obama's father simply disappear.

Obama sympathizers like to point out that although Barack Obama, Sr. was a citizen of Kenya when his son was born, he was in the United States legally at the time, admitted under a visa to attend the University of Hawaii. The argument, they insist, is equivalent to arguing that Kansas Territory was under U.S. jurisdiction when Charles Curtis was born, just as Arizona Territory was when Barry Goldwater was born. Yet the argument misses the point that simply being in the United States legally did not confer U.S. citizenship upon Barack Obama, Sr.

The point is that nothing in the 14th Amendment says a person defined as a native-born citizen is thereby automatically natural-born under Article 2, Section 1. The 14th Amendment contains no language aimed at redefining the constitutional phrase "natural-born Citizen."

The 14th Amendment's authors realized that birthplace is not the only factor determining citizenship, as evidenced by their inclusion of the clause "and subject to the jurisdiction of" as a qualification to "born or naturalized in the United States."

The same questions plaguing Obama may also surface if Republican Louisiana Governor Bobby Jindal ever runs for president. Even though he was born in Baton Rouge, Louisiana, on June 10, 1971, Jindal's parents were citizens of India when he was born, residing at that time in the United States on visa permits.

Why Obama Is Not a Natural-born Citizen Under the 14th Amendment

Supporters of illegal immigration use the 14th Amendment to argue that children of illegal aliens are automatically American citizens if they are born in the United States. Creating what is today known as "birthright citizenship," the argument relies on an interpretation of the 14th Amendment never intended or contemplated by its authors.

The controversial interpretation demands an exclusive focus on the first clause of the first sentence, but excluding the second clause, as if the sentence read: "All persons born or naturalized in the United States … are citizens of the United States and of the State wherein they reside." Advocates for illegal immigrants intentionally ignore the qualifying clause, "and subject to the jurisdiction thereof."

Read correctly, the amendment's first sentence stipulates two conditions for birth citizenship: (1) the person must be born in the United States, and (2) he must also be subject to the jurisdiction of the United States at the time he is born. Read *incorrectly,* the sentence assumes the person is under the jurisdiction of the United States just because he is born in the United States.

To understand the importance of this distinction, recall that the authors of the 14th Amendment intended that a child of foreign diplomats born in the United States would not automatically be considered a U.S. citizen. Why not? Because the parents were understood to bear their allegiance to the nation they were representing as diplomats while living in the United States. In other words, *the authors of the 14th Amendment presumed a child born in the United States would have the citizenship of the parents.* A child born in the United States to foreign nationals would be considered a citizen of the foreign nation to which the parents bore allegiance.

The author of the citizenship language of the 14th Amendment, Michigan Senator Jacob M. Howard, arose in the Senate during the 1866 debate to clarify: "This amendment which I have offered is simply declaratory of what I regard as the law of the land already, that every person born within the limits of the United States, and subject to their jurisdiction, is by virtue of natural law and national law a citizen of the United States. This will not, of course, include persons born in the United States who are foreigners, aliens, who belong to the families of ambassadors or foreign ministers accredited to the Government of the United States, but will include every other class of persons."[87]

The records of the 1866 congressional debates make clear that Senator Howard's views were shared by Illinois Senator Lyman Trumbull, who, like Howard, is considered a primary framer of the 14th Amendment. Both senators agreed that the "subject to the jurisdiction" clause was crafted to mean "sole and complete" U.S. jurisdiction, excluding anyone subject to the jurisdiction of a foreign power.

Senator Jacob Howard: [I] concur entirely with the honorable Senator from Illinois [Trumbull], in holding that the word "jurisdiction," as here employed, ought to be construed so as to imply a full and complete jurisdiction on the part of the United States, coextensive in all respects with the constitutional power of the United States, whether exercised by Congress, by the executive, or by the judicial department; that is to say, the same jurisdiction in extent and quality as applies to every citizen of the United States now.

Senator Lyman Trumbull: [T]he provision is, that "all persons born in the United States, and subject to the jurisdiction thereof, are citizens." That means "subject to the complete jurisdiction thereof." What do we mean by "complete jurisdiction thereof?" Not owing allegiance to anybody else. That's what it means.

The *Slaughter-House Cases*, 86 U.S. 36 (1873), comprised the first Supreme Court test of the 14th Amendment, adopted in 1868. The Supreme Court held for a narrow interpretation of the "jurisdiction" clause, ruling that, "The phrase, 'subject to its jurisdiction,' was intended to exclude from its operation children of ministers, consuls, and citizens of foreign States born within the United States." Similarly, in *Elk v. Wilkins*, 112 U.S. 94 (1884), the Supreme Court held that "subject to the jurisdiction" meant sole and complete jurisdiction to the United States: "The evident meaning of these last words is not merely subject in some respect or degree to the jurisdiction of the United States, but completely subject to their political jurisdiction and owing them direct and immediate allegiance."

Remember, the 14th Amendment did not confer U.S. citizenship to American Indians, the most clearly native-born among the American people, because they lived under tribal jurisdiction.

"If Obama's citizenship status at birth was 'governed' by the laws of a foreign country, how could he, at birth, be subject to *sole* and *complete* U.S. jurisdiction, which is the *essential* requirement for 14th Amendment citizenship?" asked Tonchen, author of the *Obama Presidential Eligibility – An Introductory Primer*.[88]

The point is that being born in the United States was not alone considered sufficient to grant citizenship automatically. The person born on U.S. soil must also be born under the jurisdiction of the United States, a determination that had to be made by considering the citizenship of the parents at the time the person was born.

Today much has changed, and millions of Americans incorrectly presume—and advocates for illegal immigrants successfully argue—that the 14th Amendment automatically grants "birthright citizenship" to every child born on U.S. soil, even if their parents remain foreign nationals.

Moreover, a long line of Supreme Court cases has stretched the original meaning of the 14th Amendment to the point where "birthright citizenship" is commonly accepted. For instance, writing for the majority in *United States v. Wong Kim Ark*, 169 U.S. 649 (1898), Justice Horace Gray wrote: "To hold that the Fourteenth Amendment of the Constitution excludes from citizenship the children born in the United States of citizens or subjects of other countries, would be to deny citizenship to thousands of persons of English, Scotch, Irish, German, or other European parentage, who have always been considered and treated as citizens of the United States."[89] In the last paragraph of his opinion, Justice Gray stated the decision of the court precisely:

> The evident intention, and the necessary effect, of the submission of this case to the decision of the court upon the facts agreed by the parties were to present for determination the single question stated at the beginning of this opinion, namely, whether a child born in the United States, of parents of Chinese descent, who, at the time of his birth, are subjects of the emperor of China, but have a permanent domicile and residence in the United States, and are there carrying on business, and are not employed in any diplomatic or official capacity under the emperor of China, becomes at the time of his birth a citizen of the United States. For the reasons above stated, this court is of opinion that the question must be answered in the affirmative.

So, the Supreme Court in the *Wong Kim Ark* case ruled that Ark was a U.S. citizen because he was born in the United States, even though his parents were Chinese citizens at the time of his birth. But the high court did not rule that Ark was a natural-born citizen. In the majority opinion, Justice Gray considered at length both Article 2, Section 1, and the impact of the 14th Amendment on the case. Had the Supreme Court felt the interpretation of the 14th Amendment extended to confer not just citizenship upon Wong Kim Ark, but also natural-born citizenship status, it would have said so.

Largely overlooked today is that the ruling in *United States v. Wong Kim Ark* was not meant to apply to all persons born in the United States. Viewed narrowly, the court's decision conferred U.S. citizenship on those born in the U.S. of foreign-born parents only *if* those parents were permanent U.S. residents, legally domiciled, and doing business in the United States.[90] Barack Obama's father was studying in the United States temporarily, with every intention of returning to Kenya, as he did once his academic work was completed. So, while Barack Obama, Sr. was in the United States legally, he was not domiciled here permanently, nor did he intend to conduct his business in the United States. He came to study in order to return to Kenya where he could apply his U.S. education to the advancement of Kenya.

Thus, even applying the broadest possible interpretation of the court's ruling in *United States v. Wong Kim Ark* to Obama's situation would only convey to him U.S. citizenship. There is no language in the case that could be interpreted to confer on him natural-born citizenship.[91] Indeed, Supreme Court decisions on "birth citizenship" issues have not induced the court to expand its rulings to redefine natural-born citizenship under the 14th Amendment solely according to place of birth.

Obama and his supporters should not expect to derive any additional encouragement from other federal citizenship and naturalization statutes. While Congress has passed many laws defining citizenship, no federal laws have been passed defining natural-born citizenship. In other words, the concept of natural-born citizenship derives *even today* solely from Article 2, Section 1, and the Founders' original intent for that part of the Constitution. Obama defenders who want to define him as a natural-born citizen because he is native-born and a citizen under the 14th Amendment are engaged in an effort to redefine Article 2, Section 1, away from its original natural law meaning.

Does English Common Law Make Obama a Natural-Born Citizen?

Obama supporters have reached into English common law to argue legal precedents that would establish their man as a natural-born U.S. citizen. Their justification in part derives from the extent to which the Supreme Court in *United States v. Wong Kim Ark* examined English common law in reaching its decision. A clear defect of this argument is that even though English common law continues to be used to inform arguments at the Supreme Court level, it ceased to be binding on U.S. courts once the American colonies established independence from Britain.

The basic argument is that English common law considers children born in Great Britain to be natural-born British subjects, even if their parents were foreigners. In *U.S. v. Wong Kim Ark*, Justice Gray concluded:

> It thus clearly appears that, by the law of England for the last three centuries, beginning before the settlement of this country and continuing to the present day, aliens, while residing in the dominions possessed by the crown of England, were within the allegiance, the obedience, the faith or loyalty, the protection, the power, and the jurisdiction of the English sovereign; and therefore every child born in England of alien parents was a natural-born subject unless the child of an ambassador or other diplomatic agent of a foreign state or of an alien enemy in hostile occupation of the place where the child was born.
>
> The same rule was in force in all the English colonies upon this continent down to the time of the Declaration of Independence, and in the United States afterwards and continued to prevail under the Constitution as originally established.

Obama sympathizers cite this authority to argue that English common law trumps natural law to make Obama a natural-born citizen, because he was native-born even though his father was a foreigner. The problem is that while Justice Gray made this observation in his majority opinion, the majority of the Supreme Court did not include this conclusion in its ruling. As noted above, rather than ruling Wong Kim Ark was a natural-born citizen, the Supreme Court stopped at ruling he was a simply a citizen.

What If Obama Was Not Born in Honolulu?

If Barack Obama, Jr. was not born in Hawaii, is it possible that under U.S. federal statutes he might not have been a U.S. citizen at all at the time of his birth?

During the 2008 presidential campaign, opponents of then-Senator Obama objected that he wasn't natural-born because of certain provisions in the U.S. Code that stipulate citizenship and naturalization requirements if only one parent was a U.S. citizen. Specifically, U.S. Code, Section 301 (a)(7), requires that for a person born outside America to be a U.S. citizen at birth, at least one parent must have resided in the United States for at least ten years, at least five of which had to be after the age of fourteen, for the child to be a U.S. citizen.

Stanley Ann Dunham, Barack Obama's mother, was only eighteen years old at the time of Obama's birth. So, the argument went, it was impossible for her to have lived five years after the age of fourteen in the United States before her son was born. If Obama was not born in the United States, his mother's citizenship would not have been sufficient to confer citizenship upon him, simply because she was too young, opponents concluded.

Snopes.com joined in the argument over U.S. Code, Section 301(a) (7),[92] along with other Obama supporters such as David Emery writing on the "Urban Legends" section of About.com. Snopes and Emery argued that the 14th Amendment trumped U.S. Code. In other words, because Obama was native-born, he was a citizen under the 14th Amendment, making it irrelevant to consider the age or citizenship status of his parents at the time of his birth. Both Snopes and Emery also wanted Obama to be considered a natural-born citizen simply because he was native-born to Hawaii.[93] But Snopes and Emery miss the point. At most, Snopes and Emery attempt to establish that their interpretation of birthright citizenship under the 14th Amendment means Obama was a citizen if he was born in Hawaii, regardless of Ann Dunham's age at the time. But the real question is this: What if Obama was not born in Hawaii?

Section 301 (a)(7), part of the Immigration and Nationality Act of 1952, the relevant citizenship law in effect at the time of Obama's birth, addresses the issue directly. This section of the U.S. code specifies the following conditions for conferring U.S. citizenship to a foreign-born child born with one parent an alien at the time of the person's birth:

> A person born outside the geographical limits of the United States and its outlying possessions of parents one of whom is an alien, and the other a citizen of the United States who, prior to the birth of such person, was physically present in the United States or its outlying possessions for a period or periods totaling not less than ten years, at least five of which were after attaining the age of fourteen years: Provided that any periods of honorable service in the Armed Forces of the United States by such citizen parent may be included in computing the physical presence requirements of this paragraph.

Ann Dunham, born November 29, 1942, had not yet attained nineteen years of age when Barack Obama was born August 4, 1961. Clearly, therefore, she could not have met the U.S. Code's requirement that to confer citizenship on her son she had to have lived five years in the U.S. after turning fourteen.

This means that if Obama were born outside the United States, he would not have been a U.S. citizen automatically, by virtue of his mother's age at his birth and his father being a foreign national.

Bottom line: If the suspicion that Obama was born outside the U.S. turns out to be true, the president of the United States might not have been a dual citizen at birth; he would only have been a British citizen at birth and a future citizen of Kenya after its independence, but not a citizen of the United States of America.

Not being a U.S. citizen *at all* at birth would clearly be a far greater problem than not being a natural-born citizen. Even the most partisan Obama supporters would have a difficult time arguing that a naturalized U.S. citizen could be a "natural-born Citizen."

How Obama Supporters Twist the Eligibility Argument

A close look at the argument over U.S. Code, Section 301 (a)(7), is important because it shows how far Obama sympathizers have gone to twist legal logic in their favor.

Snopes.com[94] began its defense of Obama in relation to this section of U.S. Code by arguing irrelevancies:

"A few facts of this claim immediately jump out as being far-fetched," Snopes said. "First, that a sitting U.S. Senator who has already spent a good deal of time and money securing his party's nomination for the presidency would suddenly be discovered as ineligible due to an obscure provision of U.S. law."

That a law is inconvenient to the pursuit of a partisan goal is hardly a reason for disregarding it or minimizing it as "obscure."

Next, Snopes objected "that U.S. law would essentially penalize someone who would otherwise qualify for natural-born citizenship status simply because his mother was too young." Snopes clouds the issue by implying the only impediment to Obama's eligibility under Article 2, Section 1, is whether or not he is a citizen, not specifically whether he is a natural-born citizen. Moreover, as silly as the requirement of U.S. Code Section 301(a)(7) may seem to Snopes, it was still federal law at the time Obama was born.

Snopes dismissed this concern by noting the qualifications concerning Dunham's age at the time of her son's birth "are moot because they refer to someone who was born *outside the United States.*" The italics in the original served to imply that were Obama born in the United States, that fact alone was sufficient to make him natural-born. The Web site then deduces that since Obama was born in Hawaii, the U.S. Code provision doesn't apply to him: "The Fourteenth Amendment states that 'all persons born or naturalized in the United States, and subject to the jurisdiction thereof, are citizens of the United States.' Since Hawaii is part of the United States, even if Barack Obama's parents were both non-U.S. citizens who hadn't even set foot in the country until just before he was born, he'd still qualify as a natural-born citizen." Snopes then would have no problem if a birth tourism baby born in the United States to wealthy parents, who raised the child in their foreign country, returned to the United States at thirty-five years old to run for president, even if the person spoke no English and had never lived a day in the United States since birth.

Simply stated, here is the conclusion that Obama supporters wanted to lock in the minds of the American public: If Barack Obama, Jr. were born in the United States, he was by definition a natural-born citizen under the terms of the 14th Amendment.

The goal of Obama supporters during the 2008 campaign apparently was to so blur the meaning of natural-born citizen that birthright citizenship under the 14th Amendment was considered sufficient to establish natural-born citizen status under Article 2, Section 1.

Most of these same Obama supporters were not nearly so inclusive when it came to arguing whether Senator John McCain is a natural-born citizen.

Because pro-Obama Web sites have had a tendency to remove from the Internet politically inconvenient pages once they are exposed, consider (see Exhibit 23, page 160) a screen capture of the relevant Snopes. com discussion.

David Emery at About.com[95] also attempted to obscure the argument, although with a different twist. Resorting to legal terms in Latin that are not commonly known, Emery determined (see Exhibit 24, page 161) that Obama was a natural-born citizen by *jus soli*, the right of his birthplace in Hawaii, not by *jus sanguinis*, or the right of blood, which would demand an analysis of the citizenship of Obama's parents.

Emery concluded Obama is a natural-born U.S. citizen "for the simple reason that he was born on American soil (in Hawaii, two years after it acquired statehood)." Hence, as far as Emery was concerned, the "age and citizenship status of his parents at the time of his birth have no bearing on Obama's own citizenship." Emery also accepts as established fact that Obama was born in Hawaii, a conclusion that permits him not to consider how U.S. Code Section 301(a)(7) might apply if Obama were born outside the United States.

See Exhibit 24 on page 161 for a screen capture of the relevant About.com discussion in the event it disappears from the Internet.

No wonder Obama supporters fought so hard. There was far more at stake here than simply whether or not Obama was eligible under Article 2, Section 1. Any close examination of the evidence risked raising the possibility that Obama might not have been born a U.S. citizen at all.

Were that the case, he would not be eligible to be president, since there is no serious consideration in the legal literature for including a naturalized citizen within the Founding Fathers' understanding of "natural-born citizen." The strategy was to dodge the issue that Obama's father was a foreigner by insisting the case was closed if Obama was born in Hawaii. Then, relying upon Ann Dunham being a citizen, the Obama camp planned to collapse the natural-born citizen argument into a question of birth citizenship under the 14th Amendment. In the process, Obama supporters hoped the issue of Obama's dual citizenship at birth would simply go away.

This argument had a chance of working, but success depended upon Obama supporters convincing the public that two distinct ideas—"native-born" and "natural-born"—were one and the same.

However, the two terms are firmly established in U.S. legal tradition precisely because they mean different things. "Native-born" is a term applying to an individual born on United States soil. "Natural-born" was the term the Founding Fathers applied to designate a person born on U.S. soil to two parents who were each U.S. citizens at the time of the birth. Had the Founders meant "native-born" instead of "natural-born," they would have written Article 2, Section 1, to require only that a person be born on U.S. soil in order to qualify as president.

In the final analysis, Obama's defenders were betting everything that Americans would believe the short-form Certification of Live Birth provided reliable evidence Obama was born in Hawaii. They would stress the point that Obama was a citizen at birth. If the public would only accept that "native-born" equals "natural-born," Obama's birth in Hawaii would make the age of his mother and citizenship of his father irrelevant. And that would be the end of the eligibility controversy.

There was one problem, however: Should Obama's online Certification of Live Birth be proven unreliable for any reason, the Obama camp's entire story could come crashing down.

Next, we will consider serious questions about this short-form document and the fact that it simply does not prove Obama was born in Hawaii.

OBAMA AND THE
"ONLINE BIRTH CERTIFICATE"

Obama's Short-Form Certification of Live Birth, or COLB, Debuts on the Internet

It seemed like a reasonable question. Considering Obama's promise of transparency, "Why can't the president respond to the petition requests of 400,000 American citizens by releasing a certified copy of his long-form birth certificate?" veteran White House reporter Les Kinsolving asked presidential press secretary Robert Gibbs at the May 27, 2009, daily briefing.

Instead of answering, Gibbs, along with the Washington press corps in attendance, erupted in boisterous laughter.

"Are you looking for the president's birth certificate?" Gibbs asked incredulously.

"Yes," Kinsolving replied.

"It's on the Internet, Lester," an exasperated Gibbs rejoined.

"No, no, no," Kinsolving protested, "the long form listing his hospital and physician."

More laughter ensued.

"Lester, this question in many ways continues to astound me," Gibbs intoned. "The state of Hawaii provided a copy with the seal of the president's birth. I know there are apparently at least 400,000 people (laughter) that continue to doubt the existence of and the certification by the state of Hawaii of the president's birth there, but it's on the Internet because we put it on the Internet for each of those 400,000 to download. I certainly hope by the fourth year of our administration that we'll have dealt with this burgeoning birth controversy."

For most critics of "birthers," the images of a short-form "Certification of Live Birth" that appeared in June 2008 on several pro-Obama Web sites, including DailyKos.com, FightTheSmears.com, and Politifact.com, has settled the matter of Barack Obama's presidential eligibility. Fact-Check.org also posted a photograph of someone holding a hard-copy of the document, which seemed to further cement the argument.

But has Obama actually displayed his "birth certificate"?

An original birth certificate is typically a hospital-generated long-form that lists detailed birth information, including the name of the attending physician. The short-form Certification of Live Birth, or COLB, is a computer-generated document that lists abbreviated birth information, typically not indicating the name of the hospital or the delivering doctor.

Obama has never made public his original long-form, hospital-generated birth certificate.

June 12, 2008: An Obama COLB Surfaces for the First Time Ever

According to the leftist DailyKos.com, the "birther" challenge to Senator Barack Obama can be traced back to June 2008, when a group of what were then known as "PUMAs" set out to establish that Obama was not born in the United States by demanding to see his birth certificate.[96] PUMA, a political action committee organized to support the presidential candidacy of Hillary Clinton, was registered with the FEC as People United Means Action and filed with the IRS as a 527 organization in June 2008, three months after the Senate had passed its resolution affirming that McCain was qualified under Article 2, Section 1, to run for president.

PUMA members immediately began circulating the rumor that Obama had been born in Kenya and demanded that the Obama campaign produce a birth certificate for Obama, just as the McCain campaign had produced one for its candidate.

To the rescue came the Obama-partisan Web site DailyKos.com, which on June 12, 2008, proclaimed, "In any case, here is Obama's birth certificate."[97] With this article, DailyKos was the first to publish Obama's purported Certification of Live Birth, which it trumpeted incorrectly as the candidate's "birth certificate." Again, this was months after Obama supporters had launched a serious effort to derail McCain's presidential campaign by challenging the Republican candidate's birth credentials.

What DailyKos.com published had the certificate number blacked-out, as seen in Exhibit 25, on page 162.

DailyKos gave no explanation as to how it came up with the document. It was only in response to comments on the site that DailyKos publisher Markos Moulitsas responded, "I asked the campaign. This 'journamalism' (sic) thing actually works sometimes."[98]

Almost immediately, as if to confirm the DailyKos document was official, Obama's presidential campaign Web site, FightTheSmears.com, published the identical document, (see Exhibit 26, page 163) once again incorrectly identified as "Barack Obama's Official Birth Certificate."

Within days of the COLB appearing on these two sites, a controversy flared. Janice Okubo, public information officer for the Hawaii Department of Health, told the *St. Petersburg Times* in Florida that the COLB published by DailyKos.com and FightTheSmears.com appeared to lack the embossed seal and signature necessary to authenticate the document. "I don't know that it's possible for us to even say beyond a doubt what the image on the site represents," she told the newspaper.[99]

In response, Amy Hollyfield, a reporter with PolitiFact.com, a left-leaning Web site affiliated with the *St. Petersburg Times*, e-mailed to Okubo an electronic copy of a COLB in PolitiFact.com's possession. According to Hollyfield, Okubo told her the document was "a valid Hawaii state birth certificate."[100] The COLB published by PolitiFact looked identical to that published by DailyKos and FightTheSmears, and none of these electronic copies displayed any evidence of an embossed seal or signature. Only a blue date, June 6, 2007, appeared, reading backward at the bottom right of the electronic COLB, as if it bled through from a date-stamping on the back of the document.

An article published July 3, 2008, by the Israel Insider blog raised serious questions about the source of the DailyKos COLB. "Who in the campaign would be authorized to release a personal document of Barack Obama's birth certificate?" Israel Insider asked. "Was it a paper document that they sent to Kos to scan, or did the Obama campaign scan the original and send it to Kos? If so, why not just post it on the Fight the Smears site? Or is there another possible source for the document? There is no documentation of the provenance of this image, from whom and why it was transmitted to DailyKos, and in which format. None, that is, except for the say-so of Markos Moulitsas, who said he simply asked the Obama campaign for it."[101]

Ostensibly to answer these questions, FactCheck.org published an article on June 16, 2008, claiming Obama campaign spokesman Tommy Vietor had provided FactCheck an electronic copy of the Obama COLB. FactCheck further explained the document carried a date stamp of June 6, 2007, because it was "probably a copy obtained by Obama himself at that time."[102]

Remember, FactCheck.org—a group whose very name suggests nonpartisan independence—had weighed in heavily to suggest that had McCain won the presidency, the issue of his Panama birth could still be raised in the courts.

Mainstream media sources, including the *New York Times* and the *Washington Post*, jumped in early and hard when the Internet controversy raised questions as to whether McCain's birth in the Panama Canal Zone disqualified him from being president. Yet in June 2008, the big media ignored the developing controversy Hillary Clinton's PUMA supporters had started over Obama's birth circumstances.

When the mainstream press finally weighed in, it would be utterly and totally in support of Obama. The *Los Angeles Times* on June 16, 2008, published (see Exhibit 27, page 164) the Obama COLB image posted by DailyKos and FightTheSmears. "The Obama campaign has provided at The Ticket's request what it says is a copy of the Illinois senator's official birth certificate, reproduced here, showing he was born in Hawaii on August 4, 1961, at 7:24 p.m., which means he was late for dinner, just like a politician," political commentator Andrew Malcolm wrote in the "Top of the Ticket" blog in the *Los Angeles Times*.[103]

In an update to the article, the *Times* dismissed challenges to the document's authenticity by noting that Ben LaBolt, an Obama campaign spokesman, sent the following e-mail to the newspaper: "I can confirm that that is Sen. Obama's birth certificate."

Obama Activist Jay McKinnon Forges a COLB

Shortly after the Obama COLB first appeared on DailyKos, a bizarre incident occurred. Jay McKinnon, a self-described Department of Homeland Security-trained document specialist, implicated himself in the production of an obviously fake COLB. In fact, McKinnon gave an interview to the DailyKos in which he openly admitted he had faked his document.[104] This drew a flurry of accusations that the Obama certification appearing on DailyKos.com and FightTheSmears.com had been faked from the beginning—a charge that has continued to be leveled by some document experts through the first two years of Obama's presidency.

McKinnon told the DailyKos he copied the document from the Web site's home page and proceeded to edit it in Microsoft Paint. "I copied part of the background from one section of the image and pasted it over the text," he explained. What McKinnon circulated on the Internet (see Exhibit 28, page 165) was a forged COLB that to the untrained eye looked exactly like the document produced by the DailyKos and FightTheSmears, except that it was largely blank and made for "Haye I. B. Ahphorgerie," which phonetically would read, "Hey, I Be a Forgery." It also was titled as a "Certification of Non-Torture," an invention that was meant to scorn the interrogation policies of the George W. Bush administration. The rest of the COLB fields were left blank.

McKinnon also worked off of another Hawaii-issued COLB, one a woman named Patricia Decosta had offered online to show seemingly missing elements on the posted Obama document: namely, an embossed seal clearly visible in the document's lower right quadrant and a date/signature which appeared to have bled through from the back of the document. That the border on the Decosta COLB looked different than the border on the Obama COLB posted by DailyKos and FightTheSmears provoked a host of comments on the Internet as well, along with charges the Obama certification was a fake.

To see what the Decosta COLB looked like, see Exhibit 29 on page 166.

Interestingly, the fold lines and the embossed seal show up prominently on the Decosta authentic COLB, while both features are not discernible at all on the Obama COLB's shown by DailyKos.com and by Fight-TheSmears.com, just as the features are not visible on the McKinnon "Haye I. B. Ahphorgerie" fake.

McKinnon insisted he believed Obama was born in Hawaii and that the Obama COLB was authentic. "I did not travel back in time to help Obama's parents obtain a U.S. passport with fraudulent documents, nor to provide images to the Obama campaign or Kos," he told DailyKos. "I have never counterfeited a document and I do not intend to start. I do not believe that document counterfeiters use Microsoft Paint or upload their work to Photobucket."

Many others disagreed. The Israel Insider blog described McKinnon as a twenty-five- to thirty-year-old "Democratic political activist, frequent contributor to the left wing DailyKos blog, and a fervent Barack Obama supporter" who, as far back as July 2006, had bragged on DailyKos how easily one could forge official government documents. The discussion centered around forging driver's licenses for illegal immigrants and the idea of producing "The Perfect ID Card." McKinnon was flippant, confident he could counterfeit virtually any government document, including birth certificates. "Most Americans have worse ID than illegal immigrants," he said. "So, you have a letter from a notary that says you told him you're a citizen. Is that supposed to mean something? I'm certain he would sign one saying I told him I'm a carrot. Birth certificates, are you serious? Take a look at yours. Chances are I could counterfeit it at Kinkos."[105]

Despite McKinnon's protestations that his forgery was a joke, skeptics concluded that McKinnon had managed to undermine the credibility of the Obama COLB simply by demonstrating how easy it was to forge one.

If McKinnon could produce a forgery so easily, what assurance was there that he wasn't just lying when he denied producing the Obama document? McKinnon's nonchalant attitude made it clear he considered forging official government documents to be a joke. Otherwise, he acknowledged, he would have been committing a crime to do so. But who was the joke on? Was McKinnon laughing at the Hillary Clinton PUMA supporters who first dared to raise the issue of Obama's birth credentials?

Or was he laughing at the public because he had managed to post a fake Obama COLB on DailyKos.com?

FactCheck: We "Have Now Seen, Touched, Examined" Obama Birth Document

The first to show an electronic image of an Obama COLB that appeared to be a paper copy was FactCheck.org, in "The truth about Obama's birth certificate," published August 21, 2008.[106]

Responding to claims the Obama certification was a forgery, Fact-Check crowed that its staffers "have now seen, touched, examined and photographed the original birth certificate." FactCheck failed to disclose that the Certification of Live Birth was by no stretch of the imagination an "original birth certificate," which is the long-form document hospitals generate when babies are born there.

"We conclude that it meets all the requirements from the State Department for proving U.S. citizenship," said FactCheck. Interestingly, the State Department made no such statement on its own accord. More important, as we have seen, the issue is not whether Obama is a citizen, but whether he is a *natural-born* citizen. Again, FactCheck ignored the distinction, in the process implying all that was necessary to establish Obama's presidential eligibility is that he was a U.S. citizen at birth. As explained earlier, U.S. citizenship under the 14th Amendment does not equate to natural-born citizenship as mandated for the presidency in Article 2, Section 1, of the Constitution.

"Claims that the document lacks a raised seal or a signature are false," protested FactCheck. "We have posted high-resolution photographs of the document as 'supporting documents' to this article. Our conclusion: Obama was born in the U.S.A. just as he has always said." FactCheck claimed its staffers "got a chance to spend some time with the birth certificate, and we can attest to the fact that it is real and three-dimensional and resides at the Obama headquarters in Chicago."

Look at Exhibit 30 on page 167 where the Certification of Live Birth is being "seen, touched, examined" by FactCheck.org writer Joe Miller.

Clearly FactCheck wanted viewers to see that the COLB was not just an electronic image, but an actual paper document (see Exhibit 31, page 168). This also was a goal in showing the embossed seal.

To make clear there was no conspiracy on the part of DailyKos or FightTheSmears in blacking out the COLB number when the document was first shown to the public, FactCheck produced (see Exhibit 32, page 168) a photo of the certificate number.

The folds in the FactCheck.org had not been visible in the COLB published by DailyKos.com or by PolitiFact.org.

Another FactCheck snapshot (see Exhibit 33, page 169) showed the signature of the Hawaii registrar from the reverse side of the document.

And yet another photo (see Exhibit 34, page 169) showed a close-up of the text, evidently to establish that the COLB had been printed on a laser printer.

Clearly, sources like Politifact.com and FactCheck.org did not act in an unbiased and impartial way in considering presidential candidates' constitutional birth qualifications. They attacked McCain on his birth certificate issues while defending Obama on his. The aim of online entities supporting Obama during the 2008 campaign was to spin their candidate's eligibility problem by portraying the short-form document as equivalent to a long-form birth certificate. Two years into the Obama presidency, an original birth certificate remains hidden from the American public, if it exists at all. Furthermore, Obama apologists have sought to reduce the Obama eligibility issue to a matter of convincing Americans that he was born in Hawaii, while ignoring the issue of his dual citizenship at birth.

In reality, all four of these Obama Internet supporters—PolitiFact, FactCheck, DailyKos, and FightTheSmears—were key to advancing the notion that requesting Obama's long-form birth certificate was somehow irrelevant and irrational. They were equally determined to deflect questions about how Obama could be a natural-born citizen if he was a dual citizen at birth. In the end, they all shared the same goal: declaring the Obama birth controversy over because "Obama has shown his birth certificate," when all that was ever released to the American public was a short-form, computer-generated document that raised further questions.

In 2010, the second year of his presidency, fueled by Obama's bizarre refusal to allow public and press scrutiny of his vital documents, a multitude of questions about the authenticity of the online COLB were raised in the blogosphere, most prominently by Ronald J. Polland, Ph.D. A frequent Internet poster under the username "Polarik," Polland published a series of videos on YouTube summarizing his two-year investigation seeking to prove the Obama COLB was a forgery.[107] Polland earned a doctorate in instructional systems from Florida State University in 1978, preceded by a master's degree in educational research and psychology. He has specific expertise in computer graphics and the use of computer peripherals, such as printers and scanners, to input digital images into computers.[108] His videos summarized the arguments he had made in his many Internet postings, dating back nearly to the start of the Obama eligibility controversy in June 2008.

In an online analysis, "Polarik's final report: Obama's 'Born' Conspiracy," Polland argued that the size and image resolution of the Obama COLB documents displayed by DailyKos, FightTheSmears, Annenberg's FactCheck, and PolitiFact all matched and appeared to have originated from a single forgery.[109]

Obama COLB Lists Race of Father as "African"

A close examination of the Obama COLB shows that the race of the father was listed as "African." Immediately, skeptics pointed out that "African" is not a race but a geographical identification. Further, in 1961, the year Obama was born, "Negro," not "African" would have been the most likely designation of the father's race.

To the defense of Obama's COLB on this issue came Snopes.com, the supposedly independent debunker of Internet rumors.[110]

"Aside from the inherent absurdity of such claims (i.e., that a major party presidential nominee would risk his entire candidacy on a fraud that could be uncovered simply by a check of state health records), the supposedly incriminating details don't pan out," Snopes.com wrote, after noting that the father's race had been listed as African. "The certificate is consistent with others issued in the same time and place, and the embossed seal and signature don't show through very well on the scanned front image made available on the Internet because they were applied to the back of the original document, not the front. Those who have actually touched and examined the original certificate have verified and document that it bears all the elements of a valid certificate of live birth."

In other words, the unusual designation of the father's race as "African" did not cause Obama supporters to question the document's authenticity. Why? Because otherwise, the document looks okay. Perhaps Snopes.com did not take into consideration that the Obama COLB looked good enough only to those already predisposed to be Obama supporters, including DailyKos.com, FightTheSmears.com, PolitiFact.com, Fact-Check.org, and Snopes.com itself.

Others, more creative, such as "Dr. Conspiracy" on the Obama-supporting "Obama Conspiracy Theories" Web site, stretched to argue that when asked his race, Barack Obama, Sr. told Hawaii officials that his race was "African," out of a personal identification with the Pan-Africanism of Kwame Nkruma.[111]

Hawaii Department of Health Refuses to Validate Obama COLB

In August 2009, in response to a question from WND, Janice Okubo, public information officer for the Hawaii Department of Health, refused to confirm whether the short-form Certification of Live Birth posted at Web sites such as FightTheSmears.com and FactCheck.org were authentic documents issued by the Hawaii DOH.[112]

Indeed, the Hawaii DOH has never issued an official statement affirming that any of the COLB documents posted anywhere on the Internet are authentic.

Skeptics, meanwhile, point to a September 2000 report issued by the Office of Inspector General for the U.S. Department of Health and Human Services concluding it is easy to commit birth-certificate fraud.[113]

Noting that "technological advances in the Internet, scanners, color printers, and copiers make it easier to obtain genuine birth certificates and create counterfeit ones," the inspector general concluded: "[M]any altered or counterfeit birth certificates and genuine birth certificates held by imposters may go undetected."[114]

· 6 ·

BORN IN THE U.S.A.?

Why Obama's Certification of Live Birth Doesn't Prove He Was Born in Hawaii

Even if Barack Obama's much-touted Certification of Live Birth is confirmed as an authentic document generated by the Hawaii Department of Health, it would not prove the president was born in Hawaii.

This may seem a surprising statement, until one considers that in 1961, all it took to get such a document in Hawaii was a statement by parents, grandparents, or guardians that their child was born in the state.

Since the days when Hawaii was a U.S. territory, as far back as 1911, the Hawaii Department of Health has never had the investigative resources or the inclination to research whether adults requesting Hawaiian birth certificates were telling the truth when claiming their children were born in Hawaii.

The Strange History of Hawaiian Birth Certificate Law

In 1911, when Hawaii was a U.S. territory, having been annexed in 1898, it established the Certificate of Hawaiian Birth program "to register a person born in Hawaii who was one year old or older and whose birth had not been previously registered in Hawaii," as specified by the Hawaii Department of Health.[115] Few official birth certificates existed in Hawaii at the turn of the century, and the few that were filed may have only included the person's first name. Few Hawaiians were born in hospitals, with the vast majority of births occurring at home, with no medical assistance other than a midwife. The Certificate of Hawaiian Birth program permitted a person to be registered by a parent or guardian.[116]

The program required little more than an affidavit or sworn statement that a child had been born in Hawaii. There was no verification of the information provided by the parent or guardian, as Hawaii lacked the resources to hire an investigative staff, and there were few hospital or doctor records of birth to consult. Still, under the program, the Territory of Hawaii began to capture names of citizens for the purpose of census, voting, property rights, and taxation. Sun Yat-Sen, the famous Chinese revolutionary and political leader, was issued a Hawaiian birth certificate under the Certificate of Hawaiian Birth program that stated he was born in the Hawaiian Islands in 1870, even though he was born in China in 1866.

Look at the copy of the Hawaiian birth certificate issued to Sun Yat-Sen under the Certificate of Hawaiian Birth program in Exhibit 35 on page 170.

An authoritative article by Neil L. Thomsen, archivist at the National Archives-Pacific Sierra Region, documented that Sun Yat-Sen, the "founding father" of the Republic of China, claimed to be a "native-born Hawaiian" in search of refuge because of the price he had on his head in China.[117] Sun Yat-Sen's case file maintained by the National Archives includes a handwritten, sworn, and signed testimony of both a Hawaiian farmer and of Sun Yat-Sen regarding his "birth" and early childhood on the island of Oahu.

A letter from the secretary of the Territory of Hawaii, dated March 14, 1904, (see Exhibit 36, page 171) provides evidence that Hawaii issued Sun Yat-Sen a Hawaiian birth certificate.

When Hawaii became a state in 1959, those who possessed a Certificate of Hawaiian Birth under the 1911 program could apply for an amendment, which could include an official name change. A Late Birth Certificate could then be used as an official record of Hawaiian birth, replacing the previously issued Certificate of Hawaiian Birth. The program continued from 1911 until 1971.

Even loyal Obama supporters, such as "Dr. Conspiracy" posting on the pro-Obama Web site ObamaConspiracy.org, have been forced to admit that the existence of Sun Yat-Sen's Hawaii birth certificate "remains as an indictment of the reliability of Hawaiian birth certificates."[118]

Birth Certificates Under Hawaii Territorial Law, 1955

The Hawaiian law in effect at the time of Obama's birth was the Revised Law of the Territory of Hawaii, 1955.

Under Chapter 57, "Vital Statistics," Section 9(a) opens the door for a family to make a false claim and obtain a Hawaii birth certificate for a child born *outside* the state. The relevant section of the statute provides that if neither parent of the newborn child is available to prepare a birth certificate, "the local registrar shall secure the necessary information from any person having knowledge of the birth and prepare and file the certificate." Clearly, Obama's maternal grandparents could have presented themselves to the local registrar to obtain a birth certificate for Barack Hussein Obama, Jr., even if the child were born outside Hawaii.

Furthermore, Section 57–9(b) allows the filing of a birth certificate on which the required information is simply missing, to be filled in later with a "supplementary report." When a supplementary report is filed to complete an earlier filed Hawaiian birth certificate, the resulting new document was not characterized or recorded as either "delayed" or "altered." This provision gave exceptionally wide latitude for a family to record a birth as a "Hawaiian birth" and to receive a Hawaii birth certificate.

Hawaii Territorial Law Chapter 57 makes no provision for the local registrar to investigate or otherwise corroborate information a family provides to obtain a Hawaiian birth certificate on a newborn baby. Section 57–8 specifies that "a certificate of every birth shall be filed with the local registrar of the district in which the birth occurred, by the physician, midwife or other legally authorized person in attendance at the birth; or if not so attended, by one of the parents." Then, as we saw above, Section 57–9(a) specified that if the parents were not available, anyone having knowledge of the birth could register it as a Hawaiian birth with the local registrar.

A review of the 1955 Hawaii Territorial Law leaves no doubt that a Hawaiian birth certificate was designed to be easily available to any Hawaiian family that wanted to claim a child had been born to the family in Hawaii, whether or not that was the case. If the family did not get around to filing for a birth certificate immediately, Section 57–19 provided that the family could file for a delayed certificate up to one year after the birth. Similarly, if the initial information filed needed to be changed, Section 57–19 provided that the certificate could be altered up to one year after the baby was born.

A key point is that Hawaii's official birth certification system grew from an era when many babies were born at home. Thus, Hawaii's official birth certification process functioned by accepting what amounted to the family's word.

In 2008, a private investigator asked the Hawaii DOH what proof it currently required to back up a parent's claim that a child was born in Hawaii. He was told that all the Hawaii Department of Health required was proof of residence in Hawaii. "On further enquiry, the employee that I spoke to informed me that the pre-natal and post-natal certifications had probably not been in force in the '60s," the investigator reported. "Even if they had, there is and was no requirement for a physician or midwife to witness, state or report that the baby was born in Hawaii."[119]

Hawaii Newspapers Announce Obama's Birth

Birth announcements for Barack Obama appeared in the Honolulu *Sunday Advertiser* on August 13, 1961, nine days after he was born, and in the Honolulu *Star-Bulletin* one day later.

Look at the announcement in the *Sunday Advertiser* (see Exhibit 37, page 172), as well as the *Star-Bulletin* (Exhibit 38, page 173).

The close-up (seen in Exhibit 39, page 174) makes the birth announcements easier to read, with the *Sunday Advertiser* on the left and the *Star-Bulletin* on the right.

Both announcements read identically (see Exhibit 40, page 174): "Mr.

and Mrs. Barack H. Obama, 6085 Kalanianaole Hwy, son, August 4."

Immediately, Obama supporters seized on the birth announcements as ironclad proof Obama was born in Hawaii and that "birthers" had to be drooling, ignorant conspiracists. FactCheck sarcastically dismissed any skeptics who dared to persist with doubts: "Of course, it's distantly possible that Obama's grandparents may have planted the announcement just in case their grandson needed to prove his U.S. citizenship in order to run for president someday. We suggest that those who choose to go down that path should first equip themselves with a high-quality tinfoil hat. The evidence is clear: Barack Obama was born in the U.S.A."[120]

The ridicule creates a straw-man argument suggesting anyone doubting the newspaper announcements proved Obama's birth location had to be postulating an elaborate conspiracy theory in which the family was preparing the baby at birth to run for president. In reality, totally apart from qualifying a baby as natural-born to be eligible to run for president, there are many obvious, real-world advantages to having American citizenship from birth. Illegal immigrants coming to the United States to have their babies born under claims of 14th Amendment "birthright citizenship" prove the point. Being a citizen from birth is clearly a much easier way to obtain U.S. citizenship than having to go through naturalization. Under America's ample social welfare state, a wide range of entitlement programs are available to citizens, but typically not to foreigners. Many privileges depend on being a U.S. citizen, including voting and obtaining a U.S. passport.

But the birth announcements published in the Hawaii newspapers prove only that Obama's birth was registered in Hawaii, not that he was actually born there. As we saw earlier, the Hawaii DOH would have accepted a statement from the family that the baby was born in Hawaii without demanding any proof. Hawaii vital statistics records demonstrate there were forty-two unattended births at home in Hawaii in 1961.

HAWAII 1961 BIRTHS BY ATTENDANT

	TOTAL	HOSPITAL	PHYSICIAN	MIDWIFE	UNATTENDED
TOTAL	5,418	5,406	8	0	4
NON-WHITE	12,198	12,110	50	0	38
ALL	17,616	17,516	58	0	42

(Source: Page 205, Vital Statistics of the United States, 1961, Volume 1)

All forty-two of these births had to be registered with the Hawaii DOH by the parents or the family involved, since there was no hospital record of them.

Moreover, WND determined that the announcements of Obama's birth published by the two Hawaii newspapers in 1961 do not provide solid proof of a birth in the Aloha State because of the papers' policies and procedures at the time.

The Honolulu *Star-Bulletin*, for example, reprints birth information it receives from the Hawaii DOH. "We don't have an editor who handles birth and marriage announcements. We print what we receive from the Department of Health Vital Statistics System," a *Star-Bulletin* newsroom operator told WND.[121] "This is how we've always done it."

Likewise, Marsh McFadden at the Honolulu *Advertiser* told WND that at the time of Obama's birth announcement, the newspaper got all of its information from the Hawaii DOH. "If we published it, it came from the state." McFadden said today's rules are different. Anyone can submit information for announcements, but the newspaper now requires a birth document to verify a birth in Hawaii.

In 1961, the Honolulu newspapers reported neither the name of the baby nor any additional details about whether the baby was born at home or in a hospital. The only information the newspapers published was the name of the parents, their address, whether the baby was a son or a daughter, and the date of the birth. A comparison of the Obama birth announcement in the two newspapers clearly demonstrates they are identical in every detail, including the order of other birth announcements preceding and following.

In fact, the *Advertiser* and *Star-Bulletin* should not be considered separate news agencies when it comes to reporting birth announcements. In 1961, they shared classified advertising, including information regarding birth announcements, and in mid-1962 they formed the Hawaiian News Agency to jointly publish both papers, an agreement that remains in place today.

In sum, WND interviews with the two Hawaiian newspapers revealed that:

• Neither newspaper had an editor that handled birth announcements;

• Both newspapers merely printed birth announcements, directly as received, from information published in Hawaii DOH vital statistics announcements;

• Hawaiian hospitals did not report to newspapers any birth announcement information; Hawaiian Certifications of Live Birth do not typically list hospital of birth or attending physician;

• Neither newspaper independently checked the truthfulness or accuracy of birth announcement information published by the newspapers from Hawaii DOH vital statistics records;

• Errors and misstatements in birth announcements printed in the two Hawaiian newspapers can and do result from incorrect information recorded in vital statistic information published by the Hawaiian DOH.

So, if the Obama family told the Hawaii DOH the baby was born in Hawaii, and the Health Department accepted those statements, the Hawaii DOH passed on the information to the Honolulu newspapers, and the birth announcement was printed.

In other words, the only thing proven by the much-touted Obama birth announcements in the Honolulu newspapers was that someone had registered the birth with the Hawaii DOH. They don't prove he was born in Hawaii, and they tell us nothing about who registered the birth with the Department of Health. "Was it a hospital? A doctor? A midwife? Or was it based solely on a parent's or relative's statement?" asks eligibility "Primer" author Stephen Tonchen.[122] If Obama's birth registration were based solely on a parent or relative's statement, and such statement was not independently corroborated by someone other than an immediate family member, concludes Tonchen, "we must do some further research before we can say anything for sure, one way or the other, about the circumstances of the President's birth."[123]

Who Actually Lived at the "Birth Announcement" Address?

The address listed in the birth announcements, 6085 Kalanianaole Highway, raises further questions.

Barack Obama, Sr. and Stanley Ann Dunham, President Obama's parents, apparently did not live together as husband and wife at that address at the time Barack Jr. was born, or at any other time.

It was actually the grandparents, Madelyn and Stanley Dunham, who lived there, not Mr. and Mrs. Barack H. Obama.

Indeed, there is no evidence Barack Obama, Sr. and Ann Dunham ever lived together under the same roof as a married couple.

For the entire time he was in Hawaii, Obama, Sr. lived alone at an 11th Avenue address in Honolulu, close to the university. Moreover, Dunham left Hawaii for Seattle within weeks of her son's birth, to study at the University of Washington. She did not return to Hawaii until after Obama, Sr. left Hawaii permanently in 1962 to continue his studies at Harvard.

At most, Dunham and her son lived at 6085 Kalanianaole Highway only a few weeks, and there is no evidence Obama, Sr. ever lived there.

A search of the Polk Directory of Honolulu (Polk's street directories are widely used by law enforcement and private investigators) for 1961–1962 indicates (see Exhibit 41, page 175) that 6085 Kalanianaole Highway was being rented by the grandparents: Madelyn L. Dunham, listed as a loan interviewer and escrow agent at the Bank of Hawaii, and Stanley A. Dunham, listed as a manager with Pratt Furniture.

In a separate listing (Exhibit 42, page 175), Stanley Ann Obama,

Obama's mother, is identified as a student renting an apartment at the 6085 Kalanianaole Highway address (The directory incorrectly transposed Ann's first and middle name, listing the occupant as "Obama Ann S" rather than "Obama Stanley A."); Barack H. Obama, her husband, is listed as a student living at a separate address, an apartment at 625 11th Avenue.

There is no Polk directory listing of Barack Obama, Sr. living at 6085 Kalanianaole Highway with his wife and in-laws.

A Honolulu title search (Exhibit 43, page 175) documented 6085 Kalanianaole Highway was purchased in 1958 by Orland Scott Lefforge, a University of Hawaii professor, and his wife/companion Thelma Young, who remained owners into the 1970s.

The Polk directories make clear that Lefforge and Young are first listed as living at 6085 Kalanianaole Highway in the 1963 directory, not when they purchased the home in 1958. In 1961, when Barack Obama, Jr. was born, the grandparents were renting 6085 Kalanianaole Highway from Lefforge.

A private investigator hired by WND to investigate Obama's birth provided an affidavit that supports the contention that Obama, Sr. and Ann Dunham never lived at 6085 Kalanianaole Highway as man and wife with their infant son.

Private investigator Jorge Baro's affidavit documented an interview his staff conducted with Beatrice Arakaki, who has lived at 6075 Kalanianaole Highway since before Obama was born. Arakaki told Baro's investigators she has no recollection of Obama being born or of the family living next door having a black child born to a white mother.

Very likely, Arakaki and the other neighbors interviewed by Baro's investigators did not recall the Obama family because the residents were the grandparents, Stanley and Madelyn Dunham, not the infant Barack Obama, Jr. and his parents.

Putting the Puzzle Together

The fact that 6085 Kalanianaole Highway is the address listed in the published birth announcements suggests the grandparents may have registered the birth with the Hawaii Department of Health. If Obama had a long-form birth certificate issued by a Hawaiian hospital, that document would require the listing of his mother's address, not his father's. That the birth address registered in the Hawaii newspapers was the address of the grandparents suggests Ann Dunham was not living with Barack Obama, Sr. as his wife at the 11th Avenue address.

If family members registered the birth in person with the Hawaii DOH, officials would have wanted to see records proving their residency in Honolulu, such as electric bills or telephone bills. Even if Ann Dunham were living with her parents at the time of the baby's birth, the grandparents were most likely the signers of the lease on the home on Kalanianaole Highway. Likewise, the grandparents would have been able to register the baby's birth, even without their daughter being present, because they would have had utility bills addressed to them as the home's leaseholders.

Bottom line: Birth announcements published in the Hawaii newspapers prove nothing about Obama's birth location. The Hawaii DOH would not have demanded to see the baby or the mother if the grandparents registered the baby's birth in person themselves. The baby could have been born in a foreign country and the mother not yet returned to Hawaii. All the Hawaii Department of Health would have wanted to see is the grandparents' proof that they were Hawaii residents. With electric and phone bills stretching back to August 1961 or before, the grandparents could have stated, sworn, or offered an affidavit that their grandson was born in Hawaii on August 4, 1961.

That would have been good enough for the Hawaii DOH to register the birth as having taken place in Hawaii, regardless of the actual facts. Without its own investigative unit, the Department of Health would have had no alternative but to accept the verbal say-so of the grandparents.

The short-form Certification of Live Birth would have been generated out of the birth records the Hawaii DOH had on file, even if that information consisted only of the grandparents' testimony. Because the grandparents could have been lying, the Obama short-form COLB does not prove he was born in Hawaii, even if it is authentic. Furthermore, without knowing the source of the birth information in the DOH records, it is impossible to conclude whether any officially issued short-form COLB for Barack Hussein Obama, Jr. is accurate or not.

Meet the Nordyke Twins

On July 28, 2009, the Honolulu *Advertiser* published the 1961 photo-stats of the original long-form birth certificates of twin daughters born to Eleanor Nordyke at Kapi'olani Maternity and Gynecological Hospital on August 5, 1961, one day after President Obama was supposedly born at the same hospital.[124] (Its name has since been changed to Kapi'olani Medical Center for Women & Children.)

The hospital-generated birth certificates demonstrate (see Exhibit 44, page 176) what a long-form document for Barack Obama would look like, if it indeed exists.

These genuine birth certificates include crucial information missing from the short-form document widely proclaimed to be Barack Obama's "birth certificate," including the name of the hospital, the doctor who delivered him, and considerable information about both parents, including address, race, age, birthplace, and occupation. A parent, a hospital attendant, and the local registrar all sign the long form. The date at the bottom showing when the certificate was filed is separated from the birth date of the baby listed at the top.

An examination of the birth certificates issued by Kapi'olani to the Nordyke twins further confirms that the number sequence precedes the registration number listed on President Obama's short-form COLB, even though he is supposed to have been born at the same hospital one day earlier.

- Susan Nordyke, the first twin born, was born at 2:12 p.m. local time and given File Number 151 61 10637, which was filed with the Hawaii Registrar on August 11, 1961.

- Gretchen Nordyke, the second twin, was born at 2:17 p.m. and given File Number 151 61 10638, also filed with the Hawaii Registrar on August 11.

- Barack Obama's short-form Certification of Live Birth bears a higher number than the Nordyke twins, File Number 151 1961 10641, even though he was born August 4, 1961, the day before the Nordyke twins, and his birth was filed with the Hawaii Registrar three days earlier than theirs, on August 8, 1961.

Moreover, the middle figure in Obama's purported registration is different from the Nordykes's. Obama's is 1961, indicating the year, while the Nordykes' is merely 61.

Eleanor Nordyke told WND she thinks her twins got lower numbers because she went into the hospital August 4, 1961, and was in labor for twenty hours before she delivered. She speculated that Stanley Ann Dunham came in after her and was given a later number, even though Dunham's baby was born earlier.

Look at the the birth announcement for the Nordyke twins, published in the *Honolulu Advertiser,* on August 16, 1961, in Exhibit 45 on page 176.[125]

The comparison of the Nordyke twins' newspaper birth announcements with Obama's birth announcements shows just how little actual information was referred by the Hawaii Department of Health to the newspapers for publication. The newspaper birth announcements in 1961 did not include hospital information.

To this day, no one has come forward with convincing testimony that they remember being in any Hawaii hospital when Stanley Ann Dunham was giving birth.

Nor has any photographic evidence surfaced of Barack Obama, Jr.'s birth in a Hawaii hospital.

· 7 ·

OUT OF AFRICA?

A Close Look at the Claims that Obama was Born in Kenya

In his autobiography, *Dreams from My Father*, Obama lays out a scenario of his nativity story that makes it unlikely he could have been born in Africa.

To maintain that Obama was born in Kenya, it would have to be proved against the story Obama tells in *Dreams,* that a pregnant eighteen-year-old university student—long before the age of easily accessible and affordable international travel—journeyed from Hawaii to remote Africa to visit the family of a man whose father reportedly was angered by his son's marriage to a white woman, where she had the baby, then turned up weeks later in classes at the University of Washington in Seattle.

On March 27, 2007, reporter Tim Jones told a version of the Obama nativity story in the *Chicago Tribune*[126] that buttressed the story Obama told in *Dreams*.

Jones related that Barack Obama, Sr. wrote a letter to his mother back in Africa, Sarah Hussein Onyango Obama, saying that he had met a young woman named Ann that he planned to marry. Jones neglects to mention (or did not realize) that Sarah Hussein Onyango Obama is not a blood relation to Barack Obama, Jr. She was the third wife of Obama's paternal grandfather, but not the mother of Barack Obama, Sr. At any rate, Jones relates that Obama, Sr. wrote to his stepmother, not to his father directly.

As Jones continues the story, Obama's paternal grandfather in Africa was furious because, "He didn't want the Obama blood sullied by a white woman."

Then, as Jones concludes the story, six months after Barack Obama, Sr. and Ann Dunham were married in Hawaii, a second letter arrived in Kenya, this time announcing the birth of Barack Hussein Obama, Jr. on August 4, 1961. Jones also reported that Sarah Obama said in some unspecified interview that she "was so happy to have a grandchild in the U.S."

Still, skeptics point out versions of the nativity story that derive from Obama lack independent verification.

The Obama nativity story Jones told in the *Chicago Tribune* most likely ultimately tracks back to Obama as its source, just as Obama's account of his nativity story in *Dreams from My Father* is entirely reliant on Obama's version of events. The letters Jones discusses have never surfaced, just as no marriage license for Barack Obama, Sr. and Ann Dunham has ever been found.

Alternative stories have developed from the components pieces Obama offers up in the official nativity story as told in *Dreams*.

Some skeptics attempt to argue that after traveling to Africa to win over her Kenyan in-laws, Ann Dunham was too far advanced to return to the United States before giving birth.

Those even more skeptical question whether August 4, 1961, is Obama's true date of birth, noting that the only independent verification of that date is the short-form Certification of Live Birth. If the grandparents registered the birth at the Hawaii Department of Health and the registration of the birth triggered the birth announcements in the Hawaii newspapers, how do we know for sure Obama's actual birth date could not have been earlier, allowing more time for Ann Dunham to have traveled to Kenya to give birth?

Much has also been made of a transatlantic telephone interview, conducted through an interpreter, in which Sarah Hussein Onyango Obama is said to have declared she was present at Barack Obama, Jr.'s birth in Mombasa, Kenya.

But there are many problems with the story, aside from the fact that the grandmother, interviewed by a minister who appeared to be baiting her, ended up with those interpreting for her in Kenya insisting she said the famous step-grandson was born in Hawaii.

In Kenya today, many persist in the belief that Obama was born there, even though no definitive proof of an African birth has yet been produced. Barack Obama's unwillingness to release his records, and Kenya's obvious delight in declaring him one of its own, have merged to spawn a collection of "gotcha" moments, in which African politicians, journalists, and media outlets—and Michelle Obama herself—have been cited for purportedly spilling the beans on Obama's true place of birth.

Media Reports Claim Obama Was Kenyan-Born

The first media report that Barack Obama was born in Kenya can be traced back to an article published June 27, 2004, by the *Sunday Standard* in Kenya, reporting that "Kenyan-born U.S. Senate hopeful, Barrack (sic) Obama, appeared set to take over the Illinois Senate seat after his main rival, Jack Ryan, dropped out of the race on Friday night amid a furor over lurid sex club allegations."[127]

Look at the screen capture of the article as it originally appeared (see Exhibit 46, page 177). WND calls to the newspaper were not returned, and apparently the *Sunday Standard* article was never corrected or retracted.

On October 9, 2008, a report by National Public Radio described then-Senator Barack Obama as "Kenyan-born" and a "son of Africa."[128] NPR's promotion for the story included a brief description of Western African correspondent Ofeibea Quist-Arcton, who "describes the stories that have been exciting, including the U.S. presidential race of Kenyan-born Sen. Barack Obama."

After discussing various issues developing in Africa at the time, the conversation in the NPR interview turned to Obama. At about 9:45 minutes into the audio report, interviewer Michelle Martin said, "A son of Africa, Barack Obama is poised to at least have the opportunity to become the next president of the United States." She asked, "How does this campaign look overseas?"

Quist-Arcton responded by describing Obama as a member of the Kenyan Luo tribe and reporting how Africa viewed the race. "You know [the campaign] has absolutely fired the imagination not only of American people, but of people in Africa," she said. "For a start, Barack Obama's father is from Kenya. People were very excited and because they had had a failed election in Kenya, and the opposition leader Raila Odinga comes from the same tribe as Barack Obama's father, the Luo. The joke was going around Kenya that America is going to have a Luo president before Kenya does."

She continued, "There's huge interest. All over the continent.... The fact that a black man and one with African blood has managed to get this far ... you know, I think has made young people sit up and listen and watch and follow the campaign and made the older generations who lived through the colonization and independence say, 'Well, well, well. So it can happen in America, too.'"

WND published a screen capture (see Exhibit 47, page 177) of the original NPR Web page.[129]

After the "Kenyan-born" reference was reported, NPR reposted the story with a correction that read, "An earlier summary of this story that appeared online incorrectly identified the birthplace of Barack Obama. The audio correctly states that Obama's father was born in Kenya." The new copy changed the original reference, "Kenyan-born Sen. Barack Obama," to "the U.S. presidential race of Sen. Barack Obama, whose father was born in Kenya."

Consider the screen capture of the altered NPR Web page, seen in Exhibit 48 on page 178.

On the day of the U.S. presidential election, November 4, 2008, the *Nigerian Observer* published an article that referred to Obama as Kenyan-born. Under a Solomon Asowata byline and Washington dateline, the report starts, "Americans will today go to the polls to elect their next President with Democratic Party candidate, Senator Barack Obama largely favoured to win. The Kenyan-born Senator will, however, face a stiff competition from his Republican counterpart."

Look at the WND screen capture of the 2008 article published in the *Nigerian Observer*, seen in Exhibit 49 on page 178.

Anticipating President Obama's visit to Ghana in July 2009, a report published by the newspaper *Modern Ghana* cited his birthplace on the continent of Africa. "For Ghana, Obama's visit will be a celebration of another milestone in African history as it hosts the first-ever African-

American president on his presidential visit to the continent of his birth," the report said.

Look at the the WND screen capture of the original 2009 article published in *Modern Ghana*, seen in Exhibit 50 on page 179.

Once WND pointed this out, *Modern Ghana* revised the online article (see Exhibit 51, page 179) to read "the continent of his father's birth."

On August 20, 2009, reporting on Obama's speech in Ghana, columnist Dafe Onojovwo wrote in AllAfrica.com, "Little wonder then why Kenya-born Barack Obama, America's first Black President, converted his major speech at his recent Ghana trip to a scathing upbraiding of Nigeria's irresponsible leadership!"

Again, WND screen captured the relevant passages (see Exhibit 52, page 180) in AllAfrica.com.

Kenyan Lawmakers Call Obama "Kenyan-born"

On November 5, 2008, the day after Barack Obama was elected to be the president of the United States, members of the African parliament celebrated Obama's election on the floor of the Kenyan National Assembly.[130]

Kenyan Member of Parliament Millie Odhiambo asked for a point of order to discuss the American presidential election results. According to the minutes of the Kenyan Parliamentary Debates, Ms. Odhiambo said, "Mr. Deputy Speaker, Sir, the President-elect, Mr. Obama, is a son of the soil of this country. Every other country in this continent is celebrating the Obama win. It is only proper and fitting that the country which he originates from should show the same excitement, pomp and colour. I, therefore, seek leave of the House that we adjourn to discuss the issue."

Look at the WND screen capture (see Exhibit 53, page 181) of the Kenyan Parliamentary Debates from November 5, 2008, with MP Odhiambo's remarks.

Kenyan Parliament Celebrates

The mood of the Kenyan parliament was so raucous that day that an extended debate occurred on whether or not to call the session off to celebrate Obama's victory.

"Could we allow ... Motion for Adjournment so that we could continue the celebrations of having a Kenyan rule the U.S.A.?" asked the Member of Parliament for the Ikolomani Constituency, Dr. Bonni Khalwale. Member of Parliament Affey agreed, commenting that, "For the first time, we have a leader of a great country in this world whose blood is Kenyan."

Eventually, the chair was compelled to issue an official statement of congratulations in the effort to keep the session moving forward.

Deputy Speaker Maalim Farah delivered the statement, in which he echoed Odhiambo's "son of the soil" language: "Honorable members, as you may be aware, the people of the United States have just had a historic election where the son of this soil, Barack Hussein Obama, has been elected the 44th president of the United States of America and the first African-American president in the history of that country. Please join me in registering and sending this House's congratulations to the President-elect Obama for overcoming great odds to emerge victorious."

Again, look at Exhibit 54 on page 181.

During the 2010 Kenyan parliamentary debate on a proposed new constitution, James Orengo, the country's minister of lands and a member of parliament for the Ugenya constituency, cited America's election of what he called a Kenyan-born president as an example of what can be accomplished when diverse peoples unite.[131]

Orengo asked, "If America was living in a situation where they feared ethnicity and did not see itself as a multiparty state or nation," Orengo argued, "how could a young man born here in Kenya, who is not even a native American, become the president of America?"

The United States is no longer "living in the past," said Orengo, congratulating Americans for supposedly electing a native Kenyan as their president without regard to "ethnic consideration and objectives."

The debate was recorded in the Kenyan government's official March 25, 2010, hansard—a traditional name for printed transcripts of a parliamentary debate—as continuing with no other MPs mentioning or attempting to correct Orengo's comments about Obama.

See the screen capture of the Kenyan parliament's Hansard recording Orengo's comments, featured in Exhibit 55 on page 182.

After WND published accounts of the statements in the Kenyan parliament, the relevant pages of the parliamentary debates, seen in the aforementioned screen captures, disappeared from the Internet.

Kenyan MP Asks Whether Obama Will "Repatriate"?

On April 14, 2010, the Kenyan National Assembly debated the issue of repatriation of Kenyan artifacts removed from the country by colonialists. Members of parliament wanted to know what was being done to return their artifacts, or failing their return, how Kenya would be compensated for the loss.

Bonny Khalwale of the Ikolomani Constituency posed the following question: "What commitment did [the office of President Obama] make about the compensation and more importantly, the biggest artifact in the U.S.A. today that belongs to this country is one Barack Obama. How does he intend to repatriate himself or part of the money that is realized from all the royalties that he is attracting across the whole world?"

This is the same Khalwale who declared that with the Obama presidency, a Kenyan was ruling the United States.

Look at the the relevant screen capture from the Kenyan National Assembly official report for April 14, 2010, seen in Exhibit 56 on page 182.

Did Michelle Really Say Barack Was Born in Kenya?

A video posted April 3, 2010, on YouTube.com, of Michele Obama telling a group of homosexual-rights activists that Kenya was her husband's "home country" went viral.[132]

The video shows Mrs. Obama saying, "When we took our trip to Africa and visited his home country in Kenya, we took a public HIV test." The clip comes from a June 2008 campaign speech Mrs. Obama delivered to the Gay & Lesbian Leadership Council of the Democratic National Committee in New York City, as reported by Reuters.[133]

Many who circulated a link to the video clip concluded the first lady was acknowledging her husband was born in Kenya, but the term "home country" could easily be interpreted as a reference to her husband's family heritage, not his place of birth. Whether Barack Obama was born in Kenya or not, he has Kenyan blood, assuming his father indeed was Barack Obama, Sr.

Did Obama's Grandmother Say She Was Present at His Birth in Mombasa?

Philip J. Berg, a former Pennsylvania deputy attorney general, submitted a transcript of a telephone conversation with Sarah Hussein Obama along with sworn affadavits in a filing with the U.S. Supreme Court alleging Barack Obama, Jr. was born in Mombasa, Kenya.[134] Lower courts had dismissed his August 21, 2008, case as frivolous.

American Christian minister Ron McRae, who describes himself in his affidavit as an overseer of the Anabaptist Churches in North America and a "Presiding Elder on the African Presbytery," conducted the now-famous telephone interview. McRae, who called from Detroit, said Sarah Obama was in a public setting with several hundred people listening to the telephone call on a speakerphone. The interpreter was Vitalis Akech Ogombe, the community chairman of Sarah Obama's village of Kyang'oma Kogelo in Western Kenya, thirty miles west of the Lake Victoria city of Kisumu.

"In the ensuing public conversation, I asked Ms. Obama specifically, 'Were you present when your grandson was born in Kenya?'" McRae testified in his sworn statement. "This was asked to her in translation twice, and both times she replied, Yes! Yes she was! She was present when Obama was born."

Is it possible, though, that in the crosstalk of English, Swahili, and the local Luo tribal dialogue, she could have understood McRae simply to be asking where she was when Barack Obama, Jr. was born? Moreover, she ultimately corrected herself, stating that her famous grandson was born in Hawaii, not Kenya. According to *New York Times* columnist Nicholas

Kristof, who visited her village during the presidential campaign, the grandmother is illiterate and does not know when she was born.[135]

At the end of the tape, the interpreter can be clearly heard interjecting repeatedly that the grandmother said Obama was born in Hawaii.

In an attempt to resolve the controversy, WND had the tape reviewed by two members of Sarah Hussein Obama's Luo tribe who are fluent in the local Luo dialect, Swahili, and English. One of Kenyans who listened to the tape for WND has known Sarah Hussein Obama personally, over many years. He has met with her repeatedly in her home village of Kogelo. The other Kenyan who listened to the tape for WND holds a respected position in the Kenyan government.

The WND source who knows Sarah reported: "I have keenly and attentively listened to the tape over and over again and I can confirm from Sarah's own confession that Barack Obama was born in Kenya in her presence." He continued: "I can confirm from Sarah's own testimony on the tape that Barack Obama was born in Kenya in her presence. She was asked of his actual birthplace, and she affirmed she was actually there, present in person at his birth." He further said that while the people in the room with Sarah Obama "tried as much as they could to change the tone of the whole story ... to me it seems someone is coaching her from the background and seemingly trying to guide her on what to say."

The Kenyan government source agreed. "I have listened to the tape," he said. "The preacher asked whether Barack Obama was born in Mombasa and the translator asked the same. When she said Mombasa, it was like a surprise and those there thought she could not have meant to say Mombasa." The source said that at that point those there with Sarah "began insisting Hawaii was where Barack Obama was born."

Alex Koppelman, the senior editor on Salon.com's political "War Room" blog jumped into the fray to contend, "No, Obama's grandmother didn't say he was born in Kenya."[136] In a column that attacked former-CNN television news host Lou Dobbs and radio talk show host G. Gordon Liddy, Koppelman characterized Sarah Hussein Obama's statement that Obama was born in Mombasa as "a mistake, a confusion in translation," that the family in Kenya attempted to correct, multiple times.

Dismissing the story as just another "birther myth," Koppelman explained that "people who believe in a conspiracy theory simply hear what they want to hear."

Although no documentary evidence has yet established Barack Obama was born in Kenya, the rumors and speculation continue to fly. Several clearly counterfeit attempts at a "Kenyan birth certificate," for example, remain in Internet circulation.

Ultimately, as long as Obama keeps his records under wrap, the lore surrounding the origin of the East African nation's favorite son will only grow.

PART TWO

CRACKS IN THE OBAMA NATIVITY STORY

THE MYSTERY HOSPITAL
AND THE MISSING DOCTOR

How Could Obama Be Born in Two Different Hospitals? And Who is the Missing Physician that Attended His Birth?

The mystery surrounding Barack Obama's birthplace only deepened amid conflicting reports that he was born at Queen's Medical Center and at the Kapi'olani Center for Women and Children, both in Honolulu. Obviously, it is not possible for any person to be born in two different hospitals.

Two days after highlighting the controversy in a July 7, 2009, article, "Obama Birth Mystery: More Than 1 Hospital,"[137] WND published a letter Obama purportedly sent Kapi'olani hospital only days after taking office, claiming he was born there.[138]

Until then, most Obama-supporting media sources and Internet blogs proclaimed that he had been born at Queen's Medical Center. But following a series of WND exposés beginning with the July 2009 stories, many Web sites scrubbed previous stories claiming the president was born at Queen's, substituting Kapi'olani. Apparently they took their lead from Obama's letter to Kapi'olani of January 24, 2009, deciding to bring their information in line with the official White House story.

Here we will document how far mainstream media and Internet Web sites supporting Obama have gone to scuttle investigations of his eligibility to be president under Article 2, Section 1, of the Constitution by establishing Kapi'olani as Obama's official nativity hospital, such that to suggest today as true the original version—namely, that Obama was born at Queen's Medical Center—is no longer politically correct.

Because WND anticipated Web pages stating Obama was born at Queen's Medical would soon disappear or be rewritten, WND made extensive screen captures. Indeed, some Web sites transformed Obama's birth hospital from Queen's to Kapi'olani within minutes of the appearance of WND's first story.

If Obama was born in a hospital in Hawaii, there had to be an attending physician, just as the hospital had to generate a long-form birth certificate. But no doctor has ever been identified as having been present for Obama's birth in Hawaii. After two years in office, along with refusing to authorize release of his actual birth certificate, the Obama camp has been unwilling or unable to identify the physician who delivered Obama.

The question is: If President Obama's official story does not identify the hospital where he was born and the physician who attended his birth, why should the American public accept the assertion that he was born in Hawaii?

Journalists and other investigators are trained to recognize that if one part of an official story is inaccurate or false, then the whole story should be questioned.

The *sine qua non* of Obama's birth story has been to insist he was born in Hawaii. This is the one fact he cannot afford to have uncovered as a fabrication. If Obama was born outside the United States, he almost certainly is ineligible to be president, since his father was a foreigner and his mother, at age eighteen, was too young to convey citizenship to her son under the requirements of U.S. Code, Section 301 (a)(7).

The First Hospital Birth Story: Obama was Born at Queen's

Initially, the accepted Obama birth story was that he was born at Queen's Medical Center in Honolulu. This version appeared as early as 2004 in a Hawaii high school paper and later turned up in more authoritative places such as Obama's campaign Web site and the listing of a Library of Congress genealogist.

In 2004, Obama's half-sister Maya Soetoro reportedly gave an interview to the *Rainbow Edition Newsletter*, a high school newspaper published by the Education Laboratory School in Hawaii. In the first sentence of a two-page story on Obama, titled "A New Face in Politics," reporter Benett Guira wrote, "Barack Obama was born on August 4, 1961 at the Queen's Medical Center in Honolulu."[139]

Consider the the screen capture from the 2004 story in the *Rainbow Edition Newsletter*, seen in Exhibit 57 on page 183.

An Obama-supporting Web site, BARACKRYPHAL.blogspot.com, objected that the article was written "not by a reporter, and not by a colleague of Maya Soetoro, but by a high school junior."[140] Moreover, the Web site claimed the high school reporter just copied the birth information from Wikipedia.

The collaboratively written Internet encyclopedia, which allows most of its articles to be edited by anyone with access to the site, now states Obama was born at Kapi'olani. Look at an October 2010 screen capture (see Exhibit 58, page 184) from Wikipedia.

Still, noting that the information came from Wikipedia in 2004 begs the question: Where did Wikipedia get its information? The fact remains that in 2004, the prevailing story throughout much of the media was that Obama was born at Queen's, and—significantly—there is no indication Obama or his family members made any effort to correct that story.

Genealogical Listings Citing Queen's as Obama Birth Hospital

Williams Addams Reitwiesner, a genealogist at the Library of Congress, made another early listing that Obama was born at Queen's Medical Center. Tracing Obama's lineage, Reitwiesner wrote, "Barack Hussein OBAMA was born on 4 August 1961 at the Queen's Medical Center in Honolulu, Hawaii, to Barack Hussein OBAMA, Sr. of Nyangoma-Kogelo, Siaya District, Kenya, and Ann DUNHAM of Wichita, Kansas."

Look at Reitwiesner's original entry, seen in Exhibit 59 on page 184.

Almost immediately after WND published its first story on the hospital controversy, Reitwiesner revised the Obama genealogy, published on his Web site WARGS.com, to represent that Obama was born at Kapi'olani.

See revised Reitwiesner genealogy in Exhibit 60 on page 185.

Right after the 2008 election, a lengthy blog posting on Obama's own campaign Web site, BarackObama.com, listed his birthplace as Queen's Medical Center.

Look at the campaign Web site blog image for the posting in Exhibit 61 on page 185.

Tracing Obama's lineage back to his great-great-great grandparents in the mid-1800s, the information was most likely taken from Reitwiesner's posting, as it read identically.

But after WND's first story on the Obama two-hospital controversy, the genealogy posting was deleted from the "Organizing for America" section of BarackObama.com.

Obama Letter Claims Kapi'olani as the Official Birth Hospital

The White House's attempt to belatedly establish Obama's place of birth as Kapi'olani Medical Center is traceable to a purportedly official letter signed by Obama on White House stationery January 24, 2009.

In the letter, which appeared on the Kapi'olani Web site, Obama celebrated the hospital by writing: "As a beneficiary of the excellence of Kapi'olani Medical Center—the place of my birth—I am pleased to add my voice to your chorus of supporters."

Look at Exhibit 62 on page 186 to find the Obama letter as it first appeared on the Kapi'olani Web site.

A different version of the letter, with identical text but a different format, appeared in the Spring 2009 issue of Kapi'olani Medical Center's *Inspire Magazine*.

By including the letter in a publication Kapi'olani sends to supporters and donors, Kapi'olani displayed its willingness to use it not only to proclaim the hospital as Obama's place of birth, but also as a fundraising tool. "As the hospital celebrates 100 years of pediatric care in Hawaii, we've begun a capital campaign to position the hospital for the next century of care," wrote Chuck Sted, president and CEO of Hawaii Public Health, in the edition of the magazine that featured the Obama letter. Hawaii Public Health operates Kapi'olani.

Although Kapi'olani spokeswoman Kristy Watanabe acknowledged to WND that the hospital published the letter in its magazine, she mysteriously refused to answer any questions. "Right now we have no comment. Thank you very much," she said, abruptly ending the conversation by hanging up the phone.

Consider the screen capture of the relevant *Inspire Magazine* page, seen in Exhibit 63 on page 187.

Watanabe even refused to confirm or deny the statement in Obama's letter that he was born at the hospital! "Our comment to everyone who has been calling is that federal law does not permit us to provide any more details concerning information [about President Obama's birth] without authorization from Mr. Obama," Watanabe told WND.

She admitted the hospital had not even contacted Obama for authorization. Asked why, given the large number of requests it was getting, Watanabe replied: "This is our response and we can't say anything more than that."

Both Queen's and Kapi'olani refused to answer WND questions about Obama's birth records, citing legal restrictions under the federal Health Insurance Portability and Accountability Act, or HIPAA, that protect patient privacy.

"The hospital is not allowed to give out any information to the public about patients without the patient's permission, because of federal HIPAA law restrictions," said Makana Shook, cooperate communications coordinator for Queen's.

Likewise, Kapi'olani officials said they would release any documentation they may have about the president's birth to the public only if the president gives his permission.

The Role of Obama's Pal, Neil Abercrombie, in the Birth Hospital Controversy

In January 2009, when Kapi'olani first posted the Obama birth letter, its Web site also posted a video of then-Representative Neil Abercrombie, D-HI, reading the letter on January 24, 2009, the date the letter was supposedly written by Obama in the White House, to a dinner at Kapi'olani

Medical Center of approximately seven hundred community leaders and hospital supporters celebrating the institution's 100th anniversary. A video posted on YouTube[141] shows Abercrombie introducing the letter, claiming it was the "first message to be sent from the Oval Office by President Barack Obama anywhere in the country." That Abercrombie was able to show the letter in Hawaii on the same day President Obama supposedly wrote and signed the letter suggests Abercrombie did not have a paper original of the letter received in his office for display that night.

Abercrombie's presence at the event in connection with the Obama birth letter is no surprise. During the 2008 presidential campaign, when Americans were first getting a grip on Obama's admittedly complex biography, Abercrombie stepped up to support the story that Barack Obama, Sr. and Stanley Ann Dunham did indeed meet at the University of Hawaii in a Russian language course where they fell in love. Abercrombie told the *Chicago Tribune* that he was part of a group of graduate students at the University of Hawaii along with Obama, Sr. and Dunham who spent weekends listening to jazz, drinking beer, and debating politics and world affairs.[142]

Other than Abercrombie's, there are remarkably few personal testimonies of witnesses who observed Obama, Sr. and Dunham in Hawaii together at any time, including the period of their reported dating and marriage prior to Obama's birth in 1961.

It is curious that on January 24, 2009, the date Abercrombie made public Obama's letter at the Kapi'olani anniversary dinner, he posted a notice on his congressional Web site taking credit for the letter.

The online notice is featured in Exhibit 64 on page 187.

Abercrombie's congressional Web site echoed the theme that this was "believed to be one of the first official messages of congratulations from President Barack Obama." That President Obama would make one of his first messages from the White House a letter to Kapi'olani Medical Center claiming it as his birth hospital and that Abercrombie would make such a point of this being one of the first messages from President Obama suggests both Obama and Abercrombie were aware of and trying to put to an end to the controversy over what hospital in Hawaii was Obama's birth hospital. As a side note, a declaration by Abercrombie and Obama that Obama was born in Kapi'olani, if true, would mean a long-form, hospital-generated Hawaii birth certificate must exist for Obama, even though Obama has so far refused to authorize the Hawaii Department of Health to release his birth records.

After introducing the letter, Abercrombie read it to the audience of more than seven hundred people, including children wearing T-shirts proclaiming "Born at Kapi'olani." The staging of the event made clear that a major purpose was to settle the issue once and for all and declare that Kapi'olani was the official Obama nativity hospital. Clearly, the real intent of Abercrombie presenting the Obama birth letter was to settle a lingering birth controversy. In other words, Abercrombie and Obama reduced the 100th anniversary celebration to nothing more than an occasion for the White House to establish a public record that the president was born there.

After the event, Abercrombie spokesman Dave Helfert told WND that some people have contacted Abercrombie's office "in an insane and nonsensical rage" suggesting Obama "was born somewhere else and snuck into the United States."

He said he could not understand why the public is demanding such a level of proof of natural-born citizenship. When asked why he thought Obama just doesn't end the controversy by releasing his original, long-form, hospital-generated birth certificate displaying the name of the hospital and the doctor, Helfert said he couldn't speak for the president, but added, "If that were me, I'd tell people to stick it in their ear. It's none of their business. The documents online have been certified to show he was born in the United States."

Clearly, Helfert was combatant over the Obama birth controversy.

"If you had a picture of him in the hospital [delivery room] with a hospital sign behind him, there would be a lot of people who wouldn't believe it, [thinking] that it was trick photography or something nefarious," he added. "If the hand of God appeared in the sky to write the birth certificate, they wouldn't believe it."

In his 2010 gubernatorial run, Abercrombie criticized WND for reporting that he, like Obama himself, was closely tied to the radical leftist, Marxist-oriented group Democratic Socialists of America.[143] Trevor Loudon of the New Zeal blog, a researcher of communism, had uncovered the November-December 1990 issue of the organization's official magazine, the *Democratic Left*, which listed Abercrombie as a member of the socialist party.[144] The magazine stated the group's political-action committee endorsed two congressional candidates, "DSAer Democrat Neil Abercrombie seeking to regain the House seat representing Honolulu and Vermont independent candidate Bernie Sanders."

In a section titled "Rumors and False Attacks," Abercrombie's campaign Web site claimed, "Neil has never been part of any socialist or communist organization." In a clear reference to WND, the site continued, "These rumors are being spread by Neil's political opponents and conspiracy theorists including those behind the so-called 'birther' movement who continually claim that President Obama was not born in the U.S."[145]

In his book *The Manchurian President*, WND reporter Aaron Klein documented Obama's long-term association with the Democratic Socialists of America.[146] And Stanley Kurtz, a contributing editor for *National Review Online,* produced evidence in his book, *Radical-in-Chief,* that Obama attended the 1983 Cooper Union Socialist Scholars Conference sponsored by the DSA.[147]

Kapi'olani Backtracks

The plot thickened, when WND posted a story on July 9, 2009, questioning the authenticity of the letter.[148] Within an hour of the story being posted on WND, the Kapi'olani Web site removed the image of the president's letter as well as the Abercrombie video of the anniversary dinner. The Web site provided no explanation for the changes. Viewing the Kapi'olani Web site today, a reader would have no idea the Obama letter had ever been sent.

Then, the next day, on July 10, 2009, WND reported: "The Honolulu hospital which for nearly six months proudly declared President Obama was born at its facility and used that claim as a major fundraising tool is now engaged in an active cover-up, hiding a White House letter announcing his alleged birth there and refusing to confirm such a letter even exists."[149]

The page on the *Inspire Magazine* Web site, KapiolaniGift.org, featuring the Obama birth letter was also deleted.

The WND follow-up article continued: "The Kapi'olani Medical

Center for Women and Children is electronically cloaking what it had touted as a letter dated January 24, 2008, from the president, in which the commander in chief, just four days after his inauguration, supposedly wrote, 'As a beneficiary of the excellence of Kapi'olani Medical Center—the place of my birth—I am pleased to add my voice to your chorus of supporters.'"

WND noticed that the hospital did not completely remove the image of the letter. Instead, Kapi'olani covered up the image electronically by using a hiding code called "commenting out" that maintains the material but prevents if from being seen by readers.

In the article published July 9, 2009, WND published the HTML code (see Exhibit 65, page 188) embedded in the Kapi'olani Web site to produce the Obama letter on the Web site, proving that the letter was electronically generated, not a copy of an original paper letter actually sent from the White House.

In the article published on July 10, 2009, after the letter had been removed from the Kapi'olani Web site, WND published the HTML source code that "commented out" the letter (see Exhibit 66, page 188) in a way that hid the original HTML source code in the Kapi'olani webpage, showing up now as green-colored text, as contrasted to the original HTML source code that showed up red, blue, and black when the letter appeared on the Web site.

"This was a purposeful coding in a well-known HTML code that basically removes code from showing up in the display of a Web page, but maintains it in the actual code of the page," an Internet consultant told WND. "It's just a quick way to stop things from showing up in the browser. It's typically done so that coders can hide or bring something back quickly."

Further proof that the letter was electronically created came from the letterhead and signature on the letter produced on the Kapi'olani Web site.

Look at Exhibit 67 on page 189 to see what WND saw when moving the computer cursor over the letterhead and the Obama signature.

Examining the Obama birth letter in the source code revealed that the entire text had been composed in HTML, proving without doubt that the letter displayed on the Kapi'olani Web site was an Internet construct, not a photo or scan of any original letter sent from the White House and signed by President Obama.

In the follow-up story on the letter cover-up published on July 10, 2009, WND reported that Kapi'olani spokeswoman Kristy Watanabe now refused to confirm that a letter had ever been sent from the White House on January 24, 2009. Nor would she acknowledge that the document published on the Kapi'olani Web site was an actual letter from the White House. She also dodged questions probing why the Obama birth letter did not display evidence of a presidential or White House embossed seal.

Instead, she stuck to her previous statement: "Federal law does not permit us to provide any more details concerning information [about Obama's birth] without authorization from Mr. Obama."

Asked again why the hospital's celebration of Obama's purported written declaration of his place of birth was not considered an acknowledgement of the president's authorization, Watanabe replied, "No comment."

When WND took a closer look at the image of the January 24, 2009, birth letter posted on Kapi'olani's Web site, it became clear the letter displayed online was not a photo or a scanned image of a real letter, but rather had been a pieced-together likeness of a letter constructed with HTML code routinely used to build Web sites.

WND proved this very simply by going to the hospital Web site and highlighting the letter with a cursor, and noting that the White House letterhead and Obama's signature were both individual images that had been copied separately, probably from the White House Web site, then added to give the appearance of an actual letter.

WND also noticed that the version of the Obama birth letter published in *Inspire Magazine* looked nothing like the supposedly identical letter on Kapi'olani's Web site.

See a close-up of the letter as it appeared in *Inspire* in Exhibit 68 on page 190.

Comparing the two versions reveals obvious differences, including a different font for the text, and the fact that Obama's purported signature in the magazine swoops down over his typewritten name, though the signature is completely separate from the signature in the online version, as seen in Exhibit 69 on page 190.

After several days of ignoring repeated requests for comment, Kapi'olani finally e-mailed WND what the hospital claimed was an electronic copy of the original White House correspondence.

By the time WND reported this new development in a July 16, 2009, story, "'Birth Hospital': Letter for real,"[150] Kapi'olani had removed the earlier electronic version from the hospital Web site.

Look at what Kapi'olani claimed was an electronic image of the authentic paper letter that had been sent from the White House (Exhibit 70, page 191).

"We treasure the letter, and we're delighted to share it with you," wrote Keala Peters, director of marketing and communications for Hawaii Pacific Health, which runs Kapi'olani, to WND in an e-mail.

Peters finally responded to inquiries when WND informed the hospital that the FBI and Secret Service said the matter could lead to criminal prosecution if the letter were determined to be fraudulent.

"It would be a charity fraud scheme," FBI spokesman Steve Kodak told WND. "It would be investigated by us or by the Secret Service."

Up until then, Kapi'olani spokesman Watanabe had stonewalled a week of requests for the hospital to verify the correspondence.

Peters said a reproduction of the "original letter" is on display at the hospital. "The original is something that we treasure, and we know that it came from Mr. Obama," she said, explaining only that the paper document was personally presented to the hospital by then-Rep. Abercrombie, who read its contents at the hospital's Centennial Dinner January 24, 2009, the same day the letter was dated.

In repeated visits to the hospital, Hawaii residents have reported to WND that President Obama's letter is nowhere on display, nor is there any plaque or other monument that would identify the hospital as Obama's birthplace.

Regarding the precise whereabouts of the "original" Kapi'olani letter from Obama, Peters opted not to comment, saying, "It's not anything we want to be damaged."

WND found that a close-up view of the letter photographed by the Kapi'olani Medical Center (Exhibit 71, page 192) showed an embossed presidential seal as part of the letterhead.

Why, WND asked Peters, did the hospital not post a scanned image of the paper letter to begin with, instead of the HTML version?

"We did that because we didn't want people to take it from the Web and use it for purposes other than for what it was intended," she responded. "I'm sorry it created suspicion on your part, but it was not our intention."

When asked why Kapi'olani suddenly yanked the letter off its Web site after displaying it online for nearly half a year, Peters acknowledged removing it, "not because it doesn't exist, but because it was becoming a distraction."

"The inquiries became a distraction in running our hospital," she said.

Though the hospital continues to assert the letter is indeed from Obama, the White House has refused to respond to repeated requests by phone, by e-mail, and in-person to verify its authenticity.

Secret Service spokesman Malcolm Wiley told WND, "We're not going to confirm or deny whether or not a letter exists if the White House has not confirmed it exists."

"This is something that is bearing the president's signature," he added. "It's the White House's responsibility to confirm it. So that is the first step—for the White House to determine its authenticity. We're not going to trump the White House."

When WND posed the possibility of continued stonewalling and fundraising using a presidential document that might not have originated from Obama, Wiley said, "In a case like that, it might be something we could very well investigate."

The only reason any of this matters is that President Obama has not provided simple, incontrovertible proof of his birthplace. That information would be included on his long-form, hospital-generated birth certificate, which he has steadfastly refused to release, despite not only conflicting reports, but repeated national polls showing that more than half of all Americans don't believe Obama is telling the truth about his birth.

White House Won't Verify the Letter

At a July 13, 2009, White House press conference, presidential Press Secretary Robert Gibbs refused to confirm the letter allegedly written by Obama to Kapi'olani hospital was authentic.[151]

The issue arose when Les Kinsolving, WND's White House correspondent, asked Gibbs:[152] "And my question is, can you verify this letter? Or, if not, would you tell us which Hawaiian hospital he was born in, since Kapi'olani, which used to publicize this, now refuses to confirm." By this time, Kapi'olani had already removed the alleged Obama letter from its Web site, following WND's July 7 and July 9 articles.

Instead of answering the question directly, Gibbs chose to ridicule Kinsolving for asking it.

"Goodness gracious," Gibbs responded. "I'm going to be like, like, in year four describing where it is the president was born. I don't have the letter at my fingertips, obviously, and I don't know the name of the exact hospital."

When Kinsolving asked when Gibbs could check, Gibbs responded: "I will seek to interview whoever brought the president into this world. But can we just—I want to do this once and for all, Lester. Let's just do this once and for all. You can go on this—I hope you'll take the time not just to Google 'President, January 24, Hawaii hospital, birth' and come up with this letter, but go on the Internet and get the birth certificate, Lester, and put...."

When Kinsolving pointed out that the image posted on various Web sites was not a birth certificate but an abbreviated "Certification of Live Birth" document, Gibbs said, "I know. Just a document from the state of Hawaii denoting the fact that the president was indeed born in the state of Hawaii."

Then, amid a chorus of guffaws and giggles from the White House press corps, Gibbs started lecturing Kinsolving—the second most senior correspondent on the White House beat, who has questioned every president since Nixon, and was twice nominated for a Pulitzer—about journalism.

"You know, Lester, I—I want to stay on this for a second, Lester, I want to stay on this for a second, because you're a smart man, right?" Gibbs said.

"Hypothetical," said an unidentified reporter.

"All right, all right, settle down in here. Only I get to make jokes like that," Gibbs said.

"Lester, let's finish this one. Do all your listeners and the listeners throughout this country the service to which any journalist owes those listeners, and that is the pursuit of the noble truth. And the noble truth is that the president was born in Hawaii, a state of the United States of America. And all of this incredible back-and-forth—I get e-mails today from people who inexplicably can figure out very easily the White House e-mail address, and want proof of where the president was born."

As if that was not enough abuse, Gibbs continued: "Lester, the next time you ask me a question I'm going to ask you what reporting you've done to demonstrate to your listeners the truth, the certificate, the state, so that they can look to you for that momentous search for the truth, and you can wipe away all the dark clouds and provide them with the knowing clarity that comes from that certainty."

In the exchange, Gibbs provided a textbook case for applying the advice Saul Alinsky gave political operatives in *Rules for Radicals*—to ridicule and intimidate opponents to deflect questions the operative cannot afford to answer honestly.

It is important to note that when asked about Obama's alleged letter to Kapi'olani, Gibbs refused to confirm that the president actually signed and sent the letter, and he dodged the question of whether the letter was correct in asserting Obama was born at Kapi'olani.

Obama-Supporting Web sites Scrub Queen's as Obama Birth Hospital

Obama-supporting Web sites did not initially notice the letter to Kapi'olani purportedly written by Obama, and for six months it was posted on the hospital's Web site without controversy.

But the moment WND brought the president's letter and the two-hospital birth controversy to public attention on July 9, 2009, everything changed.

Almost instantly, Web sites that previously proclaimed Obama was born at Queen's began changing the hospital to Kapi'olani. For example:

In a January 2008 Snopes.com entry examining allegations that Obama is "a radical Muslim," the site stated that "Barack Hussein Obama was born on 4 August 1961 at the Queen's Medical Center in Honolulu, Hawaii."[153]

See a screen capture of the Snopes entry, showing how the article first appeared on the Internet in Exhibit 72 on page 192.

Within ninety minutes of the WND report of July 7, 2009, Snopes changed its entry to say Obama was born at Kapi'olani.

Look at the WND screen capture of the edited Snopes article in Exhibit 73 on page 193.

Snopes gave no acknowledgment that it had changed the name of the hospital, nor did it admit to any error or explain how it now knew Obama was born at Kapi'olani.

United Press International also reacted to WND's story.

A UPI report from Election Day, November 4, 2008, stated: "Obama described his birth at Queen's Medical Center in Hawaii August 4, 1961, to a young woman from Kansas and a father of Luo ethnicity from Nyanza Province in Kenya, as an 'all-America' story transcending racial stereotypes and experience."[154]

Look at the original UPI story as it appeared online on November 4, 2008, in Exhibit 74 on page 194. And then look at Exhibit 75 on page 195, which shows the page after UPI changed its story.

As with Snopes, UPI gave no explanation for the correction, simply inserting Kapi'olani into the story in place of Queen's.

Hawaii Gov. Lingle Announces "Exact" Place of Obama Birth

More than a year and a half after Obama was elected president, then-Hawaii Gov. Linda Lingle publicly announced the alleged location of Obama's birth, saying in a radio interview on New York's WABC, "The president was, in fact born at Kapi'olani Hospital in Honolulu, Hawaii.

WND reported May 5, 2010, that the disclosure was believed to be the first time a state government official had declared the precise place where Obama was born, contradicting of course all the published claims that Obama was born at Queen's Medical Center.[155]

"It's been an odd situation," Lingle said. "This issue kept coming up so much in the campaign, and again I think it's one of those issues that is simply a distraction from the more critical issues that are facing the nation."

Lingle then claimed she had instructed the director of the Hawaii Department of Health, who she noted was a physician by background, to go personally to view Obama's birth certificate in the records of the department.

"We issued a news release at the time saying that the president was, in fact, born at Kapi'olani Hospital in Honolulu, Hawaii. And that's just a fact and yet people continue to call up and e-mail and want to make it an issue, and I think it's, again, a horrible distraction for the country by those people who continue this."

Contrary to what Lingle had represented, however, the statement issued by Hawaii health director Dr. Chiyome Fukino did not mention anything about Obama being born at Kapi'olani. In fact, the press release said nothing about the hospital where Obama was born. While we will discuss this press release in detail later, suffice it to say here that Fukino also said nothing about a long-form, hospital-generated birth certificate even existing for Obama in the vital records maintained by the Hawaii DOH.

At the time of the 2008 election, Fukino had objected to the release of any birth information about Obama, saying: "There have been numerous requests for Sen. Barack Hussein Obama's official birth certificate. State law (Hawaii Revised Statutes §338–18) prohibits the release of a certified birth certificate to persons who do not have a tangible interest in the vital record."

Ironically, Lingle's public discussion of what she asserted was Obama's birth hospital appeared to violate the provision of Hawaii law Fukino had months earlier cited as prohibiting Hawaii's government from releasing any information about Obama's birth.

In its report of Lingle's radio statement, WND also noted that Janice Okubo, the Hawaii Department of Health public information officer, had said Hawaii law prohibited her from commenting on the birth records of any specific person. Okubo also cited Hawaii Revised Statutes §338–18 pertaining to "Disclosure of Records," which states, "The department shall not permit inspection of public health statistics records, or issue a certified copy of any such record or part thereof, unless it is satisfied that the applicant has a direct and tangible interest in the record."

The Mystery Doctor

Just who delivered baby Barack Obama?

After more than two years of asking this question, no one—including the occupant of the Oval Office—has answered it with documentary proof.

Despite an in-depth search, the name of any physician or medical attendant who might have helped deliver Obama at Honolulu's Kapi'olani Hospital in 1961 remains shrouded in mystery.

The short-form Certification of Live Birth first released by DailyKos.com and placed on Obama's campaign Web site FightTheSmears.com does not indicate the delivering doctor.

And despite exhaustive research, WND has not found any medical personnel present at Kapi'olani Hospital in 1961 who can recall Ann Dunham giving birth at the hospital or who can identify the name of her doctor.

Not surprisingly, the White House also ignored WND's request to release Obama's long-form birth certificate or to obtain from the president the required permission for official medical records on his birth to be released by the hospitals and government agencies that may possess such information.

WND asked Kapi'olani spokeswoman Kristy Watanabe whether the hospital could determine from records how many babies were delivered in 1961 and whether WND could obtain a list of the physicians affiliated with the hospital that year. The goal was to see if any of the physicians there at the time could be contacted to inquire whether they remembered who attended Obama's birth.

It turns out, vital statistics maintained by the U.S. government at the time did not record the number of babies born at specific hospitals. However, one thing is certain: Each baby born at a hospital in Hawaii in 1961 generated a long-form birth certificate signed by the attending physician that specified all relevant information about the birth, including the name of the baby and parents, the hospital where the baby was born, and the baby's weight, race, and time of birth.

· 9 ·

THE STRANGE CASE OF THE

OBAMA MAMA

Ann Dunham Left Hawaii for Seattle Shortly After the Baby was Born, Leaving Obama Sr. Behind

The official narrative has it that Barack Obama's birth resulted from a love affair and marriage between his eighteen-year-old mother, Stanley Ann Dunham, and the somewhat more mature citizen of Kenya, Barack Obama, Sr., then age twenty-five.

As the story goes, Obama, Sr. came to the United States to attend college at the University of Hawaii, with the intent of returning to his native Kenya to help the nation develop economically after it became independent from Britain.

In his autobiography, *Dreams of My Father,* Barack Obama, Jr. shared with readers a romantically appealing story that his mother met his father when they were both enrolled in a Russian language class at the university.[156]

"He [Barack Obama, Sr.] was an African, I would learn, a Kenyan of the Luo tribe, born on the shores of Lake Victoria in a place called Alego," the future president tells readers in *Dreams,* explaining that though his father grew up in a poor village herding the family goats, he was smart and he won a scholarship to study in Nairobi. "In 1959, at the age of twenty-three, he arrived at the University of Hawaii as that institution's first African student."

The narrative continues: "In a Russian language course, he met an awkward, shy American girl, only eighteen, and they fell in love. The girl's parents, wary at first, were won over by his charm and intellect; the young couple married, and she bore them a son, to whom he bequeathed his name."

But the story did not end so well.

"He [Barack Obama, Sr.] won another scholarship—this time to pursue his Ph.D. at Harvard—but not the money to take his new family with him," Obama explains. "A separation occurred, and he returned to fulfill his promise to the continent. The mother and child stayed behind, but the bond of love survived the distances."

So, here is the basic outline of the official Obama nativity story:

- Barack Obama, Sr., and Stanley Ann Dunham married, after which Ann gave birth to Barack Obama, Jr. on August 4, 1961.

- The couple stayed together as man and wife until Obama, Sr. was forced by the financial limitations of his second scholarship to leave his wife and son behind in Hawaii when he moved to Cambridge, Massachusetts, in 1962.

- The family, separated in 1962, never reunited, despite the bond of love the three felt for one another, a bond that transcended the distances from Hawaii to Massachusetts, and then from Hawaii to Kenya.

The documentary evidence WND has assembled in two years of research leaves no doubt this story is a sham in every important detail.

Cracks in the Official Nativity Story

Contrary to the official Obama storyline, Dunham left Honolulu with her infant son within weeks after Barack Obama, Jr. was born, rented an apartment in Seattle and enrolling in extension courses at the University of Washington. Dunham never returned to Hawaii while Barack Obama, Sr. was there completing his studies. Instead, she continued her studies at the University of Washington by moving from the extension school to enroll as a full-time undergraduate student.

This is in direct conflict with the "authorized" story, which maintains Obama's parents lived together as husband and wife in Hawaii until Obama, Sr. departed for Harvard in June 1962.

Now that we know Barack Obama has presented false information about his early life, we must reasonably ask if the entire official nativity story is likewise a fabrication.

Dunham Quits University of Hawaii

According to records provided to WND by Stuart Lau, the registrar at the University of Hawaii at Manoa, Dunham dropped out of the university at the end of the fall term 1960 (Exhibit 76, page 196).

Lau further documented that this term ended January 31, 1961 (Exhibit 77, page 197).

That Barack Obama, Sr. continued his studies without interruption is evident from his college transcript (Exhibit 78, page 197).

From the documentary record, Barack Obama, Sr. continued his studies at the University of Hawaii, even though Dunham dropped out at the end of the first term during which they met.

Questions over Dunham's Wedding Date and Obama's Birth Date

The only documentation for Ann Dunham's marriage to Barack Obama, Sr. comes from divorce documents that list the marriage date as February 2, 1961.

No wedding certificate for the couple has ever been found or published.

"There's no record of a real wedding, a cake, a ring, a giving away of the bride," Obama wrote of his parents' wedding in *Dreams*. "No families were in attendance; it's not even clear that people back in Kansas were fully informed. Just a small civil ceremony, a justice of the peace. The whole thing seems so fragile in retrospect, so haphazard."

The only available documentation for Barack Obama, Jr.'s birthday comes from the birth date listed on the short-form Certification of Live Birth and birth announcements published in the local newspapers. As we saw in Chapter 6, the source for the birth date recorded on the COLB might simply have been testimony provided by the grandparents, Stanley and Madelyn Dunham, who were living in Hawaii at the time.

We also saw that the published birth announcements derived from the same registration of birth at the Hawaii Department of Health that led to the production of the COLB. In other words, the grandparents' verbal testimony would have been sufficient to register the birth with the Hawaii DOH, resulting in the information that was recorded in the COLB. The newspaper announcements are identical, confirming WND investigative reports that the registration of the birth with the Hawaii DOH triggered the newspaper notices. Neither the Hawaii DOH nor the Hawaiian newspapers had any investigative arm to check the veracity of information the grandparents may have presented.

Moreover, as we saw in Chapter 8, a controversy has developed over whether Barack Obama, Jr. was born in Queen's Medical Center in Honolulu, as was first reported as far back as 2004, or in Kapi'olani Medical Center, the hospital where Obama claimed he was born in the letter to Kapi'olani that first surfaced when Representative Neil Abercrombie read it to a hospital anniversary dinner in early 2009.

Until a long-form, hospital-generated birth certificate is made public and authenticated, Obama's place and date of birth must be considered as yet undocumented.

Where are the Baby Pictures?

While Obama and his supporters have made many photographs available from his childhood, key photographs are missing:

- No photographs of Dunham's marriage to Barack Obama, Sr. have ever been published;

- No photographs have yet surfaced showing Dunham pregnant in 1961;

• No photographs have surfaced showing the parents with their infant son in the hospital where he was born;

• No photographs have surfaced of the parents or the grandparents with the newly born infant after he was taken home from the hospital.

Did the Parents Ever Live Together as a Married Couple?

As we saw in Chapter 6, there is no documentary evidence that Barack Obama, Sr. and Ann Dunham ever lived together as husband and wife. Although the 1961–1962 Polk Directory for Honolulu listed students Ann S. Obama and Barack H. Obama in the same listing, indicating they were man and wife, each was listed with a separate address. Ann S. was listed as renting at 6085 Kalanianaole Highway, while Barack H. was listed as renting at 625 11th Avenue.

Separately, the Polk Directory indicated that the grandparents, Madelyn L. Dunham and Stanley A. Dunham, rented the house at 6085 Kalanianaole Highway, the address given for newborn Obama's parents in the newspaper birth announcements. Ann Dunham evidently continued living with her parents even after she was married.

Obama's Mother Resurfaces in Seattle

WND has obtained a copy of a transcript from the University of Washington in Seattle that indicates Dunham successfully completed extension courses there in the fall of 1961, on the heels of giving birth to Barack Obama, Jr.

In a letter dated July 29, 2009, Madolyn Lawson, Office of Public Records, at the University of Washington sent WND Stanley Ann Dunham's transcript records (Exhibit 79, page 198).

Two separate forms of transcript were included with this letter.

The first (Exhibit 80, page 199) appeared to be a microfiche of a transcript card. The extension course information in the lower right-hand corner seems to indicate Ann Dunham began on August 19, 1961, only fifteen days after Barack Obama, Jr. was born.

The second (Exhibit 81, page 200) appeared to be a computer printout of the transcript record, again with the initial date for extension classes listed as 8/19/1961.

However, a copy of the University of Washington's Autumn 1961 evening school bulletin (Exhibit 82, page 201) obtained by WND from the university registrar in February 2011, indicates Dunham's classes were held on the Seattle campus, beginning September 25, 1961.

The Evening Classes bulletin lists Anthropology 101, "Introduction to the Study of Man," as starting on September 25, 1961 (Exhibit 83, page 202).

The Evening Classes bulletin for the university lists Political Science 201, "Modern Government," as starting on September 26, 1961 (Exhibit 84, page 203).

Note the official transcripts obtained from the university by WND in 2009 listed the dates for Dunham's two fall 1961 courses as 08/19/61 to 12/11/61 and 08/19/61 to 12/12/61, suggesting the courses began August 19, 1961.

A controversy developed when various WND readers independently questioned the University of Washington about whether 8/19/61 indicated the date classes began.

In February 2011, interim registrar Virjean Edwards told WND she believed the initial date was entered into the student records database in error. The number for the month on the original typed transcript, she claimed, appeared to be an eight, but actually was a nine. The number was distorted, she said, because it runs up against a line in the left margin.

A close examination of the typed transcript, however, shows the number almost certainly is an eight. Nevertheless, the University of Washington sent WND a revised transcript – a computer printout from the database – that reflected the university's change of the initial date from 08/19/61 to 09/19/61, which corresponds with the date that registration began, as indicated in the class bulletin.

See a copy of the revised computer-generated transcript for Ann Dunham that the University of Washington sent WND in February 2011 (Exhibit 85, page 204).

In any case, the transcript, along with the evening course bulletin, documents that Dunham was in Seattle the month following Barack Obama's birth, if not sooner. Moreover, the documentation provided by the University of Washington substantiates previous reporting that the extension courses Ann Dunham took were night classes taught at the university's Seattle campus, not correspondence classes she may have taken while yet residing in Hawaii.

In the two fall 1961 courses, her transcript showed she received excellent grades: an A in Anthropology 100, "Introduction to the Study of Man," and a B in Political Science 201, "Modern Government." These were full-term courses, recorded at five credits each.

It is unlikely that Dunham could have obtained good grades had she missed attending in-person a large portion of either course.

In addition, the testimony of a high school friend places her and her son in the Seattle area in late August 1961.

How Dunham managed to travel from Honolulu to Seattle with a newborn baby and begin extension classes is hard to imagine.

The transcript shows she was enrolled as a "nonresident citizen," which meant she would not be able to take advantage of the tuition breaks she would have qualified for as a resident student at the University of Hawaii.

Had Dunham re-enrolled at the University of Hawaii, along with her husband, she presumably would have been enrolled as a resident student with much lower tuition.

Instead, she traveled to Seattle to enroll at the University of Washington, where she also bore the added living costs of rent and food for herself and her infant son. Had she stayed in Hawaii and re-enrolled at the University of Hawaii after the baby was born, she presumably could have continued living with her parents.

Moreover, had she stayed in Hawaii, Dunham could have looked to her parents, and presumably also her husband, to help with babysitting and housekeeping duties. No documents or family testimony suggest Barack Obama, Sr. assisted Dunham in any way with her tuition or living expenses in Seattle.

Dunham continued to take extension courses at the University of Washington into a second term that ended March 20, 1962. She then registered as a full-time student for the 1962 spring quarter, when she took three additional courses.

Barack Obama, Sr. began studies at Harvard University in Cambridge, Massachusetts, in June 1962. On June 2, reporter John Griffin ran a bylined story in the *Honolulu Advertiser* noting that Barack Obama, Sr., "the first African to graduate from the University of Hawaii," left that day for the mainland to begin his studies later that month at Harvard.[157]

One year later, Dunham was back in Hawaii, enrolled at the University of Hawaii at Manoa for the spring term of 1963.

Where Did Ann Dunham Live in Seattle?

According to the 1961–1962 Polk Directory for Seattle, Dunham, listed as a student named "Mrs. Anna Obama," took up residence at 516 13th Avenue East, Apt. 2, in the Capitol Hill area of Seattle, in a house that had been converted into what was then known as the Villa Ria Apartments.

The relevant entry form the directory can be seen in Exhibit 86 on page 205.

See at the photograph of 516 13th Avenue East, from the Washington State Archives, Pugent Sound Branch, King County Assessor Property Record Card collection, taken around 1937 (Exhibit 87, page 205).

According to HistoryLink.org, Dunham and her infant son rented Apartment No. 2 on the first floor, seen in the aforementioned picture in the three windows immediately above the garage. The 500-square-foot apartment was located in the southwest corner of the building, which included at least ten apartments at the time Dunham rented there, most of them occupied by elderly and retired residents.[158]

"It appears that [Dunham and her infant son] arrived [in Seattle] around the end of August 1961, as two of her friends recall Dunham returning to Mercer Island and visiting her and the new baby about this time," HistoryLink.org concluded. Mercer Island, a Seattle suburb, was where Dunham went to high school.

One of the high school friends Dunham visited in Mercer Island in the process of relocating from Hawaii to Seattle was Susan Blake. In a video interview, Blake recalled a "late August afternoon" visit by Dunham in 1961 when "Barry was just a few weeks old." Blake explained how she showed Dunham, an evidently inexperienced mother, how to change the baby's diaper.[159]

Another friend, Maxine Box, told *Seattle Times* columnist Nicole Brodeur she last saw Dunham in 1961, "when [Dunham] visited Seattle on her way from Honolulu to Massachusetts, where her then-husband was attending Harvard."[160]

Barack Obama, Sr., however, did not go to Harvard until 1962, and there is no record of Dunham ever visiting him there.

Box told Brodeur in the February 2008 interview that in their last visit together, Dunham "seemed very happy and very proud. She had this beautiful, healthy baby. I can see them now."

Brodeur reported that Dunham and Box were "part of a close group of girls who attended football games and sock hops but didn't really date." Dunham and Box "listened to The Limeliters, The Kingston Trio, The Brothers Four. Their parents played cards together. Dunham and Box walked home together after school, usually stopping at Box's house for mint-chocolate cake before Dunham went on to the Shorewood apartments, where she lived with her parents."

In a separate interview, Box told the *Chicago Tribune* that Dunham showed no interest in baby-sitting when they were in high school, suggesting she was surprised when Dunham ended up pregnant only a year after graduating from Mercer Island High School.[161] "She felt she didn't need to date or marry or have children," Box told the *Tribune*. Commenting on the birth of Barack Obama, Jr., Box said, "I just couldn't imagine her life changing so quickly."

Babysitter Confirms Ann Dunham was in Seattle

In an interview published in the Seattle Chat Club blog,[162] Mary Toutonghi claimed to have baby-sat the future president, who "was a really alert baby, very happy and good size."

Toutonghi was one of the other residents at 516 13th Ave. E., when Dunham and infant Obama lived there. A stay-at-home mother whose husband was taking classes at nearby Seattle University, Toutonghi told the interviewer she lived directly below Dunham and her infant son, in the level she called "the basement."

Asked why Dunham left her husband in Hawaii, Toutonghi explained that Dunham told her she and the baby would be going to Kenya when she finished her education, as she had promised her parents when she was married.

Toutonghi also added Dunham's explanation that her husband had an obligation to his tribe to take another wife who was a full-blooded Kenyan because he needed an heir. Toutonghi further commented, "I don't think I could have been that brave."

In a separate telephone interview with WND, Toutonghi said she baby-sat infant Obama "for two or three months, when he was seven months old," adding, "It was in the spring."

Given his stated birthdate of August 4, 1961, this would put the dates Toutonghi baby-sat Obama in February and March 1962.

"Ann Dunham and the baby moved in while we were there," she remembered. "We were managing the house, and the house was a great big old house. There were four rooms on the first floor. Ann Dunham had the room on the first floor to the right, immediately above the garage. Each of the rooms on that floor comprised a one-bedroom apartment.

"I couldn't figure out why she was here in Seattle while her husband was in Hawaii. She said she had promised her parents that she would finish school. Maybe the classes that she needed were here."

Toutonghi said Ann Dunham was planning to go back to join her husband in Hawaii, but Toutonghi was vague on the details and appeared confused why Dunham was in Seattle without her husband, or what exactly her future plans were.

"This was a big deal because I was taking care of the kid, but it wasn't a big deal because he was going to be president," she explained. "I was babysitting for him and she took courses in the evening at the University of Washington."

Clearly, this was a busy time for Toutonghi and babysitting for Obama was not a historic event, but a part-time job.

"I was holding down a couple of part-time jobs at that time," she recalled, "and then the babysitting in the evening. My husband was in school at Seattle University at the time. I had my own baby, so I was very busy."

There is no indication Dunham worked while attending the University of Washington, where she was enrolled in the spring 1962 term as a full-time student.

It's unclear how she paid for tuition, rent, and living expenses for herself and her infant son while she was living in Seattle from August 1961 until she returned to Hawaii, after Barack Obama, Sr. had left for Harvard.

Likewise, no evidence has surfaced that she ever returned to Hawaii to visit Barack Obama, Sr. while he continued his studies at the University of Hawaii or that Obama, Sr. ever traveled from Hawaii to visit her in Seattle.

Key Dates in Barack Obama's Birth Chronology: Toward Creating a Timeline

Here are the critical dates documenting the birth of Barack Obama Jr. as can best be determined by the limited records currently available to the public:

- Ann Dunham was born November 29, 1942, according to her Social Security card; this would have made her eighteen years old at the time Barack Obama, Jr. was born;

- Barack Obama, Jr. was born August 4, 1961, putting his date of conception at the earliest around November 4, 1960, assuming the baby went the full nine months from conception to birth;

- Records provided to WND by Stuart Lau, university registrar in the Office of Admissions and Records at the University of Hawaii at Manoa, document that Dunham's first day of instruction at the university was September 26, 1960, less than six weeks before the earliest date Barack Obama, Jr. could have been conceived;

- Dunham and Barack H. Obama, Sr.'s divorce decree states they were married February 2, 1961, in Wailuku, Maui, in Hawaii; this would mean Obama's parents were married approximately three months after Barack Obama, Jr., was conceived, if the baby went full-term;

- Instead of staying in Hawaii with her husband and new baby, Dunham began taking extension classes at the University of

Washington in Seattle only weeks after Obama was born, according to Dunham's college transcript;

• Dunham took up residence in Seattle at 516 13th Ave. E., according to the 1961–1962 Seattle Polk Directory; this residence was torn down in 1985 and is now replaced by twin Capitol Park public housing residential towers; the directory listing is for a "Mrs. Anna Obama," a variant of her name that most researchers have considered to be Ann Dunham;

• At most, Barack Obama, Sr. and Dunham lived together for approximately seven months, from February 2, 1961, the date of their marriage, until August 1961, when Dunham arrived in Seattle; there is nothing in the public record to suggest Dunham and her husband ever lived together again as a married couple;

• Nothing in the public record suggests Dunham's mother, Madelyn Dunham, accompanied her daughter to Seattle in August 1961, even though Ann Dunham was eighteen years old and responsible for a baby less than one month old;

• There is no evidence on the public record that Barack Obama, Sr. ever joined his wife in Seattle; instead, the public evidence is that Obama, Sr. remained in Hawaii to continue his studies there, while his wife and infant son established their residence in Seattle;

• Barack Obama, Sr. left Hawaii on June 2, 1962, to begin graduate studies at Harvard later that month; Dunham did not return to Hawaii until after Obama, Sr. had left the islands; Obama, Sr. never returned again to Hawaii to live there as a resident;

• Dunham did not resume her studies at the University of Hawaii at Manoa until the spring semester, beginning in April 1963, when Barack Obama, Jr. was approximately one year and five months old;

• Dunham and Obama Sr. were divorced on January 20, 1964.

Stanley Ann Dunham: The Lost Six Months

John F. Kennedy was sworn into office. Roger Maris was hitting sixty-one home runs. The Berlin Wall was erected.

Much was happening in the first six months of 1961. But an extensive WND investigation into the events leading up to the birth of Barack Obama, Jr., who would become America's first black president forty-seven years later, leaves many unanswered questions about the whereabouts and activities of his mother.

The timeline for President Obama's mother reveals an approximately six-and-a-half-month interval during which there is no record of her whereabouts—from January 31, 1961, when Ann Dunham concluded the fall term 1960 at the University of Hawaii at Manoa, until September 25, 1961, when the University of Washington at Seattle documents she was enrolled for extension courses.

Where was Dunham when she was pregnant with Obama, and what did she do?

Her pregnancy was the one time in her life that she appears to have dropped out from academic pursuits.

Assuming Barack Obama, Jr., was born August 4, 1961, and that the baby was full-term, Dunham quit the University of Hawaii when she was two-months pregnant, even though her husband-to-be continued his studies there without interruption.

One explanation is that Dunham simply left to focus her energy and time on the coming baby, even though that seems inconsistent with how quickly she returned to university studies in a distant city after the baby's birth.

No travel or passport records are available for Dunham, Barack Obama, Sr., or Barack Obama, Jr., so determining whether she remained in Hawaii during the undocumented six and a half months is difficult.

The Missing Obama Mama

Curiously, in little noticed remarks, Michelle Obama stated at a public event that her husband's mother was "very young and very single" when she gave birth.

Covering the story for WND, reporter Aaron Klein observed that Michelle Obama's comments further undermined the official story as told by President Obama—that Dunham was married to his father at the time of birth.[163]

Michelle Obama made the remarks during a July 2008 roundtable at the University of Missouri.[164] She was responding to criticism of her husband's presidential campaign speeches about fatherhood and faith-based initiatives. Michelle Obama explained her husband understood the struggles of low-income families.

"He understands them because he was raised by strong women. He is the product of two great women in his life—his mother and his grandmother," Michelle Obama said. "Barack saw his mother, who was very young and very single when she had him, and he saw her work hard to complete her education and try to raise him and his sister."

Newspaper stories in Hawaii about Barack Obama, Sr. when he lived there strongly suggest he was a bachelor during his entire time in the state.

WND, working with reporters at the *Honolulu Star-Advertiser,* accessed newspaper archives and found a series of stories written between the time Barack Obama, Sr., first arrived in Hawaii in 1959 and the time he left for Cambridge, Massachusetts, in June 1962.

The reporters in Hawaii could not find a single article published in Hawaii when Barack Obama, Sr. lived there that made any mention whatsoever of Ann Dunham, or of his infant son. Clearly, when he arrived in Hawaii he was a celebrity—the first African student to attend a Hawaiian university.

When Obama first arrived in Hawaii, the *Honolulu Star-Bulletin* reported he was living at the Atherton Branch of the YMCA near the university. The stories pointed out that Obama was a Phi Beta Kappa student at the University of Hawaii, that he was living on his personal savings, and that he intended to apply for a scholarship to finish his undergraduate school.

But nowhere in any of the published reports was there any mention that he had married a local girl and fathered a child. It should have been big news to Hawaii locals that an important student from Africa had married a local girl and had a baby born in Hawaii.

Instead, the articles present Barack Obama, Sr. as if he were a bachelor, in Hawaii only to complete his studies before returning to Kenya to share his business administration education with Kenyans who wanted to get into business.

Barack Obama, Jr. comments in *Dreams from My Father* with disappointment that his father never mentioned his mother or him in the Honolulu newspapers. On page 19, Obama says he found a clipping of an article in the *Honolulu Star-Bulletin* published at the time his father graduated from the University of Hawaii, just before Barack Obama, Sr. left Honolulu for Massachusetts in June 1962.

"No mention is made of my mother or me, and I'm left to wonder whether the omission was intentional on my father's part, in anticipation of his long departure," Obama wrote. "Perhaps the reporter failed to ask personal questions, intimidated by my father's imperious manner; or perhaps it was an editorial decision, not part of the simple story that they were looking for. I wonder too, whether the omission caused a fight between my parents."

In *Dreams*, Obama does not answer the question.

Obama, Sr.—the Bachelor Hit of the Party

Interestingly, photos of Barack Obama, Sr. attending a Hawaii party in the early 1960s, which surfaced online, show him enjoying the company of fellow students, but with no sign of Ann Dunham.[165]

While it's possible the photos were taken prior to the time Obama, Sr. met Dunham, the accompanying remarks on the Web site from Obama's fellow students make no mention that Obama, Sr. was ever associated with Dunham, then or later.

The photographs are identified as having been taken at the home of Arnie and Suzie Nachmanoff in Pearl Harbor, Hawaii, "in the early 1960s."

One photo (Exhibit 88, page 206) shows Barack Obama, Sr. smoking a cigarette and talking with an attractive young woman identified on the Web site only as "Dorothy."

Another photo (Exhibit 89, page 206) shows Obama, Sr. seated on the floor with other students attending the party.

Several reminiscences "by some old friends of Barack Obama when we were in Honolulu, Hawaii," are posted on the Web site, some noting that Obama had the historical distinction of being Hawaii's first African university student; none make any reference to his courtship with or marriage to Dunham.

The Web site on which the photos were posted, which shows support for President Obama, was created by Naranhkiri Tith, a student at the University of Hawaii's East-West Center at the same time Barack Obama, Sr. was enrolled. Tith went on to serve for twenty years on the senior staff of the International Monetary Fund.

"Although [Barack Obama, Sr.] was not an East-West Center grantee, he was always with us, especially at a Guest House owned and operated by the Asia foundation, situated on the top of a road leading to Manoa valley," Tith recalled in an essay, "Remembering my friend Barak (sic) Obama." "Atherton House was a place where most East-West Center grantees gathered for a drink or a chat."

Tith recalled that in the 1980s an IMF colleague on a mission to Kenya gave him Barack Obama, Sr.'s telephone number in Nairobi.

"Needless to say that I was very happy to be able to be in contact again with Barak (sic), after more than ten years of silence," Tith continued. "We had a long conversation, and we were able to talk to each other a few more times until one day, when I called him and his secretary told me over the phone that he had passed away of an accident."

Tith makes no reference to Dunham at the University of Hawaii or of discussing Dunham with Barack Obama, Sr. in their subsequent phone conversations after the president's father had returned to Kenya.

Robert M. Ruenitz, another student at the East-West Center when Obama, Sr. was enrolled at the University of Hawaii, had distinct recollections of the president's father living alone in Hawaii.

"For any of us to say we knew Obama well would be difficult," Ruenitz wrote. "He was a private man with academic achievement his foremost goal. He lived somewhat like a hermit in a small room up in the valleys of Manoa. I visited him there on my Lambretta and wondered how he sustained himself outside of his focused attention to his academic pursuits."

Obama's Father Not Part of Jackie Robinson Airlift

Barack Obama has always claimed his father was part of a President John F. Kennedy-era airlift arranged by Kenyan Luo politician Tom Mboya to bring Kenyan students to the United States to study in American universities.

Documents indicate, however, that Barack Obama, Sr. was not brought to Hawaii in 1959 by any airlift of Kenyan students organized by baseball great Jackie Robinson, John F. Kennedy, or the African-American Students Foundation, Inc., the AASF.

Nor was Obama Sr. on any of the three subsequently chartered airplanes in what became known as the "second airlift," organized by Mboya in 1960 after Joseph P. Kennedy contributed $100,000 to AASF.

Moreover, a thorough search of the Jackie Robinson papers at the Manuscript Division of the Library of Congress evidences no mention of Barack Obama, Sr. in the files on deposit, either as an applicant for student airlift or among those mentioned as candidates for airlift from Kenya to study in the U.S.

The manifest (Exhibit 90, page 207) of the eighty-one students airlifted from Kenya on September 9, 1959, in an airplane chartered by Robinson in conjunction with the AASF, does not contain Obama, Sr.'s name.

So, while it is true that singer Harry Belafonte and actor Sidney Poitier assisted baseball great Jackie Robinson in making possible the first Tom Mboya-organized airlift of Kenyan students to the United States in 1959, it is not true Barack Obama, Sr. was on the flight.

In Hawaii Independent of the First Student Flight

Tom Shachtman, author of the 2009 book *Airlift to America: How Barack Obama, Sr., John F. Kennedy, Tom Mboya and 800 East African Students Changed Their World and Ours,*[166] confirmed that Obama Sr. got to the United States independent of any airlift organized by JFK, Tom Mboya, or Jackie Robinson.

"In trying to make the connection between himself and President Kennedy more direct, candidate Obama, based on incomplete information, made a mistake about his own history, saying that his father's journey to America in 1959 had been aided by the Joseph P. Kennedy Jr. Foundation," Shachtman wrote on page 11 of his book. "Not exactly, fact-checkers soon found out."[167]

On pages 6–9, Shachtman wrote that Mrs. Helen Roberts and Miss Elizabeth Mooney, "a literary specialist," financially assisted Obama in leaving Kenya.

"As far as can be determined from incomplete records, Mrs. Roberts and Miss Mooney paid his [Obama Sr.'s] fare to Hawaii and provided a partial scholarship," Shachtman noted. "Mboya, while unable to transport the twenty-three-year-old, did put him on the AASF [African-American Students Foundation, Inc.] list to receive one of the handful of scholarships contributed by former baseball star Jackie Robinson, which the Scheinman foundation was administering, and encouraged him to look to the AASF for further help if needed, which he later did."

The first article documenting the presence of Barack Obama, Sr. in Hawaii was written by journalist Shurei Hirozawa and published in the *Honolulu Star Bulletin* on September 18, 1959, only nine days after the Jackie Robinson airlift.[168]

As seen in the University of Hawaii transcript at the beginning of this chapter, Obama, Sr. was enrolled for the fall term in 1959, which began on Monday, September 21.

The Hirozawa article suggested that Obama, Sr.—then fully settled in Hawaii and enrolled at the university—had used personal savings to pay for tuition and his travel from Kenya to Hawaii.

"He [Obama Sr.] clerked several years in the capital city of Nairobi to save enough for a college education and picked the University of Hawaii when he read in an American magazine about its racial tolerance," Hirozawa wrote.

"But the money [Barack Obama, Sr.] saved will only stretch out for two semesters or less because of the high cost of living in Hawaii, he found out," wrote Hirozawa. "He'll work, he says, and possibly apply for a scholarship."

The Hirozawa article makes clear that Obama Sr. had no scholarship from the university when he started at the University of Hawaii in 1959.

Shactman wrote that after he started at the University of Hawaii, the

AASF sent him checks, in increments of $50 or $150 for expenses, and $243 for tuition. Mostly, Obama, Sr. was supported by Mooney, who in 1960, married American expatriate Elmer Kirk and moved back with her husband to the United States.[169] Shactman also indicated that "some Kennedy money was later used to assist him [Obama, Sr.] in Hawaii."[170]

Leftist Activist Cora Weiss Helps Finance Obama Sr.

Cora Weiss provides the answer to who funded Obama Sr.'s education in Hawaii.

In a letter dated May 7, 2010, to the *New York Times*, Weiss acknowledges what WND proved in February, namely that Obama came to Hawaii on his own.[171]

"Barack Obama Sr., who greatly admired Mboya, did not come on the first flight, but he was a member of the airlift generation, arriving here in 1959 with the support of two American women teachers."

Weiss goes on to state that the African-American Students Foundation, Inc. provided Obama Sr. with three grants, allowing him to continue his studies at the University of Hawaii after his personal savings were exhausted.

As identified by David Horowitz's DiscoverTheNetworks.org, Weiss has served as the president of the Samuel Rubin Foundation - named for her father, the Fabergé millionaire, secret Communist Party U.S.A. member, and identified Comintern agent - since its inception in 1959.[172] Weiss was the executive director and student advisor of the African-American Students Foundation from 1959 to 1963.

Horowitz also credits Weiss with being a principal financier and board member of the Institute of Policy Studies that was founded with a 1963 grant from the Rubin Foundation. Weiss' husband, Peter, is chairman of the Institute of Policy Services board of trustees and a member of the National Lawyers Guild and the National Emergency Civil Liberties Committee, both of which were created as Communist Party front organizations. According to DiscoverTheNetworks.org, the Institute of Policy Studies had advanced leftist causes since its foundation; the Institute's headquarters in Washington, D.C., was reputedly a place for KGB agents from the nearby Soviet embassy to convene and strategize.[173]

In her May 7, 2010, letter to the *New York Times,* Weiss said the African-American Students Foundation was formed after Mboya's trip to the United States in April 1959, seeking scholarships so Kenyans and other East Africans "could secure the education never offered under British colonialism."

According to Weiss, the founders of the African-American Students Foundation included William X. Scheinman, singer Harry Belafonte, actor Sidney Poitier, Jackie Robinson, civil rights activists Frank Montero and Ted Kheel, as well as Mrs. Ralph Bunche and Mrs. Chester Bowles, "and a host of educators and me."

Candidate Obama Claims JFK Responsible for His Father Coming to the U.S.A.

Then-Senator Obama claimed in a March 4, 2007, speech from the pulpit of the historic Brown Chapel A.M.E. Church in Selma, Alabama, that President Kennedy brought his father to the United States.

A few minutes into the speech, Obama began discussing the protests in Selma and Birmingham, Alabama, that were instrumental to Martin Luther King building the civil rights movement in the 1960s.

Obama invented dialogue of Kennedy advisers, musing, "It worried the folks in the White House who said, 'You know, we're battling communism. How are we going to win hearts and minds all across the world if right here in our own country, John, we're not observing the ideals set forth in our Constitution? We might be accused of being hypocrites."

Obama continued: "This young man named Barack Obama got one of those tickets and came over to this country. He met this woman whose great-great-great-great-grandfather had owned slaves. But she had a good idea there was some craziness going on because they looked at each other and they decided that we know that [in] the world as it has been it might not be possible for us to get together and have a child."

Kennedy, however, was not in the White House until January 20, 1961, and he did not participate in origination of the September 1959 airlift.

The historical record is established by a background memorandum prepared by Senator John Kennedy's office in August 1960, while JFK was running for president.[174] The memo documents that JFK met with Mboya—but after the 1959 airlift had already occurred. Mboya met with JFK at Hyannis Port, Massachusetts, on July 26, 1960, while Kennedy was running for president. Mboya's goal was to convince JFK to fund a second airlift of African students to the United States.

The memo further documents that the State Department, despite intervention by Vice President Richard Nixon, had already turned down Mboya's request for a second airlift to bring to the United States two hundred African students who had received scholarships from U.S. schools. The Kennedy family, utilizing the Joseph P. Kennedy, Jr. Foundation, decided to give Mboya a $100,000 donation to pay for the second airlift, in memory of JFK's brother, Joseph, who was killed in World War II. Knowing the Kennedy family was going to pay for the second airlift, Nixon prevailed on the State Department to reverse its earlier negative decision.

However, the African-American Students Foundation decided to accept the Kennedy Foundation's offer, preferring the willing generosity of the privately offered financing to the obvious hostility the State Department initially had expressed. Mboya's decision was a rebuke to Nixon, who had failed to deliver the State Department until after the Kennedy family had stepped forward with funding. The State Department had originally turned down Mboya's request in deference to the government of Jomo Kenyatta, which argued that young, talented Kenyans should stay home and attend Makerere College in neighboring Uganda, instead of being trained in U.S. universities.

Still, the myth of JFK's role in bringing President Obama's father to the United States persisted, being reported again January 10, 2008, only ten days before the inauguration, by Washington-based reporter Elana Schor writing in the *Guardian* of London.[175]

On March 30, 2008, the *Washington Post* published an article by Michael Dobbs titled "Obama Overstates Kennedy's Role in Helping His Father."[176]

"Obama spokesman Bill Burton acknowledged yesterday that the senator from Illinois had erred in crediting the Kennedy family with a role in his father's arrival in the United States," Dobbs wrote. "[Burton] said the Kennedy involvement in the Kenya student program apparently 'started 48 years ago, not 49 years ago as Obama has mistakenly suggested in the past.'"

Addressing the "overstatement," Dobbs incorrectly reported that Barack Obama, Sr. had come to the United States on the September 9, 1959, first airlift organized by Jackie Robinson without the financial support of the Kennedy family.

"There was enormous excitement when the Britannia aircraft took off for New York with the future Kenyan elite aboard," Dobbs wrote of the first airlift. "After a few weeks of orientation, the students were dispatched to universities across the United States to study subjects that would help them govern Kenya after the departure of the British. Obama Sr. was interested in economics and was sent to Hawaii, where he met, and later married, a Kansas native named Ann Dunham."

Obama, Sr. Letter to Tom Mboya in 1962 Discusses Wife— in Kenya

A letter Barack Obama, Sr. wrote from Hawaii to his political benefactor in Kenya, Tom Mboya, in May 1962, discusses his wife, but does so without mentioning Ann Dunham, his Hawaiian bride and the mother of the president, Barack Obama, Jr.[177]

Toward the end of the 1962 letter, Obama wrote, "You know my wife is in Nairobi there and I would really appreciate any help you may give her."

Clearly Barack Obama, Sr. is referring to his first wife, Kezia Aoko, whom he married in 1954, when he was eighteen years old and who became pregnant with their first child when Obama left Kenya in 1959, to study in Hawaii.

He instructs Mboya that his wife Kezia was then staying with her brother, Wilson Odiawo, in Nairobi.

Look at the relevant paragraph, the third last paragraph from the end of the letter (Exhibit 91, page 208).

Obama in the letter confirms he plans to leave Hawaii for Harvard University in June 1962; as noted earlier in this chapter, Ann Dunham did not return from Seattle to Hawaii until after Barack Obama left.

Exhibit 92 on page 209 shows the beginning of the letter.

Obama makes clear that he applied himself to his studies at the University of Hawaii, having achieved a B.A. and a Masters degree in three years, as well as being awarded Phi Beta Kappa (liberal arts academic excellence), Phi Kappa Phi (overall academic excellence), and Omicron Delta Kappa (leadership) honors.

Again, there is no indication in the letter that Obama spent any time in Seattle, or anywhere else for that matter, with his wife, Ann Dunham, or their son, Barack Obama, Jr.

Unanswered Questions

If the official Obama birth story is a sham, what is the yet-undisclosed secret at the heart of the birth-certificate controversy?

Multiple speculations come to mind:

• Were Dunham and Barack Obama, Sr. ever very much in love, even at the beginning of their relationship, or was the marriage arranged merely to mask an inconvenient pregnancy?

• Were Dunham and Barack Obama, Sr. ever actually married?

• If so, did they ever live together as husband and wife? What testimony is there from neighbors at the time that would establish the residence address of Mr. and Mrs. Barack Obama, since the Polk directories indicate they lived apart?

• Where was Dunham during the undocumented six months of her pregnancy?

• Was the baby born outside of Hawaii? Could Barack Obama, Jr. have been born at sea, as his mother was bound from Honolulu to Seattle? Was he born in Seattle? Or possibly even British Columbia?

• Is President Obama's actual birth date August 4, 1961, or is that just the date the family registered with the Hawaii Department of Health?

- If Barack Obama, Jr. was born in Hawaii, what hospital was he born in and who was the attending physician?

- If a long-form, hospital-generated birth certificate exists for Barack Obama, Jr., why is it being suppressed?

- Is there a birth secret contained in the document other than the place of birth? Could it be that no father is named on the document, or that the named father is not Barack Obama, Sr.?

These and other questions inevitably arise once we understand that the official Obama birth story is a fabrication.

But if the official story is a lie, what then is the truth?

Not all possible scenarios would make Barack Obama, Jr. ineligible to be president. If his father was not Barack Obama, Sr., for example, his father could have been a U.S. citizen at the time of his birth.

Yet, Obama and his family have never wavered from the story that Barack Obama, Sr. is the father. The president's autobiography, *Dreams,* leaves no doubt that his mother and grandparents told him from the time he was old enough to understand that he was the son of the newsworthy African who came to Hawaii in 1959 as the first black university student there.

The photograph (Exhibit 93, page 210) from 1971, when ten-year-old Barack Obama, Jr. sees Barack Obama, Sr. for the first time during a return trip to Hawaii, suggests the boy accepted the African as his long-lost father.

Nevertheless, without seeing the long-form, hospital-generated birth certificate, questions about the identity of both parents remain. Where are the photographs of Ann Dunham pregnant, or of the happy parents and grandparents with the infant? Many women resist having their photos taken while pregnant, but few grandparents can resist photos of a newborn baby, especially if the baby is their first grandchild.

President Obama Presents "Nativity Myth" to School Children

In his speech to the nation's school children on September 8, 2009, President Obama repeated the official birth story told in *Dreams from My*

Father, despite documentary evidence produced by WND that the facts differ in important ways.

"I get it. I know what it's like," Obama said in the televised speech from Wakefield High School in Arlington, Virginia. "My father left my family when I was two years old, and I was raised by a single mom who had to work and who struggled at times to pay the bills and wasn't always able to give us the things that other kids had."[178]

Although WND had demonstrated that contrary to Obama's statement, his mother took him to Seattle just weeks after his birth, the story Obama told the nation's school children matches the one he told on page 126 of his autobiography.

His mother allegedly told him: "When your father graduated from [the University of Hawaii], he received two scholarship offers. One was to the New School, here in New York. The other one was to Harvard. The New School agreed to pay for everything—room and board, a job on campus, enough to support all three of us. Harvard just agreed to pay tuition. But Barack was such a stubborn bastard, he had to go to Harvard. How could I refuse the best education? he told me. That's all he could think about, proving that he was the best...."

Once having told the story in *Dreams,* Obama may have no alternative but to persist in retelling it, despite growing documentary evidence of its falseness. Does President Obama persist in perpetuating a fabricated life story intentionally, or was the truth hidden from him as a young child?

But there is a more important point here.

Having discovered a lie at the heart of the story, the American public has a right to the full truth of Obama's birth, including the right to see all relevant documentary evidence that he meets the Constitution's natural-born citizen requirement. This is a matter of law.

If President Obama's official story turns out to have been fabricated to hide a truth that would make him ineligible, the American people will demand the situation be rectified, even if it requires impeachment.

No usurper of the office of the president of the United States can be tolerated if the Constitution is to have enduring authority.

EXHIBITS

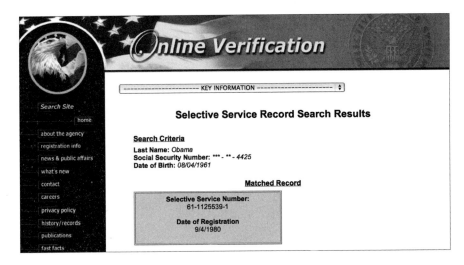

EXHIBIT I

Obama Cross-Verification, Selective Service Number with Social Security Number

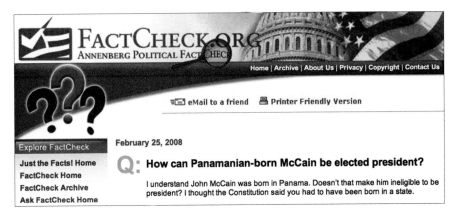

EXHIBIT 2

FactCheck.org, February 25, 2008

McCain's Canal Zone Birth Prompts Queries About Whether That Rules Him Out

From left, LOWELL P. WEICKER JR., of Connecticut, born in Paris, was told he was eligible for the Oval Office. GEORGE ROMNEY, born in Mexico, ran for the presidency in 1968. BARRY GOLDWATER was born in the Arizona territory in 1909, before it became a state. CHESTER A. ARTHUR was born in Vermont, but rumors suggested it was Canada.

By CARL HULSE
Published: February 28, 2008

WASHINGTON — The question has nagged at the parents of Americans born outside the continental United States for generations: Dare their children aspire to grow up and become president? In the case of Senator John McCain of Arizona, the issue is becoming more than a matter of parental daydreaming.

Multimedia

↖ Interactive Graphic
Milestones: John McCain

Mr. McCain's likely nomination as the Republican candidate for president and the happenstance of his birth in the Panama Canal Zone in 1936 are reviving a musty debate that has surfaced periodically since the founders first set quill to parchment and declared that only a "natural-born citizen" can hold the nation's highest office.

Almost since those words were written in 1787 with scant explanation, their precise meaning has been the stuff of confusion, law school review articles, whisper campaigns and civics class debates over whether only those delivered on American soil can be truly natural born. To date, no American to take the presidential oath has had an official birthplace outside the 50 states.

TWITTER

SIGN IN TO E-MAIL OR SAVE THIS

PRINT

REPRINTS

SHARE

Now Playing

EXHIBIT 3

New York Times, February 28, 2008

28
Feb
2008
12:07pm, EST

Oh-eight (R): Born in the USA?

MCCAIN: The campaign isn't taking chances on the issue of whether McCain was born in the U.S. Under the Constitution, a president must be natural-born. The New York Times: "Mr. McCain was born on a military installation in the Canal Zone, where his mother and father, a Navy officer, were stationed. His campaign advisers say they are comfortable that Mr. McCain meets the requirement and note that the question was researched for his first presidential bid in 1999 and reviewed again this time around."

"But given mounting interest, the campaign recently asked Theodore B. Olson, a former solicitor general now advising Mr. McCain, to prepare a detailed legal analysis. 'I don't have much doubt about it,' said Mr. Olson, who added, though, that he still needed to finish his research.'"

EXHIBIT 4
New York Times, February 28, 2008

FEBRUARY 28, 2008, 9:02 AM ET

Does John McCain Have a Birthplace Problem?

| **Article** | Comments (155) |

📧 Email   🖨 Print   🔗 Permalink   👍 Like   🔲 👥 + More   − Text +

By Dan Slater

Here's some LB Thursday morning triva: What do the following Republican presidential candidates have in common?

A) John McCain (2008)
B) George P. Weicker Jr. (1980)
C) George Romney (1968)
D) Barry Goldwater (1964)

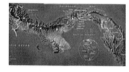 OK, so our headline sort of gives it away. Yes, they were all born on foreign soil, and therefore their basic constitutional qualifications for the presidency — a natural born citizen, at least 35 years of age with 14 years of residence — have been called into question. And now it's McCain's turn. (Here's the NYT story.)

In 1936, McCain was born at the Coco Solo Air Base, in the then-American controlled Panama Canal Zone (pictured), to Jack McCain, a Navy officer, and Roberta McCain. If McCain wins the 2008 election, he'd be the first American to take the presidential oath who has an official birthplace outside the 50 states.

"There are powerful arguments that Senator McCain or anyone else in this position is constitutionally qualified, but there is certainly no precedent," said Sarah H. Duggin, an associate professor of law at Catholic University. "It is not a slam-dunk situation."

According to the Times story, McCain's campaign recently asked Gibson Dunn's Ted Olson to prepare a detailed legal analysis. "I don't have much doubt about it," Olson told the Times, adding that he still needed to finish his research.

EXHIBIT 5

Wall Street Journal, February 28, 2008

February 28, 2008 9:04 AM

Starting Gate: The Center Holds

Posted by Vaughn Ververs   3 comments

`f Share`   0   `Digg ↑`   `Tweet`   0   Share   E-mail   Print   Font

"Something is happening in America," is how Rep. John Lewis explained his decision to cast his super delegate vote for Barack Obama over the candidate he had previously endorsed, Hillary Clinton.

Whatever is happening, New York City mayor Michael Bloomberg is hearing it too. Rather than spend up to $1 billion of his own money on an independent presidential bid, Bloomberg tells the world in a New York Times op-ed today that he will not be a candidate. "I have watched this campaign unfold, and I am hopeful that the current campaigns can rise to the challenge by offering truly independent leadership," he writes.

(AP)

Could The Supreme Court Decide Another Election? The New York Times reports on questions about John McCain's Constitutional eligibility to serve as President of the United States. The son of a U.S. Naval officer, McCain was actually born on a military base in the Panama Canal Zone where his father was stationed at the time. And the Constitution is not entirely clear on what constitutes a "natural-born citizen" – one of the few requirements needed to be met to be president.

It's a question that could conceivably end up in before the Supreme Court. And you thought counting chads was a circus.

EXHIBIT 6

CBS News, February 28, 2008

THE ⚜ TIMES
THE SUNDAY TIMES

Archive Article   Please enjoy this article from The Times & The Sunday Times archives. For full access to our content, |

From Times Online

February 29, 2008

McCain's Panama birth prompts eligibility probe by his campaign

Hannah Strange

John McCain's nomination as the Republican candidate may be an electoral near-certainty, but his campaign is investigating whether the senator's birth in the Panama Canal Zone may disqualify him from the presidency.

Mr McCain was born in 1936 while his father was stationed at a US military base and the Canal Zone was under American control. Although the question was examined during his first presidential bid in 2000, it has been revived as the senator heads towards the nomination.

The issue has also revived a centuries-old debate about the exact meaning of a constitutional clause laid down by the founding fathers in 1787, which declares that only a "natural-born citizen" can occupy the Oval Office.

VIDEO COVERAGE

> Watch the inaugural address in full
> Analysis: How good was Obama's speech?
> Taking the oath to become the 44th US president
> The First Lady passes the fashion

EXHIBIT 7

London Sunday Times, February 29, 2008

McCain's citizenship called into question

Candidate, born in Panama Canal Zone, may not qualify as 'natural born'

Below: [ ] Discussion [ ] Related

Tweet 3
Recommend 40

By Pete Williams
Justice correspondent

NBC News
updated 2/29/2008 7:21:39 PM ET   Share | Print | Font: Ⓐ A + −

Republican presidential hopeful U.S. Senator John McCain, seen in Richardson, Texas, on Thursday, was born in the Panama Canal Zone to U.S. parents.

Larry W. Smith / EPA

Sen. John McCain, R-Ariz., and his advisers are doing their best to brush aside questions — raised in the liberal blogosphere — about whether he is qualified under the Constitution to be president. But many legal scholars and government lawyers say it's a serious question with no clear answer.

The problem arises from a phrase in the Constitution setting out who is eligible to be president. Article II, which also specifies that a person must be at least 35 years old, says "No person except a natural born Citizen" can be president.

EXHIBIT 8
MSNBC, February 29, 2008

Political Punch

Power, pop, and probings from ABC News Senior White House Correspondent Jake Tapper

« Previous | Main | Next »

Legislation Introduced - by Democrats - to Declare McCain a U.S. Citizen

April 10, 2008 7:21 PM

Print   RSS | SHARE: ✉ Email 🔲 f 📷 b 🔲   [+] More

Political coverage and musings on pop culture from ABC News Senior White House Correspondent Jake Tapper and the ABC News White House team.

📶 Subscribe to this blog's feed

📶 Subscribe to Jake Tapper's "Political Punch" Podcast

🔵 Follow Jake Tapper on Twitter

Contributors

Ann Compton
National correspondent for ABC News Radio in Washington, D.C.

Sunlen Miller
Producer with the team covering the White House.

Karen Travers
Digital reporter covering the Obama White House.

Recent Posts

With questions - however serious - about whether Sen. John McCain, R-Ariz., is eligible to run for president since he was born outside U.S. borders on an American Naval base, Sens. Patrick Leahy, D-Vermont, the chairman of the Senate Judiciary Committee, and Sen. Claire McCaskill, D-Mo. today introduced a non-binding resolution expressing the sense of the U.S. Senate that McCain qualifies as a "natural born Citizen," as specified in the Constitution and eligible for the highest office in the land.

Co-sponsors include Sens. Hillary Clinton, D-NY, and Barack Obama, D-Illinois; Leahy said he anticipates it will pass unanimously.

Article II, Section 1 of the Constitution says to be eligible for the presidency a candidate must have reached the age of 35 years old, resided in the U.S. for 14 years; and must be a "natural born Citizen" of the United States.

The Constitution, however, does not define "natural born Citizen." McCain was born in the Panama Canal Zone to parents who were U.S. citizens, but some scholars have questioned if that suffices.

Earlier this month, Leahy asked Homeland Security Secretary Michael Chertoff his views on the matter during a Judiciary Committee hearing.

"My assumption and my understanding is that if you are born of American parents, you are naturally a natural-born American citizen," Chertoff said.

Leahy concurred.

The resolution introduced today states: "Resolved, That John Sidney McCain, III, is a 'natural born Citizen' under Article II, Section 1, of the Constitution of the United States."

EXHIBIT 9

ABC News, April 10, 2008

McCain's Birth Abroad Stirs Legal Debate
His Eligibility for Presidency Is Questioned

By Michael Dobbs
Washington Post Staff Writer
Friday, May 2, 2008

The Senate has unanimously declared John McCain a natural-born citizen, eligible to be president of the United States.

That is the good news for the presumptive Republican nominee, who was born nearly 72 years ago in a military hospital in the Panama Canal Zone, then under U.S. jurisdiction. The bad news is that the nonbinding Senate resolution passed Wednesday night is simply an opinion that has little bearing on an arcane constitutional debate that has preoccupied legal scholars for many weeks.

Sen. John McCain, the presumptive GOP nominee, was born on a U.S. military base in the Panama Canal Zone, which was then under U.S. jurisdiction. (By Chris Gardner -- Getty Images)

Article II of the Constitution states that "no person except a natural born citizen . . . shall be eligible to the office of president." The problem is that the Founding Fathers never defined exactly what they meant by "natural born citizen," and the matter has never been fully tested in court. At least three pending cases are challenging McCain's right to be sworn in as president.

TOOLBOX

Resize   Print   E-mail

Yahoo! Buzz

EXHIBIT 10
Washington Post, May 2, 2008

Was McCain born in the USA?

By **Robert Farley**

Published on Monday, May 12th, 2008 at 4:43 p.m.

SUMMARY: John McCain's birthplace has given rise to one of the more vexing questions of the campaign season: If McCain wasn't physically born in the United States, can he be president?

Share this article:

 Recommend 14

 Tweet 0

In a folksy Mother's Day television ad, Sen. John McCain sits across from his mother, Roberta McCain, discussing his birth.

Roberta McCain recalls that it was a Saturday when she told her husband, Navy officer John S. McCain Jr., "We're going to have this baby!"

She relates what is clearly a well-worn anecdote, that the future presidential candidate was born about noon and "the club was very close by" and "I'm told that on the table, there were 27 bottles of scotch, all presents to Johnny."

There's no mention of where this all took place. And that's probably no accident. John Sidney McCain III was born Aug. 29, 1936, in the Panama Canal Zone, where his father, a Navy officer, was stationed.

If McCain is elected president, he'd be the first born outside the 50 states.

But there's more than trivia at play. McCain's birthplace has given rise to one of the more vexing and inconvenient questions of the campaign season: If McCain wasn't physically born in the United States, can he be president?

Ultimately, the issue is rooted in legal opinions (albeit some stronger than others), not facts, and so PolitiFact's customary True-False ratings don't quite fit here. Speculation about how the Supreme Court might rule would be just that. But as the issue has been much discussed and argued, we thought it would be worthwhile to lay out some of the facts behind the main arguments.

Some Internet bloggers have speculated that McCain wasn't actually born in the Coco Solo military hospital in the Panama Canal Zone, but rather a nearby off-base hospital, in Panama.

Contrary to some jokesters who say McCain is so old his birth certificate is expired, McCain does in fact have one. He's just not releasing it publicly.

But the McCain campaign did let a *Washington Post reporter* take a peek at it. According to the reporter, the certificate records his birth in the Coco Solo "family hospital."

Exhibit II

Politifact.com, May 12, 2008

THU JUN 12, 2008 AT 05:49 PM EDT

The Bombshell on McCain's Birth Certificate

by andyfoland

🔗 Share | New | 🐦 Tweet | 0 | 👍 Like

📡 PERMALINK   🗨 149 COMMENTS

The McCain campaign is going to have no interest in releasing his birth certificate.

It's not because it will once again reinforce his age--the certificate would not change the significance, or obviousness, of that issue.

It's because one of the candidates running for President *actually wasn't* born in the United States. Though it's not exactly a secret, John McCain has done a good job keeping the public at large from catching on that **he was born in Panama**.

EXHIBIT 12

DailyKos.com, June 12, 2008

A Hint of New Life to a McCain Birth Issue

By ADAM LIPTAK
Published: July 11, 2008

🔵 TWITTER

✉ SIGN IN TO E-MAIL OR SAVE THIS

🖨 PRINT

🗐 REPRINTS

➕ SHARE

In the most detailed examination yet of Senator John McCain's eligibility to be president, a law professor at the University of Arizona has concluded that neither Mr. McCain's birth in 1936 in the Panama Canal Zone nor the fact that his parents were American citizens is enough to satisfy the constitutional requirement that the president must be a "natural-born citizen."

🔍 Enlarge This Image

The analysis, by Prof. Gabriel J. Chin, focused on a 1937 law that has been largely overlooked in the debate over Mr. McCain's eligibility to be president. The law conferred citizenship on children of American parents born in the Canal Zone after 1904, and it made John McCain a citizen just before his first birthday. But the law came too late, Professor Chin argued, to make Mr. McCain a natural-born citizen.

WIN WIN

NOW PLAYING

"It's preposterous that a technicality like this can make a difference in an advanced democracy," Professor Chin said. "But this is the constitutional text that we have."

EXHIBIT 13

New York Times, July 11, 2008

Top News

McCain not natural-born citizen, prof says

Published: July 11, 2008 at 9:36 AM

💬 Comments (0)　　✉ Email　　🖨 Print　　🔊 Listen　　**f Share**　　🐦 Tweet　0

TUCSON, July 11 (UPI) -- Research shows the circumstances of John McCain's birth don't pass constitutional muster for him to be U.S. president, a University of Arizona professor says.

A 1937 law granting citizenship to children of U.S. parents in the Panama Canal Zone came too late to apply to McCain, the U.S. senator from Arizona and likely Republican presidential nominee, The New York Times reported. The Constitution requires the president be a "natural-born citizen," but the law made McCain a citizen just before his first birthday.

"It's preposterous that a technicality like this can make a difference in an advanced democracy," professor Gabriel Chin said. "But this is the constitutional text that we have."

The law at the time of McCain's birth conferred citizenship to children born to American parents "out of the limits and jurisdiction of the United States," Chin said. The term "limits and jurisdiction" created a problem because the Canal Zone was beyond the limits of the United States but not its jurisdiction, the Times said.

File photo of presumptive Republican presidential nominee Sen. John McCain dated July 8, 2008. (UPI Photo/Roger L. Wollenberg) 🔍

Related Stories

" Opponents attest to McCain's eligibility

" McCain raises 'natural-born citizen' issue

E X H I B I T   I 4

UPI.com, July 11, 2008

Claim: John McCain does not qualify as a natural-born citizen of the U.S. because he was born in Panama.

Status: *Undetermined.*

Example: *[Collected via e-mail, July 2008]*

> I am hearing talk that Senator John McCain is not eligible to be President of the United States because he is not a natural-born citizen.

Origins: Among the few qualifications specified in Article II, Section I of the U.S. Constitution regarding eligibility for the office of President of the United States is that the office-holder must be a "natural born citizen of the United States." This qualification has not previously been an issue in U.S. politics since no one so far elected to the office of president (or who otherwise served as president) was born outside of the United States. But it has been a (minor) issue so far in 2008, as the presumptive Republican presidential nominee, Senator John McCain of Arizona, was born not in the U.S. proper but in the Panama Canal Zone. (McCain's parents were themselves U.S. citizens, and at the time of his birth they lived on a military installation in the Panama Canal Zone, where his father was stationed as a U.S. Navy officer.) If Senator McCain were deemed not to be a natural-born citizen of the United States, his name could be kept off of ballots in the 2008 presidential election, and he could be ineligible to serve as president even if won the election.

As much we'd like to dismiss this one as just another frivolous election season rumor, it's impossible to make any definitive statement about Senator McCain's presidential eligibility because the issue is a matter of law rather than a matter of fact, and the law is ambiguous. There is no disputing that, under the U.S. statutes and laws applicable to the offspring of Americans living abroad and to the Canal Zone, John McCain is a citizen of the United States. However, the difference between "citizen" and "natural-born citizen" is an important one in this case, and some of the legal distinctions between the two are still murky. (The particular sticking points in Senator McCain's case are whether the Panama Canal Zone was covered by existing citizenship laws at the time of his birth, and whether someone who was born outside the U.S. and holds U.S. citizenship status by virtue of a law passed after his birth and applied retroactively qualifies as a natural-born citizen.)

EXHIBIT 15
Snopes.com, July 2008

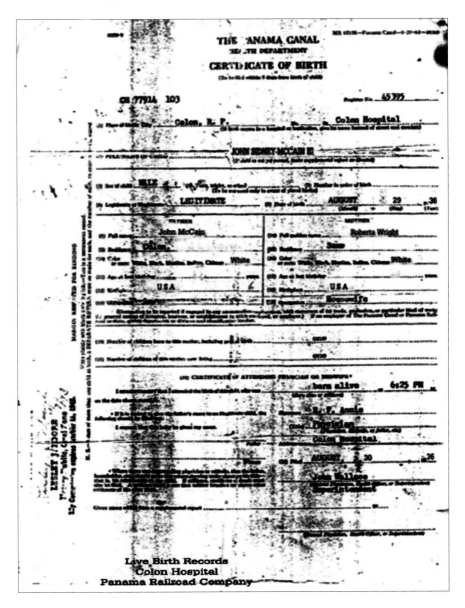

EXHIBIT 16

Senator John McCain, Long-Form Birth Certificate

PANAMA CANAL COMMISSION
COMISIÓN DEL CANAL DE PANAMÁ
CERTIFICATE OF LIVE BIRTH
CERTIFICADO DE NACIMIENTO VIVO

Name of child—Nombre del niño	Sex—Sexo	Birth Registration No.—Registro No.
John Sidney McCain III	Masc.	170027
Date of birth—Fecha de nacimiento	Place of birth—Lugar de nacimiento	
29 August 1936	Colon, Panama	
Father's name—Nombre del Padre	Father's birthplace—Lugar de nacimiento del Padre	
John McCain	U S A	
Mother's maiden name—Nombre de soltera de la Madre	Mother's birthplace—Lugar de nacimiento de la Madre	
Roberta Wright	U S A	

This is to certify that the above is a true copy of information recorded on the birth certificate on file in the records of the Panama Canal Commission at Balboa Heights, Republic of Panama. Certified copies must bear the raised impression of the seal of the Agency Records Officer, Panama Canal Commission.

Por el presente se certifica que lo anterior es copia fiel de la información que aparece en el certificado de nacimiento que se encuentra en los archivos de la Comisión del Canal de Panamá en Altos de Balboa, República de Panamá. Las copias certificadas deberán llevar la impresión en relieve del sello del Oficial de Archivos de la Agencia, de la Comisión del Canal de Panamá.

10 September 1936	E. Durfee – 28 marzo 1980
(Date Registered—Fecha de Inscripción)	(Registrar and Date Issued—Registrador y Fecha de Expedición)

WARNING: This certificate is printed on sensitized paper. Any alterations will nullify the certificate.

ADVERTENCIA: Este certificado está impreso en papel sensibilizado. Cualesquier alteraciones anularán el mismo.

EXHIBIT 17

Senator John McCain, Short-Form Birth Certificate

	6812	George Wanzer Shepard	41 51	do	Marine det., Peiping, China.
55	6813	Dallas Gilchrist Sutton	45 51	do	Naval Academy.
	6814	William Chambers	10 48 51	do	Comd. of naval hosp., Canacao, P. I.
	6815	Kent Churchill Melhorn	45 51	do	Naval hospital, San Diego.
		Joseph Albert Biello	5-abd 16	do	Staff, comdr., Battle Force, U. S. Fleet.
			41 51		
	6816	Frank Xavier Koltes	51	11 May 30	Dist. med. off., 15th nav. dist., Balboa, C. Z.
	6817	Myron Clarke Baker	51	22 Jan. 31	Comd. of nav. hosp. Parris Island.
	6818	Howard Foster Lawrence	51	do	Nav. training station, Newport.
	6819	Ernest William Brown	32 46 51	do	Mbr. Nav. Ret. Bd., Nav. Ex. Bd., for Med.
60	6820	George Carroll Thomas	51	1 Dec. 31	off. and Bd. Med. Exam., Navy Dept. Comd. of naval hospital, Washington.
	6821	Alfred Lee Clifton (E)	41 51	do	Naval hospital, Philadelphia.
	6822	Lucius Warren Johnson (C)	18 41 51	do	Relief.
65	6823	George Franklin Cottle	41 51	do	Staff, comdr. in chief, U. S. Fleet.
	6824	William Leake Mann, Jr (E)	17 48 50 51	do	Marine barracks, Quantico.
	6825	Alfred Joseph Toulon	42 51	1 Feb. 32	Navy Yard, Washington.
	6826	Glenmore Ford Clark	46 51	do	Naval hospital, Boston.
	6827	William Murray Kerr	46 51	do	Naval hospital, Portsmouth, N. H.
70	6828	John Beverly Pollard	46 51	do	Staff, comdr., Scouting Force.
	6829	George Wehnes Calver	42 46 51	30 May 34	Naval dispensary, Washington.
	6830	Andrew Blaine Davidson	51	1 July 35	Naval hospital, San Diego.
	6831	William Lorne Irvine	41 42a 44 51	do	Submarine base, Coco Solo, C. Z.
	6832	Griffith Edwards Thomas	46 51	do	Bureau of Medicine and Surgery.
75	6833	Clyde Bradley Camerer	5bc 16 43 51	do	Staff, comdr., destroyers, Battle Force, U. S. F
	6834	Gardner Ellis Robertson	38 43 51	do	Naval Medical Supply Depot, New York.
	6835	Joseph John Anthony McMullin	41 51	do	Norfolk Naval Hospital, Portsmouth.
	6836	Sankey Bacon	51	do.(Y).	Treatment, naval hospital, Washington.
	6837	Gordon Dyer Hale	46 51	do	Navy Yard, Portsmouth, N. H.

MEDICAL

EXHIBIT 18

Navy Medical Directors

FactCheck.org **Clarifies Barack's Citizenship**

"When Barack Obama Jr. was born on Aug. 4,1961, in Honolulu, Kenya was a British colony, still part of the United Kingdom's dwindling empire. As a Kenyan native, Barack Obama Sr. was a British subject whose citizenship status was governed by The British Nationality Act of 1948. That same act governed the status of Obama Sr.'s children.

Since Sen. Obama has neither renounced his U.S. citizenship nor sworn an oath of allegiance to Kenya, his Kenyan citizenship automatically expired on Aug. 4,1982."

EXHIBIT 19

FightTheSmears.com, Screen Capture Taken During 2008 Presidential Campaign

RUMORS, MYTHS AND FABRICATIONS

The Obama Birth Controversy

— By Todd Leventhal, 21 August 2009

During the past year, a number of conspiracy theorists have suggested that President Obama was not born in the United States. If this were true — which it is not — he would not be eligible to be the U.S. president, who must be a natural-born American.

On July 27, 2009, Hawaii State Health Director Dr. Chiyome Fukino confirmed that Obama was born in the U.S. state of Hawaii, stating:

> I ... have seen the original vital records maintained on file by the Hawaii State Department of Health verifying Barack Hussein Obama was born in Hawaii and is a natural-born American citizen. I have nothing further to add to this statement or my original statement issued in October 2008 over eight months ago ....

In 2008, FactCheck.org examined a copy of Obama's birth certificate held by the Obama campaign, verifying that it was a real, official document.

Nine days after Obama was born in Honolulu, Hawaii on August 4, 1961, the *Honolulu Advertiser* included among its birth notices, "Mr. and Mrs. Barack H. Obama of 6085 Kalanianaole Highway, son, Aug. 4," which it reprinted in its Aug. 17, 2009 issue. The *Honolulu Star-Bulletin* printed the identical birth notice one day later, on August 14, 1961. Its former managing editor Dave Shapiro says, "Those were listings that came over from the state Department of Health. They would send the same thing to both papers."

Interestingly, FactCheck.org determined that Obama was originally both a U.S. citizen and a citizen of the United Kingdom and Colonies from 1961 to 1963 (because his father was from Kenya, which gained its independence from the British Empire in 1963), then both a U.S. and

EXHIBIT 20

Screen Capture of State Department Web site Taken in August 2010

E X H I B I T   2 1

Screen Capture of State Department Web site Taken in August 2010

The truth about Barack's birth certificate

Lie:

Obama Is Not a Natural Born Citizen

Truth:

Senator Obama was born in Hawaii in 1961, after it became a state on August 21st, 1959. Obama became a citizen at birth under the first section of the 14th Amendment

"All persons born or naturalized in the United States, and subject to the jurisdiction thereof, are citizens of the United States and of the State wherein they reside. No State shall make or enforce any law which shall abridge the privileges or immunities of citizens of the United States; nor shall any State deprive any person of life, liberty, or property, without due process of law; nor deny to any person within its jurisdiction the equal protection of the laws."

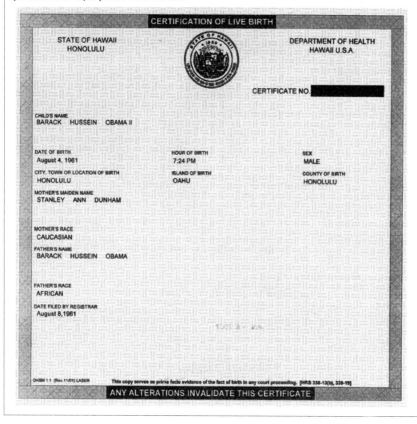

Exhibit 22

FightTheSmears.com Screen Capture, August 2009

Home --> Politics --> Barack Obama --> Native Son

Native Son

Claim: Barack Obama does not qualify as a natural-born citizen of the U.S. because his mother was too young.

Status: *False.*

The item quoted above posits that Barack Obama does not qualify as a natural-born citizen of the U.S. because the law in effect at the time he was born specified that "If only one parent was a U.S. citizen at the time of your birth, that parent must have resided in the United States for at least ten years, at least five of which had to be after the age of 16." Since Barack Obama only had one U.S. citizen parent (his mother), and his mother had not been residing in the U.S. for at least <u>five years after the age of 16</u> when Barack was born (because she herself was only 18 at the time), then he's not a natural-born citizen.

A few facets of this claim immediately jump out as being far-fetched: first, that a sitting U.S. Senator who has already spent a good deal of time and money securing his party's nomination for the presidency would suddenly be discovered as ineligible due to an obscure provision of U.S. law; and second, that U.S. law would essentially penalize someone who would otherwise qualify for natural-born citizenship status simply because his mother was too young. The fact is, the qualifications listed in the example quoted above are moot because they refer to someone who was born <u>outside the United States</u>. Since Barack Obama was born in Hawaii, they do not apply to him.

The Fourteenth Amendment states that "all persons born or naturalized in the United States, and subject to the jurisdiction thereof, are citizens of the United States." Since Hawaii is part of the United States, even if Barack Obama's parents were both non-U.S. citizens who hadn't even set foot in the country until just before he was born, he'd still qualify as a natural-born citizen.

EXHIBIT 23

Snopes.com Screen Capture, June 2008

Email: Barack Obama Isn't a Natural-Born Citizen
By David Emery, About.com Guide

See More About: barack obama rumors   u.s. citizenship   politics and politicians

Email rumor claims Barack Obama is ineligible for the presidency because by virtue of certain laws in effect at the time of his birth he is not a natural-born U.S. citizen.

Analysis: Contrary to the arguments set forth above, Barack Obama is, in fact, a natural-born citizen of the United States, for the simple reason that he was born on American soil (in Hawaii, two years after it acquired statehood). The age and citizenship status of his parents at the time of his birth have no bearing on Obama's own citizenship.

Any confusion on this point is the result of misunderstanding the legal concepts of *jus sanguinis* (right of blood) and *jus soli* (right of birthplace) as they apply to citizenship in the United States. Here's how the website of the U.S. Citizenship and Immigration Service explained the matter in 2008:

> The 14th Amendment of the U.S. Constitution **guarantees citizenship at birth** to almost all individuals born in the United States or in U.S. jurisdictions, according to the principle of jus soli. Certain individuals born in the United States, such as children of foreign heads of state or children of foreign diplomats, do not obtain U.S. citizenship under jus soli.

> Certain individuals born outside of the United States are born citizens because of their parents, according to the principle of jus sanguinis (which holds that the country of citizenship of a child is the same as that of his / her parents).

It is a fact that under the provisions of Article Two of the U.S. Constitution, *naturalized* citizens are ineligible to hold the office of president, but this disqualification does not apply to Barack Obama, who has been a citizen since birth.

EXHIBIT 24
Snopes.com Screen Capture, June 2008

CERTIFICATION OF LIVE BIRTH

STATE OF HAWAII
HONOLULU

DEPARTMENT OF HEALTH
HAWAII U.S.A.

CERTIFICATE NO.

CHILD'S NAME
BARACK   HUSSEIN   OBAMA II

DATE OF BIRTH
August 4, 1961

HOUR OF BIRTH
7:24 PM

SEX
MALE

CITY, TOWN OR LOCATION OF BIRTH
HONOLULU

ISLAND OF BIRTH
OAHU

COUNTY OF BIRTH
HONOLULU

MOTHER'S MAIDEN NAME
STANLEY   ANN   DUNHAM

MOTHER'S RACE
CAUCASIAN

FATHER'S NAME
BARACK   HUSSEIN   OBAMA

FATHER'S RACE
AFRICAN

DATE FILED BY REGISTRAR
August 8, 1961

OHSM 1-1 (Rev.11/01) LASER   This copy serves as prima facie evidence of the fact of birth in any court proceeding. [HRS 338-13(b), 338-19]

ANY ALTERATIONS INVALIDATE THIS CERTIFICATE

EXHIBIT 25
Obama Short-Form Certification of Live Birth, DailyKos.com, June 12, 2008

Exhibit 26

Obama Short-Form Certification of Live Birth, FightTheSmears.com,
Screen Capture, June 2008

Top of the Ticket

POLITICAL COMMENTARY FROM ANDREW MALCOLM

« Previous Post | Top of the Ticket Home | Next Post »

Barack Obama's birth certificate revealed here

June 16, 2008 | 1:12 am   🐦 (44)   **f** (1625)   💬 Comments (1938)

(**UPDATE:** Alan Keyes stoked the Obama birth certificate controversy anew in February 2009. See Ticket coverage here.)

[See August update here.]

Click on the certificate to enlarge for better reading.

First, last fall, there were all kinds of people, a number of them **Ron Paul** supporters, dashing from Internet site to Internet site suggesting that John McCain could not serve as president of the United States.

That was because he was born outside the United States and, therefore, not native-born, as presidents must be constitutionally.

McCain was, in fact, born in a U.S. military hospital in the Panama Canal Zone, where his father was serving in the Navy. That was, in fact, American-controlled territory at the time.

More importantly, his parents were both American citizens, so he could have been born on Mars and still been an American at birth. And a sense of the Senate resolution took care of any lingering doubts.

Now come the rumors about Barack Obama's birthplace, that he was really born in his father's native Kenya, so like Gov. **Arnold Schwarzenegger**, who was born in Austria, he can't become a U.S. president.

ＥＸＨＩＢＩＴ 27

Los Angeles Times, June 16, 2008

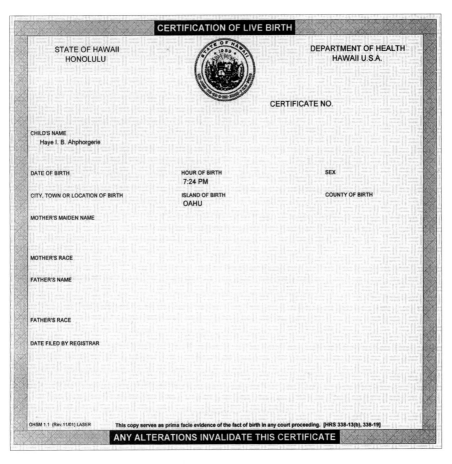

EXHIBIT 28
Jay McKinnon's Forged Obama COLB, July 2008

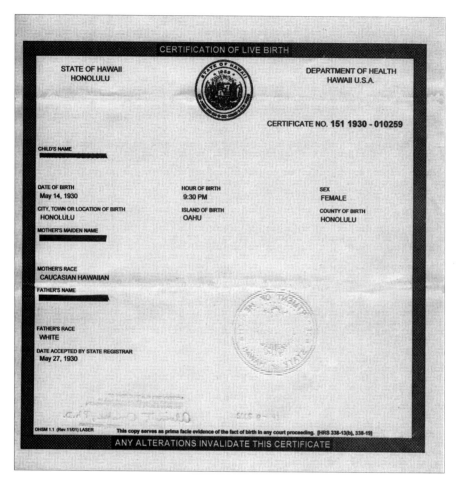

EXHIBIT 29

Authentic COLB Issued to Patricia Decosta

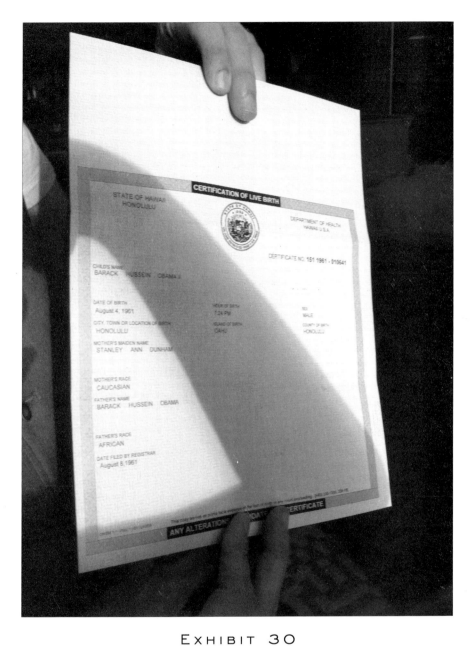

Exhibit 30

Obama COLB, FactCheck.org, August 21, 2008

Photograph of Document

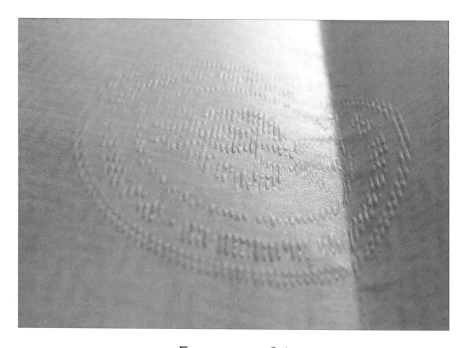

Exhibit 31

Obama COLB, FactCheck.org, August 21, 2008

Seal Visible

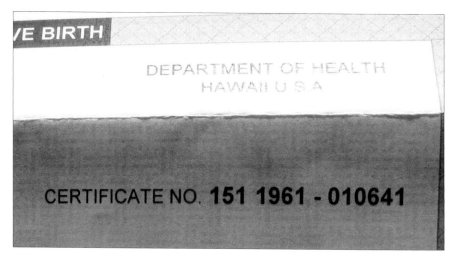

Exhibit 32

Obama COLB, FactCheck.org, August 21, 2008

Certificate Number Listed

JUN - 6 2007

I CERTIFY THIS IS A TRUE COPY OR
ABSTRACT OF THE RECORD ON FILE IN
THE HAWAII STATE DEPARTMENT OF HEALTH

STATE REGISTRAR

EXHIBIT 33

Obama COLB, FactCheck.org, August 21, 2008
Registrar Stamp, Date—on Document's Reverse Side

CITY, TOWN OR LOC.

HONOLULU

EXHIBIT 34

Obama COLB, FactCheck.org, August 21, 2008
Close-up of Printing on Document

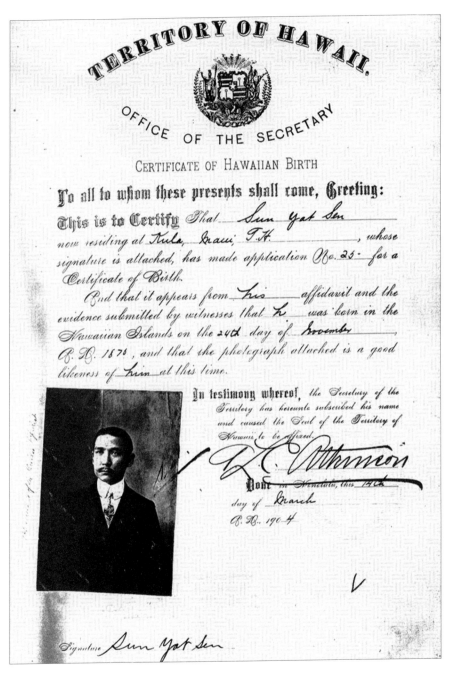

EXHIBIT 35

Birth Certificate Issued by Hawaii to Chinese Nationalist Sun Yat-Sen, 1904

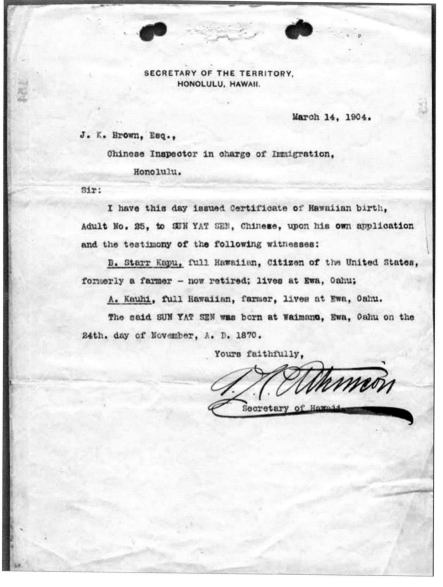

SECRETARY OF THE TERRITORY,
HONOLULU, HAWAII.

March 14, 1904.

J. K. Brown, Esq.,

Chinese Inspector in charge of Immigration,

Honolulu.

Sir:

I have this day issued Certificate of Hawaiian birth,
Adult No. 25, to SUN YAT SEN, Chinese, upon his own application
and the testimony of the following witnesses:

B. Starr Kapu, full Hawaiian, Citizen of the United States,
formerly a farmer – now retired; lives at Ewa, Oahu;

A. Kauhi, full Hawaiian, farmer, lives at Ewa, Oahu.

The said SUN YAT SEN was born at Waimano, Ewa, Oahu on the
24th. day of November, A. D. 1870.

Yours faithfully,

Secretary of Hawaii.

EXHIBIT 36

Letter Submitted to Hawaii in Support of Sun Yat-Sen's Birth Certificate Application, 1904

THE SUNDAY ADVERTISER
B-6   August 13, 1961

Beat The Hea

Health Bureau Statistics

Births, Marriages, Deaths

SERVICE ANYONE?

Yes Indee
In A Jiff

LISTED HERE IN EASY-TO-FIND ALPHABETICAL ORDER ARE
FREQUENTLY NEEDED BUSINESS AND PROFESSIONAL SERVICES.

YOU CAN USE THIS HANDY DIRECTORY EVERYDA

BIRTHS

Mr. and Mrs. Samuel K. Haae Sr., 849-A 11th Ave., son, Aug. 4.
Mr. and Mrs. Charles J. Staley, 1319 Anapa St., daughter, Aug. 6.
Mr. and Mrs. Richard R. Kitson, Apt. 11, 1635 Clark St., son, Aug. 4.
Mr. and Mrs. George P. Ayau Sr., 87-143 Liliana St., Maili, son, July 31.
Mr. and Mrs. Thaddeus J. Raymond, 1371 Haloa Drive, son, July 30.
Mr. and Mrs. Robert I. Arakawa, 935-B Houston St., son, Aug. 1.
Mr. and Mrs. Noel Y. Takaha-shi, 56 Nanea Ave., Wahiawa, daughter, Aug. 2.

LUAU SUPPLY Tents $10 up, tables, chairs, pots, pans, Japanese equipment & glasses.

58281   KANEDA'S

Mr. and Mrs. Allington K. Brown, Maunawili Road, Kailua, son, Aug. 2.
Mr. and Mrs. Cirilo V. Caharlo, 918 Puuhale Road, son, Aug. 2.
Mr. and Mrs. Samuel L. M. Mokuahi Sr., 732 Laukea St., son, Aug. 2.
Mr. and Mrs. John R. Clifford Sr., 2624 Maunawai Place, son, Aug. 4.

LUAU Food Supply Service

58281 — KANEDA'S

$2.50 per person, all you can eat.

Mr. and Mrs. Peter C. Kamealoha Jr., 441 McNeill St., son, Aug. 3.
Mr. and Mrs. Edward W. Walker, 1660 S. King St., daughter, Aug. 7.
3813 Radford Drive, son, Aug. 2.
Mr. and Mrs. Mike M. Nagaishi, 2687 Gardenia St., son, Aug. 6.

BABIES THRIVE ON CARNATION Evaporated Milk
The Milk Every Doctor Knows

Mr. and Mrs. Glenn E. Earnest, 1258 Wilhelmina Rise, son, Aug. 8.
Mr. and Mrs. Edward S. H. Chun, 45-440 Akimala St., Kaneohe, son, Aug. 5.
Mr. and Mrs. John R. Waidelich, 937 18th Ave., son, Aug. 5.
Mr. and Mrs. Emmett P. Simpson, 3792 Kahili St., daughter, Aug. 3.
Mr. and Mrs. Melvin K. F. Liu, 45-548 Kaahaala Road, Kaneohe, son, Aug. 5.
Mr. and Mrs. Richard D. Wright, 91-939 Kaiapu St., Ewa Beach, Ewa, daughter, Aug. 3.
Mr. and Mrs. Barack H. Obama, 6085 Kalanianaole Hwy., son, Aug. 4.
Mr. and Mrs. Norman Asing, 2135 Ahi Anui St., son, Aug. 4.
Mr. and Mrs. Andrew A. Hatchie, 2420 Kauluulaau St., daughter, Aug. 4.
Mr. and Mrs. Harry Y. W. Wong, 461 Lawelawe St., son, Aug. 6.

BUILDING TRADES

CARPENTRY

Home Repair Specialists. Alteration & remodeling work. Licensed. S. Moriyama, 775343, 710595.

CEMENT CONSTRUCTION

LEEWARD HOME OWNERS. Patios, tile walls. Ph. 452-072.
Tile basements, patios, drop curb driveways, tile walls including carpentry work. Fred, 95664, 814711.
FIREPLACES, patios, hollow tile fences, stone work. Ph. 83-814.
Concrete patios & driveways. Hollow tile walls. Ph. 73217.

ELECTRICAL WIRING

Licensed Contractor. Complete wiring & home appliance repair. 771315.

GENERAL CONTRACTORS

Servicing town or country. Remodeling, patios, new homes. Free estimates, drawing services included. Since 1948. Ph. ERNIE KAMISA-TO. 851-333, 240-290.

AAA GENERAL CONTRACTOR
Home building, decorating, interior & exterior painting, remodeling, repairs, roofing, large or small jobs. Fully guaranteed. 813-413.
Alterations, remodeling—LET THE EXPERTS DO IT. Complete service, planning, financing, repair & experience. ISLAND HOMES, Inc. 66238.

We Aim To Please

Remodeling, Repair, Roofing, Masonry. Call Mr. Suda, 734455, 777647.
Repairs, ALTERATIONS & GENERAL REMODELING WORK. Licensed. ROY S. MURAOKA, 893-953.
All work guaranteed. FASTEST Service & remodeling in the Islands. Free Estimate. Repairs, 995-330.
Free estimates—willing to please, 747704, 776476 eves, ask for Doug.

HOMES New & repairs, additions, remodeling, etc. TAKAHASHI, Ph. 715-410.
All kinds of Carpentry Work. Reasonable, reliable. PAUL S. NAKA-SHIMA, Ph. 900-732.
Free estimate on remodeling & house repair. T. Morimoto, Ph. 451-212.

NEW HOMES, ADDITION REPAIRS. Screens, etc. Call Stanley T. Oshiro, 921-242.

FLOORING

S. KAWAMOTO Floor sanding. Ph. office 68-074, evenings 771-992.

FLOOR WAXING

Specializing in WAXING & POLISHING. Free estimate. 771313 after 5.

GRASS

ZOYSIA MATRELLA
NARAHARA-ZOYSIA GRASS FARM
3201-H Lal Rd., Palolo Valley
Ph. 706-444, 66-757, 65-379

LANDSCAPING

For complete yard cleaning. 991-600.

LANDSCAPING

Lot clearing, grass planting, tree trimming, general yard cleaning. 991-600.

MOSS ROCK

STONE WALLS, LOT CLEARING.
Excavating. Ph. 452-645.

RUG & UPHOL CLEANING

AUTHORIZED KARPET KARE
Cleaners. Graduate of Bigelow Karpet Cleaning Institute. N.Y. 59951.

SAND & SOIL

General Hauling. Sand, top soil, fill, blue rock, coral, etc. HIRONAKA TRUCKING, 991-470, 810-533.

SAND, ROCK, CEMENT
SAND, ROCK, CEMENT & SUPPLY, LTD.
OAHU METAL & SUPPLY. 1177 N. School. 873-465, 87-779.

SAND, ROCK, CEMENT
Paradise Sales Co. Ltd.
974 Waiakamilo Rd.   Ph. 88153.

TERMITE CONTROL

ACME TERMITE SERVICE
Very reasonable. Ph. 66-753.

TOP SOIL

Top soil & fill material. Excavating, clearing & grading equipment for rent. 729-246, 226-971, 814-940.

TREE TRIMMING

Standard Tree Trimming. Free estimates. Cutting, pruning. Very reasonable. 567-981.
Hawn Tree Trimming Co. Cutting & pruning. 729-817, 756-50.

INSTRUCTION

AUTOMOBILE DRIVING
By Policeman—Safe & lawful. Guaranteed for Police tests. 995-444.

TUTORING

SPAULDING'S

AUTO RENTAL

$5 per day plus milec
for 1960 sedans. Gas & oil fu
HAWAII RENT-A-CA
2045 Kalakaua Ave.
998-121, 998-14

HOUSE TRAILER

Rent a vacation house trailer by day, week or month. California Pleasure Trailers, phone

LINEN RENTAL

For complete linen rental business, profession or home. American Linen Supply.

SEWING MACHINES

RENTALS
$4 mo. W
& Singer.
Ph. 281-619, 995-924.

WHITE SEWING MACHINE

TV & BABY FURNITURE R
DYAN'S UNITED RENTA
TV, cribs, beds. etc. by week
We deliver. Ph. 502-251, 587

TELEVISION RENTALS

VINCENT'S IN WA
7.00   Ph. 937-817
$10 per mo. option to buy.
Home Appliances. 747145, 7

REPAIR SERVICES

BICYCLES

EKI'S fine used bicycles
King. 57277.

ELECTRICAL WIRING

Stores, shops & homes. Free estimates 99/96 Electric Sales & Ice.

FURNITURE, CABINET MFG

CORBALEY'S CABINET SH
Also refinishing. 378 Cooke St

TV & RADIO REPAIR

TV UNLIMITE
1215 S. Beretania St
PHONE 503-304
TVs, Radios, Hi Fi & Car ra
ALL WORK GUARANTEE!
1 YEAR
ANTENNA INSTALLATION
Our Specialty
Also rentals with option to b

Walton's TV Servi

Exhibit 37

Obama Birth Announcement, *Honolulu Sunday Advertiser*, August 13, 1961

EXHIBIT 38

Obama Birth Announcement, *Honolulu Star-Bulletin*, August 13, 1961

August 7.
Mr. and Mrs. Wallace M. Durkin, 3813 Radford Drive, son, August 7.
Mr. and Mrs. Mike M. Nagaishi, 2687 Gardenia Street, son, August 6.
Mr. and Mrs. Glenn E. Earnest, 1258 Wilhelmina Rise, son, August 6.
Mr. and Mrs. Edward S. H. Chun, 45-440 Akimala Street, Kaneohe, son, August 5.
Mr. and Mrs. John R. Waidelich, 937 18th Avenue, son, August 5.
Mr. and Mrs. Emmett P. Simpson, 2752 Kalihi Street, daughter, August 5.
Mr. and Mrs. Melvin K. F. Liu, 45-548 Keaahala Road, Kaneohe, son, August 5.
Mr. and Mrs. Richard D. Wright, 91-939 Kalapu Street, Ewa Beach, Ewa, daughter, August 5.
Mr. and Mrs. Barack H. Obama, 6085 Kalanianaole Highway, son, August 4.
Mr. and Mrs. Norman Asing, 2135 Ani Aniku Street, son, August 4.

*

3813 Radford Drive, son, Aug. 7.
Mr. and Mrs. Mike M. Nagaishi, 2687 Gardenia St., son, Aug. 6.

BABIES THRIVE ON
CARNATION Evaporated Milk
The Milk Every Doctor Knows

Mr. and Mrs. Glenn E. Earnest, 1258 Wilhelmina Rise, son, Aug. 6.
Mr. and Mrs. Edward S. H. Chun, 45-440 Akimala St., Kaneohe, son, Aug. 5.
Mr. and Mrs. John R. Waidelich, 937 18th Ave., son, Aug. 5.
Mr. and Mrs. Emmett P. Simpson, 2752 Kalihi St., daughter, Aug. 5.
Mr. and Mrs. Melvin K. F. Liu, 45-548 Keaahala Road, Kaneohe, son, Aug. 5.
Mr. and Mrs. Richard D. Wright, 91-939 Kalapu St., Ewa Beach, Ewa, daughter, Aug. 5.
Mr. and Mrs. Barack H. Obama, 6085 Kalanianaole Hwy., son, Aug. 4.
Mr. and Mrs. Norman Asing, 2135 Ani Aniku St., son, Aug. 4.

EXHIBIT 39

Side-by-Side Comparison of Obama Newspaper Birth Announcements

91-939 Kalapu St., Ewa Beach, Ewa, daughter, Aug. 5.
Mr. and Mrs. Barack H. Obama, 6085 Kalanianaole Hwy., son, Aug. 4.
Mr. and Mrs. Norman Asing, 2135 Ani Aniku St., son, Aug. 4.
Mr. and Mrs. Andrew A. M.

EXHIBIT 40

Close-up of Obama Newspaper Birth Announcement Text

Dungate Harold (Mona) sismn Pan Am n5405 Opihi
Dunham Madelyn L Mrs loan interviewer & escrow
Bank of Hawaii r6085 Kalanianaole hwy
" Stanley A (Madelyn L) mgr Pratt Furniture h6085
Kalanianaole hwy

EXHIBIT 41

Polk's Directory of City and County of Honolulu, Hawaii, 1961–1962

Obama Ann S studt r6085 Kalanianaole hwy
" Barack H studt r625 11th av

EXHIBIT 42

Polk's Directory of City and County of Honolulu, Hawaii, 1961–1962

EXHIBIT 43

Honolulu Title Records

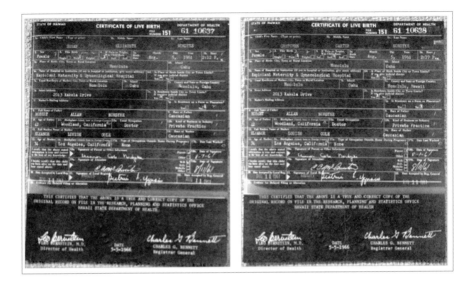

Exhibit 44

Long-Form, Hospital-Generated Birth Certificates: Nordyke Twins, Hawaii, August 1961

Exhibit 45

Newspaper Birth Announcement, Nordyke Twins,
Honolulu Advertiser, August 16, 1961

EXHIBIT 46

Screen Capture, the *Sunday Standard*, Published in Kenya, June 27, 2004

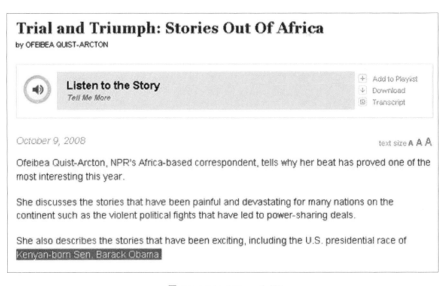

EXHIBIT 47

Screen Capture of Original NPR Web site, October 9, 2008

Trial and Triumph: Stories Out Of Africa
by OFEIBEA QUIST-ARCTON

 Listen to the Story
Tell Me More

+ Add to Playlist
↓ Download
▣ Transcript

Correction April 9, 2010
An earlier summary of this story that appeared online incorrectly identified the birthplace of Barack Obama. The audio correctly states that Obama's father was born in Kenya.

October 9, 2008   text size A **A A**

Ofeibea Quist-Arcton, NPR's Africa-based correspondent, tells why her beat has proved one of the most interesting this year.

She discusses the stories that have been painful and devastating for many nations on the continent such as the violent political fights that have led to power-sharing deals.

She also describes the stories that have been exciting, including the U.S. presidential race of Sen. Barack Obama, whose father was born in Kenya.

EXHIBIT 48

Screen Capture of Scrubbed NPR Web site, October 9, 2008

US Presidential Polls:Obama, McCain slug it out today
By SOLOMON ASOWATA WITH AGENCY REPORTS

WASHINGTON – Americans will today go to the polls to elect their next President with Democratic Party candidate, Senator Barack Obama largely favoured to win.

The Kenyan-born Senator will, however, face a stiff competition from his Republican counterpart, John McCain who has taken the presidential battle to the finishing line with vigorous campaign strategies.

The other candidates are Cynthia Mckinney (Green Party), Bob Barr (Libertarian Party), Chuk Baldwin (Constitution Party) and Ralph Nader who is running as an independent candidate.

Aiming for a last-minute upset, Republican John McCain embarked on a grueling odyssey through seven swing states yesterday while Democrat Barack Obama was headed toward three long time GOP bastions that have become Democratic-leaning battle grounds in the historic presidential contest.

EXHIBIT 49

Screen Capture of *Nigerian Observer* Web site, October 9, 2008

Mr & Mrs Obama US President Barack Obama is expected to announce a major foreign policy for Africa during his historic two-day visit to Ghana, beginning Friday, July 10, 2009.

Although Mr Obama has made foreign policy pronouncements for some parts of the world since assuming office in January, this year, he is yet to make one for Africa, and his visit to the country, which the White House describes as "one of our most trusted partners in sub-Saharan Africa", is expected to be used as a platform to unveil his foreign policy for Africa.

"It is expected that President Obama will make a major foreign policy statement on Africa", Ghana's Minister of Foreign Affairs, Alhaji Mohammed Mumuni, told the Daily Graphic.

For Ghana, Obama's visit will be a celebration of another milestone in African history as it hosts the first-ever African-American President on this presidential visit to the continent of his birth.

The Air Force One, carrying the 44th American President, his wife, Michelle and two daughters, as well as a retinue of senior US

🔍 **Have Your Say (2)** 🔅

66 what is life but a moment of consciousness and so we live and die everyday, as when we lay and die on this earth we awake another morning in another life. - By: *reuel jacques gnalega*
99

EXHIBIT 50

Screen Capture of Original *Modern Ghana* Web site, October 9, 2008

US President Barack Obama is expected to announce a major foreign policy for Africa during his historic two-day visit to Ghana, beginning Friday, July 10, 2009.

Although Mr Obama has made foreign policy pronouncements for some parts of the world since assuming office in January, this year, he is yet to make one for Africa, and his visit to the country, which the White House describes as "one of our most trusted partners in sub-Saharan Africa", is expected to be used as a platform to unveil his foreign policy for Africa.

"It is expected that President Obama will make a major foreign policy statement on Africa", Ghana's Minister of Foreign Affairs, Alhaji Mohammed Mumuni, told the Daily Graphic.

For Ghana, Obama's visit will be a celebration of another milestone in African history as it hosts the first-ever African-American President on this presidential visit to the continent of his father's birth.

66 SOMETIMES WHEN I AM ANGRY I FIND IT BETTER NOT TO SPEAK...

By: *T MANOOP*   99

More Quotes | Submit Quote

EXHIBIT 51

Screen Capture of Scrubbed *Modern Ghana* Web site, October 9, 2008

Daily Independent (Lagos)

Nigeria: Clintonian Branding

Dafe Onojovwo   20 August 2009

👍 Recommend   ❚ Be the first of your friends to recommend this.

COLUMN

Email | Print | Comment(2)

Was it right for the United States of America's Secretary of State, Mrs. Hillary Clinton, to have taken Nigeria to the cleaners, as she did last week, on our nation's own soil; was it right for an honoured guest to deliver moral tirades at the host, to his face, under the full glare of the world press, without a thought for the feeling of the host?

Share:

🔲 ❚ 🔀 ▪ 🔳 🔳

My colleague wept, with relief, as he listened to Mrs. Clinton because it became plain that the Obama administration was not hoodwinked by Nigerian government propaganda. No detail of the country's present demeaning, life-threatening disease is hidden from the US State Department. Little wonder then why Kenyan-born Barack Obama, America's first Black President, converted his major speech at his recent Ghana trip to a scathing upbraiding of Nigeria's irresponsible leadership! Clinton is implementing a tough-love state policy: to whip Nigeria's mulish leadership into line, and let verbal tact and finesse go to hell! This patient needs drastic therapy, and must endure it.

Exhibit 52

Screen Capture of Original AllAfrica.com Web site, August 20, 2009 bed capacity. Could he give a montly stipende, in the meantime to these students, so that while they are attending classes at the University of Nairobi they can use that money to pay for accommondation outside? When the Council is in place, the students can then be accommondated at the College?

Mr. Kamama: Mr. Deputy Speaker, Sir, I want to confirm to the House that if the Ministry will not receive information from the Office of the President, we will consider those options in liaison with the Joint Admissions Board.

(Mr. Affey stood up in his place)

Mr. Deputy Speaker: Order! Order, Mr. Affey! We are on Question No.462.

Mr. Bett: Mr. Deputy Speaker, Sir, it is disturbing to hear that these children cannot be admitted into the university because of beds. There are so many furniture shops in town with beds. If the Assistant Minister is unable to procure those

POINT OF ORDER

HOUSE SHOULD ADJOURN TO DISCUSS
ELECTION OF MR. BARRACK OBAMA

Ms. Odhiambo: On a point of order, Mr. Deputy Speaker, Sir. It is not on this issue. I stand on a point of order under Standing Order No.20 to seek leave for adjournment of the House to discuss the American presidential election results.

(Applause)

Mr. Deputy Speaker, Sir, the President-elect, Mr. Obama, is a son of the soil of this country. Every other country in this continent is celebrating the Obama win. It is only proper and fitting that the country which he originates from should show the same excitement, pomp and colour. I, therefore, seek

Exhibit 53

Screen Capture of Original Kenyan Parliamentary Debate Web site,
November 5, 2008, page 3275

Hon. Members, I think we had better take note of that and internalise it. We should know where our utmost loyalty is.

The Assistant Minister for Higher Education, Science and Technology (Mr. Kamama): On a point of order, Mr. Deputy Speaker, Sir. I just want to seek guidance from the Chair on this matter. Considering the fact that even His Excellency the President declared that tomorrow will be a national holiday to celebrate Obama's success, do you not think this is an urgent matter? So many man hours will be lost tomorrow because of this "Obama mania". I seek guidance on this matter.

Mr. Deputy Speaker: Hon. Members, tell me what is so urgent that you really want to discuss? Do you want to discuss the speech of Obama? What do you want to discuss on this Floor? If it is the celebrations, His Excellency the President has made tomorrow a public holiday. The House is not open to any debate on the ruling

some communication to make. As far as the interest and happiness regarding the elections that have just been concluded in the United States of America are concerned, this will put that to rest.

COMMUNICATION FROM THE CHAIR

CONGRATULATORY MESSAGE TO
PRESIDENT-ELECT BARRACK OBAMA

Hon. Members, as you may be aware, the people of the United States of America have just had a historic election where the son of this soil, Barrack Hussein Obama, has been elected the 44th President of the United States of America and the first African-American President in the history of that country, please join me in registering and sending this House's congratulations to the President-elect Obama for overcoming great odds to emerge victorious.

Exhibit 54

Screen Capture of Original Kenyan Parliamentary Debate Web site,
November 5, 2008, page 3276

The other thing that we are addressing through devolution is exclusion. What has made us suffer as a nation is exclusion. Once people feel excluded, even when you want to employ a policeman or constable or you want to build a dispensary, it must come from the centre. In the colonial days, these things were being done on the ground and they could give bursaries and build roads. I commend devolution. Those who fear devolution are living in the past. They are being guided by their ethnic consideration and objectives. They are living in the past. If America was living in a situation where they feared ethnicity and did not see itself as a multiparty state or nation, how could a young man born here in Kenya, who is not even a native American, become the President of America? It is because they did away with exclusion. What has killed us here is exclusion; that once Mr. Orengo is President, I know of no other place than Ugenya. That is why we were fighting against these many Presidencies in the past. I hope that Kenya will come of age. This country must come of age. People want freedom and nations want liberation, but countries want independence.

EXHIBIT 55

Screen Capture of Original Kenyan Hansard Web site, March 25, 2010

Mr. James Maina Kamau: Mr. Speaker, Sir, I would like to appreciate the answer given by the hon. Member but I would like to indicate to this House that there are over 2,000 lying out there, especially in the British Museum. Others are spread across the USA Museum. What are they doing? It looks like it is taking them too long to make sure that those artefacts are brought to Kenya? We need them in Kenya because they are important. They teach our young people what was happening in those days.

Mr. ole Ntimama: Mr. Speaker, Sir, as I have said in my answer, we are trying our best and the good team from my Ministry has been visiting some of these countries to try and identify all the artefacts that are there and negotiate their return. So, we are not asleep but doing our best.

Dr. Khalwale: Mr. Speaker, Sir, the Minister has told us that the office of the then Senator Obama gave him a lot of assistance. That is very good to hear. Could he tell us what commitment the same office made by way of compensation to this country because those artefacts in those museums have been attracting visitors who were paying to view them? What commitment did they make about compensation and more importantly, the biggest artefact in the USA today that belongs to this country is one Barrack Obama. How does he intend to repatriate himself or part of the money that is realized from all the royalties that he is attracting across the whole world?

EXHIBIT 56

Screen Capture of Original Kenyan National Assembly Web site, April 14, 2010

2   *Headline News*

A New Face in Politics

By BENNETT GUIRA

Barack Obama was born on August 4, 1961 at the Queen's Medical Center in Honolulu, Hawaii. Obama lived here with his parents Barack Obama, Sr. and Ann Dunham until they divorced when he was two. Obama moved back to Hawaii when he was ten and lived with his grandmother Madelyn Dunham and half-sister of our very own, Maya Soetoro. They both attended Punahou School together when they both lived here.

Ms. Soetoro explained, "He's my brother. We share the same mother, though our fathers are different. His father was Barack Obama Sr., a Kenyan economist who met our mother at the East West Center. My father was our mother's second husband after she divorced Obama. Soetoro was from Indonesia and in the late 1960s the family moved to the island of Java where I was born."

Ms. Soetoro also added, "In many ways our relationship was like that of any brother and sister. I irritated him by standing in front of the TV when he was trying to watch a basketball game. We hugged and bickered in equal measure. But since Barack is nine years older than I am and my mother and father divorced when I was nine years old, at some point he became my mentor and guide. He gave me a lot of the advice and council that a father would give. He showed me life's treasures and helped me to make fewer mistakes as I was growing up."

Photos courtesy of Ms. Soetoro

The families of Ms. Soetoro and Senator Obama dinning together after his recent election win

Obama first graduated from Columbia University with a degree in political science and a specialty in international relations. He then attended Harvard Law School and graduated magna cum laude, and he was the first African-American to be president of the Harvard Law Review.

Besides his impressive educational background, Obama has also been a great community leader in Chicago. After graduating from Columbia, he became a community organizer in Chicago's toughest neighborhoods. He assisted church groups to form job-training programs, he helped improve school areas, and improved city services. After graduating from Harvard, he became a civil rights lawyer in federal and state courts, focusing on voting rights and employment discrimination cases.

Obama, a Democrat, is now the Senator of Illinois' 13th Senate District on Chicago's South side. During his campaign for U.S. Senator of Illinois, he defeated his Democratic rival in the primary, Blair Hull. His Republican opponent, Jack Ryan was forced to dropout of the race after Republican leaders questioned his integrity.

"He showed me life's treasures and helped me to make fewer mistakes as I was growing up" -Ms. Soetoro

continued on page 15

EXHIBIT 57

Screen Capture of the Original Rainbow Edition Newsletter, 2004
Lists Queen's Medical Center as Birth Hospital

Early life and career

Main article: *Early life and career of Barack Obama*

Obama was born on August 4, 1961, at Kapiʻolani Maternity & Gynecological Hospital (now called Kapiʻolani Medical Center for Women and Children) in Honolulu, Hawaii,[4] the first President to have been born in Hawaii.[5] His mother,

E X H I B I T   5 8

Screen Capture of Wikipedia, "Barack Obama" Entry, October 2010

Barack Hussein OBAMA was born on 4 August 1961 at the ▓▓▓▓ Medical Center in Honolulu, Hawaii, to Barack Hussein OBAMA, Sr. of

Nyangoma-Kogelo, Siaya District, Kenya, and Ann DUNHAM of Wichita, Kansas. His parents met while both were attending the East-West Center of

the University of Hawaii at Manoa, where his father was enrolled as a foreign student. When Barack Obama was two years old, his parents divorced

and his father moved to Connecticut to continue his education before returning to Kenya.

When Obama was six, his mother married Lolo Soetoro, an Indonesian oil manager and moved to Jakarta, Indonesia. Obama's half-sister, Maya

E X H I B I T   5 9

Screen Capture of Original Library of Congress Genealogical Listing for Barack Obama
Lists Queen's Medical Center as Birth Hospital

Ancestry of Barack Obama	
1	*Barack* Hussein **Obama** II, U.S. Senator from Illinois, U.S. President from 2009, b. Kapiolani Medical Center, Honolulu, Hawaii, 4 Aug. 1961, m. at Trinity United Church of Christ, Chicago, 3 Oct. 1992 Michelle LaVaughn Robinson, b. Chicago 17 Jan. 1964, dau. of Frasier Robinson and of Marian Shields. Further details of her ancestry can be found here.
PARENTS	
2	Barack Hussein **Obama**, Ph. D., b. Alego, Kenya [on the shores of Lake Victoria], ... 1936, senior economist in the Kenyan Ministry of Finance, d. Nairobi, Kenya, ... 1982, bur. Alego m. Maui, Hawaii, 2 Feb. 1961, div. filed Honolulu, Hawaii Jan. 1964
3	S[tanley] *Ann* **Dunham**, b. Wichita, Kansas, 29 Nov. 1942, d. Straub Clinic, Honolulu, Hawaii, 7 Nov. 1995 [*SSDI* 535-40-8522]
GRANDPARENTS	
4	*Onyango*, later "Hussein *Onyango* **Obama**", b. ... [Luo-speaking village], Kenya, ... 1895, d. ... 1979, bur. Alego m. ... , sep. 1945
5	*Akumu*, b. ... , d. ...

EXHIBIT 60

Screen Capture of Scrubbed Library of Congress Genealogical Listing for Barack Obama Lists
Kapi'olani Medical Center as Birth Hospital

EXHIBIT 61

Screen Capture of Obama 2008 Campaign Web site: "Obama—Ancestry"
Lists Queen's Medical Center as Birth Hospital

THE WHITE HOUSE

WASHINGTON

January 24, 2009

Kapiʻolani Medical Center

Dear Friends,

I am writing to share congratulations on the centennial celebration of the Kapiʻolani Medical Center for Women & Children.

Kapiʻolani was one of Hawaiʻi's earliest hospitals, and it has served many generations of Hawaiʻi's people with distinction. The Medical Center reaches out to children of all backgrounds, and treats more than 62,000 children per year. As a beneficiary of the excellence of Kapiʻolani Medical Center - the place of my birth - I am pleased to add my voice to your chorus of supporters.

Hawaiʻi has always been a home to me, and I'm pleased to take part in your celebration. Thank you for your hard work, and I wish you all the best for the next one hundred years.

Sincerely,

Barack Obama

EXHIBIT 62

Obama Letter to Kapiʻolani as Originally Posted on Kapiʻolani Web site

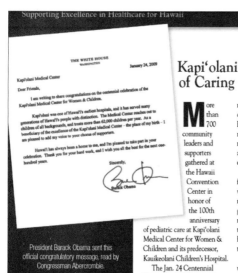

EXHIBIT 63

Screen Capture of Obama Letter in Kapi'olani Inspire Magazine

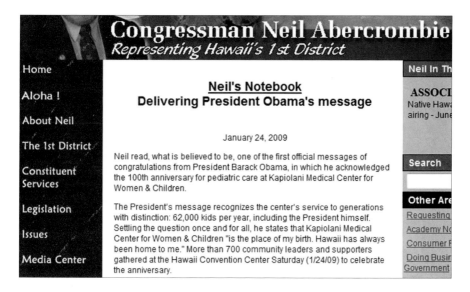

EXHIBIT 64

Screen Capture of Rep. Abercrombie Web site, January 2009

```
451  <table style="BORDER-RIGHT: #cccccc 1px solid; PADDING-RIGHT: 12px; BORDER-TOP: #cccccc 1px solid; PADDING-
     LEFT: 12px; PADDING-BOTTOM: 12px; BORDER-LEFT: #cccccc 1px solid; PADDING-TOP: 12px; BORDER-BOTTOM:
     #cccccc 1px solid" cellspacing="0" cellpadding="0" width="380" align="center" border="0">
452  <tbody>
453  <tr>
454  <td><p align="center"><img title="images/thewhitehouse.jpg" alt="images/thewhitehouse.jpg"
     src="/images/thewhitehouse.jpg" border="0" /></p>
455  <p align="center"> </p>
456  <p align="right">January 24, 2009</p>
457  <p align="right"> </p>
458  <p align="left">Kapi`olani Medical Center</p>
459  <p align="left"> </p>
460  <p align="left">Dear Friends,</p>
461  <p align="left"> </p>
462  <p align="left">          I am writing to share congratulations on the centennial celebration of the
     Kapi`olani Medical Center for Women &amp; Children.</p>
463  <p align="left"> </p>
464  <p align="left">          Kapi`olani was one of Hawai`i's earliest hospitals, and it has served many
     generations of Hawai`i's people with distinction. The Medical Center reaches out to children of all
     backgrounds, and treats more than 62,000 children per year. As a beneficiary of the excellence of
     Kapi`olani Medical Center - the place of my birth - I am pleased to add my voice to your chorus of
     supporters.</p>
465  <p align="left"> </p>
466  <p align="left">          Hawai`i has always been a home to me, and I'm pleased to take part in your
     celebration. Thank you for your hard work, and I wish you all the best for the next one hundred years.</p>
467  <p align="left"> </p>
468  <p align="right">Sincerely,                          </p>
469  <p align="right"><img title="images/barackobama_signature.jpg" alt="images/barackobama_signature.jpg"
     src="/images/barackobama_signature.jpg" border="0" /></p>
470  <p align="right"> Barack Obama                    </p>
471  </td>
472  </tr>
473  </tbody>
```

EXHIBIT 65

Second Screen Capture of Source Code, Purported Obama Letter to Kapi'olani Hospital,
Dated January 24, 2009

```
447  <!--
448  <p align="center"> </p>
449  <p align="center"><b>Read a very special congratulatory message sent by President Barack Obama and read by
     Representative Neil Abercrombie.</b></p>
450  <p align="center"> </p>
451  <p align="center"></p>
452  <table style="BORDER-RIGHT: #cccccc 1px solid; PADDING-RIGHT: 12px; BORDER-TOP: #cccccc 1px solid; PADDING-LEFT: 12px;
     PADDING-BOTTOM: 12px; BORDER-LEFT: #cccccc 1px solid; PADDING-TOP: 12px; BORDER-BOTTOM: #cccccc 1px solid"
     cellspacing="0" cellpadding="0" width="380" align="center" border="0">
453  <tbody>
454  <tr>
455  <td><p align="center"><img title="images/thewhitehouse.jpg" alt="images/thewhitehouse.jpg"
     src="/images/thewhitehouse.jpg" border="0" /></p>
456  <p align="center"> </p>
457  <p align="right">January 24, 2009</p>
458  <p align="right"> </p>
459  <p align="left">Kapi`olani Medical Center</p>
460  <p align="left"> </p>
461  <p align="left">Dear Friends,</p>
462  <p align="left"> </p>
463  <p align="left">          I am writing to share congratulations on the centennial celebration of the Kapi`olani Medical
     Center for Women &amp; Children.</p>
464  <p align="left"> </p>
465  <p align="left">          Kapi`olani was one of Hawai`i's earliest hospitals, and it has served many generations of
     Hawai`i's people with distinction. The Medical Center reaches out to children of all backgrounds, and treats more than
     62,000 children per year. As a beneficiary of the excellence of Kapi`olani Medical Center - the place of my birth - I
     am pleased to add my voice to your chorus of supporters.</p>
466  <p align="left"> </p>
467  <p align="left">          Hawai`i has always been a home to me, and I'm pleased to take part in your celebration. Thank
     you for your hard work, and I wish you all the best for the next one hundred years.</p>
468  <p align="left"> </p>
469  <p align="right">Sincerely,                          </p>
470  <p align="right"><img title="images/barackobama_signature.jpg" alt="images/barackobama_signature.jpg"
     src="/images/barackobama_signature.jpg" border="0" /></p>
471  <p align="right"> Barack Obama                    </p>
472  </td>
473  </tr>
```

EXHIBIT 66

Screen Capture of HTML Source Code "Commenting Out" the Supposed Letter Obama
Sent to Kapi'olani Hospital, Dated January 24, 2009

EXHIBIT 67
Letterhead and Signature, President Obama's Letter to Kapi'olani, Dated January 24, 2008,
Proof Letterhead and Signature Were Both Electronic Images

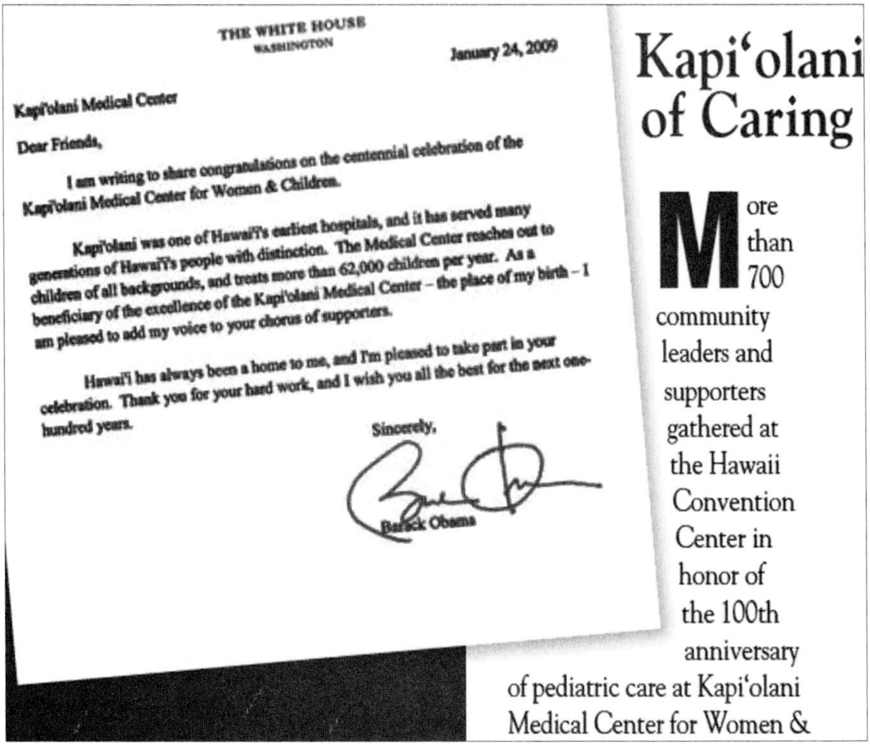

THE WHITE HOUSE
WASHINGTON

January 24, 2009

Kapi'olani Medical Center

Dear Friends,

I am writing to share congratulations on the centennial celebration of the Kapi'olani Medical Center for Women & Children.

Kapi'olani was one of Hawai'i's earliest hospitals, and it has served many generations of Hawai'i's people with distinction. The Medical Center reaches out to children of all backgrounds, and treats more than 62,000 children per year. As a beneficiary of the excellence of the Kapi'olani Medical Center – the place of my birth – I am pleased to add my voice to your chorus of supporters.

Hawai'i has always been a home to me, and I'm pleased to take part in your celebration. Thank you for your hard work, and I wish you all the best for the next one-hundred years.

Sincerely,

Barack Obama

Kapi'olani of Caring

More than 700 community leaders and supporters gathered at the Hawaii Convention Center in honor of the 100th anniversary of pediatric care at Kapi'olani Medical Center for Women &

EXHIBIT 68
Screen Capture of Obama Letter in Kapi'olani Inspire Magazine
Close-up of Obama Letter

Sincerely,

Barack Obama

EXHIBIT 69
Obama Signature in Kapi'olani Letter on Web site

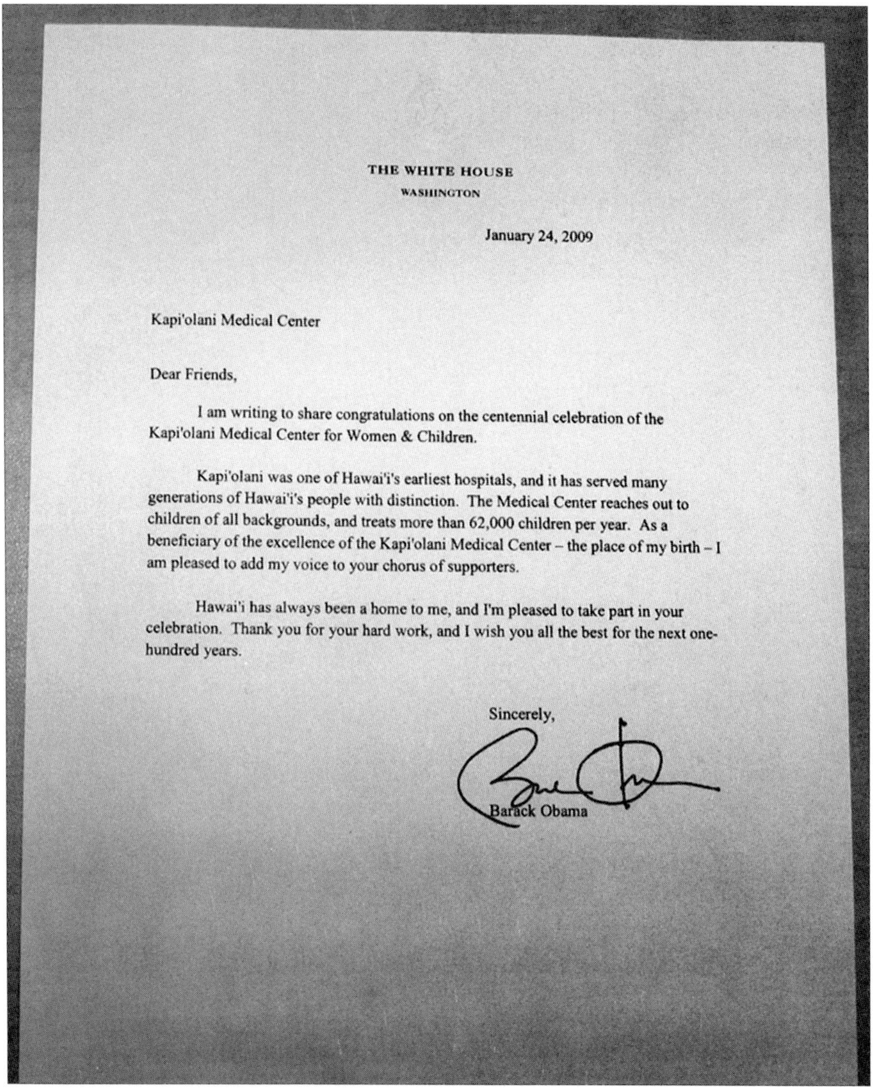

THE WHITE HOUSE
WASHINGTON

January 24, 2009

Kapi'olani Medical Center

Dear Friends,

I am writing to share congratulations on the centennial celebration of the Kapi'olani Medical Center for Women & Children.

Kapi'olani was one of Hawai'i's earliest hospitals, and it has served many generations of Hawai'i's people with distinction. The Medical Center reaches out to children of all backgrounds, and treats more than 62,000 children per year. As a beneficiary of the excellence of the Kapi'olani Medical Center – the place of my birth – I am pleased to add my voice to your chorus of supporters.

Hawai'i has always been a home to me, and I'm pleased to take part in your celebration. Thank you for your hard work, and I wish you all the best for the next one-hundred years.

Sincerely,

Barack Obama

Exhibit 70

Kapio'lani Medical Center Claimed Electronic Version of Original Obama Letter
Sent From White House

EXHIBIT 71

Embossed Seal
Kapio'lani Medical Center Claimed Electronic Version of Original Obama Letter
Sent From White House

Claim: *Barack Hussein Obama was born in Honolulu, Hawaii, to Barack Hussein Obama, Sr., a black MUSLIM from Nyangoma-Kogel, Kenya and Ann Dunh am, a white ATHEIST from Wichita, Kansas. Obama's parents met at the University of Hawaii.*

Barack Hussein Obama (Senator Obama's father) was born on the shores of Lake Victoria in Alego, Kenya. He met and married an American woman, Ann Dunham of Wichita, Kansas, while they were both attending the University of Hawaii. Their son, also named Barack Hussein Obama was born on 4 August 1961 at the Queen's Medical Center in Honolulu, Hawaii.

Although the elder Obama was raised as a Muslim, no evidence supports the claim that he was ever a "radical Muslim," and Senator Obama's family histories note that his father was an atheist or agnostic (i.e., no longer a practicing Muslim) by the time he married the younger Obama's mother. Of his mother's religious views, Senator Obama wrote:

EXHIBIT 72

Screen Capture, Snopes.com, Original Text Listing Queen's Medical Center
as Obama Birth Hospital

Claim: *Barack Hussein Obama was born in Honolulu, Hawaii, to Barack Hussein Obama, Sr., a black MUSLIM from Nyangoma-Kogel, Kenya and Ann Dunh am, a white ATHEIST from Wichita, Kansas. Obama's parents met at the University of Hawaii.*

Barack Hussein Obama (Senator Obama's father) was born on the shores of Lake Victoria in Alego, Kenya. He met and married an American woman, Ann Dunham of Wichita, Kansas, while they were both attending the University of Hawaii. Their son, also named Barack Hussein Obama, was born on 4 August 1961 at the Kapiolani Medical Center in Honolulu, Hawaii. (News accounts have also variously reported his birth as having occurred at Queen's Medical Center in Honolulu.)

EXHIBIT 73

Screen Capture, Snopes.com, Scrubbed Text
Listing Kapi'olani Medical Center as Obama Birth Hospital

Published: Nov. 4, 2008 at 11:14 PM
Order reprints

WASHINGTON, Nov. 4 (UPI) -- Sen. Barack
Obama, D-Ill., made history Tuesday by
becoming the first African-American to win
the U.S. presidency.

On a freezing day in February 2007, the first-
term U.S. senator announced his candidacy for
president outside the Old State Capitol in
Springfield, Ill., saying he could not wait until
politics "boil the hope out of him." His bestselling third book was called "The Audacity of
Hope: Thoughts on Reclaiming the American
Dream."

He said his late mother, Stanley Ann Dunham,
who died of cancer at 53, and his
grandmother, Madelyn Payne Dunham, 86,
taught him how to dream and value hard work,
and were the guiding forces of his life.

Sen. Barack Obama, D-Ill. (UPI Photo/Roger L.
Wollenberg/FILE) | Enlarge ⊕

Obama described his birth at Queen's Medical
Center in Hawaii Aug. 4, 1961, to a young
white woman from Kansas and a father of Luo
ethnicity from Nyanza Province in Kenya, as an
"all-America" story transcending orthodox racial
stereotypes and experience. Even his name --

Official GM Site
Change at GM is Under Way. Visit
Official Site to See How.
www.GMReinvention.com

Soybean Outlook Report
As demand for soybeans shifts, what

Exhibit 74

Screen Capture, United Press International, Original Text
Listing Queen's Medical Center as Obama Birth Hospital

Published: Nov. 4, 2008 at 11:14 PM
Order reprints

WASHINGTON, Nov. 4 (UPI) -- Sen. Barack
Obama, D-Ill., made history Tuesday by
becoming the first African-American to win
the U.S. presidency.

On a freezing day in February 2007, the first-
term U.S. senator announced his candidacy for
president outside the Old State Capitol in
Springfield, Ill., saying he could not wait until
politics "boil the hope out of him." His bestselling third book was called "The Audacity of
Hope: Thoughts on Reclaiming the American
Dream."

He said his late mother, Stanley Ann Dunham,
who died of cancer at 53, and his
grandmother, Madelyn Payne Dunham, 86,
taught him how to dream and value hard work,
and were the guiding forces of his life.

Obama described his birth at Kapi'olani Medical
Center for Women and Children in Hawaii Aug.
4, 1961, to a young white woman from Kansas

Sen. Barack Obama, D-Ill. (UPI Photo/Roger L.
Wollenberg/FILE) | Enlarge 🔍

ECONOMIC CRISIS!

Exhibit 75
Screen Capture, United Press International, Original Text
Listing Kapi'olani Medical Center as Obama Birth Hospital

Jerome Corsi

From: Stuart Lau [stuartl@hawaii.edu]
Sent: Monday, July 27, 2009 1:42 PM
To: Jerome Corsi
Subject: Re: Is the following informtion correct?

Dear Mr. Corsi,

The University of Hawaii at Manoa is only able to provide the following information for Stanley Ann Dunham:

Dates of Attendance:
Fall 1960
Spring 1963 – Summer 1966
Fall 1972 – Fall 1974
2nd Summer 1976
Spring 1978
Fall 1984 – 2nd Summer 1992

Degrees Awarded:
BA – Mathematics, Summer 1967 (August 6, 1967)
MA – Anthropology, Fall 1983 (December 18, 1963)
PHD – Anthropology, Summer 1992 (August 9, 1992)

Sincerely,
Stuart Lau

****
Stuart Lau
University Registrar
Office of Admissions and Records
University of Hawaii at Manoa
Ph: (808) 956-8010
****

Exhibit 76
Email from Stuart Lau, University of Hawaii, to WND
Dated July 27, 2009

From:	Stuart Lau [stuartl@hawaii.edu]
Sent:	Monday, August 03, 2009 4:46 PM
To:	jrlc@optonline.net
Subject:	Re: Dates

Dear Mr. Corsi,

The Fall 1960 term ended on January 31, 1961.

Sincerely,
Stuart Lau

EXHIBIT 77

Email from Stuart Lau, University of Hawaii, to WND, Dated August 3, 2009

Jerome Corsi

From:	Stuart Lau [stuartl@hawaii.edu]
Sent:	Friday, July 31, 2009 3:01 PM
To:	Jerome Corsi
Subject:	Re: RE: Is the following informtion correct?

Dear Mr. Corsi,

The University of Hawaii at Manoa is only able to provide the following information for Barack Obama:

Barack Obama

Dates of Attendance:
Fall 1959 – Spring 1962

Degrees Awarded:
BA – Economics, Spring 1962

Sincerely,
Stuart Lau

****
Stuart Lau
University Registrar
Office of Admissions and Records
University of Hawaii at Manoa
Ph: (808) 956-8010
****

EXHIBIT 78

Email from Stuart Lau, University of Hawaii, to WND, Dated July 31, 2009

UNIVERSITY OF WASHINGTON
Office of Public Records and Open Public Meetings
4311 11th Ave NE Suite 360, Seattle, WA 98105
Campus Mail: Box 354997

Prepared for release:

Wednesday, July 29, 2009

Jerome Corsi
World Net Daily

RE: Public Records request #09-11716

Dear Mr. Corsi:

The attached is provided in response to Public Records request #09-11716, in which you requested a copy of Stanley Ann Dunham's records.

The records responsive to your request from the University of Washington are enclosed as provided by the Public Disclosure Laws of Washington State. This concludes the University's response to your Public Records request. Please feel free to contact our office if you have any questions or concerns.

Sincerely,

Madolyne Lawson
Office of Public Records

Exhibit 79

Letter from University of Washington to WND, Dated July 29, 2009

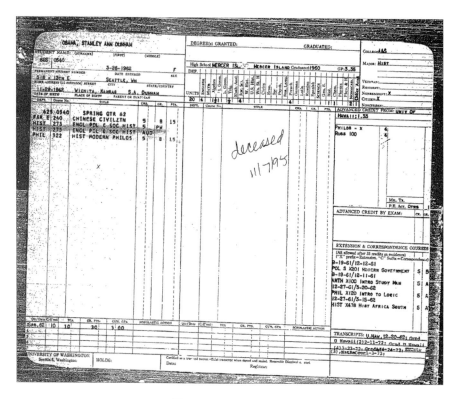

EXHIBIT 80

Ann Dunham Transcript Card, University of Washington

```
OBAMA,S1AN:    ANN DUNHAM              MERCER ISLAND HS        06/01/60    02/13/09      1

6250540                    11/29/42   NONRESIDENT CITIZEN       FEMALE      REG1524      PSEUD
                                                    NO LONGER ENROLLED (LAST QTR SPRING 1962)
FRESHMAN        Arts & Sciences
                HISTORY



****************************************************
*  ANY ALTERATION OR MODIFICATION OF THIS RECORD   *
*  OR ANY COPY THEREOF MAY CONSTITUTE A FELONY      *
*  AND/OR LEAD TO STUDENT DISCIPLINARY SANCTIONS.   *
****************************************************

HIGH SCHOOL GPA: 3.35

DETAIL OF TRANSFER CREDIT:
UNIV HAWAII: MANOA, HI (4 YEAR SCHOOL)
PHIL   1XX                     4.0
RUSS   100                     4.0
TOTAL CREDITS EARNED:          8.0 GPA:1.35

SUMMARY OF TRANSFER CREDIT:    LD      UD     TOTAL
TOTAL CREDITS EARNED:          8.0    0.0      8.0
TOTAL TOWARD DEGREE:           8.0    0.0      8.0

EXTENSION/INDEPENDENT STDY/ADVANCE PLACEMENT CREDIT:

UNIVERSITY OF WASHINGTON EXTENSION COURSES:
ANTH   100 INTRO STUDY MAN       5.0   A
 (08/19/61-12/11/61)
POL S  201 MODERN GOVERNMENT     5.0   B
 (08/19/61-12/12/61)
HIST   478 HIST AFRICA SOUTH     5.0   A
 (12/27/61-03/15/62)
PHIL   120 INTRO TO LOGIC        5.0   A
 (12/27/61-03/20/62)

TOTAL EXTENSION/CORRESPONDENCE/AP CREDIT:  20.0
TOTAL APPLIED TOWARD NEXT DEGREE:          20.0
---------------------------------------------------
                SPRING 1962          HIST   1
FAR E  240  CHIN CIVILIZATION      5.0   B
HIST   273  ENGL POL & SOC HIST    5.0   PW
PHIL   322  HIST MODERN PHILOS     5.0   B
        QTR ATTEMPTED: 10.0 EARNED: 10.0 GPA:  3.00
        QTR GRADED AT: 10.0    GRADE POINTS: 30.0
CUM ATTEMPTED: 10.0 UW EARNED: 10.0 TTL EARNED: 10.0
CUM GRADED AT: 10.0 GRADE PTS: 30.0 CUM GPA:  3.00

****************************************************
CUMULATIVE CREDIT SUMMARY:
UW CREDITS ATTEMPTED  10.0  UW CREDITS EARNED  10.0
UW GRADED ATTEMPTED   10.0  EXTENSION CREDITS  20.0
UW GRADED EARNED      10.0  TRANSFER CREDITS    8.0
UW GRADE POINTS       30.0  ------------------------
UW GRADE POINT AVG.    3.00 CREDITS EARNED     38.0
****************************************************
****************  END OF RECORD  ****************



        FOR INTERNAL USE ONLY
                                        ****************************************************
                                        ********  UNOFFICIAL DEPARTMENT COPY  ********
                                        ******  DESTROY WHEN NO LONGER NEEDED   ******
                                        ****************************************************
```

Exhibit 81

Ann Dunham Computer Transcript, University of Washington, Original Transcript,
Received by WND with Universty of Washington Letter, Dated July 29, 2009

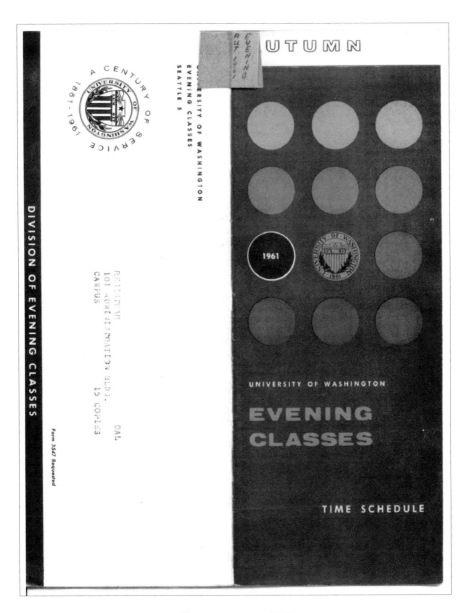

EXHIBIT 82

Bulletin, University of Washington Evening Classes, Autumn 1961

lish will present a distinguished faculty in this series designed to discuss the ideal societies of the past and the contributions writers and thinkers in this area have made to our literature and various philosophies.

Th; 7:30-9:30; October 5-November 30 (holiday, November 23); $15 ($22 family rate).

POLITICS AND THE ARTS (LS229)

In this series, coordinated by **Dr. Morton Kroll** of the Department of Political Science, we shall consider the artist and work as they relate to his political environment. Though our emphasis will be on the status, plight, and work of artists of all ages and societies, we shall focus more directly on the contemporary scene. The major art media will be considered.

W; 7:30-9:30; October 4-November 29 (classes will not meet November 22); $15 ($22 family rate).

PERSPECTIVES ON AFRICA TODAY (LS230)

The rapidity with which African states have been emerging to take their places in the family of nations is sufficient reason to take a closer look at the new developments in sub-Saharan Africa and to examine their impact upon our thought and action. **Prof. C. Edward Hopen** of the Department of Anthropology will coordinate this series which will allow experienced African observers to discuss the geographical and historical as well as contemporary problems and prospects.

T; 7:30-9:30; October 3-November 28; $15 ($22 family rate).

MAN'S VIEW OF MAN IN THE TWENTIETH CENTURY (LS231)

Prof. Melvin M. Rader and other members of the Department of Philosophy will explore recent concepts of the nature of man focusing attention on some of the major philosophies of the twentieth century. The meaning of human life and values will be discussed in relation to the conflicts and pressures of society today.

W; 7:30-9:30; October 4-November 29 (classes will not meet November 22); $15 ($22 family rate).

WITHDRAWAL INFORMATION is fully outlined in the Evening Classes Annual Bulletin. OFFICIAL WITHDRAWALS must be made by contacting the Division of Evening Classes, LAkeview 4-6000, Ext. 2501. NOTIFICATION TO YOUR INSTRUCTOR IS NOT AN OFFICIAL WITHDRAWAL.

12

CREDIT AND INFORMAL (noncredit) COURSES

FOR INFORMAL CLASSES MAIL REGISTRATION COUPON, SEE BACK COVER

ANTHROPOLOGY

X100 **Introduction to the Study of Man (5)**
Not open to students who have taken 390.
MW; 7-9:10; Sept. 25-Dec. 11; $40.

X203 **Archaeology: The Dawn of Tradition (5)**
(Formerly 103.) Prerequisite, 100 or sophomore standing.
TTh; 7-9:10; Sept. 26-Dec. 12; $40.

X211 **Oceania (3)**
MW; 7-8:30; Sept. 25-Dec. 4; $27.

ARCHITECTURE

X100 **Architectural Appreciation (2)**
M; 7-9; Sept. 25-Nov. 27; $16.

ART

X105, 106, 107 **Drawing (2 each)**
Prerequisites, 105 for 106; 106 for 107.
Sec. 1: MW; 7-10; Sept. 25-Nov. 1; $29.
Sec. 2: TTh; 7-10; Sept. 26-Nov. 2; $29.

X109, 110, 111 **Design (2 each)**
No previous experience required for 109. Prerequisites, 109 for 110; 110 for 111.
Sec. 1: MW; 7-10; Sept. 25-Nov. 1; $29.
Sec. 2: TTh; 7-10; Sept. 26-Nov. 2; $29.

X201, 202, 203 **Ceramic Art (3 each)**
Prerequisites, sophomore standing in art or permission for 201; 201 for 202; 202 or equivalent in experience for 203.
TTh; 7-10; Sept. 26-Nov. 9; $20 plus $12 materials fee ($32).

X212 **History of Western Art through the Renaissance (2)**
M; 7-9; Sept. 25-Nov. 27; $16.

X256, 257 **Painting (2 each)**
Prerequisites, 107 and 111, or permission for 256; 256 for 257.
TTh; 7-10; Sept. 26-Nov. 2; $29.

X258 **Water Color (2)**
Prerequisite, 257 or permission.
TTh; 7-10; Sept. 26-Nov. 2; $29.

X259 **Advanced Water Color (2)**
Prerequisite, 258.
TTh; 7-10; Sept. 26-Nov. 2; $29.

X261 **Elementary Interior Design (2)**
For nonmajors.
Th; 7-10:15; Sept. 28-Dec. 14; $29.

13

EXHIBIT 83

Bulletin, University of Washington Evening Classes, Autumn 1961; Listing Ann Dunham's Antrhopology Course, Extension School

X221 **Elements of Differential Equations (3)**
(Formerly 321.) Prerequisite, 126 (formerly 252) or 136
(formerly 262).
MTh; 7-8:30; Sept. 25-Dec. 4; $27.

X224 **Intermediate Analysis (3)**
(Formerly 253.) Prerequisite, 126 (formerly 252) or 136
(formerly 262).
MTh; 7-8:30; Sept. 25-Dec. 4; $27.

X324 **Advanced Calculus I (3)**
Prerequisite, 225 or 136 (formerly 262).
Sec. 1 through 3: MTh; 7-8:30; Sept. 25-Dec. 4; $27

X391 **Elementary Probability (3)**
Prerequisite, 126 (formerly 252) or 136 (formerly 262).
MTh; 7-8:30; Sept. 25-Dec. 4; $27.

X401 **Matrices (3)**
Prerequisite, 126 (formerly 252) or 136 (formerly 262) or
130.
MTh; 7-8:30; Sept. 25-Dec. 4; $27.

X427 **Topics in Applied Analysis (3)**
Prerequisite, 324 or 325.
Sec. 1 and 2: MTh; 7:30-8:30; Sept. 25-Dec. 4; $27.

Deficiency Course

XD **Survey of Plane Geometry (½ credit)**
Prerequisite, XC or departmental permission.
MTh; 7-8:30; Sept. 25-Dec. 4; $27.

MUSIC

X107 **Survey of Music (5)**
For nonmajors.
W; 6-10; Sept. 27-Dec. 13; $40.

X121 **Elementary Music Theory (2)**
For nonmajors.
M; 7-9; Sept. 25-Nov. 27; $16.

X317 **Chamber Music (2)**
For nonmajors. Prerequisite, 107 or 108.
Th; 7-9; Sept. 28-Dec. 7; $16.

OCEANOGRAPHY

X101 **Survey of Oceanography (5)**
Recommended for nonmajors.
TTh; 7-9:10; Sept. 26-Dec. 12; $40.

PHILOSOPHY

X100 **Introduction to Philosophy (5)**
(Not open to those who have taken Humanities 103.)
MW; 7-9:10; Sept. 25-Dec. 11; $40.

NONCREDIT COURSES: REGISTER BY MAIL
See inside back cover for the registration coupon.

26

PHYSICAL EDUCATION

All students assume full responsibility for their health and physical condition. Questions concerning standards of fitness should be directed to the Men's or Women's Physical and Health Education Departments.

N10 **Golf (noncredit)**
Open to men and women sixteen years of age and over.
Clubs furnished, student supplies golf balls. Fee includes
$1.50 greens fee. Golf Club, Campus.
Sec. 1: S; 10-11; Sept. 30-Dec. 9; $13.50.
Sec. 2: S; 11-12; Sept. 30-Dec. 9; $13.50.

N19 **Swimming (Men) (noncredit)**
For men sixteen years of age and over. Men's pool, behind Edmundson Pavilion.
W; 7:30-8:30; Sept. 27-Dec. 6; $12.50.

N20 **Intermediate Swimming (Men) (noncredit)**
For men sixteen years of age and over. Prerequisite, N19
or comparable experience. Men's pool, behind Edmundson Pavilion.
W; 7:30-8:30; Sept. 27-Dec. 6; $12.50.

N61, 62 **Beginning and Elementary Swimming (Women)**
(noncredit)
For women sixteen years of age and over. Prerequisite,
N61 or comparable experience for N62. Hutchinson Hall,
pool entrance.
Sec. 1: M; 7-8; Sept. 25-Nov. 27; $12.50.
Sec. 2: T; 7-8; Sept. 26-Nov. 28; $12.50.

N63, 64 **Intermediate and Advanced Swimming (Women)**
(noncredit)
For women sixteen years of age and over. Prerequisites,
N62 or comparable experience for N63; N63 or comparable experience for N64. Hutchinson Hall, pool entrance.
Sec. 1: M; 8-9; Sept. 25-Nov. 27; $12.50.
Sec. 2: T; 8-9; Sept. 26-Nov. 28; $12.50.

POLITICAL SCIENCE

X201 **Modern Government (5)**
TTh; 7-9:10; Sept. 26-Dec. 12; $40.

X470 **Introduction to Public Administration (5)**
MW; 7-9:10; Sept. 25-Dec. 11; $40.

PSYCHOLOGY

X100 **General Psychology (5)**
Sec. 1 and 2: MW; 7-9:10; Sept. 25-Dec. 11; $40.
Sec. 3: TTh; 7-9:10; Sept. 26-Dec. 12; $40.

X101 **Psychology of Adjustment (5)**
Prerequisite, 100.
TTh; 7-9:10; Sept. 26-Dec. 12; $40.

X306 **Developmental Psychology (5)**
For nonmajors only. Not open to students who have
taken 308. Prerequisite, 100.
MW; 7-9:10; Sept. 25-Dec. 11; $40.

27

EXHIBIT 84

Bulletin, University of Washington Evening Classes, Autumn 1961;
Listing Ann Dunham's Political Science Course, Extension School

UNIVERSITY OF WASHINGTON
OFFICE OF THE REGISTRAR

ACADEMIC TRANSCRIPT
THE WORD "COPY" APPEARS WHEN PHOTOCOPIED
A BLACK AND WHITE DOCUMENT IS NOT OFFICIAL

OBAMA, STANLEY ANN DUNHAM			MERCER ISLAND HS	06/01/60	08/18/09	1
6250540		11/29/42	NONRESIDENT CITIZEN		FEMALE	ONEILDL	PSEUD
FRESHMAN	Arts & Sciences HISTORY					

```
****************************************************
*  ANY ALTERATION OR MODIFICATION OF THIS RECORD   *
*  OR ANY COPY THEREOF MAY CONSTITUTE A FELONY      *
*  AND/OR LEAD TO STUDENT DISCIPLINARY SANCTIONS.   *
****************************************************


SUMMARY OF TRANSFER CREDIT:
  UNIV HAWAII: MANOA              8.0
     TRANSFER CREDIT ACCEPTED:    8.0

EXTENSION/INDEPENDENT STDY/ADVANCE PLACEMENT CREDIT:

UNIVERSITY OF WASHINGTON EXTENSION COURSES:
  ANTH   100 INTRO STUDY MAN      5.0   A
    (09/19/61-12/11/61)
  POL S  201 MODERN GOVERNMENT    5.0   B
    (09/19/61-12/12/61)
  HIST   478 HIST AFRICA SOUTH    5.0   A
    (12/27/61-03/15/62)
  PHIL   120 INTRO TO LOGIC       5.0   A
    (12/27/61-03/20/62)
  ----------------------------------------------
  TOTAL EXTENSION/CORRESPONDENCE/AP CREDIT:  20.0
  TOTAL APPLIED TOWARD NEXT DEGREE:          20.0

           SPRING 1962          HIST     1
  FAR E  240 CHIN CIVILIZATION   5.0   B
  HIST   273 ENGL POL & SOC HIST 5.0   PW
  PHIL   322 HIST MODERN PHILOS  5.0   B
           QTR  ATTEMPTED: 10.0 EARNED: 10.0 GPA: 3.00

****************************************************
CUMULATIVE CREDIT SUMMARY:
  UW CREDITS ATTEMPTED   10.0  UW CREDITS EARNED   10.0
  UW GRADED ATTEMPTED    10.0  EXTENSION CREDITS   20.0
  UW GRADED EARNED       10.0  TRANSFER CREDITS     8.0
  UW GRADE POINTS        30.0  ------------------------
  UW GRADE POINT AVG.    3.00  CREDITS EARNED      38.0
****************************************************
*****************  END OF RECORD  *****************
```

EXHIBIT 85

Ann Dunham Computer Transcript, University of Washington, Revised Transcript,
Received by WND from Universty of Washington, February 2011

Exhibit 86
1961–1962 Polk Directory for Seattle, "Mrs. Anna Obama" Listing

Exhibit 87
Photo of 516 13th Avenue East, Seattle, Taken around 1937
Source: Washington State Archives

EXHIBIT 88

Attending an East-West Center Party at University of Hawaii, Circa 1961

EXHIBIT 89

Additional Photo of Barack Obama, Sr., Attending an East-West Center
Party at University of Hawaii, Circa 1961

EIGHTY-ONE KENYA AIR-LIFT STUDENTS ARRIVED NEW YORK SEPT. 9th 1959

ALIVIDZA, Grace
Howard University,
Washington 1, D.C.

BOIT, Dorcas Chepkambol
Spelman College,
Atlanta 3, Georgia

CHANZU, Said Ambenge
Univ. of Pittsburgh,
Pittsburgh 13, Penna.

CHEGE, Henry Rigii
Cascade College,
705 North Killingsworth St.
Portland 17, Oregon

DALIZU, Fred Egambi
Lincoln University
Philadelphia, Penna.

GATHONI, Gladwell
Diablo Valley College,
Concord, Calif.

GICHOKI, Rose
Clarke College
Dubuque, Iowa

GICHURU, Mary Nyaguthii
Newton High School
Newton 60, Mass

GICHURU, Simon Mukua
St. Francis Xavier Univ.
Antigonish,
Nova Scotia, Canada

GICUHI, Evanson Ngiobi
Diablo Valley College
Concord, Calif.

GITATHA, Samuel Kinyanui
Central State College
Wilberforce, Ohio

INDAKWA, John
Lincoln University
Pennsylvania

ISIGE, Jackton Junyi
Wisconsin State College
Steven's Point, Wisconsin

KABACHIA, Venantio
LaSalle College
Philadelphia 41, Penna.

KAIRO, Simon Thue
Northeast Missouri,
State Teachers College
Kirksville, Missouri

KAJUBI, Younus Mpagi
Howard University
Washington 1, D.C.

KAMAU, Elizabeth
Diablo Valley College,
Concord, California

KAMAU, George Cachigi
Diablo Valley College
Concord, California

KANG'ETHE, John
Roosevelt University
Chicago 5, Ill.

KARUGA, Cyrus G.
Iowa Wesleyan College
Mount Pleasant, Iowa

KATUHGULU, Regina
Skidmore College
Saratoga Springs, N.Y.

KIMANTHI, Titus
Houghton College
Houghton, N.Y.

KIWINDA, Ellistone
Philander Smith College
Little Rock, Arkansas

KUNGU, James G.
Diablo Valley College
Concord, California

KWASA, Shadrack Ojuda
Howard University
Washington, D.C.

GITHAIGA, Francis Lewis
Diablo Valley College
Concord, California

MAGUCHA, Joseph Bern
Greensville College
Greensville, Ill.

MALOIY, Geofery H.
Central College
Iowa

MASEMBWA, Solomon M.
Northeast Missouri State T.C.
Kirksville, Missouri

MAUNDU, Daniel
Philander Smith College,
Little Rock, Ark

MAUNDU, Phillip
Morehouse College,
Atlanta, Ga.

MBAYAH, Mungai
New School for Social Research
66 West 12th St., N.Y.C., N.Y.

MBITHI, Johnson
Tuskegee Institute
Alabama

MBOGUA, John Peter
McGill Univ.
Montreal, P.Q., Canada

M'MUGAMBI, Andrew F.
Georgetown University
Washington 7, D.C.

MJUGUNA, Beatrice Wairimu
McKinley Continuation High School
Berkeley, California

MUGWERU, James S.
Brigham Young University
Provost, Utah

MUNGAI, Arthur Wagithuku
Bowdoin College,
Brunswick, Maine

MURAI, Stephen Macharia
St. Dunstan's Univ.
Prince Edward Island, Canada

MURATHA, Nicholas (Muga)
Warren Wilson College
Swannanoa, North Carolina

MURUNGI, Robert Wallace
College of Idaho
Caldwell, Idaho

MUTISYA, Samuel
Philander Smith College
Little Rock, Arkansas

MUYIA, Harrison Bwire
Wayne State University
Detroit 2, Mich.

MWALOZI, Dickson C.
Simpson College
Indianola, Iowa

MWANGI, Charles
Dunstan's University
Charlottetown,
Prince Edward's Island, Canada

MWANGI, Joseph Wanyoike
St. Thomas College
Chatham, H.B., Canada

MWIHIA, Francis Mbugua
Moravian College
Bethlehem, Penna.

MWIHIA, Kathleen
New York University
Adult's Education
New York, N.Y.

NABUTETE, Frank Habakuk
Philander Smith College
Little Rock, Arkansas

NGUMBI, John Mutua
Jarvis Christian College
Hawkins, Texas

NJOROGE, Raphael
St. Mary's University
Halifax, Canada

OCHIENG, Adonijah
San Francisco State College
1600 Holloway Ave.
San Francisco 27, Calif.

OCHIENG, John
Simpson College
Indianola, Iowa

OCHIENG, Philip
Roosevelt University
Chicago 5, Illinois

OCHOLA, George Philip
University of Chicago
Chicago 37, Ill.

OCHOLA, Samuel Abuna
New Paltz, State Teachers College
New York

ODEDE, Pamela
Western College
Oxford, Ohio

ODERO, Boniface
Manhattan College
Riverdale 71, N.Y.

ODINGE, Odera Barack
Northern State Teachers College
Aberdeen, South Dakota

ODODA, Patricia
Howard University
Washington 1, D.C.

ODUAR, Benjamin Enos
Central State College
Wilberforce, Ohio

OGESSA, Silvano W. Onyango
DePauw College
Greencastle, Indiana

OGOLA, Boaz Harrison
Morehouse College
Atlanta, Georgia

OLEMBO, James Reuben
Purdue University
Lafayette, Indiana

OMONDI, Raphael
St. Mary's University
San Antonio, Texas

ONYUNDO, Amram
Tuskegee Institute,
Tuskegee, Alabama

OTIENO, Olero Samuel
Morris Brown College
Atlanta, Georgia

OTIENO, Jackson
Morehouse College
Atlanta, Georgia

OTOMO, Elisha Otieno
Saint Mary's College
P.O., St. Mary, Calif.

RABALLA, Nicholas
Tuskegee Institute
Tuskegee, Alabama

RAGWAR, Jennifer Adhiamo
Spelman College
Atlanta 3, Georgia

RUENJI, Arthur
Durham High School
Durham, Conn.

SAMMA, Abdulrasul H.
Univ. of Mass.,
Amherst, Mass.

SANTIAGO, Francis Anthony
Howard Payne College
Brownwood, Texas

THAIRU, Daniel M.
Virginia Union University
Richmond, Va.

WACHIRA, Peter William
Ithaca College
Ithaca, N.Y.

WAGENA, Grace
Howard University
Washington, D.C.

WARUI, George Mbuthia
Oklahoma City Univ.
Oklahoma City 6, Oklahoma

WASHIKA, Nathan Fedha
Wisconsin State College
Superior, Wisconsin

WATATUA, Solomon
West Virginia Wesleyan College
Buchanan, West Virginia

WOKABI, Angelina W.
Clarke College
Dubuque, Iowa

EXHIBIT 90

Manifest of Kenya Student Airlift, September 9, 1959
Source: Manuscript Division, Library of Congress, Washington, D.C.

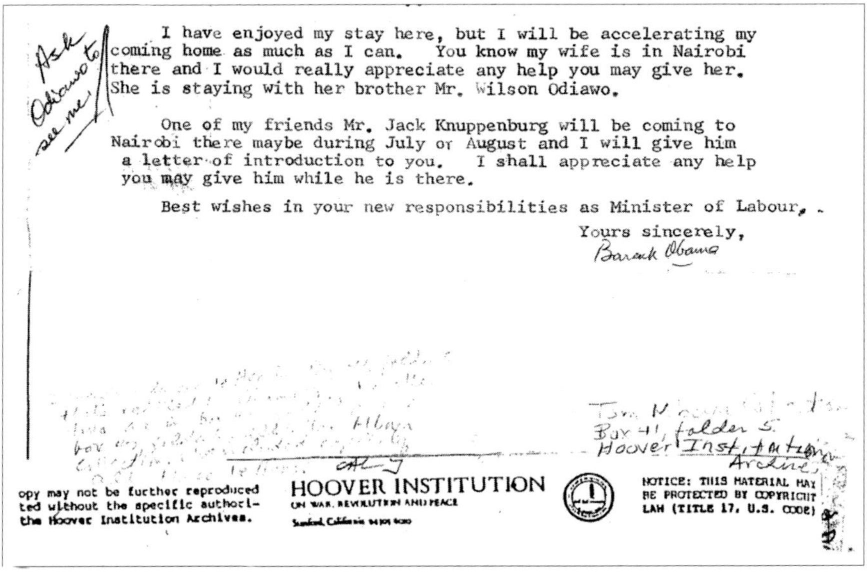

Ask Odiawo to see me

I have enjoyed my stay here, but I will be accelerating my coming home as much as I can. You know my wife is in Nairobi there and I would really appreciate any help you may give her. She is staying with her brother Mr. Wilson Odiawo.

One of my friends Mr. Jack Knuppenburg will be coming to Nairobi there maybe during July or August and I will give him a letter of introduction to you. I shall appreciate any help you may give him while he is there.

Best wishes in your new responsibilities as Minister of Labour.

Yours sincerely,

Barack Obama

Box 41, folder 5.
Hoover Institution Archives

opy may not be further reproduced
ted without the specific authori-
the Hoover Institution Archives.

HOOVER INSTITUTION
ON WAR, REVOLUTION AND PEACE

NOTICE: THIS MATERIAL MAY BE PROTECTED BY COPYRIGHT LAW (TITLE 17, U.S. CODE)

EXHIBIT 91

Letter from Barack Obama, Sr. to Tom Mboya, dated May 29, 1962

Close-up of End of Letter, Source: Hoover Institution

Barack H. Obama,
1482 Alencastre Street,
Honolulu 16, Hawaii.

29th May, 1962.

Dear Tom,

I am sorry that I have not written for such a long time, but
I fugured you were pretty busy, so I did not bother. Further I
have been busy myself and did not have time. I, however, thought
that this is the time when I feel I should thank you for the help
which you gave me when I was coming here.

As you know I have been able to finish my B.A. (hon.) degree
and done my M.A. within three years only as contrasted to the
normal four years for a B.A. and one to two years for M.A. I
have therefore been able to cut on at least two years for my B.A.
and Masters. Further during this period I have been able to get
the highest academic honours that anybody can get in America and
as for the University of Hawaii, I was the only foreign student
to get. I have been awarded the Phi Beta Kappa Honours Award,
The Phi Kappa Phi Honours Award, The Omicron Delta Kappa Honours
Award all for high attainment in scholarship and leadership.
These are the highest honours that anyone can get in the U.S.A.
for high academic attainments.

Further I am leaving here during this June for Harvard University
where I have been offered a fellowship for my PH.D. I intend to
take at least two years working on my Ph.D. and at most three years.
Then I will be coming home. I am going to write my dissertation
and thesis for the Ph.D. on the Economics of the Underdeveloped
areas. Actually I intend it to be in Economic Development and
the effect of International Trade on the countries which produce
Primary products like Kenya and on the policies that would be
necessary to offset the adverse effects that the underdeveloped
areas have been facing.

EXHIBIT 92

Letter from Barack Obama, Sr. to Tom Mboya, dated May 29, 1962

Close-up of Beginning of Letter, Source: Hoover Institution

EXHIBIT 93

Family Photograph, Barack Obama, Sr. at Honolulu Airport with Barack Obama, Jr., 1971

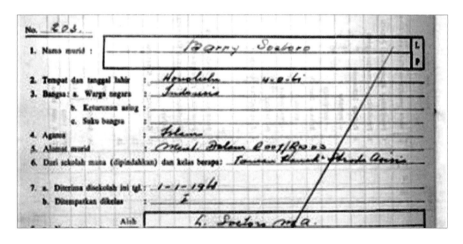

EXHIBIT 94

Barack Obama, here registered as "Barry Soetoro," Indonesian School Registration Card

United States Department of State

Washington, D.C.   20520

JUL 2 9 2010

In reply refer to:
CA/PPT/L/LE – Case Control Number: 200807238

Christopher E. Strunk
593 Vanderbilt Avenue, #281
Brooklyn, NY 11238

Dear Mr. Strunk:

The following is in response to your request to the Department of State, dated November 22, 2008, requesting the release of material under the provisions of the Freedom of Information Act (5 U.S.C. § 552).

We have completed a search for records responsive to your request. The search resulted in the retrieval of six documents that are responsive to your request. After careful review of these documents, we have determined that all six documents may be released in full.

We did not locate a 1965 passport application referenced in an application for amendment of passport that is included in the released documents. Many passport applications and other non-vital records from that period were destroyed during the 1980s in accordance with guidance from the General Services Administration.

Passport records typically consist of applications for United States passports and supporting evidence of United States citizenship. Passport records do not include evidence of travel such as entrance/exit stamps, visas, residence permits, etc., since this information is entered into the passport book after issuance.

EXHIBIT 95
State Department FOIA Letter, Ann Dunham Passport Records Before 1965 Destroyed

Obtain Copies of Passport Records

🖨 Print   ✉ Email

There are two options for obtaining copies of your passport records:

1. **Passport Records for Issuances 1925 – Present**
   a. Requesting Your Own Record
   Passport Services maintains United States passport records for
   passports issued from 1925 to the present. These records normally
   consist of applications for United States passports and supporting
   evidence of United States citizenship, and are protected by the Privacy
   Act of 1974, (5 USC 552(a)). Passport records do not include evidence
   of travel such as entrance/exit stamps, visas, residence permits, etc.,
   since this information is entered into the passport book after it is
   issued.

Exhibit 96

State Department Web site, Claim Passport Records from 1925–Present Are Preserved

P1

SOETORO (LAST NAME)

STANLEY (FIRST NAME)

ANN (MIDDLE NAME)

DUNHAM

TO BE PRINTED IN FULL

FORM APPROVED
BUDGET BUREAU NO. 47-R117.5

DEPARTMENT OF STATE	POST Djakarta, Indonesia
FOREIGN SERVICE OF THE UNITED STATES OF AMERICA	☐ REFERRED TO DEPARTMENT FOR ACTION
APPLICATION FOR	☒ RENEWED (EXXXXXX) TO Jul.18,1970
☑ RENEWAL ☐ AMENDMENT ☐ EXTENSION	☐ AMENDED AS REQUESTED
OF	$ 5.00 FEE COLLECTED
☑ PASSPORT ☐ CARD OF IDENTITY	☐ NO FEE COLLECTED
☐ REGISTRATION ☐ CERTIFICATE OF IDENTITY	

Document No. F 777788 Date Issued July 19 1965

(PLEASE PRINT NAME IN FULL)
(FIRST NAME) (MIDDLE NAME) (LAST NAME)

I, Stanley Ann Dunham Soetoro , a citizen of the United States, do hereby apply for the service indicated above. (If amendment, set forth details on REVERSE.)

DATE OF BIRTH (Month, day, year) Nov. 29, 1942   PLACE OF BIRTH Wichita, Kansas

NOW RESIDING AT Djakarta, Indonesia

UNITED STATES RESIDENCE (Street address, city, county, state)

IN THE EVENT OF DEATH OR ACCIDENT NOTIFY (Name in full, relationship, street address, city, state)

Stanley Armour Dunham, Bank of Hawaii, Honolulu

HAVE YOU EVER BEEN REFUSED A PASSPORT OR REGISTRATION AS A CITIZEN OF THE UNITED STATES?
IF THE ANSWER IS YES, EXPLAIN WHEN AND WHY

NO .

PROPOSED TRAVEL PLANS	IF RETURNING TO U. S. COMPLETE THE FOLLOWING
I INTEND TO RETURN TO THE UNITED STATES PERMANENTLY TO RESIDE WITHIN _Indefinite_ YEARS MONTHS	PORT OF DEPARTURE
I INTEND TO CONTINUE TO RESIDE ABROAD FOR THE FOLLOWING PERIOD AND PURPOSE INDEFINATE - MARRIED TO AN INDONESIAN CITIZEN	NAME OF SHIP OR AIRLINE
	DATE OF DEPARTURE

I have not (and no other person included or to be included in the passport or documentation has), since acquiring United States citizenship, been naturalized as a citizen of a foreign state; taken an oath or made an affirmation or other formal declaration of allegiance to a foreign state; entered or served in the armed forces of a foreign state; accepted or performed the duties of any office, post, or employment under the government of a foreign state or political subdivision thereof; voted in a political election in a foreign state or participated in an election or plebiscite to determine the sovereignty over foreign territory; made a formal renunciation of nationality either in the United States or before a diplomatic or consular officer of the United States in a foreign state; ever sought or claimed the benefits of the nationality of any foreign state; or been convicted by a court or court martial of competent jurisdiction of committing any act of treason against, or attempting to overthrow, or bearing arms against, the United States, or conspiring to overthrow, put down or to destroy by force, the Government of the United States,

(If any of the above-mentioned acts or conditions have been performed by or apply to the applicant, or to any other person included in the passport or documentation, the portion which applies should be struck out, and a supplementary explanatory statement under oath (or affirmation) by the person to whom the portion is applicable should be attached and made a part of this application.)

Stanley Ann Dunham Soetoro
(To be signed by Applicant)

Subscribed and Sworn to (affirmed) before me this ___13th___ day of ___August___ 13 , 19 68

(SEAL)

Vice Consul ___ of the United States at Djakarta, Indonesia

(The Department will assume that the consular officer, forwarding the application for the Department's decision, is fully satisfied as to the applicant's identity unless a notation to the contrary is made.)

FORM FS-299
7 - 64

EXHIBIT 97

First Page, Passport Application—Ann Dunham

Request to Remove Barack Obama from Mother's Passport

I have not (and no other person included or to be included in the passport or documentation has), since acquiring United States citizenship, been naturalized as a citizen of a foreign state; taken an oath or made an affirmation or other formal declaration of allegiance to a foreign state; entered or served in the armed forces of a foreign state; accepted or performed the duties of any office, post, or employment under the government of a foreign state or political subdivision thereof; voted in a political election in a foreign state or participated in an election or plebiscite to determine the sovereignty over foreign territory; made a formal renunciation of nationality either in the United States or before a diplomatic or consular officer of the United States in a foreign state; ever sought or claimed the benefits of the nationality of any foreign state; or been convicted by a court or court martial of competent jurisdiction of committing any act of treason against, or attempting by force to overthrow, or bearing arms against, the United States, or conspiring to overthrow, put down or to destroy by force, the Government of the United States.

(If any of the above-mentioned acts or conditions have been performed by or apply to the applicant, or to any other person included in the passport or documentation, the portion which applies should be struck out, and a supplementary explanatory statement under oath (or affirmation) by the person to whom the portion is applicable should be attached and made a part of this application.)

EXHIBIT 98

Close-Up of Instructions on Passport Application, First Page, Passport Application – Ann Dunham, Request to Remove Barack Obama from Mother's Passport

PAGE 2

AMEND TO INCLUDE (EXCLUDE) (WIFE)(HUSBAND)

NAME	BIRTHPLACE	BIRTHDATE

SPOUSE WAS PREVIOUSLY MARRIED TO	PREVIOUS MARRIAGE TERMINATED BY
—	☐ DIVORCE ☐ DEATH

NUMBER OF MY SPOUSE'S PREVIOUS PASSPORT	DISPOSITION OF MY SPOUSE'S PREVIOUS PASSPORT
1NDO	☐ ATTACHED ☐ CANCELED ______ (DATE)

AMEND TO INCLUDE (EXCLUDE) CHILDREN

NAMES	RESIDENCE	BIRTHPLACE	BIRTHDATE
~~Barack Hussein Obama (Soebarkah)~~			

AMEND TO READ IN MARRIED NAME

NAME

DATE MARRIED	PLACE MARRIED	MARRIED TO

CITIZENSHIP OF HUSBAND

☐ U. S. CITIZEN ☐ ALIEN-CITIZEN OF ______

OTHER AMENDMENT(S) (DESCRIBE IN DETAIL ACTION REQUESTED)

EXHIBIT 99

Second Page, Passport Application—Ann Dunham, Request to Remove Barack Obama from Mother's Passport, Ann Dunham Strikes Out Barack Obama's Name

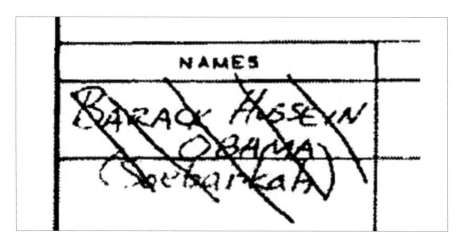

Exhibit 100

Second Page, Passport Application—Ann Dunham, Request to Remove Barack Obama from
Mother's Passport, Close-up: Ann Dunham Strikes Out Barack Obama's Name

Memorandum to file
A '4 '28 294
Sept. '4, '967

Pursuant to inquiry from Central office regarding the status
of the applicants' spouses' child by a former marriage.

The person in question is a united states citizen by virtue
of his birth in Honolulu, Hawaii Aug. 4, '96'. He is living
with the applicants' spouse in Honolulu, Hawaii. He
is considered the applicants step-child, within the meaning of
Sec. '0'(b)(')(B), of the act, by virtue of the marriage of the
applicant to child's mother on March '5, '965

W. I. Mix

Exhibit 101

Letter in Ann Dunham's State Department Passport File, Obtained by FOIA

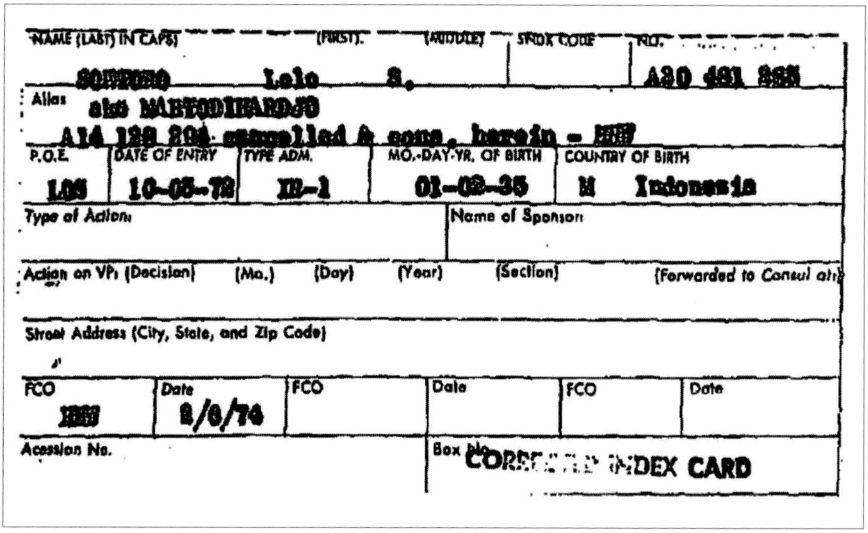

EXHIBIT 102

Card in Ann Dunham's State Department Passport File, Obtained by FOIA

1839 Poki Street, apt. 3
Honolulu, Hawaii 96822
May 1, 1974

5/16/74

T/C
Pls expedite - Treat this req as timely.

John F. O'Shea
District Director
United States Department of Justice
Immigration and Naturalization Service

Dear Mr. O'Shea,

As I informed you by telephone, the American Embassy is refusing my husband an extension of reentry permit on the grounds that he filed a 1973 non-resident tax return. This erroneous information is based on a letter sent by your office (item 1 enclosed).

My husband, prior to departing for Djakarta on business, filed a 1973 resident tax return. Enclosed is a copy of that return (item 2). The fact that it is a resident form is clearly stated at the top of the second page. In addition I have visited the downtown tax office and had them verify that it was a resident form. Non-resident forms have a special N.R. initial in the upper left-hand corner. Lastly I have enclosed copies of my husbands 1973 wage and tax statement, should you need them.

If you could clear up this mistake as soon as possible by notifying the U.S. Embassy in Djakarta it would be greatly appreciated. My husband hopes to return to Honolulu next month. If you have made a decision on the matter I would also appreciate a call from you or your secretary. You can reach me at home at 941-9958. Thank you so much for your trouble.

Mrs. Ann Soetoro

S. Ann Soetoro

Exhibit 103

Letter from Ann Dunham, "S. Ann Soetoro," to DOJ, Dated May 1, 1974, Ann Dunham's State Department Passport File, Obtained by FOIA

Exhibit 104

Close-up of Barack Obama Passport, Screen Capture from White House Web site

Exhibit 105

Photograph, Scott Inoue and Barack Obama, "Barry", Third Grade, 1969, Honolulu, Hawaii

Exhibit 106

Kindergarden Photograph, Noelani School, 1967–1968, Honolulu, Hawaii

Exhibit 107

Photograph of Holiyah "Lia" Soetoro Sobah, Honolulu, Hawaii, 1971

DEPARTMENT OF HEALTH

News Release

LINDA LINGLE
GOVERNOR

CHIYOME LEINAALA FUKINO M.D.
DIRECTOR
Phone: (808) 586-4410
Fax: (808) 586-4444

For Immediate Release: October 31, 2008   08-93

STATEMENT BY DR. CHIYOME FUKINO

"There have been numerous requests for Sen. Barack Hussein Obama's official birth certificate. State law (Hawai'i Revised Statutes §338-18) prohibits the release of a certified birth certificate to persons who do not have a tangible interest in the vital record.

"Therefore, I as Director of Health for the State of Hawai'i, along with the Registrar of Vital Statistics who has statutory authority to oversee and maintain these type of vital records, have personally seen and verified that the Hawai'i State Department of Health has Sen. Obama's original birth certificate on record in accordance with state policies and procedures.

"No state official, including Governor Linda Lingle, has ever instructed that this vital record be handled in a manner different from any other vital record in the possession of the State of Hawai'i."

###

For more information, contact:
Janice Okubo
Communications Office
Phone: (808) 586-4442

EXHIBIT 108

News Release by Dr. Fukino, Hawaii Department of Health, October 31, 2008

DEPARTMENT OF HEALTH

News Release

LINDA LINGLE
GOVERNOR

CHIYOME LEINAALA FUKINO M.D.
DIRECTOR
Phone: (808) 586-4410
Fax: (808) 586-4444

For Immediate Release: July 27, 2009   09-063

STATEMENT BY HEALTH DIRECTOR CHIYOME FUKINO, M.D.

"I, Dr. Chiyome Fukino, Director of the Hawai'i State Department of Health, have seen the original vital records maintained on file by the Hawai'i State Department of Health verifying Barack Hussein Obama was born in Hawai'i and is a natural-born American citizen. I have nothing further to add to this statement or my original statement issued in October 2008 over eight months ago."

\###

EXHIBIT 109

News Release by Dr. Fukino, Hawaii Department of Health, July 27, 2009

Loaʻa
Ka ʻĀina
Hoʻopulapula

*Applying for
Hawaiian Home Lands*

Department of Hawaiian Home Lands
State of Hawaiʻi

EXHIBIT 110

Screen Capture, Department of Hawaiian Home Lands,
Titled "Applying for Hawaiian Home Lands"

In order to process your application, DHHL utilizes information that is found only on the original ***Certificate*** of Live Birth, which is either black or green. This is a more complete record of your birth than the ***Certification*** of Live Birth (a computer-generated printout). Submitting the original ***Certificate*** of Live Birth will save you time and money since the computer-generated ***Certification*** requires additional verification by DHHL.

When requesting a certified copy of your birth certificate from the Vital Records Section of DOH, **let the clerk know you are requesting it "For DHHL Purposes," and that you need a copy of the original *Certificate* of Live Birth and not the computer-generated *Certification*. If mailing in your request form, please fill in "For DHHL Purposes" in the "Reason for Requesting a Certified Copy" section. (See example on page 6.)**

EXHIBIT III

Screen Capture, Page 4 Close-up Detail of Text, Department of Hawaiian Home Lands Titled "Applying for Hawaiian Home Lands"

First Time Applicants

🖨 Print   ✉ Email

You Must Apply in Person If:

- You are applying for your **first** U.S. passport
- You are **under age 16**
- Your previous U.S. passport was issued when you were **under age 16**
- Your previous U.S. passport was **lost, stolen, or damaged**
- Your previous U.S. passport was issued **more than 15 years ago**

- Your name has changed since your U.S. passport was issued and you are **unable** to **legally document your name change**

Before You Start, Please Note:

- Special Requirements for All Minors Under Age 16
- Special Requirements for All Minors Ages 16 & 17
- Special Requirements for Diplomatic, Official, & Regular No-Fee Passports

---

Primary Evidence of U.S. Citizenship (One of the following):

- ☑ Previously issued, undamaged U.S. Passport
- ☑ Certified birth certificate issued by the city, county or state*
- ☑ Consular Report of Birth Abroad or Certification of Birth
- ☑ Naturalization Certificate
- ☑ Certificate of Citizenship

*A **certified birth certificate** has a registrar's raised, embossed, impressed or multicolored seal, registrar's signature, and the date the certificate was filed with the registrar's office, which must be within 1 year of your birth. Please note, some short (abstract) versions of birth certificates may **not** be acceptable for passport purposes.

Exhibit 112

Screen Capture, Detail Explaining Short-Form Birth Certificates,
May Not Be Acceptable for Passport Purposes

An examination of rumors alleging that Barack Obama's birth certificate is either a forgery or an invalid 'short-form' computer print-out which fails to establish his status as a U.S. citizen.

See also: Does Obama Have a **Kenya** Birth Certificate?

THE SAGA OF Barack Obama's birth certificate is tortuous and ironic. It began with the June 2008 release of a scan of Obama's state-issued Certification of Live Birth to quell rumors speculating that his religious affiliation and/or country of origin might be other than what he claimed. Partisan scuttlebutt had it that Obama's middle name was really

Obama's Birth Certificate

CLAIM: As distinguished from a "long-form" Certificate of Live Birth, the "short-form" Certification of Live Birth issued by Hawaii and posted online by the Obama campaign isn't a "real" or "valid" birth certificate.

EXAMPLE:

Personal message from a reader dated Oct. 28, 2008:

[T]he Obama campaign did finally present a document which they claimed validated his eligibility (per the Constitution of the United States, Article II, Section I) as a "Natural born citizen" to have his name on the ballot in contention for the office of the President of the United States of America. However, contrary to what the few media outlets who are giving this outrageous claim any attention at all have concurred, what the Obama campaign supplied was not, in fact, a "birth certificate". What they supplied was actually a "Certificate of Live Birth." There is a major difference between a "birth certificate" and a "Certificate of Live Birth." Aside from the level of detail differentiating the documents (hospital of record, doctor, height, weight, etc) - in the state of Hawaii, one authenticates natural born citizenship, and the other doesn't.

STATUS: FALSE. According to both the Hawaii state government website and a June 6, 2009 article in the *Honolulu Star-Bulletin*, the computer-generated Certification of Live Birth is the *only* kind of birth record now issued by the state (original records are stored electronically), so the distinction between "short-form" and "long-form" is moot. When a citizen of Hawaii requests a certified copy of his or her birth certificate from the state, a Certification of Live Birth — what people are calling the "short-form," and what Obama released to the public — is what they get. According to Hawaii Health Department spokesperson Janice Okubo, a COLB contains "all the information needed by all federal government agencies for transactions requiring a birth certificate."

EXHIBIT 113

David Emery, About.com

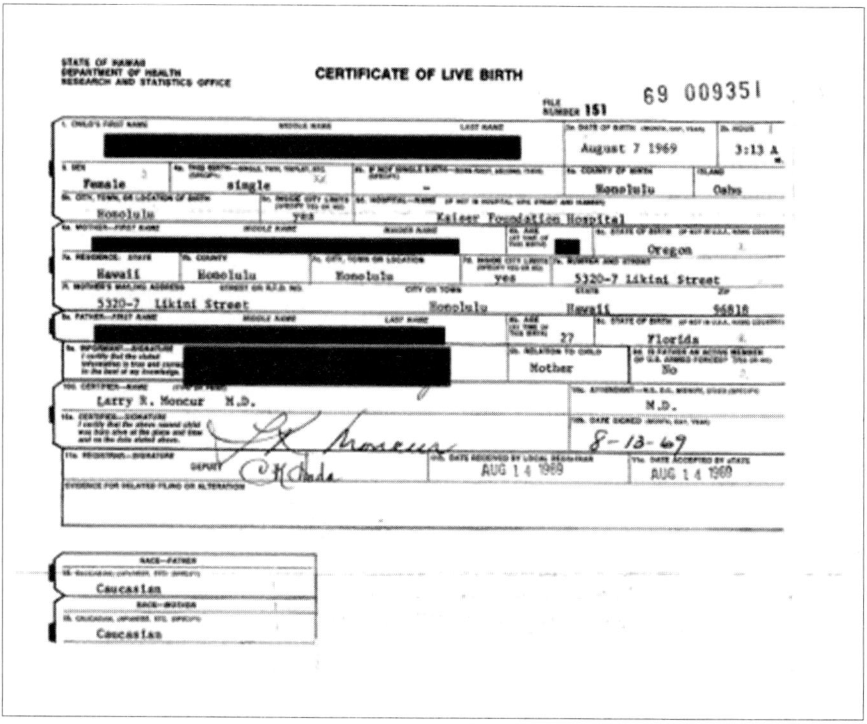

EXHIBIT 114

Long-Form Birth Certificate, Issued by Hawaii Department of Health in September 2010

State of Hawaii - Dept. of Health
288048

OFFICIAL RECEIPT

Office of Health Status Monitoring

Requestor - Mailing Address

Date	September 28, 2010
Receipt Nmbr	2010-055348
Issued By	JC
	MAIL

Legal Fees	$10.00
Postage	$.00
Total Received	$10.00
Amount Refunded	$.00

Number of Requests

Birth		Death		Marriage		Divorces		Disinterment Permits	Amendments	Test./Other
Cert.	Verif.	Cert.	Verif.	Cert.	Verif.	Cert.	Verif.			
1										

Name of Registrant:
SELF

Date of Event:
08 07 69

Place of Event:
OAHU

Father's Name:

Mother's Maiden Name:

Comments:
X; RUSH.

Amount Received	Check	Cash	Money Order $10.00	Date Completed		Non-Sufficient Funds Charge	

Courier Receipt LASER (Rev. 2/97)   Printed   9/30/2010 8:53 IM

Exhibit 115
Receipt for Long-Form Birth Certificate,
Issued by Hawaii Department of Health in September 2010

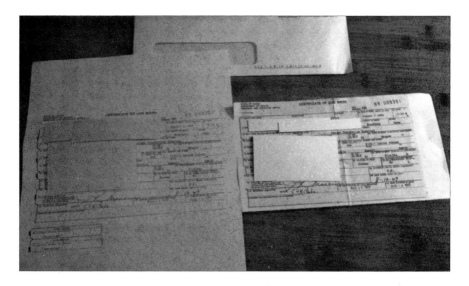

EXHIBIT 116
Photograph of Long-Form Birth Certificate,
Issued by Hawaii Department of Health, September 2010

EXHIBIT 117
Photograph of Long-Form and Short-Form Birth Certificates
Issued by Hawaii Department of Health, September 2010

DEMOCRATIC NATIONAL COMMITTEE

OFFICIAL CERTIFICATION OF NOMINATION

THIS IS TO CERTIFY that at the National Convention of the Democratic Party of the United States of America, held in Denver, Colorado on August 25 though 28, 2008, the following were duly nominated as candidates of said Party for President and Vice President of the United States respectively and that the following candidates for President and Vice President of the United States are legally qualified to serve under the provisions of the United States Constitution:

For President of the United States

Barack Obama
5046 South Greenwood Avenue
Chicago, Illinois 60615

For Vice President of the United States

Joe Biden
1209 Barley Mill Road
Wilmington, Delaware 19807

Nancy Pelosi
Chair, Democratic National
Convention

Alice Travis Germond
Secretary, Democratic National
Convention

City and County of Denver)
) ss:
State of Colorado)

Subscribed and sworn to before me in the City and County of Denver, State of Colorado, this 28th day of August, 2008.

SHALIFA A. WILLIAMSON
Notary Public
State of Colorado
My Commission Expires September 06, 2011

Notary Public

September 6, 2011
Commission expiration date

Democratic Party Headquarters ■ 430 South Capitol Street, SE ■ Washington, DC, 20003 ■ (202) 863-8000 ■ Fax (202) 863-8174
Paid for by the Democratic National Committee. Contributions to the Democratic National Committee are not tax deductible.
Visit our website at www.democrats.org.

EXHIBIT 118
Democratic Party Certification of Nomination
First Version, Includes Language Saying Obama Is Eligible

DEMOCRATIC NATIONAL COMMITTEE

OFFICIAL CERTIFICATION OF NOMINATION

THIS IS TO CERTIFY that at the National Convention of the Democratic Party of the United States of America, held in Denver, Colorado on August 25 though 28, 2008, the following were duly nominated as candidates of said Party for President and Vice President of the United States respectively:

For President of the United States

Barack Obama
5046 South Greenwood Avenue
Chicago, Illinois 60615

For Vice President of the United States

Joe Biden
1209 Barley Mill Road
Wilmington, Delaware 19807

Nancy Pelosi
Chair, Democratic National
Convention

Alice Travis Germond
Secretary, Democratic National
Convention

City and County of Denver)
) ss:
State of Colorado)

Subscribed and sworn to before me in the City and County of Denver, State of Colorado, this 28 day of August, 2008.

SHALIFA A. WILLIAMSON
Notary Public
State of Colorado
My Commission Expires September 06, 2011

Notary Public

September 6, 2011
Commission expiration date

Democratic Party Headquarters ■ 430 South Capitol Street, SE ■ Washington, DC, 20003 ■ (202) 863-8000 ■ Fax (202) 863-8174
Paid for by the Democratic National Committee. Contributions to the Democratic National Committee are not tax deductible.
Visit our website at www.democrats.org.

Exhibit 119
Democratic Party Certification of Nomination
Second Version, Omits Language Saying Obama Is Eligible

CERTIFICATE OF NOMINATIONS

State of Georgia:

We do hereby certify that at a National Convention of Delegates representing the Republican Party of the United States, duly held and convened in the City of Saint Paul, State of Minnesota, on September 4, 2008, the following person, meeting the constitutional requirements for the Office of President of the United States, and the following person, meeting the constitutional requirements for the Office of Vice President of the United States, were nominated for such offices to be filled at the ensuing general election, November 4, 2008, viz.:

TITLE OF OFFICE TO BE FILLED	NAME OF CANDIDATE	NAME OF PARTY	PLACE OF RESIDENCE OF CANDIDATE
President of the United States	JOHN McCAIN	Republican	2211 East Camelback Road Phoenix, Arizona 85016
Vice President of the United States	SARAH PALIN	Republican	1140 West Parks Highway Wasilla, Alaska 99654

IN TESTIMONY WHEREOF, we have hereunto set our hand this 4th day of September, 2008

Permanent Address of Chairman of Convention }
JOHN A. BOEHNER
7371 CHARTER CUP LANE
WEST CHESTER, OH 45069

Chairman of the 2008 Republican National Convention

Permanent Address of Secretary of Convention }
JEAN A. INMAN
457 CENTRAL STREET
AVON, MA 02322

Secretary of the 2008 Republican National Convention

John A. Boehner, being duly sworn, says that he was the presiding officer of the Convention of Delegates mentioned and described in the foregoing certificate, and that the said Jean A. Inman was the secretary of such convention, and that said certificate and the statements therein contained are true to the best of his information and belief.

Subscribed and sworn to before me this 4th day of September, 2008

Notary Public
My Commission expires on the 3rd day of 1 20 10

Jean A. Inman, being duly sworn, says that she was the secretary of the Convention of Delegates mentioned and described in the foregoing certificate, and that the said John A. Boehner was the presiding officer of such convention, and that said certificate and the statements therein contained are true to the best of her information and belief.

Subscribed and sworn to before me this 4th day of September, 2008

Notary Public
My Commission expires on the 3rd day of 1 20 10

EXHIBIT 120

Republican Party Certification of Nomination

The Only Version, Includes Language Saying Obama Is Eligible

OBAMA FOR AMERICA

PO Box 8102
Chicago, Illinois 60680

FEC Committee ID #: C00431445

This report contains activity for a Primary Election

Report type: April Monthly

This Report is an Amendment

Filed 09/15/2008

PAYEE	SUM
# 0567 LA QUINTA INN	4,100.84
# 0628 LA QUINTA INN ALBQU	49.79
#FEDEX AB# 854-073196670	26.01

Perkins Coie	261,206.69

EXHIBIT 121

Federal Election Commission, Payments from Obama for America to Perkins Coie

EXHIBIT 122

Robert Bauer and Anita Dunn at Home

607 Fourteenth Street N.W
Washington, D.C. 20005-2003
PHONE: 202.628.6600
FAX: 202.434.1690
www.perkinscoie.com

Robert F. Bauer
PHONE: (202) 434-1602
FAX: (202) 654-9104
EMAIL: RBauer@perkinscoie.com

April 3, 2009

John David Hemenway
Hemenway & Associates
4816 Rodman Street, NW
Washington, DC 20016

VIA CERTIFIED MAIL

Re: Hollister v. Soetoro et al., No. 09-5080

Dear Mr. Hemenway:

I represent President Barack Obama and Vice President Joseph Biden. I write to request that, in light of the District Court's March 24, 2009 Rule 11 order in *Hollister v. Soetoro*, No. 08-2254, you withdraw the appeal filed in the U.S. Court of Appeals for the District of Columbia, No. 09-5080. For the reasons stated in Judge Robertson's order, the suit is frivolous and should not be pursued

Should you decline to withdraw this frivolous appeal, please be informed that we intend to pursue sanctions, including costs, expenses, and attorneys' fees, pursuant to Federal Rule of Appellate Procedure 38 and D.C. Circuit Rule 38.

Very truly yours,

Robert F. Bauer

EXHIBIT 123
Letter from Attorney Robert Bauer in Hollister Case

Congressional Research Service

MEMORANDUM   April 3, 2009

Subject   Qualifications for the Office of President of the United States and Legal Challenges to the
Eligibility of a Candidate

From: Jack Maskell
Legislative Attorney
American Law Division

This memorandum was prepared to enable distribution to more than one congressional office.

This memorandum addresses inquiries from congressional offices regarding the constitutional
qualifications for the office of President of the United States, and the issue of challenges concerning
specifically the questioning of President Obama's "natural born citizenship" status.[1] Many of the inquiries
have questioned why then-Senator, and now President, Obama has not had to produce an original, so-
called "long" version of a "birth certificate" from the State of Hawaii, how federal candidates are "vetted"
for qualifications generally, and have asked for an assessment of the various allegations and claims of
non-eligibility status.

Concerning the production or release of an original birth certificate, it should be noted that there is no
federal law, regulation, rule, guideline, or requirement that a candidate for federal office produce his or
her original birth certificate, or a certified copy of the record of live birth, to any official of the United
States Government; nor is there a requirement for federal candidates to publicly release such personal
record or documentation.[2] Furthermore, there is no specific federal agency or office that "vets" candidates
for federal office as to qualifications or eligibility prior to election.[3]

The mechanics of elections of federal officials within the several states are administered under state law.[4]
The quadrennial presidential election, although required since 1845 to be held on the same day in each

---

[1] The standing qualifications to be President of the United States, at Article II, Section 1, clause 5, of the Constitution provide
that one must be at least 35 years old, a resident "within the United States" for 14 years, and a "natural born Citizen."

[2] In addition to the "natural born Citizen" requirement for President, a United States Senator must be a "citizen" of the United
States for nine years (Art. I, Sec. 3, cl. 3), and a United States Representative must be a "citizen" for seven years (Art. I, Sec. 2,
cl. 2). No general requirement exists for candidates to the United States Senate or House of Representatives to produce an
original, or a certified copy of a birth certificate.

[3] The Federal Election Commission is authorized by law to administer and seek compliance with the *campaign finance* provisions
of federal law for candidates to federal office, and to administer and seek compliance with the provisions for public financing of
the nomination and election of candidates for President, but has no duties or responsibilities with respect to judging or vetting
qualifications or eligibility of candidates to federal office. 2 U.S.C. § 437c.

[4] Article II, Section 1, cl. 2, delegates authority to the state legislatures to direct the manner of appointment of electors for
President; and Article I, Section 4, cl. 1, delegates to the state legislatures the initial authority for the "Times, Places and Manner"
of elections to Congress, with a residual authority in Congress to make such regulations.

Exhibit 124

Congressional Research Service Memo on Presidential Eligibility, Dated April 3, 2009

Exhibit 125

Kindegarten, Noelani Elementary School, Hawaii, School Year 1966–1967

· 10 ·

AN INDONESIAN CITIZEN?

In Indonesia, Obama was Registered in School as an Indonesian Citizen and a Muslim

On July 29, 2010, the U.S. State Department released two sets of documents in response to Freedom of Information Act requests for the passport files of Stanley Ann Dunham, Barack Obama's mother.[179]

The documents contained remarkable evidence strongly suggesting Obama was an Indonesian citizen when he lived in the Asian nation from the time he was about six years old until ten years old. He was there with his mother and his Muslim stepfather, Lolo Soetoro, an Indonesian by birth.

In writing *The Obama Nation*, I documented (Exhibit 94, page 210) that in Indonesia Barack Obama was enrolled in school as an Indonesian citizen and a Muslim.[180] Confirmation came with the surfacing of a 2007 Associated Press photograph by Tatan Syuflana, an Indonesian AP reporter and photographer, showing Obama's registration card at the Indonesian Francis of Assisi School, a Catholic institution that Obama attended for two years.[181]

The photograph shows Obama was registered under the name Barry Soetoro by his stepfather. The card lists Barry Soetoro as an Indonesian citizen born August 4, 1961, in Honolulu, Hawaii. His religion is listed as "Islam."

An AP spokesman confirmed to WND that the photograph of the registration card was authentic. The discovery that Obama's name was on an official record in a foreign country as a foreign citizen should have prompted a major media investigation. That the mainstream press largely ignored the issue is yet another indication of its unwillingness to hold Obama to the standards of the Constitution. In 2008, a rigorous examination of Obama's natural-born citizenship status might well have endangered his presidential candidacy.

As we saw in Chapter 1, the political bias of today's mainstream media was fully on display in the way John McCain's citizenship was pressed and Obama's ignored. To get a sense of the double standard, imagine how intensively Obama supporters, left-leaning Internet blogs, and their many mainstream-media allies would have investigated McCain had a school transcript from the Canal Zone shown up listing him as a Panamanian citizen.

If Obama received Indonesian citizenship during his sojourn there, could it disqualify him from being a "natural-born citizen" under the Constitution?

As we have seen, the entire point of the Founding Fathers in writing the "natural-born Citizen" clause was to exclude from the presidency anyone with allegiance to another nation.

And as Chapter 3 documented, Obama was a dual citizen at birth of the United States and the British Empire because his father was a citizen of Kenya when Obama was born.

Here, it is evident that Obama became a dual citizen a second time by virtue of his adoption in Indonesia by his Indonesian stepfather.

Dunham Passport Records Destroyed

In the FOIA release of passport records for President Obama's mother, the State Department claimed that a 1980s General Services Administration directive had resulted in the destruction of many passport applications and other "non-vital" passport records. Among the documents destroyed, the State Department said, were Dunham's 1965 passport application and any other passports she may have applied for or held prior to 1965.

Exhibit 95 on page 211 shows exactly how the State Department explained the problem.

The State Department made this claim despite the statement on its Web site (Exhibit 96, page 212) that it maintains records for passports issued from 1925 to the present.[182]

By destroying Dunham's application for her 1965 passport, the State Department eliminated all documentation she may have submitted to prove her son was a U.S. citizen. Typically, that documentation would have consisted of an original hospital birth certificate. The passport records released indicate Dunham had included Barack Obama, Jr. in her passport. Today, all minors regardless of age, including newborns and infants, must have their own passports when traveling internationally, but in the 1960s and 1970s, mothers frequently included their children on their U.S. passports.

Moreover, because the State Department destroyed Dunham's records, there is no way to determine if she had a passport issued prior to 1965 that she may have used to travel internationally.

Dunham's application for her 1965 passport can now join a long list of documents concerning Obama's past that are destroyed, missing, or otherwise unavailable.

"Soebarkah"

State Department documents released in two separate FOIA requests indicate that Dunham apparently identified her son with an Indonesian surname and asked the State Department to drop him from her U.S. passport.

In a passport amendment submitted in person to the State Department at the U.S. Embassy in Jakarta on August 13, 1968, less than a year after joining her second husband in Indonesia, Stanley Ann Dunham Soetoro petitioned to renew her expiring passport.

In the amendment form, she also apparently requested "Barack Obama II (Soebarkah)" be removed from her U.S. Passport No. 777788.

Exhibit 97 on page 213 shows the first page of the passport amendment form Dunham signed as "Stanley Ann Dunham Soetoro" in Jakarta to renew her passport until July 18, 1970, and to remove her son from her passport.

A close-up of the instructions above Stanley Ann Dunham Soetoro's signature indicates that if a person included or to be included in the passport, since acquiring U.S. citizenship, has subsequently been naturalized as a citizen of a foreign state or otherwise disqualified themselves from U.S. citizenship, that should be indicated by striking out the name of the person so disqualified from U.S. citizenship.

Exhibit 98 on page 214 shows the small print language above Stanley Ann Dunham Soetoro's signature.

The first paragraph reads: "I have not (and no other person included or to be included in the passport or documentation has), since acquiring United States citizenship, been naturalized as a citizen of a foreign state; taken an oath or made an affirmation or other formal declaration of allegiance to a foreign state; entered or served in the armed forces of a foreign state; accepted or performed the duties of any office, post, or employment under the government of a foreign state or political subdivision thereof; voted in a political election in a foreign state or participated in an election or plebiscite to determine the sovereignty over foreign territory; made a formal renunciation of nationality either in the United States or before a diplomatic or consular officer of the United States in a foreign state; ever sought or claimed the benefits of the nationality of any foreign state; or been convicted by a court or court martial of competent jurisdiction of committing any act of treason against, or attempting by force to overthrow, or bearing arms against, the United States, or conspiring to overthrow, put down or destroy by force, the Government of the United States."

The second paragraph reads: "(If any of the above-mentioned acts or conditions have been performed by or apply to the applicant, or to any other person included in the passport or documentation, the portion which applies should be struck out, and a supplementary explanatory statement under oath (or affirmation) by the person to whom the portion is applicable should be attached and made a part of this application.)"

On the next page of the document, Ann Dunham followed these instructions.

She struck out her son's name (Exhibit 99, page 214) in the section titled "Amend to include (exclude) children."

A close-up of the strikeout (Exhibit 100, page 215) makes clear Stanley Ann Dunham Soetoro was removing her son from her passport, following the instructions given by the form to indicate her son was now a foreign citizen who should not be included on her U.S. passport.

Until the State Department released this document in July 2010, the name "Soebarkah" had never surfaced in reference to Barack Hussein Obama, Jr. Indonesians do not typically use surnames, as is the custom in Western nations. Surnames may be used to convey ethnic information, and even within families surnames may vary. "Soebarkah" may be a variation of the "Soetoro" surname. Regardless, the surname is included in parentheses by Dunham, written under the Western name of her son, as if to indicate Soebarkah was how her son was known in Jakarta.

As noted above, filing this document required Dunham to appear in person at the U.S. Embassy in Jakarta. The signature on the document appears to be Dunham's. The strike-out on the form and the apparent Indonesian surname closely resembling "Soetoro" could indicate that Dunham was communicating that her son was now an Indonesian citizen adopted by her second husband.

Since Obama has refused to release his State Department travel and passport records, we do not know if Dunham applied for him to have his own U.S. passport in 1968, or if she felt he could travel on an Indonesian passport from that point.

It's possible that Dunham wanted her son recognized in Indonesia as an Indonesian citizen under the surname Soebarkah. After the passport amendment she submitted on August 13, 1968, there would be nothing on her passport to indicate her son was an American citizen.

Repeating the pattern of her first marriage, Dunham met Lolo Soetoro at the University of Hawaii, where they were both students. Soetoro was in the U.S. under a student visa. They married March 24, 1965.

The exact dates Barack Obama, Jr. was in Indonesia remain uncertain. But, as we will see, he returned to Honolulu shortly before Christmas 1971, when his father arrived to see him for the first time since his mother left for Seattle within weeks after he was born.

In *Dreams*, Obama typically avoids giving specific dates for key events, and establishing precise timelines for Obama remains problematic. For instance, on page 41 of *Dreams*, Obama wrote of his mother's plans to move to Jakarta with her new husband: "She tried to picture herself on the day of our arrival [in Jakarta], she a mother of twenty-four with a child in tow, married to a man whose history, whose country, she barely knew." Since Dunham was born on November 29, 1942, that would place her plans to travel to Indonesia sometime between November 1966 and November 1967. The school registration card the AP photographed in Indonesia shows "Barry Soetoro" was enrolled with serial number 203 to begin school in the Catholic Franciscan Assisi Primary School in Jakarta on January 1, 1968, and that he was enrolled in Class 1B. As we will see below, the most likely date Dunham traveled to Indonesia with her son was in October 1967.

Obama tells us he was in Indonesia for four years. "In Indonesia, I had spent two years at a Muslim school, two years at a Catholic school," he wrote on page 154 of *Dreams*.

In the FOIA-released files for Dunham, there is considerable documentation that she and Lolo Soetoro made repeated efforts to convince the State Department to allow Soetoro to remain in the United States, instead of having to return to Indonesia as required by his student visa. The principal argument Dunham and her husband made was that political instability in Indonesia made it dangerous for Soetoro to return, especially with a U.S. wife and stepson.

Indeed, beginning on September 30, 1965, a coup launched by Major General Suharto, commander of the Indonesian Army's strategic reserves, ultimately resulted in the ousting of then-President Sukarno. In the process, the Indonesian army conducted a ruthless purge in which the Muslim-backed military killed as many as 500,000 Indonesian Christians and leftists, including communists. Sukarno was not stripped of his presidential title until March 12, 1967, living under palace arrest until he died June 21, 1970. Suharto remained in office as Indonesia's second president until May 21, 1998.

Thus, it's no surprise that the State Department file contains an undated letter Soetoro submitted to Immigration and Naturalization officials at the Department of Justice in Hawaii. Apparently written in late 1965 or early 1966 when Soetoro was seeking to remain in Hawaii after his student visa had expired, the letter refers to the expulsion of the Peace Corps from Indonesia, a reference that helps date the letter, since the Peace Corps was expelled in 1965.

Soetoro explained that U.S. citizenship could be a problem in the turbulent politics of Indonesia during that time.

"My wife, Ann Soetoro, is a citizen of the United States and has resided here all her life," Soetoro wrote the immigration officials, pleading hardship should he be forced to return to his Indonesian home. "It is presently impossible for my wife to return to Indonesia with me."

What reasons did he produce to support his conclusion?

"Most importantly, anti-American feeling has reached a feverish pitch under the direction of the Indonesian communist party, and I have been advised by both family and friends in Indonesia that it would be dangerous to endeavor to return with my wife at the present time," he continued. "Of secondary importance is the fact that my wife does not yet speak Indonesian. Not only would she be forced to cut short her college education, but she would be left in a position of Isolation in the community."

Clearly, political instability in Indonesia weighed heavily on Soetoro.

"Complicated internal problems are causing the Indonesian government to crumble rapidly," he pleaded. "The anti-Western forces are gaining in strength and have brought about government conviscation (sic) of all United States industry in Indonesia as well as sacking of the United States embassy, and burning and sacking of United States Information Service libraries. The United States Peace Corps has recently been asked to leave because the Indonesian government is no longer able to guarantee the safety of corps members."

Apparently, if Dunham would not have been safe as an American citizen in the political crisis that embroiled Indonesia in these years, Barack Obama, an American child, would also have been in danger.

Soetoro's plea to the INS would suggest the prudence of legally adopting Barack Obama in Indonesia to keep him safe.

Timeline for Obama in Indonesia

The newly released State Department records establish the following timeline for Soetoro, Dunham, and Barack Obama:

SEPTEMBER 18, 1962	Lolo Soetoro, a thirty-two-year-old citizen of Indonesia, is admitted to the United States as an exchange visitor under Section 212(a) of the Immigration and Nationality Act, to participate in graduate studies at the Center for Cultural Technical Interchange Between East and West, University of Hawaii. Soetoro's program at the University of Hawaii terminates on June 15, 1964; on June 19, 1964, the university grants permission for him to remain in the United States for practical training until June 15, 1965.
MARCH 20, 1964	Stanley Ann Dunham Obama divorces Barack Hussein Obama, Sr. in the Circuit Court of the First Circuit, State of Hawaii.
MARCH 24, 1965	Dunham marries Soetoro in Molokai, Hawaii, as documented by Certificate of Marriage, License No. 80296, State of Hawaii, Department of Health, Research, Planning and Statistics Office.
JULY 19, 1965	Dunham is issued Passport No. F777788 by U.S. Department of State. It is unknown whether Dunham had a U.S. passport prior to 1965, because the State Department claims Dunham's previous passport records were destroyed in the 1980s in accordance with unspecified "guidance" from the General Services Administration.
DECEMBER 12, 1966	Soetoro's application to the U.S. State Department for a waiver of the foreign residency requirements of the student visa that allowed him to come to Hawaii is denied, as documented by a letter dated December 12, 1966, from John F. O'Shea, district director, U.S. Department of Justice, Immigration and Naturalization Service. Soetoro had requested that the hostility in Indonesia made it unsafe for his wife to travel to Indonesia and that the separation caused by forcing him to return to Indonesia would be a financial hardship for his wife. The INS rejected the argument, saying in O'Shea's letter of December 12, 1966, that the hardship Soetoro described was "usual" in such cases.
JULY 20,1966	Soetoro leaves Hawaii to return to Indonesia, according to multiple references within the DOJ and INS documents.
JUNE 29, 1967	Dunham applies to the U.S. Department of State to amend her U.S. Passport No. F777788 to change her name from Stanley Ann Dunham to her married name, Stanley Ann Soetoro; the marriage to Soetoro is listed on the amendment form as having occurred on March 13, 1965, in Molokai, Hawaii.

OCTOBER 1967	Dunham travels from Honolulu, Hawaii, to Jakarta, Indonesia, via Japan Airlines, using U.S. Passport No. F777788.
	This is documented by a request from Dunham on her return to the United States in 1971; then, she requests an exception allowing her to travel on an invalid passport that has expired; the request was granted by the U.S. State Department on October 21, 1971.
	On this, Dunham's first trip to Indonesia, we assume Obama accompanies his mother, traveling as a child named on her U.S. Passport No. F777788.
	Obama incorrectly identifies the 1967 flight with his mother to Indonesia as being on a Pan Am jet, but he recalls a three-day stopover in Japan (Source: *Dreams from My Father*, page 31).
	State Department records list no other travel to Indonesia by Dunham from 1968 to 1971.
AUGUST 13, 1968	Dunham applies from Jakarta, Indonesia, to the U.S. State Department to renew her Passport No. F777788, issued on July 19, 1965, for an additional two years. The passport is renewed until July 18, 1970, five years from the issuance of the passport.
	Under 22 USC Sec. 217(a), from 1959 through 1968, passports were initially issued for three years, but they could be renewed for an additional two years.
	In the same application, Dunham amends her Passport No. F777788 to exclude her child, identified as Barack Hussein Obama (Soebarkah), from her U.S. passport.
AUGUST 15, 1970	Obama's half-sister, Maya Soetoro-Ng, is born to Lolo Soetoro and Stanley Ann Dunham Soetoro in Indonesia.
1971 (Unidentified Date)	Barack Obama lives in Indonesia for "over three years by that time," discussing a visit with his mother to the U.S. Embassy in Jakarta at an unspecified time before he returns to the United States (Source: *Dreams from My Father*, p. 30).
	"In Indonesia, I had spent two years at a Muslim school, two years at the Catholic school" (Source: *Dreams from My Father*, p. 154).
	Obama was in Indonesia from the time he was about six years old until ten years old, from 1967–1971.

1971 (Continued)	On an unspecified date in 1971, Barack Obama returns from Indonesia to Hawaii alone, unaccompanied by his mother (Source: *Dreams from My Father*, p. 53). Obama asserts he hands his grandparents his U.S. passport upon arrival in Honolulu (*Dreams*, p. 54). "My grandparents laughed and pointed at me and waved some more until the customs official finally tapped me on the shoulder and asked me if I was an American," Obama wrote, describing his return-alone trip from Indonesia. "I nodded and handed him my passport." Nothing in the released FOIA State Department documents indicates that Dunham assisted her son in obtaining a U.S. passport in Indonesia after she amended her passport to remove his name. To date, Obama has refused to release to the U.S. public his State Department passport records and international travel documentation.
OCTOBER 21, 1971	U.S. State Department allows Dunham to enter the United States on her expired passport No. F777788. The State Department exception form notes the departure from the United States related to this trip was the October 1967 flight she took to Indonesia from Hawaii on Japan Airways.
OCTOBER 20-21, 1971	Dunham departs from Jakarta, Indonesia, on Pan American World Airways Flight No. 812, arriving October 21, 1971, in Honolulu, Hawaii, traveling on the exception granted by the State Department on October 21, 1971, to use her expired passport.
END OF OCTOBER 1971	Barack Obama, Sr. travels from Kenya to Honolulu to attend a school reunion at the University of Hawaii and to visit his son and ex-wife. Obama's father travels to Hawaii two weeks after his mother travels from Indonesia to Hawaii; his father returns to Kenya and his mother returns to Indonesia after New Year's Day, January 1, 1972. (Source: *Dreams from My Father*, p. 62).
NOVEMBER 5, 1980	The divorce becomes final between Dunham and Soetoro in the Family Court of the First Circuit, Hawaii.

Ann Dunham's Passport Records Analyzed

Ann Dunham appears to have used two different variations of her name in obtaining and amending passports while married to Loro Soetoro: Stanley Ann Dunham Soetoro and, without her maiden name, Stanley Ann Soetoro. She continued using the name Soetoro, even after her divorce with Obama's stepfather. Her passport record shows active travel between Indonesia and the United States, beginning in 1972 and continuing until the end of her life.

On January 4, 1972, Dunham applied for a U.S. passport by mail. The purpose of the trip was listed as "return home" for an indefinite stay. She listed her permanent residence as an address in Jakarta. This was the passport application Dunham filed to replace her expired passport. The application suggests she planned to return to Indonesia in 1972. She does not apply to include her son, Barack Obama, Jr., on the passport. She was issued U.S. Passport No. C030097.

On June 2, 1976, Dunham applied from Jakarta for a U.S. passport, apparently anticipating that the passport issued in 1972 would expire. She listed her current residence as Jakarta and her permanent residence as Honolulu. On the application she indicated she was planning to return to Indonesia from September 1976 through February 1977 to complete her research in Jakarta. She also filled in that she was planning to fly from Jakarta to the United States on a Pan Am flight scheduled for June 16, 1976. She applied under the name Stanley Ann Dunham Soetoro. She was issued U.S. Passport Number Z2433100, valid from June 2, 1976 until June 1, 1981.

The 1976 passport was the last passport Dunham was issued that included the surname Soetoro.

On April 27, 1981, Ann Dunham applied from Jakarta, Indonesia, for a U.S. passport, indicating that she was in Indonesia working on a two-year contract from the Ford Foundation, from January 1981 through December 1982. At that time, Ann Dunham was working on a micro-finance program for the Ford Foundation that was overseen by Peter Geithner, the father of Timothy Geithner, the current U.S. Secretary of the Treasury, while Peter Geithner was directing the Asia program at the Ford Foundation. Ann Dunham's occupation in the 1981 passport application was listed as "Program Officer, Ford Foundation." She was issued U.S. Passport No. Z3037221, valid from April 28, 1981, until April 27, 1986, under the name Stanley Ann Dunham.

On March 27, 1986, Dunham applied for a passport renewal by mail, requesting an urgent issuance of the passage because she planned to travel to the Philippines. Presumably the passport was issued, although the released records do not indicate the passport number that she was issued. She applied under the name Stanley Ann Dunham.

No passport records subsequent to 1986 for Ann Dunham were released, though presumably a passport was issued subsequent to her 1986 application, such that the ten-year period prior to expiration would extended one year past her death. Ann Dunham died on November 7, 1995, and was known to have been in Indonesia in 1994 when an Indonesian doctor first misdiagnosed the signs of the ovarian cancer that would lead to her death as indigestion.

The released documents shed no light on whether Dunham might have held a passport prior to Obama's birth that she could have used to travel to a foreign country.

Her passport records also shed no light on whether or not Obama made a trip to Indonesia on his way to Pakistan with his college roommates from Occidental, or whether Obama may have joined his mother in Indonesia, or possibly even in Pakistan, at any other time. Again, Obama has refused to release to the American public his passport and international travel records. The State Department release of Ann Dunham's passport records contained information about Obama only because Obama was listed on his mother's passport before he traveled with her to Indonesia.

Timeline Analyzed

Examining the timeline closely, it's evident that Barack Obama and his mother traveled to Indonesia to join her husband, his stepfather, in October 1967, when Obama was listed on her passport as her son and an American citizen.

When Dunham returned alone to the United States on October 20–21, 1971, the State Department forms allowing her to re-enter the United

States with an expired passport contained no reference to Obama. The only testimony that Obama returned home from Indonesia alone and on a U.S. passport is his own rendition of the story as told in his autobiography, a source proven to be unreliable in various material aspects.

In her own handwriting, Dunham completes the statement, "I intend to continue to reside abroad for the following period and purpose" on the passport amendment form filed August 13, 1968, by noting that her stay in Indonesia was "indefinite" because she was "married to an Indonesian citizen."

Soetoro also appears to have influenced Dunham to change her mind about sending Obama to school in Indonesia, something both were worried about when they were pleading for Lolo not to be forced home in 1966.

A letter to the file by INS/DOJ investigator Robert R. Schultz, dated May 24, 1967, documents a telephone conversation he had with Dunham in Hawaii on May 12, 1967.

"She also indicated that her son is now in Kindergarten and will commence the first grade next September and if it is necessary for her and the child to go to Indonesia she will educate the child at home with the help of school texts from the U.S. as approved by the Board of Education in Honolulu," Schultz wrote.

Obama would not have needed Indonesian citizenship to study in Jakarta with his mother at home.

Regarding the registration record from the Assisi school, being listed as an Indonesian citizen was useful to Obama, as his mother and stepfather's pleas to INS/DOJ officials to extend Soetoro's visa made clear the country wasn't safe for Americans.

Born in Hawaii?

The passport documents released for Dunham in July 2010 did not include any birth certificate documentation for Obama, despite one memorandum claiming he was born in Honolulu.

The released documents indicate that Soetoro petitioned the INS in 1967 to obtain a waiver to return to the United States to rejoin his wife. As the timeline above shows, Soetoro returned to Indonesia July 20, 1966, after completing his studies at the University of Hawaii; he needed to fulfill the mandatory two-year residence requirement in Indonesia before he could be granted a visa to return to America.

In an apparent attempt to establish the nationality status of Barack Obama, Jr., a person named W. I. (initial not fully legible) Mix submitted a poorly typed and difficult-to-decipher memo to the file, dated September 14, 1967, without identifying his or her official position.

Exhibit 101 on page 215 shows the relevant memo, exactly as it appeared in the released State Department documents.

The memo is written pursuant "to inquiry from Central office regarding the status of the applicants' spouses' child by a former marriage." (sic)

The next paragraph reads as follows, presented without correction, except for inserting the number "1" where the document itself types a bracket character, possibly because of a faulty typewriter:

> The person in question [Barack Obama, Jr.] is a united states citizen by virtue of his birth in Honolulu, Hawaii August 4, 1961. He is living with the applicants' spouse in Honolulu. He is considered the applicants stepchild, within the meaning of Sec. 101(b)(1)(B), of the act, by virtue of the marriage of the applicant to the childs' mother on March 15, 1965.

The person writing the document does not reference having examined any birth document in the attempt to establish the citizenship of Barack Obama, Jr. Instead, the memorandum suggests it resulted from a conversation, possibly with Obama's mother, in which the information was conveyed by her and simply accepted without documentary verification.

In contrast, various forms among the FOIA documents released clearly indicate when corroborating documents were presented. For instance, an INS/State Department official examined the divorce decree between Dunham and Barack Obama, Sr. to establish that the parents were legally divorced.

Remember also, the question is not simply whether Obama was born in Hawaii, but whether he is a natural-born citizen. The salient point here is that Obama could have been born in Hawaii, yet become an Indonesian citizen when he was in Jakarta as a child. Would that foreign citizenship compromise his natural-born citizenship status?

Lolo Soetoro Returns to the United States in 1972

The release of Dunham's passport records also inadvertently revealed much of the immigration file of Lolo Soetoro. Obama's stepfather returned to the United States in 1972, after Obama left Jakarta for good. That Soetoro returned to the United States so quickly after Obama's departure was unknown until the release of these files. In *Dreams*, Obama discusses returning home to Hawaii when his father arrived from Africa for the 1971 Christmas and New Year holidays. Obama never tells us that after his father left for Africa, his stepfather showed up in the U.S. for the 1972 holidays.[183]

On July 18, 1972, the Hawaii Police Department provided a Police Clearance Letter indicating that Lolo Martodihardjo Soetoro, a visa applicant, had no Hawaii police record. This is the first time the name "Martodihardjo" appears in the documentary record for Soetoro, a reminder of how difficult Indonesian surnames can be for Westerners to understand and decipher.

A card (Exhibit 102, page 216) in the file indicates that "Soetoro aka ('also known as') Martodihardjo" entered the United States at Los Angeles on October 5, 1972. Further, the card indicates that Soetoro's United States Immigration and Naturalization file A14–128–294 had been consolidated with A30–481–285, Soetoro's immigrant file.

The released records indicate that Dunham continued to write letters to the Immigration and Naturalization Service on behalf of her husband though 1974. Although INS had extended to Soetoro permanent resident status, that status was rescinded after Soetoro was accused of inappropriately filing a 1973 IRS income tax form as a "non-resident."

In May 1974, Dunham wrote a letter (Exhibit 103, page 217) to the INS explaining her husband intended to return to Honolulu in June 1974.

The impression Obama gives in *Dreams* is that the troubles in his mother's marriage began immediately upon their arrival in Jakarta in 1967 or 1968. "Still, something had happened between her [Ann Dunham] and Lolo in the year that they had been apart," Obama wrote on page 42 of *Dreams*. "On some nights, she [Ann Dunham] would hear him up after everyone else had gone to bed, wandering through the house with a bottle of imported whiskey, nursing his secrets," Obama continued writing onto the next page.

The released State Department documents tell a different story. Ann Dunham returned to Indonesia after 1971, presumably returning to live in Jakarta with Lolo and with their daughter Maya. Soetoro returned to the United States after 1971, even achieving permanent resident status. Through 1974, Ann Dunham continues to fight with the U.S. government to get Lolo permission to return freely and live in the United States, typically signing her letters as S. Ann Soetoro, representing herself as a loving wife.

What Is the Real Name of the President of the United States?

Is President Obama's legal name Barack Hussein Obama II, Barack Hussein Obama (without the designation "II" indicating Barack Obama, Jr.), Barry Soetoro, or Barack Hussein Obama Soebarkah?

All these names appear in the various documents produced since 2008 regarding President Obama.

The confusion continued when on August 13, 2010, the White House released a video displaying Obama's passport (Exhibit 104, page 218).[184] As seen in the exhibit, the passport displayed his name as "Barack Hussein Obama."

The question immediately arose as to why the name displayed on the passport did not match then-Senator Obama's name as displayed on the Certification of Live Birth posted on Web sites favorable to him during the 2008 presidential campaign. There, the name was rendered as "Barack Hussein Obama II." If President Obama's birth certificate was the basis for his obtaining his passport, why isn't his name listed on his passport as "Barack Hussein Obama II," the way the name appears on the COLB?

Remarkably, nearly two years into the Obama presidency, Obama's legal name remains a mystery.

As we saw earlier, the Associated Press released Obama's school registration form at St. Francis of Assisi School in Jakarta showing him listed as Barry Soetoro, an Indonesian citizen and a Muslim.

In the passport amendment submitted August 13, 1968, Dunham identified her son with a never-before-seen Indonesian surname, Soebarkah.

So, what is the president of the United States's real name? This is not an unimportant question if we are to assume the president has a legal name that should be established in documents such as a long-form, hospital-generated birth certificate, adoption papers in Indonesia, or an amended birth record filed with the Hawaii Department of Health, noting either his Indonesian adoption or the sole custody over the child that Dunham took after divorcing Soetoro in Hawaii in 1980. Obama has consented to releasing none of these documents to the American public.

Even more confusing, in *Dreams* Obama introduces an additional variation of his name on page 41, "Barry Obama," although on page 91 the author insists "Barack" is the given name, suggesting "Barry" was only used as a nickname, despite the school registration papers from Indonesia listing him as "Barry Soetoro."

Interestingly, even though *Dreams* uses the name "Barry" seventy times, and "Barack" 218 times, the name "Soetoro" does not appear in the autobiography at all, not even in the fourteen mentions the author makes of his stepsister, who is always identified only as "Maya," never as "Maya Soetoro," or by her married name, "Maya Soetoro-Ng."

In writing *Dreams*, Obama clearly avoided any mention of the name "Soetoro," perhaps so as not to draw attention to the question of whether Lolo Soetoro ever adopted him formally, conferring Indonesian citizenship on him.

Another Obama Puzzle: Third Grade in Two Different Countries?

There is yet another mystery associated with Obama's four-year stay in Indonesia: How could he have attended third grade with Scott Inoue at Noelani Elementary School in Honolulu in 1969, when he was in Indonesia at that time?

The indication that Obama attended third grade in Hawaii in 1969 comes from an old photograph (Exhibit 105, page 218) made public by Inoue, now a chiropractor practicing in Stockton, California. The informal photo shows Obama and Inoue against a background of what appear to be Christmas drawings by school children posted on a classroom bulletin board.

"The photo shows Barack Obama's arm around me in the third grade at Noelani in 1969," Inoue told WND. "My mother wrote that inscription on the bottom of the photograph at the time the picture was taken."

The inscription reads: "Scott & Barry 3rd grade 1969."

WND asked Inoue how Obama could have been with him in Hawaii in the third grade when he was supposedly in Indonesia in 1969.

"I don't have any explanation," he said.

"Truthfully, I didn't even remember that Barack Obama was in my class at Noelani until that 1966–1967 Kindergarten class photo surfaced, (Exhibit 106, page 219) showing Barack and me in it," Inoue said. "Then my mother found the picture of the two of us together in third grade, in 1969. Otherwise, I probably would never have remembered."

How Many Times Did Obama Leave Indonesia?

The State Department FOIA documents indicate Obama accompanied his mother in October 1967 when she flew on Japan Airlines to Jakarta as documented by a form Dunham filed with the State Department on October 21, 1971.

Obama was included as a child on his mother's passport until August 13, 1968, when she applied to the State Department to amend her Passport No. 777788 to exclude him.

Arriving in Indonesia in late 1967, Barry Soetoro was registered for school immediately, to start classes in January 1968.

As noted previously, the Associated Press photograph of Obama's registration card documented that "Barry Soetoro" was enrolled with serial number 203 to begin school in the Catholic Franciscan Assisi Primary School in Jakarta, Indonesia, on January 1, 1968, and that he was enrolled in Class 1B. Further, "Barry Soetoro" was listed as an Indonesian citizen whose religion was "Islam." Obama's statement on page 154 of *Dreams* that "In Indonesia, I had spent two years at a Muslim school, two years at the Catholic school," establishes, as part of the official Obama school timeline, that he had been in Indonesia from late 1967 until 1971. Remember, Obama wrote on pages 53–54 that he traveled back from Indonesia alone late in 1971 to arrive in Hawaii before his father was scheduled to visit Honolulu during Christmas 1971.

But nothing in *Dreams* suggests Obama left Indonesia twice to return to Hawaii; the only such trip ever discussed in Obama's memoir is the one in 1971 to see his father.

Noelani Elementary School refuses to release any records pertaining to Obama's school attendance there.

No Explanation

"I don't remember how long Obama was at the Noelani in 1969," Inoue said. "I'm not sure he was there the whole year. I just don't remember. It was a long time ago and my memory that far back is not very clear."

Still, Inoue is sure the photo is authentic.

"That's my mother's handwriting at the bottom of the photo," Inoue said. "She wrote that inscription at the bottom of the photo in 1969, at the time the photo was taken."

He doubted his mother would have been mistaken.

If 1966–1967 was their school year together in Kindergarten, Obama and Inoue presumably would have been in third grade during school year 1969–1970.

This timeline would have made Mrs. Inoue's inscription the correct year for third grade, except that Barack Obama left Hawaii for Indonesia in October 1967, and Barry Soetoro was enrolled on January 1, 1968, at the Catholic Franciscan Assisi Primary School in Jakarta for the first of his two years at that school.

After attending the Assisi school, the official Obama timeline has him enrolled at Sekolah Dasar Negeri Besuki, a public school in the Menteng District in Jakarta.

The exact date Barry Soetoro enrolled there remains unclear, as no school registration documents have yet surfaced.

But the official Obama timeline remains that he left Hawaii in 1967 and did not return until 1971.

Even Inoue remains confused.

In concluding the interview, he asked, "If you ever figure it out, would you please let me know?"

A Previously Unknown Obama Stepsister Dies in Indonesia

On February 26, 2010, a stepsister of Barack Obama died unexpectedly. Internet researchers[185] made the link between the president and his previously undisclosed stepsister, Holiyah "Lia" Soetoro Sobah, after translating Indonesian obituaries. The surfacing of Lia as an adopted child of Lolo Soetoro and Ann Dunham raises the question of whether Obama himself might have been adopted officially as Lolo Soetoro's stepson when Obama was in Indonesia from 1967–1971.

Even though Obama makes no mention in *Dreams* of having had an Indonesian stepsister, the Indonesian obituaries make clear that Obama slept in the same room as his stepsister while the two of them grew up together in the Soetoro home in Jakarta.

The obituaries state that Lia was born in 1957 and that she had three children with her husband Edi Sobah, with whom she lived in West Java, Indonesia.

A photograph of Lia (Exhibit 107, page 219) shows her holding a monkey doll and wearing clothes given her by Madelyn Dunham, Barack Obama's maternal grandmother, when Lia visited Hawaii for three months.[186]

Lia's visit to Hawaii apparently occurred in 1971, the year Obama left Indonesia for the last time.

While Obama has not acknowledged having had a stepsister in Indonesia, he discussed at length in *Dreams* his half-sister, Maya Soetoro-Ng, who was born in Indonesia to Lolo Soetoro and Ann Dunham on August 15, 1970.

Yet, according to the Indonesian obituaries, Barry Soetoro and Lia Soetoro were always together—playing, traveling on family vacations, and even bathing together.

There is nothing on the public record to indicate that President Obama sent any condolences or even acknowledged the death of his stepsister.

THE CONSTITUTIONAL GAMBIT

STONEWALLING IN HAWAII

How Hawaii Government Officials Have Conspired to Keep Obama's Birth Documents Hidden

The state government in Hawaii has consistently stonewalled attempts to pierce the veil of secrecy surrounding the Obama birth records.

When I was in Hawaii in October 2008, amid repeated unsuccessful attempts to find out whether or not the state possessed a copy of a long-form hospital-generated Barack Obama birth certificate, I reported that Hawaii's Republican Governor Linda Lingle had placed the then-candidate's original birth certificate "under seal" and instructed the Hawaii Department of Health to make sure no one in the press obtained access to it under any circumstances.[187]

The WND report was published after the governor's office had officially declined my written request to obtain a copy of the original birth certificate.

"It does not appear that Dr. Corsi is within any of these categories of persons with a direct and tangible interest in the birth certificate he seeks," wrote Roz Makuala, manager of constituent services in the governor's office, in an e-mailed response to WND.

According to legal criteria cited by the governor's office, those eligible to obtain a copy of an original birth certificate include the person born, or "registrant," the spouse or parent of the registrant, a descendant of the registrant, a person having a common ancestor with the registrant, a legal guardian of the registrant, or a person or agency acting on behalf of the registrant.

WND was told the official reason for denial was pursuant to a Hawaii Revised Statutes provision intended to prevent identity theft, but that the real motivation for withholding the original birth certificate was political. Furthermore, WND was informed, the Hawaii Department of Health would immediately release Obama's original birth certificate upon Obama's request, but that no such request had been received from the president or anyone acting on his account.

Hawaii Health Department Says Obama was Born in Hawaii

Although virtually all Obama-supporting news organizations, Web sites, and blogs cite the Hawaii Department of Health as affirming that Obama was born in Hawaii, on closer examination those statements by the Hawaii DOH aren't nearly as definitive as they initially seem.

Leading the spin, Snopes.com, a repeated defender of Obama in the birth certificate controversy, wrote as if Obama's Hawaiian birth was no longer in doubt once Hawaiian officials spoke up. "In October 2008 and again in July 2009, Hawaiian officials reported that they had personally verified that Barack Obama's original birth certificate was in the Hawaii State Department's files," Snopes wrote.[188] Continuing along these lines, FactCheck.org reported, "The director of Hawaii's Department of Health confirmed October 31 that Obama was born in Honolulu."[189] In an attempt to buttress the argument, FactCheck cited Associated Press reports that Chiyome Fukino, director of the Hawaii DOH, and Alvin Onaka, registrar of vital statistics, had personally verified that the health department "holds Obama's original birth certificate."

But, a closer look at Fukino's statement of October 31, 2008, makes clear that it was carefully worded to give the impression that the Department of Health possessed Obama's "original birth certificate," even though that is not what she actually said.

Exhibit 108 on page 220 features the press release in question.

What Fukino said was that she had "personally seen and verified that the Hawaii State Department of Health has Sen. Obama's original birth certificate on record in accordance with state policies and procedures."

The tricky part is the qualification "in accordance with state policies and procedures." Why didn't Fukino just say she had seen Obama's original birth certificate, or, even better, that she had seen Obama's long-form hospital-generated birth certificate? Why did she need to add the qualification "in accordance with state policies and procedures"?

The implication was that what Fukino saw was what the Hawaii DOH had on file, even if the "birth certificate" was one generated by a family statement that contained no record whatsoever of whether Obama had been born at home or in a hospital. Remember, the Hawaii DOH would have registered an abbreviated "birth certificate" for Obama even if no long-form hospital-generated birth certificate existed. All the family needed to do to get the Hawaii Department of Health to generate a "birth certificate" was to say Obama was born in Hawaii and prove they were residents.

The only conclusion we can draw from Fukino's statement is that whatever birth documents the Hawaii DOH has on file for Barack Obama, Jr., they state that he was born in Hawaii, whether or not that was actually the case.

Note that in the third paragraph, Fukino said no state official, including Gov. Lingle, had ever instructed that Obama's birth records be handled in a manner different from any other vital record held by the state agency. This seems aimed at refuting WND's claim that Lingle had sealed Obama's birth certificate records. What the statement implies is that the state holds all long-form birth certificate records secret, releasing only the limited information published on the short-form COLB.

Still, Hawaii Statutes Section 338–13 provides that the Hawaii DOH will release certified copies of any birth certificate record on file, provided the person applying has a right under Hawaii law to request the document. Despite this provision of law, WND has been repeatedly advised by well-informed sources in the Hawaiian state government that Lingle and Fukino would block requests WND might orchestrate from Obama family members.

Because Fukino's October 31, 2008, statement was so heavily qualified, questions persisted. Eight months later, on July 27, 2009, she felt it necessary to issue a second statement (Exhibit 109, page 221).

This time, Fukino said she had seen "the original vital records maintained by file by the Hawaii State Department of Health verifying Barack Hussein Obama was born in Hawaii and is a natural-born citizen." What she did not say was what documents precisely Hawaii has in the vault. Fukino's two statements amount to little more than, "Trust me."

Unfortunately, Fukino's word is not the best evidence of Obama's birth facts. If the issue were being contested in a court of law, the best evidence would be the documents themselves, not a public official's verbal representations of documents the judge and jury are not permitted to see.

Despite two statements by Fukino designed to put the Obama birth controversy to rest—and especially in light of Gov. Abercrombie's later highly publicized but unsuccessful attempts to make public Obama's original birth certificate—Americans still have no idea what documents are in the Hawaii Department of Health vaults that would independently corroborate that Obama was born there.

Question: Why did Fukino's statement on July 27, 2009, drop the earlier claim that she had seen Obama's "original birth certificate?" That she was vague about the birth documents possessed in the Hawaii DOH vault suggests the existing documents might be nothing more than statements the family made at the time. If a long-form hospital-generated birth certificate for Obama existed, why didn't Fukino say she had seen that precise document?

Still, the Hawaii DOH was obviously determined to affirm Obama was born in Hawaii. But then, the Hawaii Health Department also once affirmed that Chinese leader Sun Yat-Sen was born in Hawaii!

If a real Hawaii birth certificate exists for Barack Hussein Obama, Jr.—which it absolutely would if he were born in the Kapi'olani facility as he claims—then why doesn't President Obama authorize the Hawaii DOH to release it? This simple step would prove once and for all whether or not Obama was born in Hawaii. Does Obama not authorize the release of the document because he knows the document never existed?

Only Applicants with Long-Form Need Apply

In June 2009, WND reported that the Web site of the Department of Hawaiian Home Lands, or DHHL, clearly stated that the short-form Certification of Live Birth touted by the Obama campaign, White House press secretary Robert Gibbs and a host of other Obama defenders, was not an acceptable birth record to qualify under its program, which offers benefits to native Hawaiians.[190]

"In order to process your application, DHHL utilizes information that is found only in the original Certificate of Live Birth, which is either black or green," the DHHL Web site proclaimed at that time. "This is a more complete record of your birth than the Certification of Live Birth (a computer-generated printout). Submitting the original Certificate of Live Birth will save you time and money since the computer-generated Certification requires additional verification by DHHL."

Hawaii DOH spokeswoman Janice Okubo told WND that Hawaii policy changed in 2001, when the DOH went paperless. Since then, the agency typically issues only the computer-generated short-form COLBs when Hawaii residents request their "birth certificates." She claimed Hawaii birth certificates are now available solely in electronic form.

"At that time, all the information for births from 1908 (onward) was put into electronic files for consistent reporting," she said.

Okubo did not explain how anyone needing a standard long-form birth certificate to qualify for programs such as those offered by the Department of Hawaiian Home Lands could be fulfilled. Instead, Okubo claimed the U.S. Supreme Court has recognized the state's current Certification of Live Birth "as an official birth certificate meeting all federal and other requirements." She did not cite, however, any specific rulings, and the Supreme Court has not taken up the issue of whether the short-form Certification of Live Birth would qualify a presidential candidate under the "natural-born Citizen" clause of the U.S. Constitution.

Following publication of the WND report, the Department of Hawaiian Home Lands revised its Web site to inform applicants that short-form Certifications of Live Birth were now acceptable as proof of Hawaiian birth.

The revised DHHL Web site now reads: "The Department of Hawaiian

Home Lands accepts both Certificates of Live Birth (original birth certificate) and Certifications of Live Birth because they are official government records documenting an individual's birth."

Although the DHHL Web site has removed the original language, a DHHL brochure (Exhibit 110, page 222) titled "Applying for Hawaiian Home Lands" and archived on the Internet preserves the earlier version, documenting the WND report.

On page 7 of the brochure is the specification (Exhibit 111, page 223) that a Certification of Live Birth is not sufficient for DHHL birth certification purposes.

Still, even after changing the policy, the Department of Hawaiian Home Lands acknowledged the short-form COLB contained limited information and was less useful to DHHL in performing their mission. "The Certificate of Live Birth generally has more information which is useful for genealogical purposes as compared to the Certification of Live Birth which is a computer-generated printout that provides specific details of a person's birth," the DHHL Web site now explains. "Although original birth certificates (Certificates of Live Birth) are preferred for their greater detail, the State Department of Health (DOH) no longer issues Certificates of Live Birth. When a request is made for a copy of a birth certificate, the DOH issues a Certification of Live Birth."

The mission of the DHHL is to provide native Hawaiians with land benefits available only to native Hawaiians. To be eligible for a Hawaiian home lands homestead lease, the applicant must be at least eighteen years of age, and must be a native Hawaiian, defined as "any descendant of not less than one-half part of the blood of the races inhabiting the Hawaiian Islands previous to 1778."

The revised DHHL Web site further explains that the "general rule of thumb in determining 50 percent blood quantum is to submit enough documentation tracing your genealogy to your full Hawaiian ancestor(s). Some applicants need only go back one or two generations—that is, to their grandparents. Others may need to go back further, gathering pieces of information which eventually grow into a large family tree with roots beginning with full Hawaiian ancestors."[191] Before the WND reports, the DHHL also required a certified copy of a long-form certificate of birth for the applicant's biological father and biological mother. If the biological parents' documents failed to prove the applicant had 50 percent Hawaiian ancestry, the DHHL also required certified long-form certificates of birth for both sets of biological grandparents.

PolitiFact.com jumped into the controversy to defend Obama by arguing that the mission of the Hawaii DHHL was not specifically to prove Hawaiian birth, but Hawaiian ancestry. Lloyd Yonenaka, a spokesman for the DHHL, told Politifact the DHHL does not even care if an applicant was born in Hawaii, just so they are 50 percent native Hawaiian ancestry. He further argued that birth certificates were only the "starting point" in investigating a person's ancestry.[192]

Gov. Lingle Signs "Birther Bill," Slamming Door Shut

On May 12, 2010, Hawaii Governor Linda Lingle signed a bill authorizing the state government to ignore duplicate Freedom of Information Act requests for copies of President Obama's birth certificate.

Health Director Chiyome Fukino had complained to the press that the state was getting about fifty requests per month for the president's birth certificate from so-called "birthers," and suggested the requests were a harassment that wasted state government time and resources. "The time and state resources it takes to respond to these often convoluted inquiries are considerable," she told the press.[193]

The law was intended to permanently shut down efforts by the public and press to obtain Obama birth records on file with the department.

"The Hawaii legislature has now officially passed a measure that would allow state officials to legally ignore each month's dozens of repeated requests by persons or organizations seeking to see the infant Obama's actual birth certificate," political commentator Andrew Malcolm wrote in his *Los Angeles Times* blog.[194] "For personal privacy reasons the certificate resides under government lock and key in Hawaii and, as is his right, Obama has never authorized its release." As noted in Chapter 5, on June 16, 2008, two days after the DailyKos first posted Obama's short-form Certification of Live Birth, Malcolm was one of the first mainstream media newspaper writers to claim the document was Obama's "birth certificate," ignoring the distinction between the short-form COLB and a long-form hospital birth certificate.

So much for transparency in government—a standard neither Lingle nor Obama seem to fret over when it comes to Obama's birth records.

Hawaii Elections Clerk: "There is No Obama Long-Form Birth Certificate"

While Hawaii officials were insisting they had a record of Obama being born in the state, a former senior elections clerk for Honolulu went public with the stunning claim that Barack Obama was definitely not born in Hawaii and that a long-form, hospital-generated birth certificate for Obama does not even exist in the Aloha state.[195]

"There is no birth certificate," said Tim Adams in a June 2010 interview with WND.[196] "It's like an open secret. There isn't one. Everyone in the government there knows this."

Adams, a graduate assistant who teaches English at Western Kentucky University in Bowling Green, said he was a supporter of Hillary Clinton in the 2008 presidential campaign who ended up voting for Republican nominee John McCain when Clinton lost the Democratic nomination to Obama.

As we noted earlier in Chapter 2, Adams has since affirmed his claims in a notarized affidavit provided to WND.[197]

"I managed the absentee-ballot office," he said. "It was my job to verify the voters' identity."

Adams told WND that during the 2008 campaign when the issue of Obama's constitutional eligibility first arose, the elections office was inundated with requests to verify the birthplace of the U.S. senator from Illinois.

"I had direct access to the Social Security database, the national crime computer, state driver's license information, international passport information, basically anything you can imagine to get someone's identity," Adams explained. "I could look up what bank your home mortgage was in. I was informed by my boss that we did not have a birth record [for Obama]."

While employed as a senior elections clerk for the city and county of Honolulu, Adams oversaw a group of fifty to sixty employees. He now expects his former co-workers still working in the elections office to say little, if anything, about the nonexistent birth certificate because they fear for their jobs.

During the campaign, there were conflicting reports that Obama had been born at the Queen's Medical Center in Honolulu and at the Kapi'olani Medical Center for Women and Children across town. So Adams says his office called both facilities.

"They told us, 'We don't have a birth certificate for him [Obama]'," Adams said. "They told my supervisor, either by phone or e-mail, neither one has a document that a doctor signed off on saying they were present at this man's birth."

WND confirmed with Hawaiian officials that Adams worked in their election offices during the last presidential election.

"His title was senior elections clerk in 2008," said Glen Takahashi, elections commissioner for the city and county of Honolulu. "We hire temporary workers because we're seasonal."

However, when WND asked Takahashi if the elections office would check on birth records, he said, "We don't have access to that kind of records. [There's] no access to birth records."

Adams responded, "They may say, 'We don't have access to that.' The regular workers don't, the ones processing ballots; but the people in administration do. I was the one overseeing the work of the people doing the balloting."

Adams stressed, "In my professional opinion, [Obama] definitely was not born in Hawaii. I can say without a shadow of a doubt that he was not born in Hawaii, because there is no legal record of him being born here. If someone called and asked about it, I could not tell them that person was born in the state."

When asked about the announcements of Obama's birth published in the Honolulu newspapers, Adams responded that the announcements don't prove Obama was born in Hawaii.

"I'm sure the [maternal] grandparents were happy to put that in the paper when he was born," said Adams, who noted he spent nearly ten years on the islands and has a bachelor's degree from the University of Hawaii.

Why would Hawaii officials, including Health Director Fukino, make assertions that birth records held by the Hawaii DOH proved Obama was born in Hawaii if a long-form hospital-generated birth certificate did not exist?

Adams responded: "If they say they've seen the document, then why not produce the document? There's no need to put themselves out like that. I can't even begin to think why they did that except for some kind of political expediency. I'm too far down the totem pole [to know]."

Adams said that while he is certain Obama was not born in Hawaii, he still believes Obama is a U.S. citizen, since his mother was an American.

"You don't have to like President Obama," he said, "but it is sad he's going to have to go through this public pillory by the time all this comes out, that they did cover this up; and that's sad because the first African-American man to become president shouldn't have this blight on his term in office. That's what he'll get remembered for. It's sad."

Adams told WND he has been telling other people his information for a long time, and is free to talk about it publically since he no longer has any confidentiality restrictions from his former employer, the Honolulu government.

Adams first brought his testimony to public attention when he was interviewed by James Edwards, the host of a weekly radio show on WLRM Radio in Memphis, Tennessee.

State Department Warns: Short-Form Birth Certificates May Not Prove Citizenship

The U.S. State Department warns that not all short-form birth certificates are acceptable to prove citizenship for the purposes of obtaining a U.S. passport.[198]

See a screen capture of the relevant passport discussion from the State Department Web site in Exhibit 112 on page 224.

Clearly, the State Department even today considers short-form certifications of birth issued by the states to be suspect or insufficient. The department could have in mind the fact that states such as Hawaii will issue birth documents on the basis of family testimony, without independent investigation and without medical documents authenticating an in-state birth.

Still, Obama supporters maintain that the short-form Certification of Live Birth issued by the Hawaii Department of Health is sufficient for all purposes under the sun.

Exhibit 113 on page 225 shows an example in which David Emery on About.com argues that the Obama short-form COLB is a valid "birth certificate" because it is the only form of birth certificate that Hawaii currently issues.

In a June 6, 2009, interview with the *Honolulu Star-Bulletin*, Janice Okubo said, "You can't obtain a 'certificate of live birth' anymore, because the Hawaii DOH went paperless in 2001 and the only birth documents currently issued are short-form Certifications of Live Birth, or COLBs, issued electronically." All information for births from 1908 until 2001 had been put into electronic files "for consistent reporting," she said.

She further indicated that under current procedures, information about births is transferred electronically from hospitals to the department.

"The electronic record of the birth is what (the Health Department) now keeps on file in order to provide same-day certified copies at our help window for most requests," Okubo said.

Okubu added that the Health Department "does not have a short-form or long-form certificate." Arguing that the Hawaii birth certificate form had been modified over the years to conform to national standards, Okubo emphasized that the COLB "contains all the information needed by all federal government agencies for transactions requiring a birth certificate." Moreover, she said, the U.S. Supreme Court has recognized the state's current electronic COLB "as an official birth certificate meeting all federal and other requirements," although she neglected to cite any specific Supreme Court cases.

Although Okubo said birth certificates before 2001 had been "put into electronic files" so the long-form certificates were no longer available, in an interview one year earlier, published July 28, 2008, by the *Honolulu Advertiser*, Okubo told reporters that President Obama's original August 4, 1961, birth certificate was in storage, even though she didn't specify whether that "birth certificate" was an original long-form, hospital-generated paper certificate of birth, a Photostat of a long-form, hospital-generated certificate of birth, or some other type of document.

"We don't destroy vital records," Okubo said. "That's our whole job, to maintain and retain vital records."[199]

Okubo was trying to put an end to questions that Obama's original paper birth records may have been destroyed when the Hawaii DOH went electronic in 2001. Still, she did not specify whether the "original Obama birth certificate," whatever she meant by that, was now an electronic copy of the original or the original paper document locked away in the Health Department's vault.

Hawaii Long-Form, Hospital-Generated Birth Certificate Available for $10

On October 13, 2010, a contributor with the username "Danae" posted on FreeRepublic.com a copy of her long-form birth certificate originally issued in 1969, but which the Hawaii Department of Health had mailed to her on September 28, 2010, after the payment of a $10 legal fee.[200]

Exhibit 114 on page 226 shows the birth certificate the Hawaii DOH mailed "Danae."

And Exhibit 115 on page 227 shows the copy of the receipt "Danae" was sent on September 28, 2010, by the Hawaii DOH, documenting the payment of the $10 legal fee to receive her long-form, hospital-generated birth certificate displayed immediately above.

Questioned on FreeRepublic about the authenticity of the copy of her birth certificate sent by the Hawaii DOH, "Danae" posted a photograph of her original long-form, hospital-generated certificate of live birth side-by-side with the copy she was sent, as evidence.

Exhibit 116 on page 228 shows the photograph.

As if that were not enough, "Danae" posted the two documents together with a short-form COLB that she had also asked the Hawaii DOH to produce.

Exhibit 117 on page 228 shows that photograph.

"Danae" obtained her long-form, hospital-generated certificate of birth to win a $200 bet another poster on FreeRepublic, operating under the username "STARWISE," had made. STARWISE dared someone to prove he or she could get a long-form birth certificate from the Hawaii DOH after 2001, when the Hawaii DOH went electronic and Okubo claimed they quit issuing such documents.

Perhaps the Hawaii DOH would be well advised to review the Hawaii Revised Statutes §38–13(a) that specify regarding birth certificates: "The department shall, upon request, furnish an applicant a certified copy of any certificate, or the contents of any certificate, or any part thereof." Further, §338–13(c) allows that copies of birth certificates "may be made by photography, dry copy reproduction, typing, computer printout or other process approved by the director of health."

Reading Hawaii's law, one point is abundantly clear: If the Hawaii Department of Health has a birth certificate, including a long-form, hospital-generated certificate of birth, the person whose birth is recorded or a person who has a tangible interest in the birth documents as defined by Hawaii law, can request and receive a certified copy. The argument advanced by Obama supporters that the Hawaii DOH currently issues only electronic short-form COLBs is patently false.

· 12 ·

DEMOCRATS DODGE ELIGIBILITY

**Democratic Party Pretends Eligibility Issue Doesn't Exist,
While Obama Hires Lawyers**

Rather than respect the American public by producing definitive documentary evidence that Barack Obama is legally eligible to occupy the office of president, the Democratic Party has instead stonewalled the issue and hired lawyers.

Increasingly controlled by the New Left that arose in the Bill Ayers era of 1960s anti-war, anti-America radicals, the Democratic Party has attempted to dodge questions about Obama's eligibility. Moreover, the Democratic Party and its supporters in the mainstream media and blogosphere have resorted to Saul Alinsky-style tactics of ridiculing anyone who dares raise the issue.

The Democratic Party took advantage of gaps in U.S. law that allowed it to avoid presenting evidence to the public that Obama was constitutionally qualified to be placed on the presidential ballot in 2008. And through Obama's first two years in office, the White House has spent more than a million dollars hiring lawyers to fight lawsuits filed by citizens to contest his eligibility. In court, the hired-gun attorneys have filed motion after motion to dismiss the lawsuits, largely on procedural grounds.

Now that it is apparent how many fabrications Obama's official life story contains, citizens demanding that courts examine his eligibility remain determined to press forward, despite continued stonewalling by the Democratic Party as well as the extreme reluctance of U.S. courts to litigate election issues.

Democrats File Questionable Certifications of Nomination

Each state requires political parties to file certificates of nomination to place their candidates on the ballot. In presidential elections, the states typically require that parties certify a candidate is qualified under the natural-born citizen requirement of Article 2, Section 1.

After the 2008 presidential election, researchers found that the Democratic Party had prepared two different forms to submit to the states as certificates of nomination for Barack Obama. One required party officials to swear that Obama was eligible under the Constitution to run for president; the other certificate omitted the language, allowing officials to swear Obama was their presidential candidate without also having to specifically swear he was eligible under the Constitution.

Exhibit 118 on page 229 shows what the first Democratic Party Certification of Nomination looked like in 2008, including the language that Obama was eligible to run for president.

It reads: "THIS IS TO CERTIFY that at the National Convention of the Democratic Party of the United States of America, held in Denver, Colorado on August 25 through 28, 2008, the following were duly nominated as candidates of said Party for President and Vice President of the United States respectively and that the following candidates for President and Vice President of the United States are legally qualified to serve under the provisions of the United States Constitution."

The second version (Exhibit 119, page 230) of the Democratic Party Certification of Nomination in 2008 excluded the language about constitutional eligibility.

"THIS IS TO CERTIFY that at the National Convention of the Democratic Party of the United States of America, held in Denver, Colorado on August 25 through 28, 2008, the following were duly nominated as candidates of said Party for President and Vice President of the United States respectively." Gone is the language in the first version specifying explicitly that the candidates were eligible under the provisions of the Constitution.

House Speaker Nancy Pelosi, chairwoman of the Democratic National Convention, and Alice Travis Germond, the convention secretary, swore to both of these Certifications of Nomination. The same Colorado notary public, Shalifa A. Williamson, certified both documents.

In contrast, the Republican National Convention prepared only one version of the Certification of Nominations, as it titled its document. Exhibit 120 on page 231 shows the document as submitted by the RNC to the secretary of state in Tennessee.

The Republican Party "Official Certificate of Nominations" for Senator John McCain and Governor Sarah Palin included the language that the candidates were eligible under the provisions of the Constitution, stating: "We do hereby certify that at a national convention of Delegates representing the Republican Party of the United States, duly held and convened in the city of Saint Paul, State of Minnesota, on September 4, 2008, the following person, meeting the constitutional requirements for the Office of President of the United States, and the following person, meeting the constitutional requirements for the Office of Vice President of the United States, were nominated for such offices to be filled at the ensuing general election, November 4, 2008, viz:"

Rep. John Boehner and Jean Inman, chairman and secretary respectively of the 2008 Republican National Convention, swore to the certificate.

The controversy over why the Democrats prepared two different versions of the certification of nomination document reached national attention when political commentator J.B. Williams published an article on September 10, 2009, in the *Canada Free Press*, publishing the above documents for the public to see.[201]

Evidently the Democratic National Committee had sent the abbreviated letter, without the language about being eligible under the Constitution, to forty-nine states, with only Hawaii getting the longer letter, specifying Obama was eligible under the Constitution.

The suspicion was that the Democrats had sent Hawaii the certification with the eligibility statement because Hawaii was openly claiming to be Obama's state of birth. The concern was that the Democrats had cleverly sent the other forty-nine states a certification of nomination that did not include the Constitutional eligibility statement because Nancy Pelosi knew Obama was not eligible and the Democratic Party was trying to dodge the issue.

Who Checks Eligibility?

The Democrats' preparation of two different versions of their certification of nomination was first reported by legal blogger jbjd on jbjd.org in 2009.

While the J.B. Williams article brought the issue to national attention in September 2010, the controversy had been brewing in various Internet blogs for almost two years before then.

The Democratic National Committee, jbjd reported, sent the abbreviated certification to forty-nine states, with only Hawaii getting the longer letter, which specified Obama was eligible under the Constitution. But jbjd had a different reason why the Democrats sent Hawaii the form specifying Obama was eligible.

Hawaii, it turned out, was unusual in that its law requires each party to specifically certify in writing that the presidential candidate is constitutionally eligible. "Under the laws in every state, once election officials receive the Official Certification of Nomination, the name of the nomination for [president of the United States] from the major political party is automatically entitled to appear on the state's general election ballot," jbjd wrote. "That is, in every other state in the union except [Hawaii]. In [Hawaii], just identifying the name of the nominee does not guarantee his name will be placed on the ballot. No; in order to get [Barack Obama's] name on the ballot in just that state, [Nancy Pelosi] also had to swear he was Constitutionally eligible for the job."[202]

DNC rules dictate that the candidate for the Democratic nomination for president "shall meet those requirements set forth by the United States Constitution and any law of the United States."[203] By swearing that Obama was "duly nominated" to be president, the shorter Democratic Party Certification of Nomination was in effect affirming that Obama was constitutionally eligible to be president. Obama, jbjd concluded, was "duly nominated" or "Constitutionally eligible for the job" was "a distinction without a difference."[204] By specifying Obama was "duly nominated," jbjd argued, the DNC was stating that Obama was a "natural-born citizen" under the requirements of Article 2, Section 1.

But in researching how presidential candidates get on state ballots, jbjd discovered a much deeper problem. Even in states such as Hawaii, South Carolina, Texas, and Georgia, where the state law specifies that a presidential nominee must be eligible under the Constitution, there is no provision that requires anyone in government to actually *check*. Once election officials in each state receive a Certification of Nomination from the Republican or Democratic Party in an acceptable format, the state officials place the nominee's name on the state ballot for president as requested, without determining for themselves whether or not the nominee actually is constitutionally eligible.

So, jbjd decided to ask Pelosi and the Democratic National Committee what steps had been taken at their level to ascertain Obama's constitutional eligibility. The blogger had letters addressed and hand-delivered to Pelosi and 2008 convention secretary Alice Germond, asking what documentation was used to determine Obama's constitutional eligibility before the Certification of Nomination sworn letters were sent to the states. Neither responded. Instead, jbjd got a letter from DNC General Counsel Joseph E. Sandler, who argued the DNC "is not a state agency subject to the open records or freedom of information statutes of any state."[205]

This response did not sit well with jbjd. "Of course, by focusing on the fact, [Sandler] cannot be legally compelled to turn over these records, Mr. Sandler qua the DNC, thumbs his nose at the voters from the states all across the country, who have enacted laws permitting their state to expend its public resources to print on state ballots the name of the nominee for POTUS from this private club," jbjd wrote. "In exchange, these voters only required the major political party *to ascertain their nominee is eligible for the job*."[206]

Objecting that the Democratic Party was stonewalling, jbjd used words such as "hubris" and "obfuscation" to describe Pelosi and the DNC, claiming their non-responsiveness "insults the integrity and intelligence of the voters."

On March 5, 2010, jbjd filed a memorandum of complaint with Maryland Attorney General Douglas F. Gansler, charging Pelosi, Germond, Sandler, and Howard Dean, the former DNC chairman, with election fraud.[207]

The complaint charged that at the time the DNC certified Barack Obama as the party's 2008 nominee for president that Pelosi, Germond, and the DNC had not ascertained that Obama was a natural-born citizen.

"Citizens from several states, concerned that members of the Democratic Party had submitted to their state election officials these unauthenticated Certificates of Nomination, contacted the DNC to see the documentation on which they had based this Certification," the complaint read. "Ms. Pelosi ignored all such requests. Mr. Sandler, claiming he was responding to requests that were directed to Ms. Germond, said, 'The Democratic National Committee is not a state agency subject to the open records or freedom of information statutes of any state.' And based on the fact, no law required him to produce the requested documentation; he chose not to produce this documentation."

In bold letters, the complaint argued: "Such display of hubris by members of any political party confronted by citizens concerned as to the legitimacy of the electoral process cannot be tolerated in our Constitutional Republic."

This then was the cover-up: Not that Pelosi and the DNC sent Certification of Nomination letters that neglected to swear Obama was constitutionally eligible to be president, but that they refused to produce for the public the documentation the DNC had relied upon to conclude that Obama is a natural-born citizen.

In addition, jbjd initiated election fraud complaints in Virginia,[208] South Carolina,[209] Texas,[210] Georgia,[211] and Hawaii.[212]

The complaint filed with the attorney general in Virginia noted that the Democratic National Committee had filed with state election officials a Certification of Nomination claiming Obama was "duly nominated." On that basis alone, Virginia election officials placed Obama's name on the state presidential ballot in 2008. The complaint continued: "However, overwhelming circumstantial evidence points to the fact that at the time [Pelosi and Germond] signed and forwarded this Certification, neither of them could have ascertained Mr. Obama is a NBC (natural-born citizen). And in Virginia, swearing to election officials he is a NBC without ascertaining he is, in order to secure a place on the ballot, constitutes election fraud."

Obama Hires Lawyers to Defeat Eligibility Court Cases

Instead of releasing relevant birth documents, the Obama White House has spent more than a million dollars hiring lawyers to defeat eligibility challenges in court.

The No. 1 hired gun of the White House legal effort is Robert Bauer. It turns out that Bauer is married to yet another White House hired gun, Anita Dunn, who was White House communications director and attacker of Fox News. Bauer is chairman of the political law group at Perkins Coie, the Seattle law firm hired by the White House to defend Obama in court cases contesting his eligibility. So successful was Bauer at fighting off legal challenges to Obama's eligibility that on November 12, 2009, he was appointed to serve as White House counsel.[213] Virtually the same day Bauer moved into the White House, Dunn resigned, largely over the dust-up she had spearheaded against Fox News.

But while Dunn targeted Fox with criticisms emanating from the Obama administration that the leading cable news organization was not a real news organization, her husband did his best to prevent the American public from ever seeing a wide range of Obama's records that could resolve whether he is legally eligible to occupy the Oval Office.

Dunn was on the record claiming that Obama's 2008 presidential campaign focused on "making" the news media cover certain issues by controlling messages through videos produced and distributed by campaign operative David Plouffe.

"Very rarely did we communicate through the press anything we didn't absolutely control," said Dunn. "One of the reasons we did so many of the David Plouffe videos was not just for our supporters, but also because it was a way for us to get our message out without having to talk to reporters. We just put that out there and made them write what Plouffe had said as opposed to Plouffe doing an interview with a reporter. So it was very much we controlled it as opposed to the press controlled it."

Dunn summed up the strategy as, "Making the press cover what we were saying."[214]

On October 12, 2009, calling Fox News "a wing of the Republican Party," Dunn further charged that Fox merely took Republican Party "talking points and opposition research" and put them on the air as news.

"And that's fine," Dunn said. "But let's not pretend they're a news network the way CNN is."[215]

Dunn summed up her White House-directed attack on Fox News by charging that the network is "opinion journalism masquerading as news."[216] Perhaps calling Fox a "part of the Republican Party" was the last straw in her controversial tenure as White House communications director.[217]

Bauer has a history of providing legal advice to Obama since Obama was sworn in as a U.S. senator in 2005. Prior to that, Bauer served as the general counsel to the Democratic National Committee.

On May 7, 2010, the White House posted an ethics waiver on the White House Web site exempting Bauer from the requirements of Executive Order 13490: "Ethics Commitments by Executive Branch Personnel," which prohibits political appointees from participating in activities of political parties that are directly and substantially related to former employees.[218]

The waiver allowed Bauer to remain White House counsel to the president while continuing to work with Perkins Coie in defending Obama against eligibility lawsuits.[219]

"If the ethics pledge were literally applied, when representing the interests of the President and the United States as Counsel to the President, Mr. Bauer would not be able to advise the President appropriately on particular matters that are directly and substantially related to Perkins Coie's representation of the president in his personal capacity," the waiver posted on the White House Web site read.

In October 2009, WND reported that Federal Election Commission records showed Obama for America made $1,352,378.95 in payments to Perkins Coie through the third quarter 2009.[220] The payments were made for the firm to defend Obama in various court cases that have sought to obtain his long-form birth certificate. Nor did the payments to Perkins Coie stop once Bauer became White House counsel. In the first quarter 2010, after Bauer had been appointed White House counsel, Obama for America (Exhibit 121, page 232) dispersed $261,206.69 to Perkins Coie to continue defending Obama against eligibility lawsuits.[221]

In January 2009, Obama for America, Obama's 2008 political campaign, merged with the Democratic National Committee and is now known as Organizing for America. This grassroots army that some refer to as "Obama 2.0" continues to solicit financial contributions on the BarackObama.com Web site.

Together, Bauer and Dunn (Exhibit 122, page 232) demonstrated the aggressive combination of media attack and legal stonewalling Obama used during the 2008 presidential campaign and which he has continued using in the White House to prevent any serious inquiry into his history and his leftist politics. While Bauer and Dunn present themselves as professionals in their respective fields, they function as Washington-insider attack dogs for Obama, ridiculing and abusing opponents' arguments both in the media and in the courts.[222]

Bauer, a Democratic Party partisan, has a long history of defending party ambitions as legal counsel. His biography posted on the Perkins Coie Web site in 2009 indicated he was general counsel to the Democratic National Committee during the presidential campaign of Senator John Kerry and served as counsel to Senator Tom Daschle, the Democratic Senate majority leader, during the impeachment of President Bill Clinton.

During the 2008 presidential campaign, Bauer functioned as an "attack lawyer," threatening with FEC complaints groups wanting to run television ads critical of Obama. As counsel for the Obama campaign, Bauer wrote letters to television station managers and to Department of Justice Assistant Attorney General John Keeney arguing that airing an anti-Obama ad linking Obama to Weather Underground radical Bill Ayers would violate federal election rules.[223] He also intervened on behalf of his client Senator Obama to block the California-based American Leadership Project—a group supporting the presidential candidacy of Hillary Clinton—from running a TV ad campaign in Indiana claiming that Obama's Indiana campaign had been funded by unions, including the Service Employees International Union.[224] Filing a complaint with the FEC, Bauer charged that the television campaign was illegal under federal election laws.

During the 2008 presidential campaign, Bauer was also at the center of the controversy over Obama's decision to go back on his promise to accept public financing for his presidential campaign. The decision came after a meeting with McCain attorney Trevor Potter in which Bauer charged that the Republican nominee did not want to reach a compromise on the issue. At that time, McCain campaign communications director Jill Hazelbaker argued that Obama "has revealed himself to be just another typical politician who will do and say whatever is most expedient for Barack Obama." The McCain campaign sharply criticized Bauer's characterization of the meeting.[225]

In June 2007, Bauer authored a piece in the *Huffington Post* arguing that liberals should not oppose a White House pardon for Vice President Dick Cheney's chief of staff, Scooter Libby, who was convicted of perjury. He wrote that a pardon would draw President Bush directly into the case, warning that the "presidential fingerprints" would become politically explosive.[226]

In short, Bauer was clearly the right attorney to stonewall every court challenge to Obama's eligibility. His defense strategy was predicated on making plaintiffs look like fringe lunatics, while refusing to provide to courts any proof of Obama's eligibility other that what had already been offered, namely the COLB first posted by DailyKos and the Hawaii newspaper birth announcements published in 1961.

A Look at the Legal Challenges to Obama's Eligibility

An exhaustive coverage of the many lawsuits filed by citizens challenging Obama's presidential eligibility is beyond the scope of this book. But the brief summary of the lawsuits presented here should make it clear why the courts do not want to take the case—that is, U.S. appellate courts have been very reluctant to take on political cases that could determine the outcome of an election. An exception was the Supreme Court decision in the 2000 presidential election, *Bush v. Gore*, in which the court effectively ended the Florida recount in favor of the Republican presidential nominee, George W. Bush. Since then, many Bush opponents have asserted the former Texas governor was "selected" as president, not elected.

Courts have rejected most of these lawsuits based on the determination that the plaintiffs do not have "legal standing." Plaintiffs must be able to demonstrate they have suffered harm as a result of a breach of law. But if it turns out that President Obama is not eligible to be president because he is not a natural-born citizen, the integrity of the vote for all Americans is compromised. In a common-sense understanding, if Obama turned out to be a "usurper" of the Oval Office, the damage done to voters should be sufficient to give *every one of them* legal standing.

By refusing to hear eligibility cases, courts are also denying plaintiffs the opportunity to engage in discovery, a legal process in which the president could be subpoenaed to release documents about his birth and his life that have been kept from public view.

Here then is a brief discussion of the major court eligibility cases that have been brought against Barack Obama. They illustrate the generally disappointing results citizens have obtained in the extensive effort to get courts to resolve the controversy:

Philip J. Berg

One of the earliest litigants was attorney Philip J. Berg, former deputy attorney general of Pennsylvania and a Democratic supporter of Hillary Clinton. Obama supporters like to characterize Berg as an extremist, activist attorney who in 2004 filed a RICO (Racketeer Influenced and Corrupt Organizations Act) case on behalf of a World Trade Center maintenance worker, charging the Bush administration was complicit in the 9/11 attacks.

U.S. District Judge R. Barclay Surrick dismissed Berg's case on October 24, 2008—just before the presidential election in November—for lack of legal standing, issuing a court order accompanied by a thirty-four-page legal memorandum.[227] In the memorandum, Judge Surrick wrote that to grant standing to Berg such that the case could be heard would "derail the democratic process by invalidating a candidate for whom millions of people voted and who underwent excessive vetting during what was one of the most hotly contested presidential primaries in living history."

Surrick misses the point that there was no governmental mechanism in place to determine Obama was a natural-born citizen within the meaning of Article 2, Section 1. Moreover, the eligibility issue was not settled simply because Obama was elected president. Eligibility is not a question that can properly be settled by voting. Eligibility is a yes or no determination that can only be made after a duly constituted and appointed authority has examined the birth facts to rule whether or not the candidate is a natural-born citizen.

By ruling that Berg did not have standing to have the case heard, Judge Surrick dodged having to rule on the substance of the case. Ultimately the case settled nothing, except to suggest that filing lawsuits was not likely to resolve the Obama eligibility issue.

Alan Keyes

Former Reagan administration ambassador Alan Keyes filed a lawsuit on November 14, 2008, demanding that Obama provide documentation that he is a natural-born citizen. The suit had some weight in that Keyes himself was a presidential candidate that year, first contending for the Republican Party nomination, and then running under the banner of the American Independent Party.

On October 25, 2010, Justice Arthur G. Scotland of the U.S. Court of Appeals of California for the Third District in Sacramento, writing for the three-judge panel, ruled that the California secretary of state "does not have a duty to investigate and determine whether a presidential candidate meets eligibility requirements of the United States Constitution." Judge Scotland contended that if the fifty states were at liberty to issue injunctions restricting certification of duly elected presidential electors, "the result could be conflicting rulings and delayed transition of power in derogation of statutory and constitutional deadlines." Instead, the judge contended, the eligibility investigation was best left to the political parties, noting that the parties "presumably will conduct the appropriate background check or risk that its nominee's election will be derailed by an objection in Congress, which is authorized to entertain and resolve the validity of objections following the submission of electoral votes."[228]

But we now know the Democratic National Convention pronounced Obama "duly nominated" without conducting any check into his birth credentials. Moreover, a Democratic Party-controlled Congress is not inclined to take an eligibility challenge to its presidential candidate seriously, especially if the candidate had already won the election.

Orly Taitz

Orly Taitz, a Russian-born, California-based dentist and attorney, has perhaps drawn the most media attention among the lawyers challenging Obama's eligibility.

After having several of her eligibility court cases dismissed, Taitz achieved one of the few victories in the controversy. Representing U.S. Army Major Stefan Frederick Cook, a U.S. Army reservist who objected to deployment in Afghanistan because he believed Obama was not eligible to be commander-in-chief, Taitz filed the case in the U.S. District Court for the Middle District of Georgia on July 8, 2009, seeking a temporary restraining order and conscientious objector status for Cook. The case became moot on July 15, 2009, when the U.S. Army revoked Cook's orders to report to MacDill Air Force Base for mobilization. Lt. Col. Maria Quon told the *Atlanta Journal-Constitution* that she could not say why the deployment orders were revoked.[229]

While the Army refused to explain why it changed Cook's orders, many Obama critics believed the Army capitulated to stop the eligibility case from going forward. A U.S. military officer refusing to obey orders to deploy to a combat zone was more likely to have legal standing in court because refusal to obey would result in a military court martial. Being found guilty of refusing orders at a military court martial would have caused Cook considerable harm, including the possibility of dishonorable discharge and a prison sentence. Whether or not the decision to drop the case came from the White House cannot be proved. Still, that the Army did not pursue the case strongly suggested Pentagon officials were concerned that the U.S. District Court might agree to hear the case. Any federal court agreeing to hear a plaintiff's case would also grant to the plaintiff the right to discovery.

In other cases, Taitz was less fortunate.

In October 2009, U.S. District Judge Clay Land fined Taitz $20,000 for what he called "frivolous" court actions, mocking her concerns over Obama's eligibility.[230] The case was brought in Georgia, with Taitz defending U.S. Army physician Captain Connie Rhodes, who had sought a restraining order for her deployment to Iraq on grounds similar to those of Cook, charging Obama was not eligible to be commander-in-chief.

Judge Land rejected Taitz's argument that the judiciary should be "the arbiter of any dispute regarding the President's constitutional qualifications." Without specifying the governmental mechanisms he had in mind, Land wrote: "Our founders provided opportunities for a President's qualifications to be tested, but they do not include direct involvement by the judiciary."

The judge suggested impeachment was the only remedy to remove an ineligible president from the White House. "In addition to the obvious opportunity that exists during a presidential campaign to scrutinize a candidate's qualifications, the framers of the Constitution provided a mechanism for removing a President who 'slips through the cracks,' which is how counsel [Taitz] describes President Obama," Land continued. "Upon conviction by the Senate of treason, bribery or other high crimes and misdemeanors, the President can be removed through impeachment. Thus, if the President were elected to the office by knowingly and fraudulently concealing evidence of his constitutional disqualification, then a mechanism exists for removing him from office." Again, the court wanted nothing to do with adjudicating the eligibility questions.

Along with fining Taitz for "misconduct," Land also ridiculed her pursuit of the case. "Although counsel's present concern is the location of the President's birth, it does not take much imagination to extend the theory to his birthday," Land wrote. "Perhaps, he looks 'too young' to be President, and he says he stopped counting birthdays when he reached age thirty. If he refused to admit publicly that he is older than the constitutional minimum age of thirty-five, should Ms. Taitz be allowed to file a lawsuit and have a court order him to produce his birth certificate?"

Even this was not enough for Land. "Or perhaps an eccentric citizen has become convinced that the President is an alien from Mars, and the courts should order DNA testing to enforce the Constitution," he continued. "Or, more to the point, the Court should issue a nationwide injunction that prevents the U.S. Army from sending any soldier to Iraq or Afghanistan or anywhere else until Ms. Taitz is permitted to depose the President in the Oval Office."

Land was clear in his view that the federal courts "were not established to resolve such purely political disputes or to assist in the pursuit of a political fishing expedition, particularly when that intrusion would interfere with the ability of the U.S. Army to do its job."

Lt. Col. Terrence Lakin

Lt. Col. Terrence Lakin, a veteran flight surgeon in the U.S. Army Medical Corps, refused to obey orders to deploy to Afghanistan, arguing that Obama is not legally the commander-in-chief because he has not proved his eligibility to be president.

At a military hearing on September 2, 2010, Col. Denise Lind, the officer assigned to be the military judge in Lakin's court-martial, ruled that it was "not relevant" for the military to consider claims over Obama's eligibility, and that the laws allegedly violated by Lind were valid on their face. She further ruled that the chain of command that led up to the Pentagon should have been sufficient for Lakin. So, the only question Lind would allow at the court-martial was whether Lakin obeyed his orders or not.

In so ruling, Lind denied Lakin the right of discovery, saying that opening up the White House to a subpoena for eligibility documents could be an "embarrassment" to the president. She did not explain the basis for her conclusion that being forced to produce relevant birth documents at the court-martial would embarrass Obama. Still, Lind expressed her concurrence with federal civil court cases that had dismissed various eligibility lawsuits, saying that it was up to Congress to call for the impeachment of a sitting president.

On December 15, 2010, a military jury found Lakin guilty of refusing to obey orders, dismissed him from the Army, stripped him of all Army benefits including his retirement benefits, and sentenced him to six months in military prison.

Hollister v. Soetoro, et al

The case *Hollister v. Soetoro, et al*,[231] was made on behalf of a retired Air Force colonel by attorney Philip Berg. After losing *Berg v. Obama* over a lack of legal standing, Berg represented Gregory Hollister, believing a military officer would more clearly have legal standing in challenging the eligibility of the commander-in-chief. Hollister, who served honorably for twenty years and retired in 1998, based his lawsuit on his continued participation in the Individual Ready Reserve and challenged Obama's legal authority to recall him to duty. John D. Hemenway, an attorney in Washington, D.C., also represented Hollister in the case, which was brought in the U.S. District Court for the District of Columbia.

On April 3, 2009, before he joined the White House as counsel for the president, Robert Bauer wrote a letter to Hemenway, addressed from Bauer's law firm, Perkins Coie, in Washington, D.C., and representing the defendant in the case, "Barry Soetoro," aka President Barack Obama. The letter (Exhibit 123, page 233) threatened Hemenway with sanctions unless Hemenway agreed "to withdraw this frivolous appeal" of the original ruling.

Hemenway, a former Rhodes Scholar who was eighty-two years old at the time, had taken the Hollister case for what he considered to be patriotic reasons.[232]

On March 5, 2009, U.S. District Court Judge James Robertson dismissed the case, writing, "This case, if it were allowed to proceed, would deserve mention in one of those books that seek to prove that the law is foolish or that America has too many lawyers with not enough to do. Even in its relatively short life the case has excited the blogosphere and the conspiracy theorists. The right thing to do is to bring it to an early end."[233]

Judge Robertson claimed in his memorandum that the real plaintiff in the Hollister case was Philip J. Berg, "a lawyer who lives in Lafayette Hill, Pennsylvania, and who has pursued his crusade elsewhere, see *Berg v. Obama*, 574 F. Supp. 2d 509 (E.D. Pa. 2008), invoking the civil rights statutes, the Federal Election Campaign Act, the Freedom of Information Act, the Immigration and Nationality Act, and the law of promissory estoppel." The judge also claimed Hollister was "Mr. Berg's fallback brainstorm, essentially a straw plaintiff, one who could tee Mr. Berg's native-born issue up for decision on a new theory." Evidently Robertson saw no need to distinguish between "native-born" and "natural-born." Still, he dismissed the case and reprimanded attorney Hemenway for taking it.

Ultimately, the U.S. Court of Appeals for the District of Columbia Circuit upheld the dismissal and the reprimand of Hemenway.

This case is important not just for demonstrating the animosity federal judges have shown in virtually every eligibility case brought to challenge Obama, but also for the weakness of the case Bauer and his attorneys at Perkins Coie produced to defend their client.

Legal blogger jbjd, who analyzed the DNC Certification of Nomination letters, had been predicting that the only evidence the White House would produce to support Obama's eligibility would be the Certification of Live Birth generated during the 2008 presidential campaign by Obama-supporting Web sites. In reading the Motion to Dismiss produced by Bauer and Perkins Coie in the Hollister case, jbjd focused on a footnote in which the president's defense attorneys had asserted that Obama had "publicly produced a certified copy of a birth certificate showing that he was born on August 4, 1961, in Honolulu, Hawaii." Furthermore, Bauer and the Perkins Coie attorneys neglected to present the court with the "original" COLB so the court clerk could mark up the document as evidence and place it in the case record. Instead, Bauer and the Perkins Coie attorneys tried to authenticate the Internet-posted COLB by asking the court to take "notice" that the Annenberg-funded Web site FactCheck. org had concluded the document was "genuine."

Jbjd was astounded to have been correct.[234] The only evidence Obama's defense attorneys were producing to support his claim of presidential eligibility was the COLB, offered as if it were a "certified copy of a birth certificate." Furthermore, Bauer and the defense attorneys at Perkins Coie were asking the federal court to take the word of partisan Web sites such as DailyKos.com and FactCheck.org that the document was authentic.

To buttress their argument, Bauer and Perkins Coie also cited the announcements of Obama's birth that were published in the Honolulu newspapers at the time.

"He is truly trying to put one over on the court," jbjd concluded.

"Thankfully, the only thing the court granted [Barack Obama] in *Hollister* was a dismissal," jbjd wrote. "But beginning back in July 2008, I surmised, the strongest piece of evidence [Obama] could produce to verify his Constitutional eligibility for POTUS, is that COLB he posted on [FightTheSmears.com], which means nothing. By placing that footnote in his Motion to Dismiss, [Obama] validated my suspicions. If he had 'evidence' of eligibility with more gravitas that a photocopied COLB, or a phantom image of a newspaper birth announcement, he would have asked the federal judge to take judicial notice of that."

Even more astounding, jbjd noted, was that Bauer and Perkins Coie did not consider the Certification of Nomination forms signed by House

Speaker Nancy Pelosi on behalf of the Democratic National Convention proof that Obama was eligible to be president.

Evidently, the defense attorneys were aware that Pelosi and the DNC had nothing better to go on themselves, other that the COLB, the Honolulu newspaper birth announcements, and Obama's word that he was born in Hawaii.

· 13 ·

A FEDERAL MANDATE AND THE STATES' RIGHTS SOLUTION

Instituting Governmental Procedures to Implement the "Natural-born Citizen" Requirement of Article 2, Section 1, of the Constitution

If the courts, in their reluctance to take up political questions, will not allow presidential eligibility to be adjudicated, then new governmental procedures need to be instituted to make sure all serious presidential candidates are "natural-born citizens" under the meaning of the U.S. Constitution.

In the final analysis, the question is: How is it possible that Barack Obama was allowed to fabricate key facts in his official birth narrative without being held accountable under Article 2, Section 1?

What Obama's case demonstrates is that a popular candidate from the political left will be given a pass on the question of presidential eligibility, with the winking complicity of a politicized establishment press. While news outlets such as the *New York Times* and the *Washington Post* were happy to publish articles raising questions about whether John McCain was a natural-born citizen, those same sources demonized anyone who dared ask the same questions about Obama as "birthers".

Nor can the Democratic Party be counted on to rigorously examine birth credentials of popular candidates. In truth, many on the political left consider Article 2, Section 1, just another archaic constitutional provision that needs to be abandoned in an age when Democrats champion the idea that illegal immigrants have a right to vote and international laws should be equivalent to U.S. law in determining the precedents applied in Supreme Court decisions.

As we have seen, Article 2, Section 1, did not set up any governmental institution or mechanism to examine and certify presidential candidates' birth credentials. That loophole was all Obama needed to sponsor a resolution in Congress to affirm that McCain is a natural-born citizen, while refusing to present his own birth credentials for a similar resolution.

If American voters are resolved to take seriously constitutional requirements, then either Congress or the state legislatures must craft new laws specifying precisely how birth credentials of presidential candidates will be examined.

In addition to Congress passing a law requiring the presentation of birth credentials for all presidential candidates, the federal mandate specified under Article 2, Section 1, will only be secure when a states-rights solution is put in place. Why? Because in the federal system specified by the Constitution, state electors are responsible for choosing the president. The secretaries of state in each state thus hold the final responsibility for placing presidential candidates on the ballot. For this reason, state laws must be crafted, in addition to a federal law, requiring that the political parties certify to the secretaries of state in each state the basic constitutional credentials for their presidential candidates.

Congressional Research Service Covers for Obama

As noted in Chapter 2, a congressional document surfaced on the Internet two years after the 2008 presidential election officially confirming explicitly that no one in the federal government ever bothered to check Obama's birth credentials during the campaign.

The document, written by the Congressional Research Service, admitted that no one in the federal government, including Congress, ever asked to see Obama's long-form, hospital-generated birth certificate. Why? Because, the CRS explained, there were no federal or state laws requiring officials to demand that the document be submitted.

Technically, the CRS is a public policy research arm of the United States Congress, organized as a legislative branch agency within the Library of Congress. The CRS works exclusively for members of Congress, congressional committees and congressional staff in an advisory capacity.

The CRS memorandum, published and distributed to congressional offices on April 3, 2009, was written to explain to senators and members of the House how they could answer constituents who were demanding to see Obama's birth certificate.

Authored by Jack Maskell, the legislative attorney in the American Law Division of the Congressional Research Service, the document was a memorandum headlined: "Qualifications for the Office of President of the United States and Legal Challenges to the Eligibility of a Candidate"[235] The CRS began by stating the problem:

> Many of the inquiries have questioned why then-Senator, and now President, Obama has not had to produce an original, so-called "long" version of a "birth certificate" from the State of Hawaii, how federal candidates are "vetted" for qualifications generally, and have asked for an assessment of the various allegations and claims of non-eligibility status.

In other words, senators and members of the House could not explain why nobody ever saw Obama's long-form, hospital birth certificate, and they needed a ready answer to give angry constituents who were writing, e-mailing, faxing, and telephoning their offices.

The second full paragraph of the CRS memo is astonishing and needs to be read in its entirety to comprehend that *no one in Congress or anywhere else in the federal government* concerned themselves with Obama's eligibility to be president. This is the most important paragraph in the document:

> Concerning the production or release of an original birth certificate, it should be noted that there is no federal law, regulation, rule, guideline, or requirement that a candidate for federal office produce his or her original birth certificate, or a certified copy of the record of live birth, to any official of the United States Government; nor is there a requirement for federal candidates to publicly release such personal record or documentation. Furthermore, there is no specific federal agency or office that "vets" candidates for federal office as to qualifications or eligibility prior to election.

In other words, Obama got a pass from Congress and the federal government as a whole. No one in government sought to look for Obama's birth certificate because no law or regulation required them to look.

The CRS document is so startling in this admission that a screen capture of the document's first page is presented in Exhibit 124 on page 234.

Next, the CRS memo recognized that federal elections are administered under state law. This is apparent to lawyers and legal scholars, though for typical American voters the admission is hard to understand.

> The mechanics of elections of federal officials within the several states are administered under state law. The quadrennial presidential election, although required since 1845 to be held on the same day in each state is, in an administrative and operational sense, fifty-one separate elections in the states and the District of Columbia for presidential electors. States generally control, within the applicable constitutional parameters, the administrative issues, questions, and mechanisms of ballot placement and ballot access.

So the states control federal elections, including the balloting for president. However, state law, like federal law, does not require any state to examine the birth qualifications of presidential candidates.

While states may have discretionary authority to question a candidate's eligibility to run for federal office, there is no requirement in state law to do so when it comes to examining birth records.

Once more, here is the memo's relevant language:

> In *Keyes v. Bowen*, the California Supreme Court discussed a suit against the Secretary of State that challenged President Obama's eligibility and the California electoral votes for him, finding that: "Petitioners have not identified any authority *requiring* the Secretary of State to make an inquiry into or demand detailed proof of citizenship from Presidential candidates," and thus mandamus (a writ of mandate) was not granted. However, although no "ministerial duty" or mandatory requirement exists to support a mandamus action, there may still exist discretionary authority in such elections official.

In the last chapter we saw that the court dismissed this lawsuit brought by Ambassador Alan Keyes. A writ of mandamus in this case would have involved a court order being issued by the secretary of state of California demanding that Obama produce his long-form, hospital-generated birth certificate to get his name on the state's presidential ballot in 2008.

What the CRS is saying is that since there was no state law demanding Obama show his birth certificate, the court could not demand he do so. It was entirely up to the California secretary of state, who had discretion to ask for the document or not.

In practical terms, the CRS was also saying to Congress that Obama could refuse to show his real birth certificate because no state or federal law required him to do so.

Here, the CRS shows how Obama and his campaign saw the legal loophole and took full advantage of it:

> Despite the absence of any formal administrative or legal requirement or oversight at the federal level, or specific state requirement to produce a birth certificate for ballot placement, it may be noted here briefly that the only "official" documentation or record that has been presented in the matter of President Obama's eligibility has been an official, certified copy of the record of live birth released by the Obama campaign in June of 2008, as an apparent effort by then-candidate Obama to address rumors and innuendos concerning the place of his birth.

The CRS memo makes the following conclusion clear: If the birth requirements of Article 2, Section 1, are to be taken seriously, new laws at the federal and state levels *must* be passed to institutionalize government procedures requiring presidential candidates to come forward with their birth certificates.

A Federal Law Designed to Implement Article 2, Section 1

On May 15, 2009, Rep. Bill Posey, R-FL, introduced H.R. 1503, "The Presidential Eligibility Act," a bill designed to amend the Federal Election Campaign Act to require, beginning in 2012, that a candidate for president submit a birth certificate to the Federal Election Commission at the same time the campaign submits a statement of organization to the FEC.[236]

Posey's suggestion works because the federal government does regulate the formation of presidential campaigns and campaign contributions, even though the states control the presidential balloting process.

In seeking to amend 2 U.S. Code §433(b), Posey's H.R. 1503 states its purpose as follows:

> To amend the Federal Election Campaign Act of 1971 to require the principal campaign committee of a candidate for election to the office of President to include with the committee's statement of organization a copy of the candidate's birth certificate, together with such other documentation as may be necessary to establish that the candidate meets the qualification of eligibility to the Office of the President under the Constitution.

The bill also provides:

> Congress finds that under … the Constitution of the United States, in order to be eligible to serve as President, an individual must be a natural-born citizen of the United States who has attained the age of 35 years and has been a resident within the United States for at least 14 years.

So, when registering a national campaign to run for president, a candidate would also be forced to deliver his or her birth certificate and any other relevant birth documents to the FEC. This would close the loophole of Article 2, Section 1, with a clear, specific federal requirement of proof that a presidential candidate is a natural-born citizen.

Posey's goal was to have H.R. 1503 become effective for the 2012 presidential election, requiring President Obama to present his birth certificate to the FEC to run for re-election. The legislation garnered twelve co-sponsors in the House before languishing in committee.

Passing H.R. 1503 would eliminate the possibility that a candidate like Obama could avoid presenting to the American public a long-form, definitive birth certificate, if such a document exists.

Hawaii has verified that no birth records on file with the Hawaii Department of Health have been destroyed. Hawaii law permits Obama to obtain and release to the public any birth records on file with the Hawaii DOH. Therefore, Obama should have no problem complying with the requirements of this proposed legislation.

If the Hawaii DOH is telling the truth that Obama's birth records validate that he was born in Hawaii as he claims, then why would the president object to meeting the requirements of H.R. 1503 when he organizes his re-election committee ahead of the 2012 campaign?

The States' Rights Solution

Bills have been introduced in several state legislatures requiring candidates to submit their birth certificates to the state secretary of state to get their names on the ballot.

If the secretary of state decided that the documents submitted did not prove the presidential candidate was a natural-born citizen, he or she would possess the authority to keep that candidate's name off the presidential ballot for that state.

Arizona, Oklahoma, and Georgia head a list of about a dozen states in various stages of passing presidential eligibility legislation.

Given that state law controls balloting in presidential elections, the secretary of state in each state is the appropriate control point for eligibility determinations. Typically, no name appears on any state ballot without the approval of that state's secretary of state.

The Arizona bill, HB 2441, "Presidential candidates; proof of qualifications," is rapidly becoming the model of state eligibility legislation for presidential elections.[237]

Arizona HB 2441 contains the following provisions:

- The national political party committee for a candidate for president must present to the Arizona secretary of state written notice of that political party's nomination of its candidates for president and vice-president;

- Within ten days after the submittal of the names of the candidates, the national political party committee shall submit an affidavit of the presidential candidate in which the presidential candidate states the candidate's citizenship and age;

- Appended to the affidavit must be documents that prove the candidate's age, and prove that the candidate is a natural-born citizen under the requirements prescribed in Article 2, Section 1, of the U.S. Constitution;

- The Arizona secretary of state will review the affidavit and other documents submitted by the national political party committee;

- If the Arizona secretary of state has reasonable cause to believe that the candidate does not meet the citizenship, age, and residency requirements prescribed by law, the Arizona secretary of state shall not place that candidate's name on the presidential ballot.

To guard against forgery, a state law should give the secretary of state the authority to examine in person all original documents, including short-form or long-form birth certificates, submitted to establish eligibility for candidates seeking to be placed on the state's presidential ballot.

Additionally, a state law should impose these identical requirements on all candidates for the vice presidency as well, since in the event of the president's death, the vice president ascends to the presidency. In effect, the vice president is a candidate for president.

Passing such eligibility laws at the state level is the states rights solution to instituting a governmental mechanism to implement the requirements of Article 2, Section 1.

In fact, the states rights solution would work by itself, even if the Congress fails to pass a law such as that proposed by Rep. Posey.

If just one state were to have an eligibility law in place for the 2012 election, that might be enough to force Obama to either show the public his long-form birth certificate and all other documentation relevant to his natural-born citizen status or withdraw from seeking re-election.

If HB 2441, or a law similar to it, is in place in Arizona for the 2012 presidential election, Obama and the Democratic Party will have no choice but to present all relevant birth and citizenship documents to the Arizona secretary of state to get Obama's name on the state's 2012 presidential ballot.

No candidate for president could afford to be taken off the presidential ballot of even one state, and President Obama should not be given a pass on complying with state eligibility laws simply because he is already president.

WHAT WILL HAPPEN IN 2012?

The test in the upcoming presidential election of 2012 is whether or not President Obama will get a second pass on having to present his eligibility credentials to the American people.

At stake is nothing less than the U.S. Constitution.

Will the American public demand to see Obama's genuine, hospital birth certificate this time around? What about the other documents that relate to Obama's citizenship, including adoption papers from Indonesia, an amended Hawaii Certification of Live Birth that reflects Obama's Indonesian adoption, as well as his State Department travel and passport file that could reflect foreign citizenship and possibly an Indonesian passport? Will voters demand to see these as well?

Americans should not wait until 2012. In the event it is proven conclusively that Obama was not born in Hawaii, he should immediately be removed from office by impeachment simply because he lied and was elected president fraudulently. The same should hold true if Obama became an Indonesian citizen by adoption when he was a child, or if he used an Indonesian passport to travel to Pakistan with his college roommates. The American people would be outraged if they learned Obama received scholarships to attend college after applying as a foreign student. Is this the reason Obama refuses to make the relevant documents public?

Readers should be shocked to learn that the president's mother, Ann

Dunham, took him as an infant and left Hawaii within weeks of his birth to enroll in extension classes at the University of Washington in Seattle. This inconvenient fact was never disclosed in Obama's autobiography *Dreams of My Father,* nor in any of the many stories about his childhood Obama has told and retold in his public life. What we have been led to believe is that Dunham stayed in Hawaii until her husband, Barack Obama, Sr., left for Harvard. The truth could not be more different: Dunham left her husband in Hawaii and never returned until after Obama, Sr., had left the state for good.

Will the public demand that Obama finally tell the whole truth about his birth, about his childhood, and about his citizenship? The lies are material because Article 2, Section 1, demands we know the truth about a person's life if that person wants to be president of the United States.

If Obama is a usurper, lying to cover up material facts about his life that would have made him legally ineligible to be president, then he should be removed from office, regardless of the consequences.

At the very least, Congress and the states must pass laws to demand that all future candidates—including Obama, should he run for re-election in 2012—must present all relevant birth and citizenship documentation to have their names placed on the presidential ballot.

The point is that not holding Obama accountable to the "natural-born citizen" requirements of Article 2, Section 1, will have serious consequences, not only to the credibility of the presidency, but to the future meaning of U.S. citizenship, and to the integrity of the Constitution itself.

The Push to Eliminate Article 2, Section 1

Amending the Constitution to eliminate the "natural-born citizen" clause is not feasible in the short time remaining before the 2012 presidential election because the lengthy process requires a two-thirds vote of the House and Senate, as well as ratification by three-fourths of the states.

Yet, in order to support Obama's eligibility to be president, the political left would like to see the definition of "natural-born citizen" reduced to the equivalent of "native-born citizen." Obama's supporters have argued that he is a "natural-born citizen" under the meaning of Article 2, Section 1, simply if it can be proved conclusively that he was born in Hawaii.

In the Congressional Research Service memo written to defend Obama's eligibility, Jack Maskel, legislative attorney for the CRS American Law Division, summed up the argument as follows: "The constitutional history and relevant case law indicate that one born 'in' the United States, and subject to its jurisdiction, that is, when one's parents are not official diplomatic personnel representing a foreign nation in the United States, would be considered a U.S. citizen 'at birth' or 'by birth,' and thus a 'natural-born Citizen' of the United States, regardless of the citizenship status of that individual's parents."[238]

In other words, "birth citizenship"—the fact of being born in the United States—is all that Obama supporters want to be relevant. Once birth citizenship can be established, the 14th Amendment is rolled out to argue that a native-born citizen equals a "natural-born citizen" under the meaning of Article 2, Section 1. The distinction between "citizen" and "natural-born citizen" is intentionally blurred since Obama supporters want any citizen not naturalized to be a natural-born citizen by definition. Their goal is to make the terms "native-born" and "natural-born" equivalent, such that "natural-born citizens" are no longer a more restrictive subset of "native-born citizens" under the 14th Amendment.

Obama supporters also aim to strike out as irrelevant that Obama was a dual citizen of the British Empire at birth because of his father's Kenyan citizenship. Equally irrelevant, Obama partisans would argue, is the possibility Obama became an Indonesian citizen as a child because his Indonesian stepfather adopted him. Even if Obama had an Indonesian passport, they argue, Obama was a child and had no say in a decision made by his stepfather and mother.

As we proceed down this slippery slope, we have to ask if future generations will even demand that a president be a citizen. If globalism is the vogue perspective, future generations might ask, why limit the talent pool for prospective presidents to U.S. citizens only? How about someone talented from the United Nations to resolve wars, or the International Monetary Fund to take care of a perceived economic crisis?

Already, the goal of those who promote Austrian-born former California Gov. Arnold Schwarzenegger for president is that naturalized citizens should have the chance to run for president. If "native-born" can be made equivalent to "natural-born," then why isn't it sufficient that a presidential candidate simply be a U.S. citizen, even if he or she is naturalized? That is the argument being made for Schwarzenegger.

Arnold Schwarzenegger for President

Don't be fooled into thinking the issue is only about Barack Obama.

If the Democrats ignored Article 2, Section 1, in 2008 because they were confident Obama would win the presidency, would Republicans do the same if they thought Arnold Schwarzenegger might someday be their sure-win presidential candidate? The only obstacle is that Schwarzenegger was born in Austria.

On November 30, 2004, when presenting Schwarzenegger with the 2004 George Bush Award for "excellence in public service," President George H.W. Bush suggested as much during the award ceremony at Texas A&M University. "In regard to [Schwarzenegger] ever being president of the United States, my advice to you Aggies and to any of those doubters, don't bet against Arnold Schwarzenegger," the former president told the 2,500 people attending the award ceremony.[239]

But Article 2, Section 1, cannot be repealed or otherwise negated by legislation or judicial rulings, not even by an act of Congress or a decision of the Supreme Court. A constitutional amendment is required.

Yet, an online petition calling for changing the Constitution to enable Schwarzenegger to run for president argues that Article 2, Section 1, is unfair: "There are great leaders out there who were not born in the United States. Some of those leaders who became U.S. citizens love and appreciate this country more than many of those who were born here and take it for granted. They have lived life outside the U.S. and know what it means to be an American citizen. Know what it means to live free and have their families live in a free world. I believe Arnold Schwarzenegger as President of the United States of America is almost like Mr. Schwarzenegger as President of the world. I realize this is a bold statement, but the man is loved and admired all over the world. People listen to him. People respect him. This is the kind of person we need running these great United States."[240]

Noting that Schwarzenegger's victory in the California gubernatorial recall-election of 2003 prompted calls to amend Article 2, Section 1, to allow naturalized citizens to be eligible for the presidency, attorney Sarah Herlihy demeaned the eligibility provision, noting it has been called the "stupidest provision" in the Constitution, "decidedly un-American," "blatantly discriminatory," and the "Constitution's worst provision."[241] She went on to argue that the natural-born citizenship requirement "discriminates against naturalized citizens, is out-dated and undemocratic, and incorrectly assumes that birthplace is a proxy for loyalty."

She based her argument on globalization: "Today, unlike in 1789, discriminating against naturalized citizens based solely on the fact that they were not born in the United States is no longer justified because globalization has lessened the differences between natural-born citizens and foreign-born citizens." She argued that the increase in travel, the growth of a global economy, and the increase in the number of people who are multi-lingual minimizes differences among cultures because people throughout the world "now have access to the same information, buy and sell the same products, and frequently travel or move out of their 'home' countries during their lifetimes."

What Herlihy's argument boils down to is that keeping Article 2, Section 1, demonstrates America's fear of foreigners. "It is an unfortunate truth that many Americans are racist," she wrote. Perhaps John W. Dean, the former counsel to President Nixon who was disgraced for his role in Watergate, expressed Herlihy's conclusion best when he wrote, "Show me a person who believes that the natural-born qualification clause should remain in the Constitution, and I will show you a bigot, pure and simple."[242]

On October 29, 2004, in an appearance on CBS-TV's *60 Minutes*, Schwarzenegger told Morley Safer that he would like to see an amendment to the Constitution: "I think, you know, because why not? Like with my way of thinking, you always shoot for the top."[243] Again, on April 29, 2010, Jay Leno asked Schwarzenegger on *The Tonight Show* if he would make a run for the White House if Article 2, Section 1, were changed. Schwarzenegger again replied in the affirmative, "Without any doubt."[244]

Birth Tourism

By promoting multicultural diversity and open borders, the political left has pushed for decades to blur distinctions even between illegal immigrants and U.S. citizens. Leftists continually push for illegal immigrants and their children to be given ready access to a wide range of social welfare benefits, including the education of their children at taxpayer expense in public schools and the right to vote in state and national elections. How much of an extension would it be for those on the left to see no objection in having someone as president who was known not to be a natural-born citizen?

But Republicans in recent years also have not held the line on U.S. citizenship. This was demonstrated by the determination of President George W. Bush and Senator John McCain to join hands twice with Senator Ted Kennedy in their mutual enthusiasm to pass "comprehensive immigration reform" legislation. Many conservatives continue to believe "comprehensive immigration reform" amounts to nothing more than a euphemistic phrase meaning support of amnesty.

"Since 2003, more than 12,000 Turkish children have been born in the U.S., giving them instant citizenship, under the 14th Amendment," wrote reporter Dave Gibson in the Examiner.com.[245] "They are part of a growing trend known as 'birth tourism.'"

The idea is that a foreign national expecting a baby makes travel plans through a "birth tourism" agency to travel to the United States in time for the birth. Put simply, U.S. citizenship was up for sale to foreign expectant mothers.

Flourishing in countries like Turkey, companies in the birth tourism business arrange trips to New York, Los Angeles, Chicago, and other U.S. cities at a price ranging from $25,000 to $40,000, including transportation, city tours, living accommodations for several months, and hospital expenses.

Birth tourism relies on the lax interpretation of the 14th Amendment that Hispanic immigrants entering the United States through Mexico have used to argue Hispanic children born in the United States to illegal immigrants are "birthright citizens."

As we saw in Chapter 4, the 14th Amendment was ratified in 1868 to make sure citizenship rights went to the native-born African-Americans whose rights were being challenged because they were recently freed slaves. Even more specifically, the 14th Amendment was aimed at preventing a state government from denying native-born African-Americans the rights they were entitled to as U.S. citizens.

Still, since hospitals typically issue birth certificates for every baby born in the hospital, and because birth certificates are the key proof required for other official documentation, including drivers licenses and passports, being born in the United States has been the backdoor for illegal immigrants to get their children rights as U.S. citizens.

The number of children in the U.S. born to illegal immigrants on American soil jumped to 4 million in 2009, up from 2.7 million in 2003, according to a report by the Pew Hispanic Center. About 8 percent of the 4.3 million babies born in the U.S. in 2008 alone came from illegal immigrant parents, the report said.

Mark Krikorian, director of the Center for Immigration Studies, points out that consular officers are not permitted to turn down a visa application simply because a woman will soon give birth.

Indeed, the current system allows foreigners to decide completely on their own who will and will not be a citizen of the United States, Krikorian explains.

Thus, in June 2010,[246] New York's first "birth tourism" hotel opened a new hospitality niche in mid-town Manhattan. The Marmara Manhattan, part of a Turkish hospitality chain, is a high-rise suites hotel located in New York's Upper East Side. Offering a one-bedroom suite accommodation for $5,100, plus taxes, for a month, with airport transfer, baby cradle and a gift set for the mother, the hotel arranged medical fees separately, at a cost of around $30,000. The Marmara Manhattan marketed the program as "an exclusive package for new mothers that wish to give birth in the U.S.A.," with the added benefit that the newborn baby is a native-born U.S. citizen from the moment of birth.[247]

Companies have sprung up around the globe to promote birth tourism to those foreign nationals who can afford it. U.S. hospitals offering birth packages to affluent foreign expectant mothers typically market the service by stressing technology and downplaying the attraction of instant U.S. citizenship. According to bloggers who follow the issue, the potential for birth tourism to become a black market criminal activity has developed in several nations, including Jamaica.[248]

So, if the only requirement for Barack Obama to be constitutionally eligible to be president is that he was born in Hawaii, how does that extend to birth tourism? Let's say a pregnant mother and her husband fly in from a foreign nation, perhaps Great Britain, and have their baby in the United States. Under the 14th Amendment, the baby is deemed to be a "native-born" birthright U.S. citizen. The child returns to Britain with his parents and grows to adulthood as an active British. So the child is a dual citizen of the United States and Britain, both at birth and into adulthood.

Now let's say that, as an adult, this person moves to the United States and establishes a residence for fourteen years, without renouncing citizenship in Britain where the parents are yet living. As an adult, the person votes in U.S. elections in person and votes in British elections by absentee ballot. He or she runs for U.S. president and is elected.

For supporters of Barack Obama, there would be nothing wrong with this scenario. The person in the birth tourism example is a native-born U.S. citizen, hence a natural-born U.S. citizen under the 14th Amendment, despite the foreign citizenship of the parents.

For supporters of the Constitution, however, it would be incomprehensible that we have deviated so far from the principles of the Founding Fathers that a person could be elected president of the United States while still a citizen of Great Britain, the very nation against whom Americans fought the Revolutionary War to gain independence.

The only key difference between the birth tourism example above and Obama's situation is that Barack Obama, Sr. came to Hawaii on a temporary basis to study and only one of the parents was a foreign citizen.

In the final analysis, the attack on Article 2, Section 1, of the Constitution is an attack on the sovereignty of the United States and her Founding Fathers' determination that the chief executive and commander in chief of the nation be born on U.S. soil to parents who were U.S. citizens at the time of birth. The Founding Fathers specifically designed the "natural-born Citizen" clause to make sure no future chief executive and commander-in-chief of the United States would have a divided loyalty to another nation.

Those valuing the Constitution have to be vigilant or those whose vision is multicultural globalism will redefine Article 2, Section 1, to their liking, with or without a constitutional amendment—either by court decisions that continually redefine citizenship, or by new laws passed in Congress, or simply by running ineligible candidates and blurring the lines while refusing to submit documentation, much as Obama has already done.

"Birthers" Demonized

In Chapter 1, we documented that the first "birthers" in the 2008 election were supporters of Barack Obama that challenged whether John McCain was a natural-born citizen.

Despite the glaring hypocrisy, the Obama supporters who challenged McCain's constitutional eligibility to be president demonized anyone who dared raise similar challenges to Obama, ridiculing opponents rather than dealing with the facts. Yet, in so doing, they have ridiculed those of us who continue to take seriously the importance of U.S. citizenship, the allegiance to a sovereign United States of America, and the value of the U.S. Constitution as written and intended by our Founding Fathers.

The attacks have been brutal, and intentionally demeaning—arguing virtually that those of us upholding Article 2, Section 1, are too backward or too stupid to understand how useless and antiquated our views are in today's global political economy and multicultural world.

Ben Smith, writing in the increasingly left-leaning Politico.com, described the "birthers" as "a new culture of conspiracy," and argued that the challenges to Obama's eligibility "have no grounding in evidence."[249] To support that contention, Smith argued, "Courts across the country have summarily rejected the movement's theory—that Obama can't be a citizen because his father wasn't—as a misreading of U.S. law." Smith evidently felt no need to understand that the argument was not whether Obama is a citizen, but whether Obama is a natural-born citizen.

Mark Ambinder, the politics editor of the *Atlantic* and chief political consultant to CBS News, argued that "birthers" were a fringe movement "because no important Republicans believe it, and most are offended by it."[250]

Richard Cohen, president of the Southern Poverty Law Center, a group that regularly attacks anything to the right of Karl Marx, wrote a letter dated July 24, 2009, to Jonathan Klein, then-president of CNN, demanding that CNN take Lou Dobbs off the air because "in taking up the birthers' claims," Dobbs "is adopting an unsubstantiated conspiracy theory that originated on the radical racist right."[251]

Leftist attack site Gawker.com assailed the author of this book, claiming "Jerome Corsi, bizarre all-purpose conspiracy theory and smear artist, has done more than perhaps anyone else to further the Birther movement. As the superstar co-author of the anti-John Kerry Swift Boat book, he had a platform and an audience of die hard crazies willing to promote anything he wrote." Gawker further charged that I write for "WorldNetDaily, a daily repository of conspiracies, lies, and insanity. The right-wing 'news' site publishes a new piece on the Obama birth conspiracy *every day*."[252]

PolitiFact.com, one of the left-leaning Web sites that attacked McCain on eligibility issues but supported Obama on the Hawaiian short-form COLB, attacked WND as "the conductor of the Birther train."[253] In a separate piece, PoltiFact.com issued the following pronouncement: "At PolitiFact, we have explored several of the birthers' claims, and have concluded that there is ample evidence that President Obama was born in Hawaii."[254]

FactCheck.org, another Web site that pursued McCain's eligibility issues but steadfastly defended Obama's, attacked "birthers" in no uncertain terms. As FactCheck director Brooks Jackson wrote on November 1, 2008, just days before the 2008 presidential election: "Of all the nutty rumors, baseless conspiracy theories that we've dealt with at FactCheck.org during campaign 2008, perhaps the goofiest is the claim that Barack Obama is not a 'natural-born citizen' and therefore not eligible to be president under the constitution."[255]

Then, DailyKos.com, the first Web site to publish the Obama COLB, came forward with a survey that evidently it thought would settle the issue. Defining the 11 percent of respondents who did not think Obama was born in the United States as "Obama-hating conspiracy theorists," DailyKos founder Markos Moulitsas proclaimed the results showed "birthers are mostly Republican and Southern," evidently a characterization he considered the ultimate insult.[256]

Phil Griffin, president of MSNBC, said it more directly: "It's racist. Just call it for what it is."[257] MSNBC reporter Donny Deutsch upped the ante, calling birthers on air not only "racist," but also "hate-mongering" and "fear-mongering." Ultimately Deutsch was booted from his week-long anchoring stint on MSNBC for criticizing Keith Olbermann, before Olbermann was suspended for making campaign contributions to Democratic candidates in the 2010 mid-term elections.[258]

The abuse extends even to Kenya.

"They are living in denial," wrote Kenneth Ogosia and Kevin Kelly in Kenya's *Nation*, describing "birthers" as "lunatics."[259]

The vitriol heaped upon "birthers" from Obama supporters on the political left is endless. Why is their reaction so extreme? Are Obama supporters so insecure regarding their position that Alinskyite ridicule and *ad hominem* attacks are their only line of defense? These attacks are meant to place anyone at risk of their reputation just because they continue to inquire about Obama's eligibility to be president. Where are the journalists who championed Bob Woodward and Carl Bernstein when as young reporters for the *Washington Post* they dared question President Richard Nixon over Watergate?

None of these vituperative bombasts and personal assaults would be needed if only Obama would release his long-form, hospital-generated birth certificate and the other documents pertaining to his citizenship.

Instead, Obama chooses to stand behind his vile-mouthed defenders, preferring to remain the undocumented worker in the Oval Office.

"Just the Facts, Ma'am. All We Want are the Facts."

Jack Webb, playing police detective Joe Friday in the 1950s TV series *Dragnet*, became famous for the line, "All we want are the facts."

The same applies to those of us who dare to continue inquiring into President Obama's eligibility to hold the office under the requirements of the supreme law of the land, the U.S. Constitution.

In the end, the request is simple and the stonewalling is hard to understand or justify. Why would Obama and his determined supporters protest so much unless there was something to hide?

Far from losing this argument, we are winning. By now the American public has caught on that the foul language of the left is hurled forth to stop inquiry, demonstrating once again how fearful leftists truly are of any serious First Amendment-protected investigation of their leaders.

Increasingly, the original small group of "birthers" is becoming an army of eligibility "proofers" who are tired of the abuse and the excuses, the calumny and the rhetoric.

All proofers want is the same thing Detective Joe Friday wanted: the facts.

In October 2010, former House Speaker Newt Gingrich told Spanish-language TV that Obama has an "obligation to figure out why so many Americans doubt his life story. If I were the president, that would really concern me, not because of Fox News or talk radio or Rush Limbaugh, but what is there that he's doing that would let that many people be confused?," Gingrich said on Univision's *Al Punto*,[260]

Although Gingrich said he believes that Obama was "absolutely" born in the United States and is a Christian, he also insisted the president needs to consider what he's doing that leads people to suspect he is Muslim.

"I think some of this stuff is just a sign of how much fear and anxiety has built up," Gingrich said, "but I think the president has an obligation to slow down and say, if you're president of all the people, what is it the White House is doing that so frightens a third of the Republican Party and they don't even believe something as simple and as obvious as his self-professed religious belief."

A prominent array of commentators, including Rush Limbaugh, Sean Hannity, Michael Savage, Mark Levin, Lou Dobbs, Chuck Norris, and Pat Boone have all said unequivocally and publicly that the Obama eligibility issue is legitimate and worthy of inquiry.[261]

Because the White House continues to stonewall legitimate requests to produce eligibility documentation, six out of ten Americans now doubt Obama's birth story. If the stonewalling continues, the number of proofers is sure to grow.

History has not been kind to U.S. presidents that have attempted to hide behind a lie.

At some point, even President Richard Nixon had to face the truth.

At some point, President Barack Obama will have to do the same.

ACKNOWLEDGEMENTS

After the success of *The Obama Nation: Leftist Politics and the Cult of Personality*, in 2008—No.1 on the *New York Times* bestseller list for a month—Elizabeth Farah asked if I would consider returning to write books for WND, where I am a senior staff reporter.

Then, when Elizabeth and Joseph Farah suggested a good topic would be Obama's eligibility to be president, I decided to give their request serious consideration. Since 2008, WND has led the press coverage of the Obama eligibility issue, running billboards across the country asking, WHERE'S THE BIRTH CERTIFICATE?

A continuing series of hard-hitting investigative reports, including many I authored, explored cracks in the Obama nativity story, convincing me over time that Obama is not eligible to be president.

While I knew I would take abuse from the mainstream media and the Soros-funded far left for writing this book, the courage Elizabeth and Joseph Farah have demonstrated in setting WND editorial policy gave me the confidence I needed to know WND was the only publisher in America that could do this book justice.

Truthfully, without the assistance of the WND staff, this book would not have been possible.

Managing Editor David Kupelian and Art Moore, one of WND's most accomplished editors and staff writers, edited the manuscript meticulously, sharpening the analysis by demanding the text stick closely to what we could document.

Assignment editor Robert Unruh has guided my research over the past three years, assigning me many pieces that were the original building blocks of the chapters you read here. Chelsea Schilling, Joe Kovacs, and Drew Zahn conducted investigations of their own that have contributed importantly to the argument presented here.

Aaron Klein worked with me both as a colleague and close friend to share unselfishly his extensive knowledge of how the far left has operated in United States politics, and particularly in Hawaii, since the 1950s.

WND White House correspondent Les Kinsolving dared to raise the issue of Obama's constitutional eligibility during White House press briefings and each time graciously weathered the ridicule of then-Obama spokesman Robert Gibbs.

Megan Byrd, the head of WND books, set the project parameters and fixed the deadlines for guiding this work from outline, though manuscript drafts to final copy-edited galleys.

Thanks also to WND Books editor John Perry.

Mark Karis, the book designer, is to be congratulated for a book cover design and format that captures the message of the book.

Finally, the book would not have been possible without the many sacrifices my wife, Monica, and my daughter, Alexis, graciously made to allow me the time necessary for reflection and the days required to write this book.

— *Jerome R. Corsi, Ph.D., March 30, 2011*

THE MISSING OBAMA DOCUMENTS

Barack Obama's refusal to produce his authentic birth certificate typifies the amazing and wholly unprecedented lack of documentation provided by Obama to the American public about his personal history and political life. The footprints of the president's own history have largely either vanished or remain hidden from public view.[262]

Below is a list of important missing documents and reasons making them public remains important.

Long-Form, Hospital-Generated Birth Certificate

This document would list the hospital where Obama was born and the physician who attended the birth. If Obama was born in a Hawaiian hospital, as he claims, this document would absolutely exist and would provide definitive proof.

The document should also settle the controversy over whether Obama was born in Queen's Medical Center in Honolulu, as initially claimed, or in Kapi'olani Medical Center, as the White House now claims.

Neither Obama nor the Hawaii Department of Health has ever affirmed that a Hawaiian long-form, hospital-generated birth certificate document exists for Barack Obama.

Adoption Records

The Hawaii Department of Health has refused to answer questions about whether Obama's birth records on file were amended to reflect an adoption in Indonesia by Obama's Indonesian stepfather.

A registration card at the St. Francis of Assisi School in Jakarta shows Obama was registered as an Indonesian citizen and as a Muslim. He was listed as "Barry Soetoro," with the surname of his stepfather.

In 1968, Ann Dunham, Obama's mother, filed a request with the U.S. State Department to have her son removed from her passport. Dunham further listed her son's name as Barack Hussein Obama (Soebarkah), an apparent Indonesian surname Obama has never publically acknowledged or discussed.

Kindergarten Records

The *Maui News* reported that Obama attended Kindergarten at the Noelani Elementary School in Honolulu during the school year 1966–1967.[263] The newspaper released a photo (Exhibit 125, page 235) of two teachers, Katherine Nakamoto and Aimee Yatsushiro, with five students. The teachers claim one of the students is Barack Obama.

According to the Hawaii Department of Education, students must submit a birth certificate to register. Parents may bring a passport or student visa if the child is from a foreign country.[264]

So far, the school has released no records. Noelani Elementary School officials have not responded to WND's request for comment.

Punahou School Records

Obama attended the Punahou School in Honolulu, one of Hawaii's most expensive private schools. He enrolled in the sixth grade when he was ten years old, immediately after returning from Indonesia in 1971, and remained until he finished high school.

The *Boston Globe* reported that in 1979, the year Obama graduated, tuition for high school students at Punahou was $1,990, a sizable expense given that Hawaii's median family income that year was around $22,750.[265]

Obama reportedly received a scholarship to attend Punahou, although the school has refused to release Obama's financial records. At issue is whether or not Obama applied for financial aid by registering at Punahou as a foreign student. Did Obama qualify for foreign aid because he had been adopted by his Indonesian stepfather and had been registered for four years in Jakarta schools as an Indonesian citizen?

Occidental College Records

Obama attended Occidental College, a small liberal arts school in Los Angeles for two years, beginning in the fall of 1979. He attended the school on a scholarship.

During the 2008 presidential campaign, Obama acknowledged that at the end of his time at Occidental he traveled to Indonesia and Pakistan with his Pakistani roommates at Occidental.

Again, the unanswered question is whether Obama applied for financial aid from Occidental as a foreign student. Occidental refuses to release any information about Obama's application to the college, as well as grade or financial records regarding his two years there.

In a legal action, handled largely by attorney Gary Kreep of the U.S. Justice Foundation, officials at Occidental College were served with a demand to produce records concerning Obama's attendance.

"The gravamen of the petition is the question as to whether United States Senator Barack Hussein Obama, of Illinois, is eligible to serve as president of the United States pursuant to the requirements for that office in the United States Constitution," Kreep wrote. "The records sought may provide documentary evidence, and/or admissions by said defendant, as to said eligibility or lack thereof."

College officials then contacted Obama's lawyers, who argued to the court that the election was over and that future concerns should be addressed to Congress.

Kreep's petition argued that the records could reveal under what name

Obama attended classes at Occidental—"Barry Soetoro" or "Barack Obama" or some other variation—and whether he attended on scholarship money intended for foreign students.

A judge granted a motion made by Obama's attorneys to quash Kreep's request for subpoena power to force Occidental to release the requested documents.

"Obama's attorneys bent over backward to block us," Kreep told WND. "Obama doesn't want anyone to see those records. He's trying to hide them."

State Department Passport and Travel Records

Obama has refused to release his U.S. State Department passport and travel records.

His initial passport application to the State Department should have included birth-certificate documentation that he was a U.S. citizen.

Released State Department documents confirmed that Obama was listed in his mother's 1965 passport until 1968, when she requested he be removed.

The State Department reported that Dunham's 1965 application for a passport was destroyed in a purge of passport records during the 1980s in accordance with guidance from the General Services Administration. Along with the destruction of Dunham's 1965 passport application was the loss of any birth documents she would have submitted to the State Department to establish her son's U.S. citizenship.

Without Obama's passport records, it is impossible to determine when and how he received his own U.S. passport after his mother removed him from hers in 1968.

Also, it is not known whether the State Department has a record of Obama being adopted by his stepfather in Indonesia or being an Indonesian citizen, as listed on the school records in Jakarta.

Nor is it possible to determine if the State Department carried the surname "Soebarkah" forward in Obama's passport records, or whether or not Obama ever had an Indonesian passport.

Did Obama use a U.S. passport when he returned from Indonesia to Hawaii in 1971? If so, when was that passport issued and what birth information, if any, was contained in his passport application?

Did Obama travel to Pakistan at the end of his two years at Occidental on a foreign passport?

Did Obama make any other, yet undisclosed trips to Indonesia and Pakistan?

Again, without a release of Obama's State Department passport and travel records, it is impossible to determine.

What other countries did Obama visit after he returned to Hawaii from Indonesia in 1971, and what passport or passports did he use?

Columbia University Records

Obama transferred from Occidental College to Columbia University in 1981 at the age of twenty.

Columbia has refused to release any records regarding Obama's attendance, including his application to attend, his grades, and his financial aid records, if any exist. Without documentation, it is impossible to determine if Obama applied to Columbia or received financial aid as a foreign student.

According to the *New York Times*, Obama "suggests in [*Dreams from My Father*] that his years in New York were a pivotal period: He ran three miles a day, buckled down to work and 'stopped getting high,' which he says he had started doing in high school. Yet he declined repeated requests to talk about his New York years, release his Columbia transcript or identify even a single fellow student, co-worker, roommate or friend from those years."[266]

Then-campaign spokesman Ben LaBolt explained to the *Times*, "[Obama] doesn't remember the names of a lot of people in his life."

"Mostly, my years at Columbia were an intense period of study," Obama told *Columbia College Today* in a 2005 alumnus interview. "When I transferred, I decided to buckle down and get serious. I spent a lot of time in the library. I didn't socialize that much. I was like a monk."[267]

Still, a *Wall Street Journal* editorial in September 2008, titled "Obama's Lost Years," noted that Fox News contacted some 400 of Obama's classmates at Columbia and found no one who even remembered him.[268]

The *Wall Street Journal* noted that Obama received a degree in political science without honors and recalled what Obama had told his biographer David Mendell: "For about two years there, I was just painfully alone and not really focused on anything, except maybe thinking a lot."

The *New York Sun* said the Columbia University chapter in Obama's life remains largely blank.

"The Obama campaign has refused to release his college transcript, despite an academic career that led him to Harvard Law School and, later, to a lecturing position at the University of Chicago," the *Sun* reported in September 2008. "The shroud surrounding his experience at Columbia contrasts with that of other major party nominees since 2000, all of whom have eventually released information about their college performance or seen it leaked to the public."[269]

The *Sun* also reported that the Obama campaign did not offer an explanation as to why his Columbia records were not released to the public, although the newspaper speculated that Obama was reluctant to let the public know he was admitted to the university as an affirmative-action student.

Columbia Thesis, "Soviet Nuclear Disarmament"

Obama is said to have written a senior thesis at Columbia on Soviet nuclear disarmament, but it has never been released.

The *New York Times* reported in September 2008 that Obama "barely mentions Columbia, training ground for the elite, where he transferred in his junior year, majoring in political science and international relations and writing his thesis on Soviet nuclear disarmament."[270]

Columbia University said it did not retain a copy of that paper, and Obama's campaign spokesman Ben LaBolt said Obama does not have a copy. In an interview with NBC News, one of Obama's Columbia professors, Michael Baron, said he saved Obama's thesis for years and even hunted for it again in July 2008 in some boxes. But, said Baron, the search did not produce the paper, and now he thinks he threw it out during a move in 2000.[271]

Harvard Law School Records

Harvard Law School has refused to release Obama's application, his grades, and any information about financial assistance he may have received.

As was the case with Punahou, Occidental and Columbia, Obama's unwillingness to authorize the release of his Harvard Law School records prevents the public from seeing documents that would disclose whether he applied for or received financial aid as a foreign student.

Furthermore, Obama's unwillingness to allow the public to see his Harvard records prevents resolution of a continuing controversy over whether radical Islamic influences promoted his admission and financed his legal education there.

In an appearance on the New York-produced *Inside City Hall* TV show, octogenarian Harlem lawyer Percy Sutton, among whose clients was Malcolm X, explained that Islamic radical Khalid Abdullah Tariq al-Mansour, "one of the world's wealthiest men," asked him to write a letter of recommendation to Harvard Law School for then relatively unknown Barack Obama.[272]

In the video, Sutton says he was introduced to Obama by Saudi citizen al-Mansour, who "was then raising money" for Obama.

Describing al-Mansour as being from Texas, Sutton commented that al-Mansour was the "principal advisor to one of the world's richest men."

Sutton also says al-Mansour told him about Obama, noting in a letter, "There's a young man that has applied to Harvard. I know that you have a few friends left there because you used to go up there to speak. Would you please write a letter in support of him?"

In the interview, Sutton confirmed he did write the letter, telling his friends at Harvard, "I thought there was going to be a genius that was going to be available, and I certainly hoped they would treat him kindly."

During the 2008 presidential campaign, Politico's Ben Smith reported that the Obama campaign flatly denied Sutton's story.[273]

Smith was not able to contact Sutton, whose advanced age had raised questions about whether his memory of writing the letter of recommendation was confused.

But Smith did reach al-Mansour, who confirmed that Sutton was "a dear friend, his health is not good."

On July 20, 2009, WND e-mailed the following to Obama spokesman Tommy Vietor in the White House: "WND requests that the White House authorize Harvard University to release the Law School records of President Obama. Ben Smith at Politico chose to rely upon the word of Khalid al-Mansour in the above linked story. Mr. al-Mansour's word is not the best evidence on the question—President Obama's records at Harvard Law School are."

During the 2008 presidential campaign, Vietor was a frequent spokesman for the Obama campaign's "Fight the Smears" Web site, which subsequently has been removed from the Internet.

WND received no response from Vietor or from the White House press office.

Before he abandoned his "slave name," al-Mansour was known as Don Warden, an African-American radical who was founder of the Afro-American Association in the San Francisco Bay Area and was instrumental in creating the Black Panthers.

The University of California Berkeley Library's Social Activism Sound Recording Project identifies Warden as being the "mentor" of Black Panther co-founder Huey Newton.[274]

Harvard Law Review Articles

In 1990, Obama beat out 18 other contenders to become the first black president of the *Harvard Law Review*, where he spent at least 50 hours a week editing submissions from judges, scholars, and other legal authors.[275]

According to Politico, there were "eight dense volumes [of the *Harvard Law Review*] produced during his time in charge there—2,083 pages in all."[276]

Campaign spokesman Ben LaBolt told Politico that Obama did not write any articles for the *Law Review*, though his two semesters at the helm "did produce a wide range of edited case analyses and unsigned 'notes' from Harvard students."

Susan Estrich, the first female president of the *Harvard Law Review*, who served 14 years earlier than Obama, said Obama must have had something published that year, even if his campaign denied it.

"They probably don't want [to] have you [reporters] going back" to examine the *Review*, Estrich told Politico.

However, Politico later reported it had unearthed a 1990 unsigned and previously unattributed article that "offers a glimpse at Obama's views on abortion policy and the law during his student days."[277]

The six-page summary answers a legal question about whether fetuses should be allowed to file lawsuits against their mothers.

"Obama's answer, like most courts': NO," Politico reported. "He wrote approvingly of an Illinois Supreme Court ruling that the unborn cannot sue their mothers for negligence, and he suggested that allowing fetuses to sue would violate the mother's rights and could, perversely, cause her to take more serious risks with her pregnancy."

The report continued, "His article acknowledged a public interest in the health of the fetus, but also seemed to demonstrate his continuing commitment to abortion rights, and suggested that the government may have more important concerns than 'ensuring that any particular fetus is born.'"

Despite its earlier statement, the Obama campaign later confirmed Obama's authorship of the article and claimed it was the only piece he had written for the *Harvard Law Review*.

University of Chicago Scholarly Articles

Obama lectured from 1992 until 2004 at the University of Chicago Law School, a top institution where the faculty is known for voluminous scholarly publishing.[278]

The university offered Obama a full-time tenure-track position, an honor typically reserved for published instructors. However, reporters have been unable to find any scholarly articles authored by him.

Matthew Franck noted in National Review Online, "A search of the HeinOnLine database of law journals turns up exactly nothing credited to Obama in any law review anywhere at any time."[279]

Frank was emphatic: "Let me say that again. There appears to be not one single article, published talk, or comment of any kind, anywhere in the professional legal literature, under Barack Obama's name, notwithstanding an apparent eleven-year teaching career in constitutional law at a top-flight school."

Obama declined the tenure offer.

Susan Galer, news editor at the law school and Harris School of Public Policy at the University of Chicago, told WND, "President Obama wrote *Dreams from My Father* while at the law school but did not produce any scholarly articles, as far as I know."

Emmy-award-winning writer and producer Jack Cashill has made a convincing case that skilled editor and writer Bill Ayers of radical Weather Underground fame was the primary author of important sections of Obama's autobiography and editor of the work as a whole.[280]

Obama has never released to the public manuscript pages from *Dreams* that might help authenticate his authorship of the book.

Medical Records

During his first presidential campaign in 1999, Senator John McCain released 1,500 pages of medical and psychiatric records collected by the Navy, and in 2008, he allowed reporters to spend three hours sifting through 1,200 pages of health records.

Obama, however, refused to release his medical records during the 2008 campaign.

Instead, he simply provided a six-paragraph note from his physician briefly summarizing twenty-one years of doctor's visits and heath information.[281]

By not releasing his complete medical records, any history of foreign medical treatments or inoculations is not available, denying to the public yet another source of possible information about Obama's foreign travels.

Chicago Law Practice Records: 1993–2004

In 1993, Barack Obama took a job at the Chicago law firm of Davis, Miner, Barnhill and Galland. He remained with the law firm until 2004, although his law license became inactive in 2002.

The firm did legal work for Antoin "Tony" Rezko, who is now a federal felon. Allison S. Davis, the lead partner in the firm when Obama joined, was such a close associate of Rezko that he left the firm to go into business with Rezko.

The *Chicago Sun-Times* identified fifteen building projects that Rezko defrauded while represented by Davis, Miner, Barnhill and Galland during the time Obama was a lawyer working for the firm.[282]

"Obama has been friends with Rezko for 17 years," investigative reporter Tim Novak wrote in the *Chicago Sun-Times* in 2007. "Rezko has been a political patrol patron to Obama and many others, helping to raise millions of dollars for them through his own contributions and by hosting fundraisers in his home."[283]

Novak continued: "Obama, who has worked as a lawyer and a legislator to improve living conditions for the poor, took campaign contributions from Rezko even as Rezko's low-income housing empire was collapsing, leaving many African-American families in buildings riddled with problems—including squalid living conditions, vacant apartments, lack of heat, squatters and drug dealers."

Obama has never released his billing or client records for his time with Davis, Miner, Barnhill, and Galland.

State Senator Records: 1997–2004

Obama was elected to the Illinois Senate in 1996; he served until 2004, when he was elected to the U.S. Senate.

Obama has never released his calendar or appointment records for the time he spent in the Illinois legislature.

On November 11, 2007, during a broadcast of NBC's *Meet the Press*, host Tim Russert asked Obama, "You talked about Senator Clinton having records released from the Clinton Library regarding her experience as first lady, and yet when you were asked about 'What about eight years in the state senate of Illinois,' you said, 'I don't know.' Where, where are the—where are your records?"[284]

Obama answered: "Tim, we did not keep those records. I ..."

Surprised, Russert interrupted: "Are they gone?"

Obama did his best to backpedal: "Well, let's be clear. In the state

Senate, every single piece of information, every document related to state government was kept by the state of Illinois and has been disclosed and is available and has been gone through with a fine-toothed comb by news outlets in Illinois. The, the stuff that I did not keep has to do with, for example, my schedule. I don't have a schedule. I was a state senator. I wasn't intending to have the Barack Obama State Senate Library. I didn't have 50 or 500 people, to help me archive these issues. So ..."

Russert pressed Obama: "But your meetings with lobbyists and so forth, there's no record of that?"

Obama responded: "I did not have a scheduler, but, as I said, every document related to my interactions with government is available right now. And, as I said, news outlets have already looked through them."

In March 2008, public interest watchdog organization Judicial Watch reported that as a result of a FOIA request, a letter from the Illinois Office of the Secretary of State refuted Obama's contention that records of his state legislature service were available.

"The ISA [Illinois State Assembly] does not maintain Senator Obama's personal records or papers. [Nor] does the ISA maintain records generated by his office," the Illinois secretary of state explained. "In addition, the ISA has received no requests from Senator Obama to archive any records formerly in his possession."[285]

The List Goes On, as Does the Double Standard

Many other Obama records are missing, lost or being withheld. No wedding license has ever been found for Barack Obama, Sr. and Ann Dunham. No baptism records are available for Barack Obama at Reverend Wright's Trinity United Church of Christ in Chicago.

Obama has never answered questions about irregularities with his Social Security number and his Selective Service number.

Independent investigators have released other documents, after Obama refused to do so, including the divorce records of Dunham and Barack Obama, Sr. and of Dunham and Lolo Soetoro.

Today, a compliant and politically motivated press establishment largely gives Obama a pass on his unreleased records. To comprehend the extreme double standard, compare the lengths to which the mainstream media went to investigate Governor Sarah Palin after she was nominated to run for vice president.

On September 3, 2008, Palin delivered her acceptance speech to the Republican National Convention in Saint Paul, Minnesota. Less than two weeks later, a *New York Times* hit squad of three experienced investigative reporters dispatched to Alaska began reporting "background stories" on Palin.

On September 13, 2008, *New York Times* reporters Jo Becker, Peter S. Goodman and Michael Powell co-authored an article datelined from Wasilla, Alaska, "Once Elected, Palin Hired Friends and Lashed Foes."[286]

Becker, Goodman, and Powell had been busy.

"Throughout her political career, she has pursued vendettas, fired officials who crossed her and sometimes blurred the line between government and personal grievance, according to a review of public records and interviews with 60 Republican and Democratic legislators and local officials," the three *New York Times* reporters wrote.

The *Times* launched no similar investigative effort to search Obama's background in Hawaii, Illinois, or anywhere else.

WND TIMELINE: BREAKING THE
BIRTH CERTIFICATE ISSUE

June 10, 2008 – Is Obama's candidacy constitutional?

Bloggers begin raising questions about then-Illinois Senator Barack Obama's qualifications to be U.S. president, because of the secrecy over his birth certificate and the requirement presidents be "natural-born" U.S. citizens.

July 8, 2008 – Obama birth certificate: Real or phony baloney?

Investigative work done by the Israel Insider raises the possibility that an image purporting to be Barack Obama's birth certificate posted on the Daily Kos Web site, and an image later on the Obama campaign site, lack authenticity. Jay McKinnon, a self-described Department of Homeland Security-trained document specialist, successfully produces fake Hawaii birth certificate images nearly identical to the document the Obama campaign provided.

Aug. 8, 2008 – 2 campaigns seek 'truth' about Obama's birth

Israel Insider reports that analysts working separately determine the birth certificate posted on the Daily Kos Web site and on then-Senator Barack Obama's campaign Web site is fraudulent. An online petition to the Federal Election Commission asks the agency to verify Obama's eligibility, and lawsuits are filed in several states against the secretaries of state to prevent Obama from appearing on the 2008 ballot until his eligibility can be confirmed.

Aug. 23, 2008 – Democrat sues Senator Obama over 'fraudulent candidacy'

Philip J. Berg, a prominent Pennsylvania Democrat, sues Senator Barack Obama, the Democratic National Committee and the Federal Election Commission, claiming that Obama is not a natural-born citizen and, therefore, is not eligible to be president of the United States.

Oct. 4, 2008 – DNC steps in to silence lawsuit over Obama birth certificate

Lawyers for Obama and the DNC file a joint motion to dismiss Berg's lawsuit. Berg believes his party's leaders have ignored his pleas for proof in order to favor their chosen candidate over a rank-and-file constituent.

Oct. 21, 2008 – Obama 'admits' Kenyan birth?

Berg now cites Rule 36 of the Federal Rules of Civil Procedure, arguing that by failing to respond to the lawsuit and produce proof of his natural-born citizenship status, Obama has legally "admitted" to the lawsuit's accusations, including the charge that the Democratic candidate was born in Mombosa, Kenya.

Oct. 23, 2008 – Democrat: Obama's grandma confirms Kenyan birth

Berg announces he has a recording of a telephone call from Obama's paternal grandmother confirming his birth in Kenya and affirming she "was in the delivery room in Kenya when he was born Aug. 4, 1961."

Oct. 25, 2008 – Judge dismisses Obama birth certificate lawsuit

Federal judge R. Barclay Surrick concludes that ordinary citizens can't sue to ensure that a presidential candidate actually meets the constitutional requirements of the office and dismisses Berg's lawsuit.

Oct. 26, 2008 – Obama's birth certificate sealed by Hawaii governor

Jerome Corsi travels to Hawaii, and Hawaii's Gov. Linda Lingle places Obama's birth certificate under seal, instructing the state's Department of Health to make sure no one in the press obtains access to the original document under any circumstances.

Oct. 30, 2008 – Supremes asked to halt Tuesday's vote
The U.S. Supreme Court is asked to help the nation avoid a constitutional crisis by halting the 2008 election until Democratic presidential nominee Barack Obama documents his eligibility to run for the top office in the nation.

Nov. 2, 2008 – Doubts persist about Obama birth certificate
Gov. Lingle's office leaves ambiguous whether the Obama birth certificate on file with the Department of Health was originally generated by a Hawaii doctor after giving birth to Obama in Hawaii, or generated in Kenya and subsequently *registered* by the Obama family in Hawaii.

Nov. 4, 2008 – Will Supreme Court have say in presidency?
U.S. Supreme Court Justice David Souter rejects an emergency appeal for the court to halt the tabulation of the 2008 presidential election results until Democratic presidential nominee documents his eligibility to run for the office, but he sets a schedule for a response from Obama to the challenge from Berg.

Nov. 13, 2008 – Obama camp: Lawsuits by citizens are 'garbage'
An Obama campaign spokeswoman tells WND more than half a dozen legal challenges to Obama's citizenship status are unfounded: "All I can tell you is that it is just pure garbage."

Nov. 14, 2008 – 'Constitutional crisis' looming over Obama's birth location
A California court petition filed on behalf of former presidential candidate Alan Keyes and others argues that the California secretary of state should refuse to allow the state's 55 Electoral College votes to be cast in the 2008 presidential election until Obama verifies his eligibility to hold the office.

Nov. 20, 2008 – Supremes to review citizenship arguments
A case brought by Leo C. Donofrio against Nina Wells, secretary of state in New Jersey, challenges Obama's name on the 2008 election ballot and is scheduled for a "conference" at the U.S. Supreme Court.

Nov. 21, 2008 – Petition to see the birth certificate

WND launches an online petition designed to enlist the public's help in demanding evidence of Obama's constitutional eligibility for office.

Nov. 25, 2008 – Orders from new president spark lawsuit every time

Lawyer Gary Kreep, chief of the United States Justice Foundation, organizes plans to challenge, even after the inauguration, every order, every proposal, every piece of paperwork generated by Obama until questions about his citizenship are resolved.

Nov. 25, 2008 – Embassy: Obama *not* born in Kenya

Three Detroit radio hosts are surprised when their light-hearted interview with Kenyan Ambassador Peter N.R.O. Ogego reignites suspicions that Obama may have been born in Kenya since the ambassador called Obama's birthplace a "well-known" attraction in Kenya. Ogego later tells WND he was misunderstood.

Dec. 1, 2008 – FedEx the Supremes about Obama's eligibility

WND launches a FedEx campaign that sends letters to the Supreme Court just before justices review a case challenging Obama's eligibility to be president.

Dec. 1, 2008 – Obama, DNC elude citizenship lawsuit deadline

Obama and the Democratic National Convention let a Dec. 1 deadline slip by without responding to Berg's petition for writ of certiorari demanding Obama produce a legitimate birth certificate to document his eligibility for office.

Dec. 1, 2008 – Imaging guru: 'Certification' of birth time, location is fake

Ron Polarik, a document expert contends the "Certification of Live Birth" Barack Obama's campaign posted online is criminally fraudulent.

Dec. 2, 2008 – Print, TV ads demand citizenship proof from Obama

Concerned citizens fund a full-page "Open letter to Obama" in an issue of the Chicago Tribune asking Obama, "Are you a natural born citizen of the U.S.?" and "Are you legally eligible to hold the office of the president?"

Dec. 2, 2008 – Democrat asks Supreme Court to halt electors
Berg files an emergency motion for immediate injunction to keep the
Electoral College from meeting Dec. 15 and casting votes for Obama.

Dec. 5, 2008 – Will Supremes review citizenship arguments?
With protesters gathering and praying on the front steps, the U.S.
Supreme Court meets in conference to discuss whether to hear Donofrio's
case arguing that Obama does not meet the Constitution's Article 2, Section 1, "natural-born citizen" requirement for president because of dual
citizenship at birth.

Dec. 8, 2008 – Supreme Court denies 1st eligibility challenge
The U.S. Supreme Court decides against bringing Donofrio v. Wells
before a full hearing.

Dec. 8, 2008 – Eligibility dispute, Part 2, scheduled by Supremes
Within minutes of denying a request to listen to arguments in the case
Donofrio v. Wells, the Supreme Court confirms that another conference
is scheduled on another case, Cort Wrotnowski v. Susan Bysiewicz, Connecticut secretary of state, which also makes a dual citizenship argument.

Dec. 11, 2008 – Supremes turn down request to stop Electoral vote
The Supreme Court rejects a request to stop the Electoral College from
selecting the 44th president until Obama documents his eligibility for office.

Dec. 11, 2008 – Electors challenged to investigate birth dispute
Activist organization Democratic-Disaster.com posts a YouTube video
challenging members of the Electoral College to investigate the dispute
over Obama's birth certificate and eligibility for office.

Dec. 13, 2008 – Thousands advise electors to check eligibility
Nearly 4,000 concerned citizens participate in a WND effort to deliver
letters to every elector, urging them to investigate Obama's eligibility for
office, following an earlier campaign among WND readers that sent more
than 60,000 letters by overnight delivery to the U.S. Supreme Court when
a case contesting Obama's eligibility for the Oval Office was pending.

Dec. 15, 2008 – Supreme Court refuses 2ⁿᵈ challenge to eligibility

The Supreme Court rejects a second challenge to the presidency of Obama, denying an application for a stay or an injunction in a case from Connecticut brought by Cort Wrotnowski.

Dec. 16, 2008 – Obama citizenship issue has merit, AOL poll says

With more than 90,000 national votes in an unscientific AOL poll, 52 percent of nationwide respondents believe people should be concerned about Obama's citizenship, 42 percent say the controversy has no merit and 6 percent of voters remain undecided.

Dec. 16, 2008 – Investigator casts doubt on Obama's birth residence

Private investigator Jorge Baro releases to WND an affidavit that shows long-time Honolulu resident Beatrice Arakaki (neighbor to address listed in Obama's birth announcement) has no recollection of Obama being born or of the family living next door having a black child born to a white mother, casting doubt on whether Obama's family lived at the address in 1961.

Dec. 17, 2008 – More challenges fail in Supreme Court

Supreme Court Justice Anthony Kennedy denies without comment an appeal by Berg which alleged Obama is a citizen either of Kenya or Indonesia and thus ineligible.

Dec. 19, 2008 – Supreme Court to talk about Obama 3ʳᵈ time

Another case brought by attorney Philip J. Berg is set for a conference in the Supreme Court on Jan. 9.

Dec. 30, 2008 – Eligibility case finds 'standing'?

In Washington state's Broe v. Reed case, plaintiff's attorney Stephen Pidgeon argues a unique state statute grants everyday citizens the required standing to challenge the election of a candidate if the candidate at the time of the election was ineligible to hold office.

Dec. 30, 2008 – Berg files new challenge to eligibility

Berg, who already has two conferences pending before the U.S. Supreme Court on the issue of Obama's eligibility, files a new lawsuit on behalf of retired military colonel Gregory S. Hollister.

Dec. 31, 2008 – Most covered-up stories of 2008: Natural-born citizen

An annual WND survey shows charges that Obama is not a natural-born citizen of the U.S. and, therefore, constitutionally ineligible to serve as president top the list of the 10 most "spiked" or underreported stories of 2008.

Jan. 8, 2009 – Watch Obama commercial they don't want you to see

CNBC, MSNBC, Headline News, CNN and Fox refuse to sell time for a 60-second commercial to publicize information about the eligibility concerns.

Jan. 8, 2009 – Eligibility issue to follow Obama into Oval Office

The Supreme Court announces that a fourth case on the eligibility issue, Gail Lightfoot et al v. Debra Bowen, California Secretary of State, will be reviewed by justices Jan. 23.

Jan. 12, 2009 – Latest eligibility challenge rejected

Berg's case challenging Obama's eligibility to be president is turned back by the Supreme Court.

Jan. 18, 2009 – Eligibility battle rages on 3 fronts

Officials at Occidental College in Los Angeles are served with a demand to produce records of Obama's attendance there during the 1980s to determine whether he was registered as a foreign national.

Jan. 23, 2009 – President's meeting with judges questioned

Orly Taitz, a lawyer working on a case before the Supreme Court that challenges Obama's eligibility, raises concerns over a private meeting between Obama and eight of the justices who are expected to review it.

Jan. 27, 2009 – What did president tell Supreme Court?

Supreme Court justices deny Taitz' case a hearing on its merits after they reportedly held a private meeting with the president, prompting Taitz to demand records of the secretive discussions.

Jan. 31, 2009 – Congress sued to remove prez from White House

A new eligibility lawsuit brought by attorney Mario Apuzzo of New Jersey targets Congress as a defendant for its "failure" to uphold the constitutional demand to make sure Obama qualified before approving the Electoral College vote that actually designated him as the occupant of the Oval Office.

Feb. 10, 2009 – Eligibility issue: McCain checked but not Obama

Eligibility lawsuit brought by Apuzzo adds claims of rights violations, including unequal treatment, because Congress investigated eligibility of GOP candidate Senator John McCain and not whether Obama had been eligible for office.

Feb. 13, 2009 – 'Sanctions' sought in eligibility case

A high-powered team of attorneys representing Obama suggests there should be "monetary sanctions" against attorney Gary Kreep of the U.S. Justice Foundation, whose clients brought a complaint alleging Obama doesn't qualify for the Oval Office under the Constitution.

Feb. 16, 2009 – Keyes: President 'has something to hide' about eligibility

Alan Keyes, a 2008 presidential candidate who is a plaintiff in one of the many eligibility lawsuits, warns the tactics adopted by lawyers for the president confirm there is an issue for the courts to investigate.

Feb. 20, 2009 – States reviewing 'eligibility' challenges

Campaigners who have brought dozens of lawsuits challenging Obama's eligibility turn their attention to state legislatures, which could require their states to verify such information about candidates.

Feb. 22, 2009 – Eligibility petition hits quarter-million mark

A WND petition created in late November calling on all controlling legal authorities to ensure that Obama is constitutionally eligible to serve as president quickly receives more than 250,000 signatures and 3,000 new signups every day.

Feb. 22, 2009 – Senator questions Obama eligibility

Senator Richard Shelby, R-Ala., tells constituents he has never seen proof Obama was actually born in Hawaii, saying, "Well, his father was Kenyan and they said he was born in Hawaii, but I haven't seen any birth certificate. You have to be born in America to be president."

Feb, 23, 2009 – Soldier questions eligibility, doubts president's authority

Active duty U.S. Army officer, Scott Easterling, stationed in Iraq, calls Obama an "impostor" in a statement in which he affirms plans to join as plaintiff in a challenge to Obama's eligibility to be commander in chief.

Feb. 24, 2009 – 2nd U.S. soldier in Iraq challenges eligibility

A second U.S. soldier on active duty in Iraq joins a challenge to Obama's eligibility to be commander-in-chief, citing WND's report on 1st Lt. Scott Easterling, who has agreed to be a plaintiff in a lawsuit over the issue, as his inspiration.

Feb. 25, 2009 – Eligibility lawyer argues for president's deportation

Berg, a Democrat who served as deputy attorney general in Pennsylvania and is leading a number of lawsuits over the eligibility of Obama, tells radio talk show host Michael Savage that not only is Obama not eligible to be president, he's probably an illegal alien and should be deported.

Feb. 26, 2009 – Major general says president's eligibility needs proof

On the heels of two active duty members of the U.S. military serving in Iraq calling for Obama to prove his eligibility to be president, a retired major general agrees to join the case, saying he just wants "the truth."

March 2, 2009 – More military officers demand eligibility proof

Military officers from the U.S. Army, Navy, Air Force and Marines working California attorney Orly Taitz, citing Quo Warranto, a legal right established in British common law nearly 800 years ago and recognized by the U.S. Founding Fathers to demand documentation that may prove – or disprove –Obama's eligibility to be president.

March 3, 2009 – U.S. soldier gagged on prez' eligibility

A member of the U.S. military whose suspicions about Obama's eligibility to be president prompted him to sign onto a legal demand sent to Attorney General Eric Holder has been ordered by commanding officers not to speak with media.

March 4, 2009 – Senator: Eligibility is up to the voters

Senator Mel Martinez, R-Fla., suggests to his constituents that voters have made Obama eligible to occupy the Oval Office, whether or not he meets the constitutional mandate of being a "natural born" citizen.

March 6, 2009 – Republican senator says Snopes settled 'eligibility'

Senator Jon Kyl, R-Ariz., refers constituents raising concerns over Obama's eligibility to occupy the Oval Office to Snopes.com, an online "fact" organization that relies for its answer partly on information from the Obama campaign.

March 7, 2009 – Judge: Eligibility issue thoroughly 'twittered'

Federal Judge James Robertson throws out a lawsuit brought by Gregory Hollister questioning Obama's eligibility to be president, because the issue already has been "blogged, texted, twittered and otherwise massaged."

March 8, 2009 – Wikipedia scrubs Obama eligibility

Wikipedia, the online "free encyclopedia" mega-site written and edited entirely by its users, deletes within minutes any mention of eligibility issues surrounding Obama's presidency, with administrators kicking off anyone who writes about the subject.

March 10, 2009 – Scalia: You need 4 votes for Obama eligibility case

Orly Taitz, a lawyer lobbying the U.S. Justice Department and the U.S. Supreme Court for a review of Obama's qualifications to be president, says Justice Antonin Scalia hinted that another conservative justice has been voting against hearing the dispute.

March 12, 2009 – Did Supreme Court *clerk* torpedo eligibility cases?

Orly Taitz, whose emergency submission to the U.S. Supreme Court on Obama's eligibility was turned back without a hearing or comment, submits a motion for re-hearing, alleging some of her documentation may have been withheld from the justices by a court clerk.

March 13, 2009 – Court: No need for state to check prez' eligibility

A California court rules that apparently anyone can run for president on the California ballot – whether or not they are eligible under the Constitution of the United States.

March 13, 2009 – Eligibility bill hits Congress

Rep. Bill Posey, R-Fla., a freshman representative, introduces a bill to the U.S. Congress that would require presidential candidates to provide a birth certificate and other documents to prove their eligibility to occupy the Oval Office.

March 14, 2009 – Chief justice accepts 'eligibility' petition

Orly Taitz confronts U.S. Chief Justice John Roberts with legal briefs and a WND petition bearing names of more than 325,000 people asking the court to rule on whether or not the sitting president fulfills the Constitution's "natural-born citizen" clause.

March 21, 2009 – Man critical of Obama case judge visited by marshals

A Washington, D.C., man who believes Obama probably isn't eligible to be president – and colorfully stated as much to a federal judge who dismissed a case challenging Obama's residency in the White House – says he got a visit from U.S. marshals for his exercise of free speech.

March 23, 2009 – Suggesting eligibility proof gets congressman scorned

Rep. Bill Posey, R-Fla., proposes a bill that would require future presidential candidates to document their eligibility – a move that earns him scorn and ridicule from TV personalities and Rep. Neil Abercrombie, D-Hawaii.

March 25, 2009 – Eligibility lawyer says Homeland Security shadowing him

Stephen Pidgeon, a lawyer spearheading the effort in Washington State to bring light to the issue of Obama's eligibility to be president, says he was shadowed all day today by officers with the federal Department of Homeland Security, the Snohomish County sheriff's office and the Everitt city police department.

March 25, 2009 – Federal criminal complaint contends Obama ineligible

Retired U.S. Navy officer Walter Francis Fitzpatrick III raises the stakes in the ongoing dispute over Obama's eligibility to be president, filing a criminal complaint against the "imposter" with the U.S. attorney's office for the Eastern District of Tennessee.

March 26, 2009 – Keyes to appeal case on Obama's eligibility

A lawsuit filed on behalf of Ambassador Alan Keyes, a candidate for president on California's general election ballot in 2008, will be appealed.

March 31, 2009 – Citizen grand jury indicts Obama

A citizen grand jury in Georgia indicts the sitting president and delivers the indictment to state and federal prosecutors.

April 1, 2009 – Eligibility judge backs off sanctions threat

Federal Judge James Robertson, who threw out a lawsuit by a retired military officer challenging Obama's eligibility to be president because the subject had been "blogged, texted, twittered and otherwise massaged," backs off threats to impose financial sanctions on the officer's attorney, John D. Hemenway.

April 4, 2009 – What about the hospital of his 'birth'?

Hawaii lawmakers vote to advance a resolution to make the apartment building where Obama grew up a national landmark, yet there is still no move to recognize any island hospital as his birthplace.

April 9, 2009 – 'Twittered' eligibility case lawyer faces threat of sanctions

A Washington, D.C., law firm defending Obama in a lawsuit challenging his eligibility to be president that earlier was tossed by a district judge because the issue already had been "twittered" threatens sanctions against opposing counsel if he doesn't withdraw his appeal of that decision.

April 10, 2009 – Kentucky elections officer wants eligibility investigated

An official in the office of Kentucky's elections chief refers to state Attorney General Jack Conway for investigation the issue of Obama's eligibility to be president.

April 15, 2009 – Did state election papers include eligibility perjury?

Tens of thousands of faxes and letters are sent to attorneys general in all 50 states asking them to investigate whether Obama's state elections submissions included an affirmation that he is qualified and eligible to hold the office of president – and whether those statements constitute perjury.

April 22, 2009 – Is Obama campaign cash quashing eligibility suits?

Federal Election Commission records reveal Obama may be using campaign funds to stomp out eligibility lawsuits brought by Americans, as his campaign pays more than $1 million to his top eligibility lawyer since the election.

May 13, 2009 – 2nd congressman: Prove eligibility

Rep. Bob Goodlatte, R-Va., signs onto a measure in Congress that would require presidential candidates to verify their eligibility to hold the highest elected office in the United States.

May 19, 2009 – U.S. bonkers for Obama birth certificate billboards
WND, the only news agency in the world to relentlessly pound the eligibility questions, launches its "Where's the birth certificate?" campaign, which is an instant hit with WND readers in its first 24 hours.

May 21, 2009 – Grand juries cite Obama for ineligibility, treason
Hundreds of "presentments" – or accusations assembled by citizen grand juries – are given to courts, sheriffs, prosecutors, judges and legislators across the United States by July 4 alleging that Obama is ineligible to be president and his occupancy in the Oval Office constitutes treason.

May 27, 2009 – Obama flack laughs off birth certificate question
When asked by WND White House correspondent Les Kinsolving why the president would not release his long-form birth certificate, spokesman Robert Gibbs guffaws in unison with members of the Washington press corps about the concerns of 400,000 petitioners who have demanded it.

May 28, 2009 – New bid to unseal Obama's birth certificate
Andy Martin, a Chicago activist who has pursued a challenge to Obama's eligibility since before the 2008 election, asks an appeals court in Hawaii to order the release of the president's original birth certificate, explaining that state officials waived their ability to claim it is a private document.

May 29, 2009 – Appeals court dumps eligibility arguments
Arguments that had been expected to be taking place before the 3rd U.S. Circuit Court of Appeals in Berg vs. Obama are pushed off at least four months by the federal court.

May 31, 2009 – Obama asks which public records you want to see
The White House launches a Web site on "open government dialogue" with a forum open to the public, but more than 70 percent of citizen responses are calls on Obama to release his elusive "long-form" birth certificate.

June 2, 2009 – White House 'dialogue' site scrubbed of eligibility posts

With more than 200 individual threads and thousands of citizen comments on the eligibility issue, moderators of the White House Web site on "open government dialogue" work tirelessly to scrub the dialogue about Obama's birth certificate.

June 7, 2009 – Obama's 'birth certificate' not acceptable in Hawaii?

According to the Department of Hawaiian Home Lands, the Hawaiian certification of live birth Obama posted on his campaign Web site is not suitable as a form of identification and would not be accepted as a "birth certificate" even for some Hawaiian state government eligibility issues.

June 8, 2009 – Door slams on Hawaiian hospital records

Kapi'olani Medical Center for Women and Children and Queen's Medical Center, both separately cited as the birth hospitals in 1961 of Obama, refuse to comment or decline to return any of several WND messages.

June 9, 2009 – Obama: Where have all his records gone?

Aside from the long-form birth certificate, more than a dozen other documents remain unreleased or otherwise blocked from the public eye by the Obama administration, including: elementary school records, Occidental College records, Columbia University records, Columbia thesis "Soviet Nuclear Disarmament," Harvard Law School records, Harvard Law Review articles, University of Chicago scholarly articles, passport and medical records, law client lists and other documents.

June 12, 2009 – Appeal promised of eligibility lawsuit

Philip Berg says he'll appeal a judge's ruling in a case citing the False Claims Act and accusing Obama of defrauding the United States Treasury "by illegally being a U.S. senator from Illinois" without proof of citizenship for nine previous years and "fraudulently receiving a salary and benefits of nearly $1 million."

June 15, 2009 – Gibbs gets 2nd shot at eligibility question

Obama press secretary Robert Gibbs is given another chance to respond to a question regarding the documentation of Obama's eligibility, but instead of laughing at it like the last time it was raised, he simply ignores it.

June 22, 2009 – Farah's $10,000 birth certificate challenge

WND Editor and Chief Executive Officer Joseph Farah offers a $10,000 reward to anyone who can prove he or she was present at the birth of Obama.

June 26, 2009 – Judge: Eligibility dispute is 'serious'

U.S. Magistrate Judge Joel Schneider in Camden, N.J., a judge hearing one of the cases challenging Obama's eligibility, takes the unusual step of describing the dispute as a serious constitutional issue and begins adding letters of comment from the public to the court record.

June 28, 2009 – Hawaii paper turns down ad probing Obama's birth

The Honolulu Star-Bulletin rejects WND Editor and Chief Executive Officer Joseph Farah's efforts to buy a full-page ad soliciting assistance in finding documentary evidence of Obama's birth.

July 2, 2009 – 'Citizen grand jury' organizers deliver accusations

Documents assembled by 172 volunteer "citizen grand jury" members alleging Obama is ineligible to serve as president are delivered to the White House, the FBI, members of Congress and the court system in Washington, D.C.

July 4, 2009 – Holder 'conflict' cited in eligibility case

After months of delay, Attorney General Eric Holder's staff confirms its decision not to pursue an investigation and requests that one of Berg's cases – alleging Obama fraudulently held the position of Illinois' senator – be dismissed.

July 6, 2009 – Hospital won't back Obama birth claim

The Kapi'olani Medical Center for Women and Children in Honolulu, the hospital in Hawaii where Obama claims he was born, refuses to produce any documentation – or even confirm the claim – without permission of the president himself.

July 7, 2009 – Obama calls Jakarta his 'old hometown'

In a press briefing, Obama refers to Jakarta, Indonesia, as his old home town, raising questions as to whether Obama ever possessed Indonesian citizenship, with the subject first being broached by WND after a photograph emerged of Obama's school registration papers as a child in Indonesia showing the presidential candidate listed as a "Muslim" with "Indonesian" citizenship.

July 8, 2009 – Hawaii upgrades 'certification of live birth'

Hawaii, which had excluded the controversial "certification of live birth" document as proof of native Hawaiian status, changes its policy and makes a point of accepting the documents "because they are official government records documenting an individual's birth."

July 9, 2009 – Eligibility claims attracting high-level interest

California attorney Orly Taitz attracts high-level attention, with the Justice Department trying to add itself onto one of her cases and the legal counsel for the Joint Chiefs of Staff being assigned to review military justice code complaints filed by members of the military challenging Obama's eligibility.

July 9, 2009 – Hawaii Supremes asked to take 'action' on WND report

Chicago activist Andy Martin, who has asked Hawaii courts to unseal Obama's birth certificate, urges the state's Supreme Court to take action following a WND report documenting conflicting reports on the president's birth location.

July 9, 2009 – Obama birth letter: Is this thing for real?

Honolulu's Kapi'olani Medical Center for Women and Children removes from its Web site a letter purportedly sent by Obama in which the commander in chief outright declares his birth at the facility.

July 11, 2009 – U.S. office demands answer: Is Army 'corps of chattel slaves?'

A U.S. Army Reserve major from Florida with orders to report for deployment to Afghanistan within days files a court demand to be classified as a "conscientious objector" because without proof of the commander in chief's eligibility for office, the entire Army "becomes merely a corps of chattel slaves under the illegitimate control of a private citizen."

July 12, 2009 – Just who delivered baby Barack Obama?

Despite an in-depth search, the name of any physician or medical attendant who might have helped deliver the baby Barack Obama at Honolulu's Kapi'olani Hospital in 1961 remains shrouded in mystery.

July 13 – 2009 – Now White House joins 'birth hospital' cover-up

White House Press Secretary Robert Gibbs refuses to confirm that a letter posted by the Kapi'olani Medical Center for Women and Children in Honolulu – purportedly from President Obama claiming the facility as his birthplace – is, in fact, real.

July 13, 2009 – Eligibility arguments to get court hearing

U.S. District Judge David O. Carter in California plans a hearing on the merits of Orly Taitz' federal court case questioning Obama's eligibility to be president.

July 14, 2009 – Bombshell: Orders revoked for soldier challenging prez

Maj. Stefan Frederick Cook, a U.S. Army Reserve soldier from Florida scheduled to report for deployment to Afghanistan within days, has his military orders revoked after arguing he should not be required to serve under a president who has not proven his eligibility for office.

July 15, 2009 – Pentagon orders soldier fired for challenging prez

The Department of Defense allegedly compels a private employer to fire Maj. Stefan Frederick Cook from his civilian job after he has his military deployment orders revoked for arguing he should not be required to serve under a president who has not proven his eligibility for office.

July 16, 2009 – 'Begone!' Georgia judge orders fired reservist
In Georgia, U.S. District Judge Clay Land dismisses a case brought by
Maj. Stefan Frederick Cook, whose orders to deploy to Afghanistan were
pulled when he challenged Obama's eligibility, telling the officer's lawyer
the case would be handled better in Florida where the reservist lives.

**July 16, 2009 – Lib talker, Lou Dobbs now asking eligibility
questions**
Lynn Samuels, longtime New York radio talker, and talk format icon
Lou Dobbs begin taking note of the the doubts about and challenges to
President Obama's eligibility to occupy the Oval office.

July 16, 2009 – 'Birth hospital': Letter for real
After days of sustained silence, the Kapi'olani Medical Center for Women
and Children, the Honolulu hospital that trumpeted – then later concealed
– a letter allegedly written by President Obama in which he ostensibly
declares his birth at the facility claims the letter is, in fact, real.

July 17, 2009 – Another paper changes 'Obama's origin'
The Modern Ghana, an African news agency that reported extensively on
Obama's visit to Ghana, changes its archived article that describes Africa
as "the continent of his birth" to "the continent of his father's birth."

July 20, 2009 – Birth records get murky when adoption involved
Jerry Fuller and Mike Persons of the passport services division of the U.S.
State Department explain that a move overseas as a child, coupled with
Obama's apparent adoption, could impact a his birth certificate, possibly
resulting in dual citizenship.

July 20, 2009 – Limbaugh: 'Obama has yet to prove he's a citizen'
Top-rated radio host Rush Limbaugh, upset that he's forced to report his
every movement to tax authorities, blasts Obama for failing to prove he
is natural-born citizen of the United States.

**July 20, 2009 – Obama's online 'birth cert' misses
'proving' eligibility**

The "Certification of Live Birth" posted online and presented by Barack Obama as documentation of his reported Hawaiian birth doesn't "prove" his birth alone and must meet certain requirements, State Department officials explain to WND.

July 22, 2009 – Hawaiian newspapers don't prove birthplace
The announcements of Obama's birth printed by two Hawaii newspapers in 1961 do not provide solid proof of a birth in the Aloha State because the newspapers' "proof" of birth could be based on a state-issued "Certification of Live Birth," which is insufficient alone, even for some State Department officials, to document the birthplace.

July 26, 2009 – White House stonewalling on 'birth letter'
Despite numerous, repeated requests for more than two weeks, the White House refuses to verify the authenticity of a letter allegedly sent by Obama in which he ostensibly declares Kapi'olani Medical Center for Women and Children in Honolulu as his birthplace.

July 27, 2009 – Gibbs: 10,000 more important issues than eligibility
White House Press Secretary Robert Gibbs admits that the questions about Obama's eligibility to be president simply won't go away, even though he contends there are 10,000 things "more important" for Americans to worry about.

July 27, 2009 – Fax blast asking states to investigate eligibility
Just as Obama's Aug. 4 birthday approaches, a law firm handling one of the legal challenges to his eligibility to be president arranges for a fax blast to attorneys general in all 50 states pointing out their obligation to investigate possible perjury during the 2008 election and citing evidence that suggests Obama may have been born in what now is Kenya.

July 27, 2009 – Hawaii health official: Trust me
In another carefully worded statement, Hawaii health director Chiyome Fukino claims to have seen "original vital records" that prove "Barrack [sic] Hussein Obama was born in Hawaii and is a natural-born American citizen."

July 28, 2009 – $100,000 offered for proof of eligibility

Jason Hommel, a man who runs a silver business and offers stock investment advice, announces he's offering a reward of $100,000 for proof that Obama is a "natural born" citizen of the United States and, therefore, eligible to be president.

July 28, 2009 – Congressional support for proof of eligibility grows

Ten U.S. representatives sponsor and co-sponsor H.R. 1503, legislation requiring that presidential candidates provide proof – more than just a sworn statement – that they are eligible to occupy the Oval Office.

July 28, 2009 – New doubts revealed in Obama's nativity story

More cracks appear in the official story of Obama's family life, with the revelation in school documentation from the University of Washington that Ann Dunham most likely left her husband, Barack Sr., within weeks of the baby's birth in 1961 – while the official story claims Dunham relocated to Seattle late in 1962.

July 28, 2009 – Lou Dobbs: Just produce birth certificate

After being attacked by groups for relentlessly calling on Obama to prove his eligibility for office, CNN's Lou Dobbs renews his calls for Obama to produce his long-form birth certificate that would settle doubts about where he was born and offered that the president's actions could actually be "illegal."

July 28, 2009 – Unveiled! Hawaii's 1961 long-form birth certificates

Images of two 1961 Hawaii long-form birth certificates of twin daughters born at Kapi'olani Maternity and Gynecological Hospital Aug. 5, 1961, one day after Obama was supposedly born at the same facility, include information missing from Obama's short-form document, such as the name of the hospital, the name of the attending physician, name and address of the parents, the race of the parents and the race of the baby.

July 31, 2009 – Will Hawaii destroy Obama's birth certificate?

The state of Hawaii makes a series of procedural changes that would allow officials to destroy President Obama's original long-form birth certificate, concealing its contents forever, and accept the short-form "Certification of Live Birth" as a formal authentication document.

July 30, 2009 – No. 11 signs onto demand for eligibility proof
Rep. Louis Gohmert, R-Texas, a former judge now serving in Congress, agrees to cosponsor H.R. 1503, a bill demanding that future presidential candidates provide proof that they are eligible to hold the office.

Aug. 2, 2009 – Is this really smoking gun of Obama's Kenyan birth?
California attorney Orly Taitz, who has filed a number of lawsuits demanding proof of Obama's eligibility, releases a copy of what purports to be a Kenyan certification of birth and files a new motion in U.S. District Court for its authentication.

Aug. 2, 2009 – Andrew Sullivan: Release the birth certificate
One of the most influential bloggers, pundits and columnists in America, Andrew Sullivan, joins the rising chorus of voices across the political spectrum calling for Obama to release his original, long-form birth certificate.

Aug. 2, 2009 – Hawaii refuses to verify president's online COLBs
In response to direct questioning from WND, the Hawaii Department of Health refuses to authenticate either of the two versions of Obama's short-form Certification of Live Birth, or COLB, posted online – neither the image produced by the Obama campaign nor the images released by FactCheck.org.

Aug. 3, 2009 – Farah's birthday challenge: A $10,000 gift to hospital
In another bid to persuade Obama to release his long-form birth certificate publicly, WND Editor and Chief Executive Officer Joseph Farah says he will donate $10,000 to the birth hospital listed on the document.

Aug. 3, 2009 – Harry Reid: Not 1 minute for 'phony issue' of birth
The Senate plunges into the eligibility dispute and gives the issue a permanent spot in the official Congressional Record after Senate Majority Leader Harry Reid declares, "Let's be clear. It's a phony issue and does not deserve even a minute of our attention on the floor of the United States Senate."

Aug. 3, 2009 – Now Glenn Beck slams Obama birth issue
Fox News Channel host Glenn Beck insists people should be focusing on

the goals Obama is pursuing and the way he is reaching them instead of questioning his eligibility to be president.

Aug. 3, 2009 – 1,200 send Obama request for records

More than 1,200 personalized letters are dispatched to Obama for the occasion of his 48th birthday, all asking him to overcome his obstinacy and release his original long-form birth certificate and other records.

Aug. 4, 2009 – Kenyan document ignites firestorm over authenticity

A document unveiled by California attorney Orly Taitz in her quest to determine Obama's place of birth is condemned as a forgery by critics who deride as nonsense the challenges that have been raised to the president's eligibility for office.

Aug. 4, 2009 – The birth certificate movie every American must see

The first DVD documentary about the hottest issue in America, "A Question of Eligibility," is produced and edited to release Aug. 4, the date Obama claims as his 48th birthday.

Aug. 6, 2009 – Obama birth doc update: Kenya sources weigh in

The Kenyan birth document released by California attorney Orly Taitz is probably not authentic, according to WND's investigative operatives in Africa, though officials in Nairobi do not rule out the possibility Obama may indeed have been born in their country.

Aug. 7, 2009 – Bill would force Obama to reveal birth documents

Hawaii state Senator Will Espero, a Democrat, confirms plans to introduce legislation through which the state's lawmakers would force the public disclosure of all Obama's birth documents held by the Hawaii Department of Health, including Obama's long-form original birth certificate.

Aug. 10, 2009 – Obama law tab up to $1.4 million

Obama may be using his political action committee funds to stomp out eligibility lawsuits brought by Americans, as he pays more than $1.35 million to his top eligibility lawyer since the election.

Aug. 7, 2009 – Blogger: I created Kenya document
A blogger who maintains anonymity claims to have generated a Kenyan birth certificate for the president that appears similar to the one unveiled by Orly Taitz.

Aug. 9, 2009 – Globe: Obama's Hawaiian birth document fake
The supermarket tabloid the Globe features a cover story proclaiming Obama's "official birth document" a fake and suggesting the president may actually have been born in Canada.

Aug. 9, 2009 – Evidence challenges claim over Obama's birth address
Documents uncovered by WND strongly suggest Barack Obama Sr. and Stanley Ann Dunham, President Obama's parents, did not live at 6085 Kalanianaole Highway in Hawaii, even though birth announcements in local newspapers listed that address.

Aug. 12, 2009 – Federal judge calls soldier's Obama challenge 'frivolous'
Maj. Stefan Cook, a U.S. Army soldier questioning the eligibility of President Obama to hold office, has his latest legal challenge dismissed "as frivolous and wholly without merit," though the basic constitutional issue has yet to have a legal ruling.

Aug. 13, 2009 – Gibbs stumbles explaining Obama's birthplace
Obama Press Secretary Robert Gibbs stumbles over the explanation about Obama's birthplace, saying, "I can't tell you why somebody believes, despite all preponderance of the evidence, that the president was born ... uhm ... in ... uhh, uhh ... was born here and not somewhere else. I've stopped trying to explain that."

Aug. 16, 2009 – Obama mama: 6 lost months
The timeline for Obama's mother, Ann Dunham, reveals an approximately six-and-a-half month interval in which there is no documentation for her whereabouts, from Jan. 31, 1961, when she concluded the fall term at the University of Hawaii at Manoa, until Aug. 19, 1961, when the University of Washington at Seattle documents she was enrolled for extension courses.

Aug. 17, 2009 – Obama's MySpace page: I'm 52 years old, not 48

Obama's official MySpace page declares his age is 52, thus placing his birth year at 1957 instead of 1961 as has been claimed.

Aug. 18, 2009 – Eligibility billboard campaign goes viral

Americans pick up on WND's "Where's the birth certificate?" billboard campaign by creating their own homemade versions of the signs and displaying them on highways, byways and on their own properties.

Aug. 18, 2009 – Obama's parents didn't live at newspaper birth address

More documents uncovered by WND support a previous report that Obama's parents did not live together as husband and wife at the Honolulu address listed in birth announcements in two local newspapers.

Aug. 19, 2009 – Tom Delay – proud 'birther'

Asked if he's a "birther," former House Majority Leader Tom DeLay tells Chris Matthews on his "Hardball" show, "Well, I'd like the president to produce his birth certificate. I can. Most illegal aliens here in America can. Why can't the president of the United States produce his birth certificate?"

Aug. 24, 2009 – Did Obama's grandmother say he was born in Kenya?

Although no other evidence has surfaced placing Barack Obama's mother in Kenya at the time of the president's birth, a taped telephone conversation in which his Kenyan step-grandmother purportedly claims he was born in the coastal city of Mombasa becomes an Internet hit since its submission as evidence in a lawsuit challenging the president's eligibility.

Sept. 7, 2009 – Panic in D.C.? Justice urges birth suit tossed

The U.S. Justice Department urges Judge David Carter, a federal judge in California, to dismiss a lawsuit brought by attorney Orly Taitz challenging the constitutional eligibility of Obama to hold the office of president.

Sept. 11, 2009 – Eye-popper: Is Nancy Pelosi in on eligibility cover-up?

A Canada Free Press commentator says he has obtained copies of two documents apparently prepared by Democrats to certify Barack Obama as their nominee for president in 2008 that suggest House Speaker Nancy Pelosi knew there was an unresolved issue with his eligibility under the U.S. Constitution.

Sept. 14, 2009 – Soldier ordered not to challenge Obama's eligibility?

Capt. Connie Rhodes, a medical doctor and Army officer who claimed her superiors had prevented her from attending her previous, emergency court hearing, stands before a judge to question the constitutional eligibility of her commander in chief.

Sept. 15, 2009 – Legislator takes eligibility question to election officials

New Hampshire State Rep. Laurence Rappaport, R-Colebrook, meets with New Hampshire's secretary of state, William Gardner to demand answers and give him a pair of allegedly genuine, Kenyan birth certificates that declare Obama was born in Africa, and not in the U.S.

Sept. 6, 2009 – Judge ridicules eligibility case

Judge Clay Land, the same judge who earlier dismissed a similar case filed by Maj. Stefan Frederick Cook, rejects another request for restraining order preventing Army Capt. Connie Rhodes' deployment overseas and threatens sanctions against attorney Orly Taitz if she files any future "frivolous" actions regarding Obama's eligibility status with his court.

Sept. 19, 2009 – Judge threatens eligibility lawyer with $10,000 fine

Judge Clay Land, the judge who dismissed a lawsuit over President Obama's eligibility and was accused by the attorney of exhibiting "subservience" to that "same illegitimate chain of command," threatens lawyer Orly Taitz with a $10,000 fine.

Sept. 30, 2009 – Was Obama's birth out of wedlock?

Former Time magazine contributing editor Christopher Andersen raises once again the question of whether Obama's parents were ever officially married, writing in his book: "Barack Obama and Ann Dunham were reportedly married in a civil ceremony on the island of Maui, although there are no official records showing that a legal ceremony ever took place."

Oct. 1, 2009 – Senator says Obama's birth location doesn't matter

In a letter to a constituent, Senator Tim Johnson, D-S.D., declares Barack Obama "a natural born citizen of the United States regardless of the location of his birth."

Oct. 13, 2009 – Eligibility attorney mocked, fined $20,000

U.S. District Judge Clay Land blasts attorney Orly Taitz, who has handled a number of court challenges to Obama's eligibility, fining her $20,000 for what he called "frivolous" court actions and mocking her concern over Obama's background.

Oct. 15, 2009 – Obama from Kenya, archived report says

A 2004 archived article from the Sunday Standard in Kenya on Barack Obama's run for the U.S. Senate in Illinois describes the relative political newcomer as "Kenyan-born," providing further fuel for speculation over the president's eligibility for office.

Oct. 21, 2009 – Judge tosses eligibility case against Congress

Judge Jerome Simandle, a federal judge in New Jersey, dismisses a lawsuit filed by Charles F. Kerchner Jr. and others against Congress, alleging members of that institution failed in their constitutionally specified responsibility to evaluate Obama and make sure of his eligibility to occupy the Oval Office.

Oct. 27, 2009 – Obama law tab up to $1.7 million

President Obama pays nearly $1.7 million to his top eligibility lawyer since the election.

Oct. 27, 2009 – Appeal filed in Obama eligibility argument

A case led by attorney Mario Apuzzo alleging Congress failed in its constitutional duties by refusing to investigate the eligibility of Obama to be president is sent on appeal to the 3rd U.S. Circuit Court of Appeals.

Oct. 27, 2009 – Michelle contradicts Obama nativity story

Michelle Obama contradicts Obama's official birth story, stating at a public event that her husband's mother, Ann Dunham, was "very young and very single" when she gave birth to the future U.S. president.

Oct. 29, 2009 – Does eligibility court clerk have ties to Obama?

Bloggers buzz about a law clerk who purportedly works in the same California court that's hearing a lawsuit challenging Barack Obama's eligibility to be president – and his ties to the former law firm of Obama's top eligibility lawyer.

Oct. 29, 2009 – Judge dismisses California eligibility challenge

California Judge David Carter, who recently hired a law clerk out of the law firm that has been paid nearly $1.7 million to defend Obama, dismisses a complaint challenging Obama's eligibility to be president citing the "birth certificate from the state of Hawaii" that apparently refers to an Internet image of a "Certification of Live Birth" released during Obama's campaign.

Dec. 4, 2009 – Palin: OK to press Obama's eligibility

Former Alaska Gov. Sarah Palin declares on "The Rusty Humphries Show" that the public is "rightfully" making questions about Barack Obama's eligibility to be president into an issue, because "I think that members of the electorate still want answers."

Jan. 4, 2010 – Beck on birther issue: 'Dumbest thing I've ever heard'

On the air, popular radio host Glenn Beck mocks "birthers" and claims there is a concerted campaign to get those questioning Obama's constitutional eligibility onto the airwaves – a strategy Beck said would actually benefit Obama.

Jan. 7, 2010 – Report: Congressman challenges Obama eligibility

Rep. Nathan Deal, R-Ga., writes to President Obama asking him to prove his eligibility to hold the office of president.

Jan. 12, 2010 – White House mum on eligibility demand

The White House confirms that a member of Congress formally has requested that President Obama document information regarding his birth and, therefore, his eligibility to occupy the Oval Office.

Jan. 12, 2010 – Birthers, is Secret Service watching you?

In blogs, interviews and e-mails, "birthers" around the country report surveillance and visits from the U.S. Secret Service, whose agents have questioned – or, as some say, intimidated – them over their insistence that Barack Obama prove his constitutional eligibility to serve as president.

Jan. 18, 2010 – 3 dozen lawmakers want proof of Obama eligibility

Three dozen lawmakers in Arizona propose a law that would require state officials to begin independently verifying the accuracy of newly required documents affirming the constitutional eligibility of any candidate for the U.S. presidency in 2012.

Jan. 19, 2010 – Obama's eligibility becomes war among the states

The demand for documentation of Obama's eligibility to occupy the Oval Office surges, with lawmakers in several states working on legislation that could be used to require future presidential candidates to reveal precisely how they are qualified under the U.S. Constitution's demand for a "natural born citizen."

Jan. 24, 2010 – Hawaii launches defense to Obama birth queries

The state of Hawaii, overwhelmed or perhaps annoyed at the number of inquiries about the birth records of President Obama, launches a new Web page with the information it wants the public to know about its Obama records, including the fact that state law does not "require agencies to respond to all questions asked of the agency."

Jan. 27, 2010 – Democrats suddenly interested in Obama birth certificate

Democratic Senatorial Campaign Committee chief Robert Menendez distributes a memo to U.S. Senate campaign offices stating that Democrats need to demand that their political opponents answer a series of questions, including, "Do you believe that Barack Obama is a U.S. citizen?"

Feb. 4, 2010 – Obama's prayer: 'Don't question my citizenship'
At the National Prayer Breakfast, President Obama raises the issue of his own eligibility for office, saying people shouldn't be questioning his "citizenship."

Feb. 13, 2010 – Attorney facing penalties wants birth docs for defense
California lawyer Orly Taitz, who has shepherded several of the high-profile legal challenges to Barack Obama's eligibility to be president, files a pleading to Chief Judge Royce Lamberth of the U.S. District Court for the District of Columbia, saying she faces a $20,000 penalty and a threat to her law license and needs the president's birth documents to defend herself.

Feb. 24, 2010 – Lawyer who challenged Obama: Ineligibility could prove costly
Gary Kreep of the United States Justice Foundation, an attorney whose legal brief in a case challenging Barack Obama's eligibility revealed the Supreme Court can remove an ineligible chief executive, releases an analysis confirming that if Obama isn't eligible, he could be charged under several felony statutes.

March 5, 2010 – Arizona lawmakers a joke to prez?
While nearly half the members of the Arizona House of Representatives sign on in support of a measure that would require presidential candidates to document their constitutional eligibility for the office in 2012, Obama spokesman Robert Gibbs jokes about their efforts.

March 7, 2010 – Rep. Broun wonders if Obama 'citizen'
U.S. Rep. Paul Broun, R-Ga., says he doesn't know if President Obama is a "citizen."

March 16, 2010 – Virginia questions Obama's eligibility
An unearthed recording reveals Virginia Attorney General Kenneth T. Cuccinelli explaining how Obama's eligibility could be tested in the courts by a lawyer defending a client against an accusation brought under legislation signed by the president.

March 25, 2010 – Court told 'citizen' Obama may actually be alien

A filing in the 3rd Circuit Court of Appeals in the case Kerchner v. Obama argues that Obama may not even be a "citizen" because "under the British Nationality Act of 1948 his father was a British subject/citizen and not a United States citizen, and Obama himself was a British subject/citizen at the time Obama was born."

March 30, 2010 – Obama: Tea party based on eligibility issue

President Obama tells the "Today" show the tea-party movement is based on those who doubt his eligibility to occupy the Oval Office, adding, "There are some folks who just aren't sure I was born in the United States, whether I was a socialist."

March 31, 2010 – Army 'showdown' at eligibility corral

Lt. Col. Terry Lakin, an active-duty flight surgeon charged with caring for Army Chief of Staff Gen. George Casey's pilots and air crew, says he's refusing all orders until President Barack Obama finally releases his long-form, hospital-generated birth certificate to prove his eligibility to serve as commander in chief.

April 1, 2010 – Army suggests brain scan for eligibility challenger

The U.S. Army unofficially suggests a brain scan and medical evaluation for Lt. Col. Terry Lakin, who announced he would refuse to follow further orders until and unless President Obama documents his constitutional eligibility to be commander in chief.

April 4, 2010 – Eligibility challenger: Don't touch my brain!

U.S. Army flight surgeon Lt. Col. Terry Lakin, who posted a video indicating his complete rejection of all orders from the military unless Barack Obama documents his eligibility for office, refuses an "unofficial" suggestion from the Army for a brain scan and medical evaluation.

April 5, 2010 – Did Michelle say Barack born in Kenya?

A video of Michelle Obama telling a group of homosexual-rights activists that Kenya was her husband's "home country" goes viral.

April 5, 2010 – Officer questioning eligibility faces new threats from Army

The Army threatens to dismiss and jail flight surgeon Lt. Col. Terry Lakin, who says he won't obey military orders until he knows that President Obama is in the Oval Office as a constitutionally eligible president.

April 8, 2010 – NPR archive describes Obama as 'Kenyan-born'

National Public Radio archives reveal that its 2008 report described then-Senator Barack Obama as "Kenyan-born" and a "son of Africa."

April 10, 2010 – Petition demanding birth certificate surges past 500,000

More than half a million people sign a petition demanding proof Barack Obama is eligible for office.

April 13, 2010 – Officer to Army: Bring it on!

Lt. Col. Terry Lakin faces imminent court-martial charges because of his decision to refuse orders to report for a Middle East deployment until President Obama's eligibility is documented.

April 14, 2010 – Officer challenging Obama 'reassigned'

Lt. Col. Terry Lakin is "reassigned" at Walter Reed Army Hospital after he refuses to deploy to Afghanistan as scheduled until President Obama's eligibility is documented.

April 17, 2010 – Justice Clarence Thomas: We're 'evading' eligibility

U.S. Supreme Court Justice Clarence Thomas tells a House subcommittee that when it comes to determining whether a person born outside the 50 states can serve as U.S. president, the high court is "evading" the issue.

April 22, 2010 – Army charges Lt. Col. Lakin

The U.S. Army files two charges against Lt. Col. Terry Lakin, who earlier posted a video inviting that action, over his refusal to follow orders until Barack Obama documents his eligibility to be commander in chief.

April 23, 2010 – Retired Army general: Lt. Col. Lakin has a 'valid point'

Maj. Gen. Paul Vallely, a retired Army general and national-security-policy expert, says Lt. Col. Terry Lakin has "a valid point" and suggests he use his "right to discovery" to force the Obama administration to produce proof of his natural-born-citizenship status.

April 23, 2010 – Army to 'inquire' into charges against Lakin

The U.S. Army claims it will "inquire" into the "truth" of the charges filed against Lt. Col. Terry Lakin, who refused to follow orders until Barack Obama documents his eligibility to occupy the Oval Office, and ultimately will "determine what disposition should be made of the case in the interest of justice and discipline."

April 23, 2010 – Another state considers Arizona eligibility plan

Georgia begins considering a law like an Arizona plan approved by the state House that would require presidential candidates to document their eligibility for office before being allowed on the election ballot.

April 27, 2010 – Eligibility sponsor fears GOP protecting Obama

A bill in Arizona that would require candidates for president to document their constitutional eligibility needs only an affirmative vote from the state Senate to advance to the governor, but its sponsor, Rep. Judy Burges, R-Skull Valley, says she's concerned GOP leadership will end up protecting President Obama's secrets.

May 5, 2010 – Hawaii governor announces 'exact' place of Obama birth

More than a year and half after Barack Obama was elected commander in chief, the governor of Hawaii publicly voices the alleged exact location of Obama's birth, saying "the president was, in fact, born at Kapi'olani Hospital in Honolulu, Hawaii."

May 10, 2010 – Obama waives ethics rules for eligibility lawyer

President Obama waives ethics rules for White House counsel Robert Bauer, his personal and campaign lawyer and the same attorney who has defended

Obama in lawsuits challenging his eligibility to be president, allowing him to continue participating in lawsuits and legal matters related to former clients, such as Obama and the Democratic National Committee.

May 10, 2010 – Elections chief: Constitution 'important'
South Dakota's chief elections officer, Chris Nelson, says the issue of President Obama's eligibility is a huge concern among voters in the state, and he thinks the constitutional qualifications for the office are supremely important to the nation.

May 11, 2010 – Investigators: Obama uses Connecticut Soc. Sec. Number
Two private investigators working independently ask why President Obama is using a Social Security number issued between 1977 and 1979 and set aside for applicants in Connecticut while there is no record he ever had a mailing address in the state.

May 12, 2010 – Google hides Obama's Social Security number story
Internet giant Google hushes up the new dispute over President Obama's strange Social Security number by diverting searches for news reports on the issue to unrelated stories about Elena Kagan, oil, Tampa and the Federal Reserve.

May 23, 2010 – U.S. Selective Service in Obama cover-up
The U.S. Selective Service System appears to block access to President Barack Obama's online Selective Service registration records, as the federal database suddenly begins posting an "error" message in place of the matched record.

June 4, 2010 – Recusal sought for 'Twitter' judge in eligibility case
Attorney John D. Hemenway files a motion for recusal against Judge James Robertson, the federal judge who threw out a lawsuit questioning Barack Obama's eligibility to be president because the issue already has been "blogged, texted, twittered and otherwise massaged."

June 3, 2010 – Army slams door on Obama details

An Army "investigating officer" banishes evidence about the controversy over President Obama's eligibility to be commander in chief from a pending hearing for Lt. Col. Terrence Lakin, a military doctor who announced he is refusing orders until Obama documents his constitutional status.

June 10, 2010 – Hawaii elections clerk: Obama not born here

Tim Adams, a college instructor who worked as senior elections clerk for the city and county of Honolulu in 2008 makes the stunning claim Barack Obama was definitely not born in Hawaii as the White House maintains, and that a long-form, hospital-generated birth certificate for Obama does not even exist in the Aloha State.

June 10, 2010 – Gibbs sidesteps Obama's Social Security Number

Press secretary Robert Gibbs refuses to answer questions about President Obama purportedly using a Social Security number set aside for applicants in Connecticut, while there is no record Obama ever had a mailing address there.

June 11, 2010 – Officer to Army: See you in court

Lt. Col. Terrence Lakin, who invited his own court-martial to resolve for the nation questions about Barack Obama's eligibility to be president, waives a preliminary military hearing in his case after an Army hearing officer bans Lakin from bringing in evidence about Obama's birth as well as testimony from Hawaii officials.

June 13, 2010 – Election official: I'd testify Obama not born in Hawaii

Tim Adams, former Honolulu elections clerk, says President Obama was "definitely" not born in Hawaii and has no birth certificate from any hospital in the Aloha State, and Adams says he's willing to testify in court to those facts.

June 15, 2010 – Army disses officer challenging Obama

Military officials go back into their records and alter their previously positive evaluations of Lt. Col. Terrence Lakin, chastising him for not having "the sound judgment required of a senior officer" after he refuses deployment orders until Obama documents his eligibility.

July 8, 2010 – Has 'standing' been created in hunt for Obama birth doc?

Judges Dolores Sloviter, Maryanne Trump Barry and Thomas Hardiman of the 3rd U.S. Circuit Court of Appeals dismiss as "frivolous" an appeal of a lower-court decision throwing out questions about whether the British Nationality Act of 1948 made Obama, at his birth to an American mother and Kenyan father, a subject of the British crown, thus possibly making him ineligible under the Constitution's requirement that a president be a "natural born citizen."

July 12, 2010 – Senator: Resolve eligibility in court

Louisiana Republican Senator David Vitter says the dispute over Barack Obama's eligibility to be president should be resolved in court and that he supports conservative legal organizations and others who would bring the issue to court.

July 17, 2010 – Eligibility challenger Army convicted me without trial

Lt. Col. Terrence Lakin, an Army officer who chose to stake his career on a demand that Barack Obama document his eligibility to be president, charges that the Army convicted him without a trial.

July 25, 2010 – Judges evade Obama birth-certificate query

Judges on the 3rd U.S. Circuit Court of Appeals suddenly abandon plans to assess damages against an attorney Mario Apuzzo, whose clients are challenging Barack Obama's eligibility to be president, after he argued that if there was to be punishment, he would have the right to know whether the defendants could have mitigated their injury by publicly releasing Obama's birth documentation.

Aug. 1, 2010 – Oops! Obama mama passport 'destroyed'

Responding to a Freedom of Information Act request, the State Department releases passport records of Stanley Ann Dunham, President

Obama's mother, but records for the years surrounding Obama's 1961 birth are missing.

Aug. 4, 2010 – New documents point to Indonesian citizenship

Documents released by the State Department in two separate Freedom of Information Act requests bolster evidence Barack Obama became a citizen of Indonesia when he moved to the Southeast Asian nation with his mother and stepfather in the late 1960s.

Aug. 7, 2010 – Another Obama puzzle: 3rd grade in 2 countries?

State Department documents give new life to the puzzle of how Barack Obama could have attended third grade in Hawaii, as claimed by a classmate, while he stated he was living in Indonesia at the time.

Aug. 8, 2010 – No birth certificate among passport documents

Passport documents for Stanley Ann Dunham Soetoro released by the State Department do not include any birth-certificate documentation for Barack Obama, despite a memorandum in the file claiming he was born in Honolulu.

Aug. 9, 2010 – Congressman: Obama 'enjoying' eligibility dispute

U.S. Rep. Brian Bilbray, R-Calif., tells WND that he believes President Obama is enjoying the dispute over his background.

Aug. 10, 2010 – Retired general: Congress should give Obama ultimatum

Maj. Gen. Jerry Curry, a decorated combat veteran who ran an abbreviated campaign for the presidency in 2008, says Congress should deliver an ultimatum to President Obama: Prove your eligibility or quit.

Aug. 19, 2010 – How many names does the president have?

At least four names appear in various documents produced since 2008 regarding Obama's life story and his passport records: Barack Hussein Obama II, Barack Hussein Obama (without the designation "II" indicating Barack Obama Jr.), Barry Soetoro and Barack Hussein Obama Soebarkah.

Sept. 27, 2010 – Key Dem: GOP to shut down government to probe eligibility

House Majority Whip James Clyburn, D-S.C., tries to drum up support for his party by warning voters that if the GOP moves into the majority in November, Republicans will issue subpoenas over every possible issue they can assemble, including Barack Obama's eligibility for office.

Sept. 4, 2010 – Battle-scarred judge says Lakin decision ignores Constitution

Lt. Col. Terrence Lakin is denied permission by Army Col. Denise R. Lind to obtain evidence that could document Obama is not eligible to occupy the Oval Office, noting that it could be "embarrassing" to request his birth and education records.

Oct. 15, 2010 – U.S. attorney: Nothing Americans can do about eligibility

A team of U.S. attorneys based in California argues to the 9th U.S. Circuit Court of Appeals that there essentially is nothing the American public can do to determine if Barack Obama is qualified under the U.S. Constitution's demand for a "natural born citizen" in the Oval Office, and if they are injured, at least they are all injured alike.

Oct. 10, 2010 – Gingrich sounds off on Obama eligibility

Former House Speaker and potential GOP presidential hopeful Newt Gingrich uses an appearance on Spanish-language television to sound off on questions surrounding President Obama's birthplace and religious faith, declaring the president has an "obligation" to figure out why so many Americans doubt his life story.

Oct. 23, 2010 – D.C. rally boldly blasts Obama as 'fraud'

A rally of a couple hundred people called by Philip Berg at the U.S. Capitol declares President Barack Obama an "imposter" and "fraud" who should resign before a constitutional crisis of his own making rips apart the nation.

Nov. 4, 2010 – Eligibility attorney asks to join case before Supremes

Gary Kreep of the United States Justice Foundation, a prominent lawyer who has argued several legal challenges to Barack Obama's eligibility to be president asks to join an appeal by attorney Mario Apuzzo on behalf of his client, Charles Kerchner Jr., that's already pending before the U.S. Supreme Court.

Nov. 8, 2010 – Congress report concedes Obama eligibility unvetted

A congressional document posted by the Congressional Research Service, a research arm of the U.S. Congress, openly admits no one in the federal government, including Congress, ever asked to see Obama's long-form, hospital-generated birth certificate.

Nov. 11, 2010 – How Congress was prepped to dismiss 'birthers'

The Congressional Research Service confirms it issued a memo to prepare members of Congress to rebut and defuse questions constituents were asking regarding Barack Obama's presidential eligibility under the "natural born citizen" requirement of the Constitution.

Nov. 17, 2010 – Show birth certificate, or don't get on ballot

Texas Rep. Leo Berman, R-Tyler, files a bill that would require candidates for president or vice president to show their birth certificates to the secretary of state before being allowed on the ballot.

Nov. 21, 2010 – Old papers tell different tales on Obama's past

Contributing to the impression of shifting sands in Barack Obama's official biography, two newspaper articles from 1990, apparently based on interviews with Obama, reported that the future president left Hawaii for Indonesia when he was 2 years old, not 6 years old, as he relates in his autobiography.

Nov. 18, 2010 – 1962 Obama articles don't mention wife, son

Two Hawaii newspaper articles published in June 1962, the month Barack Obama Sr. left the islands to attend classes at Harvard University, make no reference to his wife, Ann Dunham, or his then 10-month-old son, Barack Obama Jr.

Nov. 29, 2010 – Supremes again punt on Obama eligibility

The U.S. Supreme Court announces it will not hear Kerchner v. Obama, a case that argues that the writers of the Constitution believed the term "natural-born citizen" to mean a person born in the United States to parents who were both American citizens.

Nov. 30, 2010 – Investigator: Government fogging Obama's Connecticut ties

Without addressing questions regarding the apparent assignment of a Connecticut-based Social Security number to President Barack Obama, who reportedly spent his growing-up years in Hawaii and Indonesia, the federal agency moves quickly to randomize all future Social Security numbers.

Dec. 6, 2010 – Rush on WikiLeaks: Where's Obama's birth certificate?

With global secrets dripping out from WikiLeaks, radio host Rush Limbaugh wonders where "the real good stuff" is, including President Obama's original, long-form hospital-generated birth certificate, which has still never been released two years into his presidency.

Dec. 8, 2010 – Obama's birth-certificate guardian out of job

Hawaii Department of Health Director Chiyome Fukino, M.D., the primary gatekeeper for those who would like to explore President Obama's original birth documentation on file with the state, leaves her post.

Dec. 15, 2010 – Court martial convicts Lakin

Lt. Col. Terrence Lakin, the officer who raised questions about Barack Obama's eligibility to be president only to be struck down by a military court's banishment of evidence about his concerns, is convicted on three counts of disobeying orders after missing a flight scheduled to take him to a new assignment.

Dec. 16, 2010 – Lakin sentenced: Dismissal, 6 months

Lt. Col. Terrence Lakin is sentenced to six months in prison, forfeiture of pay and dismissal from the Army after exposing himself to court martial in an effort to validate the military chain of command by determining whether President Barack Obama is constitutionally eligible to serve as commander in chief.

Dec. 28, 2010 – Chris Matthews: Release Obama's birth certificate
Chris Matthews, anchor of MSNBC's "Hardball" program, calls for Barack Obama to release his original, long-form, hospital-generated birth certificate to put to rest any doubts about the president's constitutional eligibility to hold office.

Dec. 30, 2010 – New eligibility challenge reaches the Supreme Court
Another legal challenge to Barack Obama's eligibility to occupy the White House is docketed for consideration before the U.S. Supreme Court, and the plaintiff, Gregory S. Hollister, a retired military officer, asks that the justices appointed by Obama, the "respondent" in the case, be excluded.

Dec. 28, 2010 – Hawaii guv suddenly 'mum' on Obama birth 'certificate'
Although Hawaii's newly elected Democrat governor, Neil Abercrombie, has given a flurry of high-profile media interviews condemning "birthers" who question Barack Obama's constitutional eligibility to occupy the Oval Office, suddenly he is declining to answer a few hard questions from WND, which has reported more on the controversy than any other news source in the world.

Jan. 11, 2011 – Ineligible president cited as reason to kill Obamacare
A lawsuit brought by former financial company executive Nicholas E. Purpura and Donald R. Laster Jr., acting as their own attorneys, argues *since* Obama is not legally president, his Obamacare takeover of the nation's health-care industry should be voided.

Jan. 11, 2011 – Resolving Obama's eligibility now has dollars-and-sense plan
Montana state Rep. Bob Wagner proposes legislation that would require candidates for president to document their constitutional eligibility in his state, but his plan takes the controversy one step beyond other state

proposals by providing state law protections for the taxpayers to prevent them from being billed for "unnecessary expense and litigation" involving the failure of "federal election officials" to do their duty.

Jan. 18, 2011 – Hawaii governor can't find Obama birth certificate

Hawaii Gov. Neil Abercrombie suggests in an interview with the Honolulu Star Advertiser that a long-form, hospital-generated birth certificate for Barack Obama may not exist within the vital records maintained by the Hawaii Department of Health and that the continuing eligibility controversy could hurt the president's chances of re-election in 2012.

ENDNOTES

Preface

1 Shannon Travis, "CNN Poll: Quarter Doubt Obama Was Born in U.S.," CNN Politics, August 4, 2010, at http://politicalticker.blogs.cnn.com/2010/08/04/cnn-poll-quarter-doubt-president-was-born-in-u-s/.

2 NBC News, "Full Transcript: Obama Interview with NBC News—President Speaks on Fifth Anniversary of Hurricane Katrina," August 29, 2010, at http://www.msnbc.msn.com/id/38907780.

Introduction

3 "Obama Passport Files Violated; 2 Workers at State fired; 1 Rebuked," *Washington Times*, March 20, 2008, at http://www.washingtontimes.com/news/2008/mar/20/obama-passport-files-violated-2-workers-at-state-f/.

4 Helene Cooper, "Passport Files of 3 Candidates Were Pried Into," *New York Times*, March 22, 2008, at http://www.nytimes.com/2008/03/22/us/politics/22passport.html.

5 "Passports Probe Focuses on Worker," *Washington Times*, March 22, 2008, at http://www.washingtontimes.com/news/2008/mar/22/passports-probe-focuses-on-worker/.

6 United States Department of State and the Broadcasting Board of Governors, Office of Inspector General, Office of Audits, "Review of Controls and Notification for Access to Passport Records in the Department of State's Passport Information Electronic Records System (PIERS)," AID/IP-08-29, July 2008.

7 Ken Timmerman, "Obama's Intelligence Adviser Involved in Security Breach," NewsMax.com, January 12, 2009, at http://www.newsmax.com/KenTimmerman/brennan-passport-breach/2009/01/12/id/337482.

8 Officer William A. Smith, Jr., *Affidavit of Criminal Complaint vs. Lieutenant Quarles Harris, Jr.*, DOB 3/7/84, U.S. District Court for the District of Columbia, Case Number 08-215-11-01, dated March 25, 2008, and filed March 26, 2008, at http://acc-tv.com/sites/wjla/news/stories/

videos/harrischargingdoc.pdf. Note: the correct spelling of Harris' first name is "Leiutenant," distinct from the spelling of the military rank, "lieutenant." Despite this, the criminal complaint uses the incorrect spelling, listing the suspect as "Lieutenant Quarles Harris, Jr."

9 "Key Witness in Passport Fraud Case Fatally Shot," *Washington Times*, April 19, 2008, at http://www.washingtontimes.com/news/2008/apr/19/key-witness-in-passport-fraud-case-fatally-shot/.

10 Mayhill Fowler, "Obama: No Need for Foreign Policy Help from V.P.," *Huffington Post*, April 7, 2008, at http://www.huffingtonpost.com/mayhill-fowler/obama-says-no-to-foreign_b_95357.html.

11 Jake Tapper, "Obama's College Trip to Pakistan," ABC News Blog "Political Punch," April 8, 2008, at http://blogs.abcnews.com/politicalpunch/2008/04/obamas-college.html.

12 Social Security Administration, "Social Security Number Verification Service (SSNVS)," "Social Security Number Allocations," at http://www.socialsecurity.gov/employer/stateweb.htm.

13 "Here's the Scoop: Obama Has Worked in the Ice Cream Business, Among Many Others," PolitiFact.com, April 7, 2009, at http://www.politifact.com/truth-o-meter/statements/2009/apr/15/joe-scarborough/heres-scoop-obama-has-worked-ice-cream-business-am/.

14 Jerome R. Corsi, "Investigators: Obama Uses Connecticut Soc. Sec. Number," WND, May 11, 2010, at http://www.wnd.com/?pageId=152773.

Chapter 1

15 Jonathan Turley, on his blog "Res Ipsa Loquitur ('The Thing Itself Speaks')," in the "Bio" section, at http://jonathanturley.org/about/.

16 Jonathan Turley, "Does John McCain Have an Alexander Hamilton Problem? A Constitutional Challenge May Loom Over McCain's Eligibility for President," February 28, 2008, JonathanTurley.org, at http://jonathanturley.org/2008/02/28/does-john-mccain-have-an-alexander-hamilton-problem-a-constitutional-challenge-may-loom-over-mccains-eligibility-for-president/.

17 Jonathan Turley, "McCain's Constitutional Dilemma: Native Son But Not Natural-born," February 29, 2008, JonathanTurley.org, at http://jonathanturley.org/2008/02/29/mccains-constitutional-dilemma-native-son-but-not-natural-born/.

18 Jonathan Turley, "Arnold Schwarzenegger and the Constitutional Ban on Foreign Born Presidents," August 20, 2007, JonathanTurley.org, at http://jonathanturley.org/2007/08/20/arnold-schwarzenegger-and-the-constitutional-ban-on-foreign-born-presidents/.

19 Gabriel J. Chin, "Why Senator John McCain Cannot Be President: Eleven Months and a Hundred Yards Short of Citizenship," Arizona Legal Studies, Discussion Paper No. 08-14, August 2008, James E. Rogers College of Law, University of Arizona, at http://papers.ssrn.com/sol3/papers.cfm?abstract_id=1157621. Also, available at http://www.scribd.com/doc/9258498/Why-Sen-John-McCain-Cannot-Be-President.

20 Jonathan Turley, "The Supreme Redux: Is John McCain Ineligible to Be President?" March 6, 2008, JonathanTurley.org, at http://jonathanturley.org/2008/03/06/the-supreme-redux-is-john-mccain-ineligible-to-be-president/.

21 Opinion of Laurence H. Tribe and Theodore B. Olson, March 19, 2008, at http://www.scribd.com/doc/23193402/Opinion-of-Laurence-H-Tribe-and-Theodore-B-Olson-03-19-2008-re-McCain-Eligibility.

22 "How Can Panamanian-born McCain Be Elected President?" FactCheck.org, February 25, 2008, at http://www.factcheck.org/askfactcheck/how_can_panamanian-born_mccain_be_elected_president.html.

23 Ronald J. Polland, Ph.D. did ground-breaking work identifying the campaign waged by the political left to challenge McCain's eligibility to be president. See Polland's video: "Fraud in

the U.S.A. (Chapter 1, Part 1): The Greatest Birth Certified Fraud in History," YouTube, April 30, 2010, at http://www.youtube.com/watch?v=f2-2E65uFHM. Polland's series of videos on Obama's eligibility can be found on YouTube at http://www.youtube.com/user/TheDrRJP#p/a/u/1/f2-2E65uFHM. Polland often posts on the Internet under the username "Polarik."

24 Carl Hulse, "McCain's Canal Zone Birth Prompts Queries About Whether That Rules Him Out," *New York Times*, February 28, 2008, at http://www.nytimes.com/2008/02/28/us/politics/28mccain.html?_r=5&adxnnl=1&oref=slogin&ref=politics&pagewanted=print&adxnnlx=1204172107-YSe.

25 "Oh-eight(R): Born in the U.S.A.?" published in "First Read" on NBC News, February 28, 2008, at http://firstread.msnbc.msn.com/_news/2008/02/28/4436045-oh-eight-r-born-in-the-usa.

26 Vaughn Ververs, "Starting Gate: the Center Holds," CBS News, February 28, 2008, http://www.cbsnews.com/8301-502163_162-3886167-502163.html.

27 Hanna Strange, "McCain's Panama Birth Prompts Eligibility Probe by His Campaign," *Sunday Times*, February 29, 2009, at http://www.timesonline.co.uk/tol/news/world/us_and_americas/us_elections/article3460276.ece.

28 Pete Williams, Justice Correspondent, NBC News, "McCain's Citizenship Called into Question," Nightly News on NBC, MSNBC.MSN.com, February 29, 2008, at http://www.msnbc.msn.com/id/23415028/.

29 Jake Tapper, "Legislation Introduced—by Democrats—to Declare McCain a U.S. Citizen," in the "Political Punch" blog at ABCNews.com, April 10, 2008, at http://blogs.abcnews.com/politicalpunch/2008/04/legislation-int.html.

30 Ashby Jones, "Clinton, Obama Agree: McCain's a 'Natural-born Citizen,'" Law Blog, *Wall Street Journal*, April 11, 2008, at http://blogs.wsj.com/law/2008/04/11/clinton-obama-agree-mccains-a-natural-born-citizen/tab/article/.

31 Michael Dobbs, "McCain's Birth Abroad Stirs Legal Debate," *Washington Post*, May 2, 2008, at http://www.washingtonpost.com/wp-dyn/content/article/2008/05/01/AR2008050103224.html.

32 Robert Farley, "Was McCain Born in the U.S.A.?" Politifact.com, May 12, 2008, at http://www.politifact.com/truth-o-meter/article/2008/may/12/born-usa/.

33 "The Bombshell on McCain's Birth Certificate," posted by blogger "andyfoland," on DailyKos.com, June 12, 2008, at http://www.dailykos.com/story/2008/6/12/17219/6245/58/534894.

34 Adam Liptak, "A Hint of Life to a McCain Birth Issue," *New York Times*, July 11, 2008, at http://www.nytimes.com/2008/07/11/us/politics/11mccain.html?_r=2&adxnnl=1&oref=slogin&partner=rssuserland&emc=rss&pagewanted=all&adxnnlx=1215800111-BJ41WXhHTAsrQ7oybs7UFg.

35 Clay Waters, "The NY Times Presents: John McCain, Disqualified at Birth—the Sequel," NewsBusters.com, July 11, 2008, at http://newsbusters.org/blogs/clay-waters/2008/07/11/ny-times-presents-john-mccain-disqualified-birth-sequel.

36 "McCain Not Natural-born Citizen, Prof Says," UPI.com, July 11, 2008, at http://www.upi.com/Top_News/2008/07/11/McCain-not-natural-born-citizen-prof-says/UPI-86721215783410/.

37 "Claim: John McCain Does Not Qualify as a Natural-born Citizen of the U.S. Because He Was Born in Panama," Snopes.com, July 2008, at http://www.snopes.com/politics/mccain/citizen.asp.

38 "Claim: Barack Obama Does Not Qualify as a Natural-born Citizen of the U.S. Because His Mother Was Too Young," Snopes.com, June 2008, at http://www.snopes.com/politics/obama/citizen.asp.

39 Tony Mauro, "Judge Rules McCain's U.S. Citizenship Is 'Highly Probable,'" Law.com, September 18, 2008, at http://www.law.com/jsp/article.jsp?id=1202424594348.

40 See, for instance: Nolu Chan, "John McCain and His Mythical Birth Certificate," The

People's Forum, September 20, 2009, at http://www.the-peoples-forum.com/cgi-bin/readart. cgi?ArtNum=14500.

41 Franklin D. Roosevelt, Executive Order 8981, Naval Hospital Area, Coco Solo, Canal Zone, December 17, 1941, at http://www.presidency.ucsb.edu/ws/index.php?pid=60931.

42 Dr. Conspiracy, "The Birth Certificate Is a forgery!" ObamaConspiacyTheories.com, February 27, 2009, http://www.obamaconspiracy.org/2009/02/the-birth-certificate-is-a-forgery/; and Dr. Conspiracy, "John McCain's Fake Birth Certificate," ObamaConspiracyTheories.com, April 24, 2010, at http://www.obamaconspiracy.org/2010/04/john-mccains-fake-birth-certificate/.

43 Michael Dobbs, "John McCain's Birthplace," on the blog "The Fact Checker," *Washington Post*, May 20, 2008, at http://voices.washingtonpost.com/fact-checker/2008/05/john_mccains_birthplace.html.

Chapter 2

44 Jack Maskell, Legislative Attorney, American Law Division, "Qualifications for the Office of President of the United States and Legal Challenges to the Eligibility of a Candidate," Congressional Research Service, April 3, 2009, at http://www.scribd.com/doc/41131059/CRS-Congressional-Internal-Memo-What-to-Tell-Your-Constituents-Regarding-Obama-Eligibility-Questions.

45 Brooks Baehr, "Abercrombie Offended by Obama Citizenship Questions," Hawaii News Now, KGMB and KHNL, December 25, 2010, at http://www.hawaiinewsnow.com/Global/story. asp?S=13739513.

46 Sheryl Gay Stolberg, "Hawaii's Governor Takes On 'Birthers,'" *New York Times*, December 24, 2010, at http://www.nytimes.com/2010/12/25/us/25hawaii.html?_r=2.

47 Ed Henry, Senior White House Correspondent, "Governor Vows to End Birther Controversy," CNN Politics, December 27, 2010, at http://whitehouse.blogs.cnn.com/2010/12/27/governor-vows-to-end-birther-controversy/.

48 Michael A. Memoli, Washington Bureau, "For Hawaii Governor, Discrediting Anti-Obama 'Birthers' Is a Top Priority," *Los Angeles Times*, December 24, 2010, at http://articles.latimes. com/2010/dec/24/nation/la-na-obama-birthers-20101224.

49 "Chris Matthews: Why Doesn't Obama Demand a Copy of His Birth Certificate? (VIDEO)," *Huffington Post*, December 28, 2010, at http://www.huffingtonpost.com/2010/12/28/chris-matthews-obama-birthers_n_801818.html.

50 Jerome R. Corsi, "Unveiled! Hawaii's 1961 Long-form Birth Certificates," WND, July 28, 2009, at http://www.wnd.com/index.php?fa=PAGE.view&pageId=105347.

51 "'This Is a Collaborative Endeavor,'" *Honolulu Star Advertiser*, January 18, 2011, at http://www. staradvertiser.com/editorials/20110118_This_is_a_collaborative_endeavor.html.

52 Jerome R. Corsi, "Hawaii Governor Can't Find Obama Birth Certificate," WND, January 18, 2011, at http://www.wnd.com/index.php?pageId=252833.

53 Russell Goldman and Devin Dwyer, "Hawaii Gov. Says Proof of Obama's Birth Certificate Exists but Hasn't Produced the Document," ABC News/Politics, January 20, 2011, at http://abcnews.go.com/Politics/obama-birth-hawaii-gov-proof-presidents-birth-certificate/story?id=12721552.

54 "Hawaii Gov Says State Has Obama Birth Form," United Press International, January 20, 2011, at http://www.upi.com/Top_News/U.S./2011/01/20/Hawaii-gov-says-state-has-Obama-birth-form/UPI-32381295552740/.

55 Daily Mail Reporter, "Hawaii Governor Claims Record of Obama's Birth 'Exists in Archives' but Can't Produce the Vital Document," *Daily Mail*, Mail Online, January 20, 2011, at http://www.dailymail.co.uk/news/article-1348916/Hawaii-governor-says-Obamas-birth-

record-exists-produce-it.html.

56 Rush Limbaugh, Transcript, "Governor of Hawaii Can't Find Barack Obama's Birth Certificate?" RushLimbaugh.com, January 21, 2011, at http://www.rushlimbaugh.com/home/daily/site_012111/content/01125106.guest.html.

57 James Taranto, "Birther Turnabout," in the "Best of the Web" blog, *Wall Street Journal*, December 28, 2011, at http://online.wsj.com/article/SB1000142405297020351320457604774105767656.html.

58 Goldman and Dwyer, *op.cit.*, supra at note #50.

59 Robert Paul Reyes, "Gov. Neil Abercrombie Has Utterly Failed to Prove He Was Born in Hawaii," *Hawaii Reporter*, January 20, 2011, at http://www.hawaiireporter.com/gov-neil-abercrombie-has-utterly-failed-to-prove-obama-was-born-in-hawaii/123.

60 Jerome R. Corsi, "Obama Birth Certificate 'Egg on Face' for Guv," WND, January 25, 2011, at http://www.wnd.com/index.php?pageId=255769.

61 Jana Winter, "Celebrity Journalist: I Never Spoke to Hawaii Gov About Obama Birth Certificate," Fox News, January 26, 2011, at http://www.foxnews.com/politics/2011/01/26/celebrity-journalist-says-he-never-talked-hawaii-governor-obama-birth/.

62 Bob Unruh, "Abercrombie's Buddy Promises to Grill Guv on Birth Certificate," WND, January 27, 2011, at http://www.wnd.com/?pageId=256365.

63 Jack Cashill, *Deconstructing Obama: The Life, Loves, and Letters of America's First Postmodern President* (New York: Threshold Editions, 2011).

64 Jack Cashill, "Still More Prevaricating from Abercrombie Pal," American Thinker, January 27, 2011, at http://www.americanthinker.com/blog/2011/01/still_more_prevaricating_from.html.

65 Memoli, *op.cit.*, supra note #46.

66 Mark Niesse, Associated Press, "Neil Abercrombie to Release Proof in Battle Against Birthers," *Huffington Post*, December 28, 2011, at http://www.huffingtonpost.com/2010/12/29/neil-abercrombie-seeking-_n_802245.html.

67 "Law Stops Effort to Document Obama's Birth," Associated Press, published by the *New York Times*, January 22, 2011, at http://www.nytimes.com/2011/01/23/us/politics/23hawaii.html.

68 Jerome R. Corsi, "Hawaii Official Now Swears: No Obama Birth Certificate," WND, January 24, 2011, at http://www.wnd.com/index.php?pageId=254401.

69 Barack Obama, *Dreams from My Father: A Story of Race and Inheritance* (New York: Crown Publishers, 1995), 345.

Chapter 3

70 Thomas C. Reeves, *Gentleman Boss: The Life of Chester Arthur* (New York: Knopf, 1975).

71 Statement of Forest McDonald, Professor of History, University of Alabama, before Subcommittee on the Constitution, Committee on the Judiciary, House of Representatives, July 24, 2000.

72 Christina S. Lohman, "Presidential Eligibility: The Meaning of the Natural-Born Citizen Clause," *Gonzaga Law Review*, Volume 36, 2000, 349.

73 Benjamin Franklin to: Charles William Frederic Dumas, *Delegates to Congress: Letters to Congress, 1774–1789, Volume 2, September 1775–December 1775*, Electronic Text Center, University of Virginia Library, at http://etext.lib.virginia.edu/etcbin/toccer-new2?id=DelVol02.xml&images=images/modeng&data=/texts/english/modeng/parsed&tag=public&part=459&division=div1.

74 Mario Apuzzo, "The Natural-born Citizen Clause of Our U.S. Constitutions Requires that Both of the Child's Parents Be U.S. Citizens at the Time of Birth," Puzo1.BlogSpot.com, September 8, 2009, at http://puzo1.blogspot.com/2009/09/natural-born-citizen-clause-requires.html.

75 Dr. Conspiracy, "The Law of Nations and the Law of the United States," published under "Obama Conspiracy Theories" on the blog ObamaConspiracy.org, February 21, 2009, at http://www.obamaconspiracy.org/2009/02/the-law-of-nations-and-the-law-of-the-united-states/.

76 "Q: Does Barack Obama Have Kenyan Citizenship?" FactCheck.org, August 29, 2008, at http://www.factcheck.org/askfactcheck/does_barack_obama_have_kenyan_citizenship.html.

77 "Things You Might Not Know about Barack Obama," *Rocky Mountain News*, August 6, 2008, at http://www.rockymountainnews.com/news/2008/aug/06/things-you-might-not-know-about-barack-obama/?partner=yahoo_headlines.

78 "The Truth About Barack Obama's Citizenship," FightTheSmears.com, at http://fightthesmears.com/articles/5/birthcertificate.

79 "Conspiracy Theories and Misinformation," State Department, America.gov, at http://www.america.gov/conspiracy_theories.html.

80 Jerome R. Corsi, "State Dept. confirms Obama Dual Citizen," WND, August 24, 2010, at http://www.wnd.com/index.php?fa=PAGE.view&pageId=195441.

81 Rob Crilly, "Kenyans Hail Election of Savior Barack Obama," *Sunday Times*, January 21, 2009, at http://www.timesonline.co.uk/tol/news/world/us_and_americas/us_elections/article5556295.ece.

82 Jake Tapper, "In Ghana, President Obama Gives Tough Love," ABC News "Political Punch" Blog, July 11, 2009, at http://blogs.abcnews.com/politicalpunch/2009/07/in-ghana-president-obama-gives-tough-love.html.

83 Peter Baker, "Obama Delivers Call for Change to a Rapt Africa," *New York Times*, July 11, 2009, at http://www.nytimes.com/2009/07/12/world/africa/12prexy.html?_r=2.

84 Observer Staff, "'I Don't See Africa as a World Apart'—Says President Obama," *Daily Observer*, August 6, 2010, at http://www.liberianobserver.com/node/7692.

85 "The Proposed Constitution of Kenya, May 6, 2010," published by *The Nation* in Kenya, at http://www.nation.co.ke/blob/view/-/913208/data/157983/-/l8do0kz/-/published+draft.pdf.

Chapter 4

86 Stephen Tonchen, "Obama Presidential Eligibility—An Introductory Primer," Revised, October 8, 2010, at http://people.mags.net/tonchen/birthers.htm.

87 Congressional Globe, 39th Congress (1866), 2890. The actual page is archived on the Internet at http://www.14thamendment.us/articles/anchor_babies_unconstitutionality.html.

88 Ibid., 32. Emphasis in original.

89 *United States v. Wong Kim Ark*, 169 U.S. 649 (1898).

90 Stephen Tonchen, "Obama Presidential Eligibility—An Introductory Primer," Revised October 8, 2010, at http://people.mags.net/tonchen/birthers.htm.

91 Ibid.

92 "Claim: Barack Obama Does Not Qualify as a Natural-born Citizen of the U.S. Because His Mother Was Too Young. Status: False," Snopes.com, June 2008, at http://snopes.com/politics/obama/citizen.asp.

93 David Emery, "Email Claims Barack Obama Isn't a Natural-Born Citizen," in the "Urban Legends" section of About.com, June 2008, at http://urbanlegends.about.com/od/barackobama/a/obama_citizen.htm.

94 "Claim: Barack Obama Does Not Qualify as a Natural-born Citizen of the U.S. Because His Mother Was Too Young," Snopes.com, June 2008, at http://www.snopes.com/politics/obama/citizen.asp.

95 David Emery, "Email Rumor Claims Barack Obama Is Ineligible for the Presidency by Virtue of Certain Laws in Effect at the Time of His Birth He Is Not a Natural-born U.S. Citizen," About.com, June 2008, at http://urbanlegends.about.com/od/barackobama/a/obama_citizen.htm.

Chapter 5

96 An interview conducted by a poster with the username "opendna" conducted with Jay McKinnon, "Beyond a Reasonable Doubt," DailyKos.com, July 5, 2008, at http://www.dailykos.com/story/2008/7/5/15947/95667/125/547039. McKinnon typically posted under the name "opendna," a username meant to suggest "open-DNA."

97 Kos, "Obama's Birth Certificate," DailyKos.com, June 12, 2008, at http://www.dailykos.com/story/2008/6/12/11012/6168/320/534616.

98 "Comments," DailyKos.com, "by kos," June 12, 2008, at 08:46:03 AM PDT, at http://www.dailykos.com/comments/2008/6/12/11012/6168/172#c172.

99 Israel Insider Staff, "As Obama Stonewalls on Uncertified Birth Certificate, Official Doubts Mount," IsraeliStreams.com, June 28, 2008, at http://israelstreams.com/?israelinsider.html?http://israelinsider.com/Articles1/Politics/12944.htm. The original article in the *St. Petersburg Times* appears to have been removed from the Internet.

100 Amy Hollyfield, "Obama's Birth Certificate: Final Chapter," PolitiFact.com, June 27, 2008, at http://www.politifact.com/truth-o-meter/article/2008/jun/27/obamas-birth-certificate-part-ii/.

101 Israel Insider Staff, "Blogger Manipulates Birth Certificate Image, Undermining Obama Claims," July 3, 2008, at http://israelstreams.com/?israelinsider.html?http://israelinsider.com/Articles1/Politics/12956.htm.

102 "Has Obama's Birth Certificate Been Disclosed?" FactCheck.org, June 16, 2008, at http://www.factcheck.org/askfactcheck/has_obamas_birth_certificate_been_disclosed.html.

103 "Barack Obama's Birth Certificate Revealed Here," published in the "Top of the Ticket" blog, *Los Angeles Times*, June 16, 2008, at http://latimesblogs.latimes.com/washington/2008/06/obama-birth.html.

104 *Op.cit.,* An interview conducted by a poster with the username "openda" conducted with Jay McKinnon, "Beyond a Reasonable Doubt," DailyKos.com, July 5, 2008, above at note #96.

105 Posted by "opendna," a user name commonly used by Jay McKinnon, "Off-Peak Immigration Series #1," DailyKos.com, July 17, 2006, at http://www.dailykos.com/story/2006/7/18/14428/4104.

106 "The Truth About Obama's Birth Certificate," FactCheck.org, August 21, 2008, at http://www.factcheck.org/elections-2008/born_in_the_usa.html.

107 The series of videos posted by Ronald J. Polland, Ph.D., on Obama's eligibility can be found on YouTube at http://www.youtube.com/user/TheDrRJP#p/a/u/1/f2-2E65uFHM. Polland often posts on the Internet under the username "Polarik."

108 Bob Unruh, "Imaging Guru: 'Certification' of Birth Time, Location Is Fake," WND, December 1, 2008, at http://www.wnd.com/index.php?fa=PAGE.view&pageId=82503.

109 "Polarik's Final Report: Obama's 'Born' Conspiracy," posted on FreeRepublic.com, November 23, 2008, at http://www.freerepublic.com/focus/bloggers/2136816/posts.

110 "Claim: A Certification of Live Birth Document Provided by the Obama Campaign Is a Forgery," Snopes.com, June 2008, at http://www.snopes.com/politics/obama/birthcertificate.asp.

111 Poster using "Dr. Conspiracy" username, "The African Race," ObamaConspiracy.com, April 3, 2009, at http://www.obamaconspiracy.org/2009/04/the-african-race/.

112 Jerome R. Corsi, "Hawaii Refuses to Verify President's Online COLBs," WND, August 2, 2009, at http://www.wnd.com/?pageId=105817.

113 June Gibbs Brown, Inspector General, Office of Inspector General, Department of Health and Human Services, "Birth Certificate Fraud," September 2000, Report, EI-07-99-00570, at http://www.oig.hhs.gov/oei/reports/oei-07-99-00570.pdf.

114 Ibid., ii.

Chapter 6

115 "Who Is Eligible to Apply for the Issuance of a Late Birth Certificate in Lieu of a Certificate of Hawaiian Birth?" Department of Health, State of Hawaii, at http://hawaii.gov/health/vital-records/vital-records/hawnbirth.html.

116 "Obama's 'Birth Certificate'—the Devil's in the Details," posted on "Article 2, Sect 1, Clause 5 (Natural-born Citizen), November 28, 2008, at http://art2sect1clause5.blogspot.com/2008/11/obamas-missing-link-hawaiian-birth_28.html.

117 Neil L. Thomsen, "No Such Sun Yat-Sen: An Archival Success Story," at Asian America Media, Chinese-America" History and Perspectives (1997), at http://www.asianamericanmedia.org/separatelivesbrokendreams/sunintro1.html.

118 Dr. Conspiracy, "Hawaiian Birth Certificate: It's a Fraud!" ObamaConspiracy.org, January 25, 2009, at http://www.obamaconspiracy.org/2009/01/hawaiian-birth-certificate-its-a-fake/.

119 "Clearing the Smoke on Obama's Eligibility: An Intelligence Investigator's June 10 Report," *Western Journalism*, June 10, 2009, updated July 18, 2009, at http://www.westernjournalism.com/exclusive-investigative-reports/clearing-the-smoke-june10/.

120 "Born in the U.S.A.: The Truth about Obama's Birth Certificate," FactCheck.org, first published August 21, 2008, updated November 1, 2008, at http://www.factcheck.org/elections-2008/born_in_the_usa.html.

121 Drew Zahn, "Hawaiian Newspapers Don't Prove Birthplace," WND, July 22, 2009, at http://www.wnd.com/?pageId=104678.

122 Stephen Tonchen, "Obama Presidential Eligibility—An Introductory Primer," Revised October 8, 2010, 107, at http://people.mags.net/tonchen/birthers.htm.

123 Ibid.

124 Dan Nakaso, "Hawaii Officials Confirm Obama's Original Birth Certificate Still Exists," *Honolulu Advertiser*, July 28, 2009, at http://the.honoluluadvertiser.com/article/2009/Jul/28/ln/hawaii907280345.html.

125 "Presenting … The Nordyke Twins Newspaper Birth Announcement," MyVeryOwnPointOfView.WordPress.com, posted January 14, 2010, at http://myveryownpointofview.wordpress.com/2010/01/07/editing/.

Chapter 7

126 Tim Jones, "Barack Obama: Mother Not Just a Girl from Kansas," *Chicago Tribune*, March 27, 2007, at http://www.chicagotribune.com/news/politics/obama/chi-0703270151mar27-archive,0,2623808.story?page=1.

127 Drew Zahn, "Kenyan Official: Obama Born Here," WND, April 11, 2010, at http://www.wnd.com/?pageId=139481.

128 Bob Unruh, "NPR Archive Describes Obama as 'Kenyan-born,'" WND, April 8, 2010, at http://www.wnd.com/?pageId=138293.

129 Ibid.

130 Drew Zahn, "Kenyan Officials Affirm: Obama 'Son of This Soil," WND, April 12, 2010, at http://www.wnd.com/?pageId=139725.

131 Drew Zahn, "Kenyan Official: Obama Born Here," WND, April 11, 2010, at http://www.wnd.com/index.php?fa=PAGE.view&pageId=139481.

132 "Michelle Obama: Barack's Home Country Is Kenya," YouTube.com, posted April 3, 2010, at http://www.youtube.com/watch?v=HLDHDfPNBME&feature=player_embedded.

133 "Michelle Obama Speaks to Gay Democrats," Reuters, June 26, 2008, at http://blogs.reuters.com/frontrow/2008/06/26/michelle-obama-speaks-to-gay-democrats/.

134 Jerome R. Corsi, "Did Obama's Grandmother Say He Was Born in Kenya?" WND, August 24, 2009, at http://www.wnd.com/?pageId=107524.

135 Nicholas D. Kristof, "Obama's Kenyan Roots," *New York Times*, February 24, 2008, at http://www.nytimes.com/2008/02/24/opinion/24kristof.html.

136 Alex Koppelman, "No, Obama's Grandmother Didn't Say He Was Born in Kenya," posted on the "War Room" blog, Salon.com, July 23, 2009, at http://www.salon.com/news/politics/war_room/2009/07/23/liddy.

Chapter 8

137 Joe Kovacs and Jerome Corsi, "Obama Birth Mystery: More Than 1 Hospital," WND, July 7, 2009, at http://www.wnd.com/?pageId=103306.

138 Joe Kovacs, "Obama's Birth Letter: Is This Thing for Real?" WND, July 9, 2009, at http://www.wnd.com/index.php?fa=PAGE.view&pageId=103503.

139 Bennett Guira, "A New Face in Politics," *The Rainbow Edition*, Education Laboratory School, Vol. 2, Issue 3, at http://www.radiodujour.com/people/berg_philip/pdf/057_2%20 Exhibit%20Charter%20Schools%20Rainbow%20Edition%20Newsletter.pdf.

140 "Birther Mythbusting: Maya Soetoro and The Rainbow Edition Newsletter," BARACK-RYPHAL.blogspot.com, February 6, 2010, at http://barackryphal.blogspot.com/2010/02/birther-mythbusting-maya-soetoro-and.html.

141 "Suspicious Letter Regarding Obama's Birth," YouTube.com, posted July 9, 2009, at http://www.youtube.com/watch?v=Trqfq9FY1Ig.

142 Tim Jones, "Barack Obama: Mother Not Just a Girl from Kansas," *Chicago Tribune*, March 27, 2007, at http://www.chicagotribune.com/news/politics/obama/chi-0703270151mar27-archive,0,2623808.story?page=1.

143 Aaron Klein, "Hawaii Guv Candidate Member of Socialist Group?" WND, July 12, 2010, at http://www.wnd.com/index.php?pageId=178049.

144 Trevor Loudon, "Obama File 107: Neil Abercrombie, Yet Another Covert Socialist in the Obama 'Orbit,'" NewZeal.blogspot.com, July 12, 2010, at http://newzeal.blogspot.com/2010/07/obama-file-107-neil-abercrombie-yet.html.

145 Aaron Klein, "Obama Pal Slams WND for Eligibility Reporting," WND, July 21, 2010, at http://www.wnd.com/?pageId=182233.

146 Aaron Klein, *The Manchurian President: Barack Obama's Ties to Communists, Socialists and Other Anti-American Extremists* (Washington, D.C.: WND Books, 2010), 146.

147 Stanley Kurtz, *Radical-in-Chief: Barack Obama and the Untold Story of American Socialism* (New York: Threshold Editions, 2010), 1–7, 62–64, 85–87.

148 Joe Kovacs, "Obama's Birth Letter: Is This Thing for Real?" WND, July 9, 2009, at http://www.wnd.com/index.php?fa=PAGE.view&pageId=103503.

149 Joe Kovacs, "Obama 'Birth Hospital' in Astonishing Cover-up," WND, July 10, 2009, http://www.wnd.com/index.php?fa=PAGE.view&pageId=103633.

150 Joe Kovacs, "'Birth Hospital': Letter for Real," WND, July 16, 2009, at http://www.wnd.com/index.php?fa=PAGE.view&pageId=104146.

151 "Press Briefing by Press Secretary Robert Gibbs," White House Web site, WhiteHouse.gov, July 13, 2009, at http://www.whitehouse.gov/the_press_office/Briefing-by-White-House-Press-Secretary-Robert-Gibbs-7-13-09/.

152 Joe Kovacs and Bob Unruh, "Now White House Joins 'Birth Hospital' Cover-up," WND, July 13, 2009, at http://www.wnd.com/?pageId=103898.

153 "Claim: Barack Obama Is a 'Radical Muslim' Who 'Will Not Recite the Pledge of Allegiance," Snopes.com, January 2008, at http://www.snopes.com/politics/obama/muslim.asp.

154 United Press International, "Sen. Barack Obama, Democrat of Ill.," UPI.com, November 4,

2008, at http://www.upi.com/Top_News/2008/11/04/Sen-Barack-Obama-Democrat-of-Illinois/UPI-33901225647000/.

155 Joe Kovacs, "Hawaii Governor Announces 'Exact' Place of Obama Birth," WND, May 5, 2010, at http://www.wnd.com/?pageId=150125.

Chapter 9

156 Barack Obama, *Dreams from My Father: A Story of Race and Inheritance* (New York: Crown Publishers, 1995), 8–9.

157 John Griffin, "First UH African Graduate Gives View on E-W Center," *Honolulu Advertiser*, June 22, 1962.

158 http://www.youtube.com/watch?v=advfrQEeIBY.

159 Phil Dougherty, "Barack Obama Moves to Seattle in August or Early September 1961," HistoryLink.org Essay #8926, last updated on March 21, 2009, at http://www.historylink.org/index.cfm?DisplayPage=output.cfm&file_id=8926.

160 Nicole Brodeur, "Memories of Obama's Mother," *Seattle Times*, February 5, 2008, at http://seattletimes.nwsource.com/html/localnews/2004164387_brodeur05m.html.

161 Tim Jones, "Barack Obama: Mother Not Just a Girl from Kansas," *Chicago Tribune*, March 27, 2007, at http://www.chicagotribune.com/news/politics/obama/chi-0703270151mar27-archive,0,2623808.story?page=1.

162 Charlette LeFevre and Philip Lipson, "Baby Sitting Barack Obama on Seattle's Capitol Hill," January 28, 2009, archived on Seattle Chat Blog, at http://www.seattlechatclub.org/News.html.

163 Aaron Klein, "Michele Contradicts Obama Nativity Story," WND, October 27, 2009, at http://www.wnd.com/index.php?fa=PAGE.view&pageId=114259.

164 Michael Bersin, "Michelle Obama in Kansas City—Remarks," ShowMeProgress.com, July 11, 2008, at http://blog.showmeprogress.com/showDiary.do?diaryId=1297.

165 "Reminiscences: Barack Obama, Before He Was the 'Old Man,'" published on Cabodiana.org, no date, at http://cambodiana.org/MainreasonsofmysupportofObama.aspx.

166 Tom Shachtman, *Airlift to America: How Barack Obama, Sr., John F. Kennedy, Tom Mboya, and 800 East African Students Changed Their World and Ours* (New York: St. Martin's Press, 2009).

167 Ibid., 11.

168 Shurei Hirozawa, "Young Men from Kenya, Jordan and Iran Here to Study at U.H.," *Honolulu Star Bulletin*, Saturday, September 19, 1957.

169 Shachtman, *op.cit.*, 9.

170 Ibid., 11.

171 Cora Weiss, "From Kenya to America," *New York Times*, letter to editor, May 7, 2010, at http://www.nytimes.com/2010/05/09/books/review/Letters-t-FROMKENYATOA_LETTERS.html.

172 David Horowitz, "Cora Weiss," DiscoverTheNetworks.org, at http://www.discoverthenetworks.org/individualProfile.asp?indid=1677.

173 David Horowitz, "Institute for Policy Studies," DiscoverTheNetworks.org, at http://www.discoverthenetworks.org/groupProfile.asp?grpid=6991.

174 "The Facts on Grant to American Students Airlift," includes background memorandum prepared by Senator Kennedy's Office, August 1960, at http://www.jfklink.com/speeches/jfk/misc60/jfk010860_africangrant.html.

175 Elana Schor, "The Other Obama-Kennedy Connection," *Guardian*, January 10, 2008, at http://www.guardian.co.uk/world/2008/jan/10/usa.uselections2008.

176 Michael Dobbs, "Obama Overstates Kennedys' Role in Helping His Father," *Washington Post*, March 30, 2008, at http://www.washingtonpost.com/wp-dyn/content/article/2008/03/29/

AR2008032902031.html.

177 Barack Obama, Sr. to Tom Mboya, May 29, 1962, Tom Mboya Papers, Box 41, Hover Institution Archives, at http://hooverinstitutionla.blogspot.com/2010_02_01_archive.html.

178 "Remarks by the President in a National Address to America's Schoolchildren: Wakefield High School, Arlington, Virginia," Office of the Press Secretary, The White House, September 8, 2009, at http://www.whitehouse.gov/the_press_office/Remarks-by-the-President-in-a-National-Address-to-Americas-Schoolchildren/.

Chapter 10

179 Stanley Ann Dunham Obama Soetoro Passport Application File, *Strunk v. Dept. of State*, FOIA Release, July 29, 2010, at http://www.scribd.com/doc/35163631/Stanley-Ann-Dunham-Obama-Soetoro-Passport-Application-File-Strunk-v-Dept-of-State-FOIA-Release-7-29-10; and Lolo Soetoro U.S. Records, *Allen v. DHS State* and *Allen v. USCIS*, FOIA Releases, Final, July 29, 2010, at http://www.scribd.com/doc/35192432/Lolo-Soetoro-U-S-Records-Allen-v-DHS-State-and-Allen-v-USCIS-FOIA-Releases-Final-7-29-10.

180 Jerome R. Corsi, *The Obama Nation: Leftist Politics and the Cult of Personality* (New York: Threshold Editions, 2008), 50–56.

181 Aaron Klein, "Was Young Obama Indonesian Citizen?" WND, August 17, 2008, at http://www.wnd.com/?pageId=72656.

182 "Obtain Copies of Passport Records," Travel.Gov.State, A Service of the Bureau of Consular Affairs, U.S. Department of State at http://travel.state.gov/passport/services/copies/copies_872.html.

183 John N. Sampson, SI Consulting and Investigations, LLC, Strasburg, Colorado, "Memorandum of Investigative Findings—Subject: Review of U.S. CIS Alien File Relating to Lolo Soetoro, and U.S. Dept. of State Passport File Relating to Stanley Ann Dunham," September 12, 2010.

184 White House, "West Wing Week: Mailbag Day Summer Edition," August 13, 2010, archived on YouTube.com at http://www.youtube.com/watch?v=GtUkeVHfj5w.

185 "'Lia' Obama's Adopted Sister Died Suddenly," posted on WTPOTUS.WordPress.com by "Bridgette," August 7, 2010, at http://wtpotus.wordpress.com/2010/08/07/liaobamas-adopted-sister-died-suddenly/.

186 Ibid.

Chapter 11

187 Jerome R. Corsi, "Obama's Birth Certificate Sealed by Hawaii Governor," WND, October 26, 2008, at http://www.wnd.com/?pageId=79174.

188 "Claim: A Certification of Live Birth Document Provided by the Obama Campaign Is a Forgery," Snopes.com, June 2008, at http://www.snopes.com/politics/obama/birthcertificate.asp.

189 "Born in the U.S.A.: The Truth about Obama's Birth Certificate," *op.cit.*, above at note #120.

190 "Obama's 'Birth Certificate' Not Acceptable in Hawaii," WND, June 7, 2009, at http://www.wnd.com/index.php?fa=PAGE.view&pageId=100451.

191 "Applying for Hawaiian Home Lands," on the Web site of the Hawaiian Department of Hawaii Home Lands, at http://hawaii.gov/dhhl/applicants/appforms/applyhhl.

192 Robert Farley, "Obama's Birth Certificate: Final Chapter. This Time We Mean It," PolitiFact.com, July 1, 2009, at http://www.politifact.com/truth-o-meter/article/2009/jul/01/obamas-birth-certificate-final-chapter-time-we-mea/.

93 Brian Montopoli, "Hawaii to Birthers: Enough Already," in the "Political Hotsheet" blog, CBS News "Politics," May 13, 2010, at http://www.cbsnews.com/8301-503544_162-20004908-503544.html.

94 Political Commentary from Andrew Malcolm, "Hawaii Legislature OKs Measure to Ignore Requests for Disclosure of Barack Obama's Birth Certificate," in the "Top of the Ticket" blog, *Los Angeles Times*, April 28, 2010, at http://latimesblogs.latimes.com/washington/2010/04/barack-obama-birth-certificate-linda-lingle.html.

95 Joe Kovacs, "Hawaii Elections Clerk: Obama Not Born Here," WND, June 10, 2010, at http://www.wnd.com/?pageId=165041.

96 Ibid.

97 Jerome R. Corsi, "Hawaii Official Now Swears: No Obama Birth Certificate," WND, January 24, 2011, at http://www.wnd.com/?pageId=254401.

98 U.S. Department of State, "Passports: First Time Applicants," at Travel.State.gov, at http://travel.state.gov/passport/get/first/first_830.html.

99 Dan Nakaso, "Hawaii Officials Confirm Obama's Original Birth Certificate Still Exists," *Honolulu Advertiser*, October 26, 2010, archived at About.com at http://urbanlegends.about.com/gi/o.htm?zi=1/XJ&zTi=1&sdn=urbanlegends&cdn=newsissues&tm=949&f=11&su=p284.9.336.ip_p504.3.336.ip_&tt=2&bt=1&bts=1&zu=http%3A//the.honoluluadvertiser.com/article/2009/Jul/28/ln/hawaii907280345.html.

200 The relevant post on Free Republic is listed as #1,181 on a thread begun by a poster named "BuckeyeTexan" posted an article under the headline, "LTC Lakin's Appeal Denied," on FreeRepublic.com, October 12, 2010, at http://freerepublic.com/focus/f-news/2606951/posts?q=1&;page=1151#1181.

Chapter 12

201 J.B. Williams, "The Theory Is Now a Conspiracy And Facts Don't Lie," Canada Free Press, September 10, 2009, at http://www.canadafreepress.com/2009/williams091209.htm.

202 Ibid.

203 JBJD, "Back Up, Birthers!" posted on JBJD.org, October 12, 2010, at http://jbjd.org/2010/10/12/back-up-birthers/.

204 JBJD, "If Drowning Out Opposing Facts Is "un-American" Then Ignoring Unpleasant Facts Must bB Un-American, Too," posted on JBJD.org, on August 13, 2009, at http://jbjd.org/2009/08/13/if-drowning-out-opposing-facts-is-un-american-then-ignoring-unpleasant-facts-must-be-un-american-too/. The posting on the Internet of the DNC two variations of the Certification of Nomination letter appears to have occurred first in this article on JBJD.org, not in the J.B. Williams article published in Canada Free Press on September 10, 2009.

205 JBJD, "The Cheese Stands Alone," posted on JBJD.org, on September 20, 2009, at http://jbjd.org/2009/09/20/the-cheese-stands-alone/.

206 Ibid., emphasis in original.

207 Memorandum of Complaint of Election Fraud against Howard Dean, (former) Chair, DNC Services Corporation ("DNC"); and Joseph E. Sandler, (former) DNC General Counsel; and The Honorable Nancy Pelosi, Acting in a Non-Governmental Role as Chair, 2008 DNC Convention; and Alice Travis Germond, Secretary, DN; and Request for Investigation by Maryland Attorney General, March 5, 2010, archived on Scribd.com at http://www.scribd.com/doc/21675349/jbjd.

208 Memorandum of Complaint of Election Fraud against The Honorable Nancy Pelosi, Acting in a Non-Governmental Role as Chair, 2008 DNC Convention; and Alice Travis Germond, Secretary, DNC; and Request for Investigation by Virginia Attorney General, January 28, 2010, archived on Scribd.com at http://www.scribd.com/doc/24321780/jbjd.

209 Memorandum of Complaint of Election Fraud against Howard Dean, (former) Chair, DNC Services Corporation ("DNC"); and Joseph E. Sandler, (former) DNC General Counsel; and Carol Fowler, Chair, South Carolina Democratic Party and Kathy Hensley, (former) Treasurer; and The Honorable Nancy Pelosi, Acting in a Non-Governmental Role as Chair, 2008 DNC Convention; and Alice Travis Germond, Secretary, DNC; and Request for Investigation by Attorney General of South Carolina, March 5, 2010, archived on Scribd. com at http://www.scribd.com/doc/21676023/jbjd.

210 Memorandum of Complaint of Election Fraud against Boyd L. Richie, Chair, Texas Democratic Party and Request for Investigation by Attorney General of Texas, April 8, 2010, archived on Scribd.com at http://www.scribd.com/doc/21675344/jbjd.

211 Memorandum of Complaint of Election Fraud against The Honorable Nancy Pelosi, Acting in a Non-Governmental Role as Chair, 2008 DNC Convention; and Alice Travis Germond, Secretary, DNC; and Request for Investigation by Georgia Attorney General, March 5, 2010, archived on Scribd.com at http://www.scribd.com/doc/21675349/jbjd.

212 Memorandum of Complaint of Election Fraud against Brian E. Schatz, Chair, Democratic Party of Hawaii and Request for Investigation by Attorney General of Hawaii, March 5, 2010, archived on Scribd.com at http://www.scribd.com/doc/22419525/jbjd.

213 Mark Ambinder, "White House Counsel: Craig Out, Bauer In," *The Atlantic*, November 12, 2009, at http://www.theatlantic.com/politics/archive/2009/11/white-house-counsel-craig-out-bauer-in/30115/.

214 Aaron Klein, "White House Boasts: We 'Control' News Media," WND, October 18, 2009, at http://www.wnd.com/index.php?fa=PAGE.view&pageId=113347.

215 "White House Escalates War of Words with Fox News," FoxNews.com, October 12, 2009, at http://www.foxnews.com/politics/2009/10/12/white-house-escalates-war-words-fox-news/.

216 Michael Scherer, "Calling 'Em Out: The White House Takes on the Press," *Time*, October 8, 2009, at http://www.time.com/time/politics/article/0,8599,1929058,00.html.

217 Peter Nicolas, "White House Communications Chief Anita Dunn to Depart," *Los Angeles Times*, November 11, 2009, at http://articles.latimes.com/2009/nov/11/nation/na-dunn11.

218 Norman L. Eisen, Special Counsel to the President and Designated Agency Ethics Official, "Limited Waiver Pursuant to Section 3 of Executive Order 13490," May 7, 2010, White House Web site at http://www.whitehouse.gov/sites/default/files/rss_viewer/bauer_ltd_pledge_waiver.pdf.

219 Chelsea Schilling, "Obama Waives Ethics Rules for Eligibility Lawyer," WND, May 10, 2010, at http://www.wnd.com/?pageId=152177.

220 Chelsea Schilling, "Obama Law Tab Up to $1.7 Million," WND, October 27, 2009, at http://www.wnd.com/?pageId=114202.

221 Federal Elections Commission, "Obama for America: Dispersements by Payee," FEC Committee ID #: C00431445, Filed April 15, 2010, at http://query.nictusa.com/pres/2010/Q1/C00431445/B_PAYEE_C00431445.html.

222 Photo source: Daylife.com at http://www.daylife.com/photo/05JjcLO638cEH. The photograph appears to have been removed from the Web site.

223 Jim Kuhnhenn, Associated Press, "Obama Seeks to Silence Ad Tying Him to 60s Radical," August 25, 2008, at http://www.breitbart.com/article.php?id=D92PL7400.

224 Dan Morain, "Clinton Backers Fund Anti-Obama Ads," *Los Angeles Times*, May 1, 2008, at http://articles.latimes.com/2008/may/01/nation/na-money1.

225 Shailagh Murray, "Obama Opts Out of Public Financing," *Washington Post*, June 19, 2008, at http://blog.washingtonpost.com/44/2008/06/19/obama_opts_out_of_public_finan.html.

226 Robert F. Bauer, "The Progressive Case for a Libby Pardon," *Huffington Post*, June 13, 2007, at http://www.huffingtonpost.com/robert-f-bauer/the-progressive-case-for-_b_51983.html.

227 District Judge Surrick, "Memorandum and Order," in *Philip J. Berg, v. Barack Obama, et al.,* Civil Action No. 08-4083, U.S. District Court E.D. Pennsylvania, October 24,

2008, at http://scholar.google.com/scholar_case?case=3807085678376493081&hl=en&as_sdt=8000000002&as_vis=1.

228 Judge Arthur G. Scotland, writing the decision of the court in *Alan Keyes v. Debra Bowen*, U.S. Court of Appeals of California, Third District, Sacramento, Case No. C062321, filed October 25, 2010, at http://www.leagle.com/xmlResult.aspx?xmldoc=In%20CACO%20 20101025033.xml&docbase=CSLWAR3-2007-CURR.

229 Alyse Knorr, "Soldier's Suit against Obama Presidency Dismissed," *Atlanta Journal-Constitution*, July 16, 2009, at http://www.ajc.com/news/soldiers-suit-against-obama-92933.html.

230 Judge Clay D. Land, writing the order of the court in *Connie Rhodes v. Thomas D. McDonald*, U.S. District Court for the Middle District of Georgia, Columbus Division, Case No. 4:09-CV-106 (CDL), October 13, 2009, archived on the Internet at Scribd.com at http://www.scribd.com/doc/20997067/Taitz-Fined-20-000.

231 *Gregory Hollister v. Barry Soetoro, et al.*, U.S. Court of Appeals, D.C. Circuit, Case No. 09-5080, filed March 18, 2009, at http://dockets.justia.com/docket/circuit-courts/cadc/09-5080/.

232 Bob Unruh, "'Twittered' Eligibility Case Lawyer Faces Threats of Sanctions," WND, April 9, 2009, at http://www.wnd.com/index.php?fa=PAGE.view&pageId=94409.

233 James Robertson, U.S. District Judge, "Memorandum," *Gregory S. Hollister v. Barry Soetoro, et al.*, Civil Action No. 08-2254 (JR), U.S. District Court for the District of Columbia, Case 1:08-cv-02254-JR, filed March 5, 2009, at http://www.obamaconspiracy.org/wp-content/uploads/2009/02/hollister-soetoromemorandum.pdf.

234 JBJD, "Rumors, Lies, and Unsubstantiated 'Facts,'" posted on JBJD.org, August 14, 2009, at http://jbjd.org/2009/08/09/rumors-lies-and-unsubstantiated-facts/.

Chapter 13

235 Jack Maskell, Legislative Attorney, American Law Division, Congressional Research Service, "Memorandum, Subject: Qualifications for the Office of President of the United States and Legal Challenges to the Eligibility of a Candidate," April 3, 2009, archived on the Internet at Scribd.com, at http://www.scribd.com/doc/41192270/CRS-Members-of-Congress-Internal-Memo-What-to-Tell-Your-Constituents-in-Answer-to-Obama-Eligibility-Questions.

236 U.S. Congressman Bill Posey, "The Presidential Eligibility Act (H.R. 1503)", May 15, 2009, at http://posey.house.gov/News/DocumentSingle.aspx?DocumentID=130248.

237 Arizona State Legislature, HB 2441, "Presidential Candidates; Proof of Qualifications," at http://www.azleg.gov/DocumentsForBill.asp?Bill_Number=hb2441.

Conclusion

238 Jack Maskell, Legislative Attorney, American Law Division, Congressional Research Service, "Memorandum, Subject: Qualifications for the Office of President of the United States and Legal Challenges to the Eligibility of a Candidate," April 3, 2009, 14, archived on the Internet at Scribd.com, at http://www.scribd.com/doc/41192270/CRS-Members-of-Congress-Internal-Memo-What-to-Tell-Your-Constituents-in-Answer-to-Obama-Eligibility-Questions.

239 Clay Robison, "California Governor Honored: Senior Bush sSuggests that Schwarzenegger Could Someday Become President," *Houston Chronicle*, November 30, 2004, at http://www.chron.com/disp/story.mpl/metropolitan/2926290.html.

240 Rob Gagnon, "Arnold Schwarzenegger for President," no date, at http://www.petitiononline.com/robnlisa/petition.html.

241 Sarah Herlihy, "Amending the Natural-born Citizen Requirement: Globalization as the Impetus and the Obstacle," Chicago-Kent Law Review, 2006, Vol. 81, 275, archived on the

Internet at Scribd.com, http://www.scribd.com/doc/12873456/Amending-the-Natural-Born-Citizen-Requirement-Sarah-p-Herlihy-Feb-22-2006.

242 John W. Dean, "The Pernicious 'Natural-born' Clause of the Constitution: Why Immigrants Like Governors Schwarzenegger and Granholm Ought to Be Able to Become Presidents," Find Law, October 8, 2004, at http://writ.news.findlaw.com/dean/20041008.html.

243 Rebecca Leung, "President Schwarzenegger? Calif. Governor, Film Star Tells 60 Minutes He'd Like to Run," CBSNews.com, October 29, 2004, at http://www.cbsnews.com/stories/2004/10/28/60minutes/main652046.shtml.

244 "Arnold Schwarzenegger Wants to Be President," *Huffington Post*, April 29, 2010, at http://www.huffingtonpost.com/2010/04/30/arnold-schwarzenegger-wan_n_558275.html.

245 Dave Gibson, "Turkish Travel Agencies Selling U.S. Citizenship to Expectant Mothers," Examiner.com, March 17, 2010, at http://www.examiner.com/x-35821-Immigration-Reform-Examiner-y2010m3d17-Turkish-travel-agencies-selling-U.S.-citizenship-to-expectant-mothers.

246 Jerome R. Corsi, "Welcome to Hotel Anchor Baby!" WND, June 21, 2010, at http://www.wnd.com/?pageId=169049.

247 "New York Hotel Pioneers Birth Tourism," BreakingTravelNews.com, June 10, 2010, at http://www.breakingtravelnews.com/news/article/new-york-hotel-pioneers-birth-tourism/.

248 Posted by "Digger" username, "American Citizenship Part of 'Birth Tourism' Black Market for Foreign Women," DiggersRealm.com, October 1, 2010, at http://www.diggersrealm.com/mt/archives/002496.html.

249 Ben Smith, "Culture of Conspiracy: the Birthers," Politico.com, March 1, 2009, at http://www.politico.com/news/stories/0209/19450.html.

250 Mark Ambinder, "Should the GOP Take the Birther Threat Seriously? Rush does ..." *The Atlantic*, July 21, 2009, at http://www.theatlantic.com/politics/archive/2009/07/should-the-gop-take-the-birther-threat-seriously-rush-does/21787/.

251 Richard Cohen, "SPLC President Calls on CNN to Remove Lou Dobbs from Air, Cites Newsman's Support for Extremist-Inspired 'Birther' Claims," Southern Poverty Law Center, July 24, 2009, at http://www.splcenter.org/get-informed/news/splc-president-calls-on-cnn-to-remove-lou-dobbs-from-air-cites-newsmans-support-fo.

252 "The Birthers: Who Are They and What Do They Want?" Gawker.com, July 22, 2009, at http://gawker.com/5320465/the-birthers-who-are-they-and-what-do-they-want.

253 "'Birthers' Claim Gibbs Lied When He Said Obama's Birth Certificate Is Posted on the Internet," PolitiFact.com, July 28, 2009, at http://www.politifact.com/truth-o-meter/statements/2009/jul/28/worldnetdaily/birthers-claim-gibbs-lied-when-he-said-obamas-birt/.

254 "Alleged Obama Birth Certificate from Kenya Is a Hoax," PolitiFact.com, August 21, 2009, at http://politifact.com/truth-o-meter/statements/2009/aug/21/orly-taitz/alleged-obama-birth-certificate-kenya-hoax/.

255 Brooks Jackson, "It's Official: Obama 'Born in the U.S.A.,'" FactCheck.org, November 1, 2008, at http://www.factcheck.org/2008/11/its-official-obama-born-in-the-usa/.

256 Markos Moulitsas, posting under the "Kos" username, "Birthers Are Mostly Republican and Southern," DailyKos.com, July 31, 2009, at http://www.dailykos.com/story/2009/7/31/760087/-Birthers-are-mostly-Republican-and-Southern.

257 Quoted by Media Matters, "MSNBC President Calls Birthism 'Racist,'" MediaMatters.com, July 24, 2009, at http://mediamatters.org/blog/200907240043.

258 Video Clip on Media Matters, "On MSNBC, Deutsch Calls Birtherism "Hate-mongering," "Fear-mongering," "Racist," MediaMatters.com, July 28, 2009, at http://mediamatters.org/mmtv/200907280045. Also: Rick Moran, "MSNBC's Deutsch Booted for Criticizing Olby," April 22, 2010, at http://www.americanthinker.com/blog/2010/04/msnbcs_deutsch_booted_for_crit.html.

259 Kenneth Ogosia and Kevin Kelly, "Anti-Obama Lunatics Living in Denial," *Nation*, August 5, 2009, at http://www.nation.co.ke/News/-/1056/635400/-/ull727/-/index.html.

260 Bridget Johnson, "Gingrich: Obama 'Absolutely' a Citizen and Christian, but May Confuse People," *The Hill*, October 10, 20010, at http://thehill.com/blogs/blog-briefing-room/news/123531-gingrich-obama-absolutely-a-citizen-and-christian-but-may-be-confusing-people.

261 "The Big List of Eligibility 'Proofers,'" WND, October 15, 2010, at http://www.wnd.com/?pageId=215797.

Appendix

262 Chelsea Schilling, "Obama: Where Have All His Records Gone?" WND, June 9, 2009, at http://www.wnd.com/?pageId=100613.

263 Claudine San Nicolas, "Retired Teachers on Maui Recall Young, 'Cute' Student Barry," *Maui News*, January 21, 2009, at http://www.mauinews.com/page/content.detail/id/513898.html?nav=5074.

264 Hawaii Department of Education, "Registering for School: What to Bring ...." at http://doe.k12.hi.us/register/index.htm.

265 Sudhin Tanawala, Associated Press, "Obama Worked to Fit in at Elite School," *Boston Globe*, March 26, 2008, at http://www.boston.com/news/nation/articles/2008/03/26/obama_worked_to_fit_in_at_elite_school/.

266 Janny Scott, "Obama's Account of New York Years Often Differs From What Others Say," *New York Times*, October 30, 2007, at http://www.nytimes.com/2007/10/30/us/politics/30obama.html.

267 Shira Boss-bicak, "Barack Obama '83: Is He the New Face of the Democratic Party?" *Columbia College Today*, January 2005, at http://www.college.columbia.edu/cct_archive/jan05/cover.php.

268 Editorial, "Obama's Lost Years," *Wall Street Journal*, September 11, 2008, at http://online.wsj.com/article/SB122108881386721289.html.

269 Ross Goldberg, "Obama's Years at Columbia are a Mystery," *New York Sun*, September 2, 2008, at http://www.nysun.com/new-york/obamas-years-at-columbia-are-a-mystery/85015/.

270 Janny Scott, *op.cit.*

271 "Paper Trail," Snopes.com, last updated October 25, 2009, at http://www.snopes.com/politics/obama/columbiathesis.asp.

272 "Obama and Khalid Mansour," YouTube.com, August 21, 2008, at http://www.youtube.com/watch?v=4EcC0QAd0Ug&eurl=http%3A%2F%2Fatlasshrugs2000.typepad.com%2Fatlas_shrugs%2F2008%2F08%2Fobamas-benefact.html&feature=player_embedded.

273 Ben Smith, "Obama Camp Denies Sutton Story," Politico.com, September 4, 2008, at http://www.politico.com/blogs/bensmith/0908/Obama_camp_denies_Sutton_story.html.

274 University of California at Berkeley, "Social Activism Sound Recording Project: The Black Panther Party," UC Berkeley Library, at http://www.lib.berkeley.edu/MRC/pacificapanthers.html.

275 Fox Butterfield, "First Black Elected to Head Harvard's Law Review," *New York Times*, February 6, 1990, at http://www.nytimes.com/1990/02/06/us/first-black-elected-to-head-harvard-s-law-review.html.

276 Jeffrey Ressner and Ben Smith, "Obama Kept Law Review Balanced," Politico, June 23, 2008, at http://www.politico.com/news/stories/0608/11257.html.

277 Ben Smith and Jeffrey Ressner, "Exclusive: Obama's Lost Law Review Article," Politico, August 22, 2008, at http://dyn.politico.com/printstory.cfm?uuid=E99B0FC2-18FE-70B2-A8749734EF6D25D9.

278 "Media Inquiries: Statement Regarding Barack Obama," University of Chicago Law School, no date, http://www.law.uchicago.edu/media.

279 Matthew J. Franck, "Obama the Titan, or the Cipher?" *National Review*, February 12, 2008, at http://www.nationalreview.com/bench-memos/51166/obama-titan-or-cipher/matthew-j-franck.

280 Jack Cashill, "Who Wrote 'Dreams from My Father'?" WND, at http://www.wnd.com/index.php?fa=PAGE.view&pageId=79392.

281 Lawrence K. Altman and Jeff Zeleny, "Obama's Doctor, Praising His Health, Sees No Obstacles to Service," *New York Times*, May 30, 2008, at http://www.nytimes.com/2008/05/30/us/politics/30obama.html.

282 "Rezmar Deals Involving Davis Miner Law Firm," *Chicago Sun-Times*, April 23, 2007, at http://www.suntimes.com/news/metro/353777,CST-NWS-rezside23.article.

283 Tim Novak, "Obama and His Rezko Ties," *Chicago Sun-Times*, April 23, 2007, at http://www.suntimes.com/news/metro/353829,CST-NWS-rez23.article.

284 Transcript, "'Meet the Press' Transcript for November 11, 2007: Barack Obama," MSNBC.msn.com, November 11, 2007, at http://www.msnbc.msn.com/id/21738432/.

285 "Illinois State Archives Letter Raises Questions About Obama's Records Claim," Judicial Watch, March 27, 2008, at http://webcache.googleusercontent.com/search?q=cache:6W0w5PJg94wJ:www.judicialwatch.org/illinois-state-archives-letter-raises-questions-about-obama-s-records-claim+tom+fitton+%2B+judicial+watch+%2B+Obama+%2B+state+senate+records+lost&cd=3&hl=en&ct=clnk&gl=us.

286 Jo Becker, Peter S. Goodman and Michael Powell, "Once Elected, Palin Hired Friends and Lashed Foes," *Wall Street Journal*, September 13, 2004, at http://www.nytimes.com/2008/09/14/us/politics/14palin.html.

INDEX

WND Books has a history of publishing provocative, current-events titles, including many *New York Times* bestsellers.

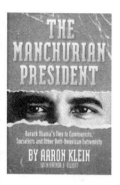

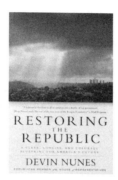

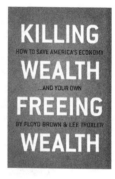

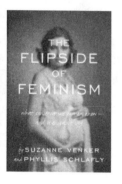

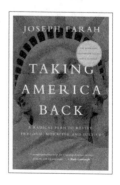

WND Books • a WND Company • Washington, DC • www.wndbooks.com

"A compelling indictment of Obamacare."
~ Ron Paul, M.D.

"A remarkable essay on life, medicine,
health care, politics and Congress."
~ Newt Gingrich

WITH A FOREWORD BY **NEWT GINGRICH**

DOCTOR$_x$
in the HOUSE

A PHYSICIAN-TURNED-CONGRESSMAN OFFERS HIS PRESCRIPTION
FOR SCRAPPING OBAMACARE... AND SAVING AMERICA'S MEDICAL SYSTEM

MICHAEL C. BURGESS, *M.D.*
MEMBER *of the* HOUSE *of* REPRESENTATIVES

WND Books

WND Books　　•　　a WND Company　　•　　Washington, DC　　•　　www.wndbooks.com

"A fascinating inside tale of politics, power, expediency and intimidation."
~ *Newt Gingrich*

"Experience one of our nation's greatest crises through the eyes of a key witness."
~ *David P. Schippers*

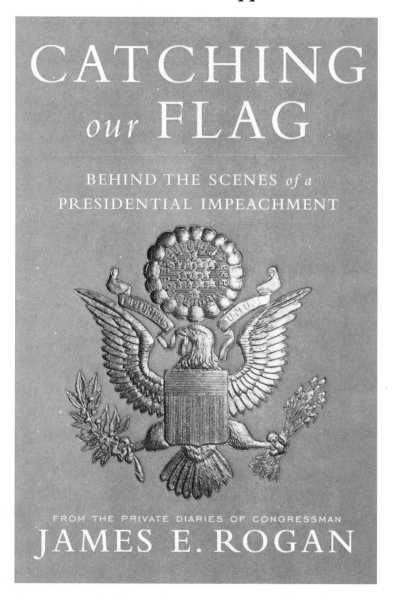

CATCHING *our* FLAG

BEHIND THE SCENES *of a* PRESIDENTIAL IMPEACHMENT

FROM THE PRIVATE DIARIES OF CONGRESSMAN

JAMES E. ROGAN

WND Books

WND Books • a WND Company • Washington, DC • www.wndbooks.com

"Vadum warns that despite the defunding of ACORN, they have only feigned death."
~ *Michele Bachmann*

"There is no way liberals will be able to whitewash the evils of ACORN."
~ *Hannah Giles*

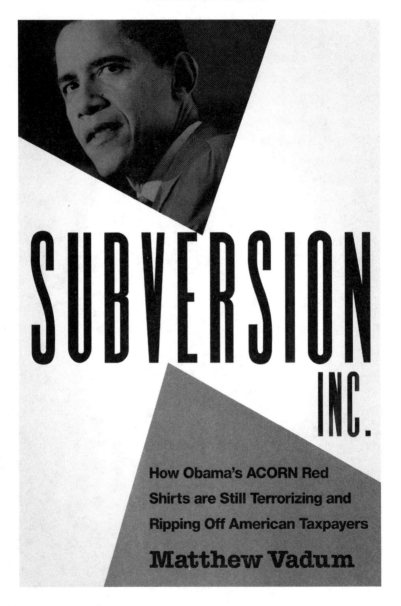

SUBVERSION INC.

How Obama's ACORN Red Shirts are Still Terrorizing and Ripping Off American Taxpayers

Matthew Vadum

WND BOOKS

WND Books   •   a WND Company   •   Washington, DC   •   www.wndbooks.com